EVALUATIVE SEMANTICS

Evaluation, from connotations to complex judgements of value, is probably the most neglected dimension of meaning. Calling for a new understanding of truth and value, this book is a comprehensive study of evaluation in natural language, at lexical, syntactic and discursive levels.

Jean Pierre Malrieu explores the cognitive foundations of evaluation and uses connectionist networks to model evaluative processes. He takes into account the social dimension of evaluation, showing that ideological contexts account for evaluative variability. A discussion of compositionality and opacity leads to the argument that a semantics of evaluation has some key advantages over truth-conditional semantics and, as an example, Malrieu applies his 'evaluative semantics' to a complex Shakespearean text. His connectionist model yields a mathematical estimation of the consistency of text with ideology, and is particularly useful in the identification of subtle rhetorical devices such as irony.

Evaluative Semantics proposes a strongly postmodernist theory of cognition, ideology and discourse, in which the structure and internal consistency of ideology resemble those of evaluative knowledge in the mind. The strength of this book is to go beyond purely theoretical claims and to propose an original connectionist model of evaluative interpretation. Jean Pierre Malrieu's new semantics, based upon a sociological approach to meaning, makes a unique contribution to the literature of cognitive science, linguistics and discourse analysis.

Jean Pierre Malrieu is based at Jean Dautet College, La Rochelle, France and a member of the research group 'Language and Connectionism' at the Centre National de la Recherche Scientifique. His research interests are evaluation in natural language and connectionist modelling in semantics.

ROUTLEDGE FRONTIERS OF COGNITIVE SCIENCE
Series Adviser Tim Valentine

1. DECISION MAKING
Cognitive models and explanations
Edited by Rob Ranyard, W. Ray Crozier and Ola Svenson

2. THE NATURE OF CONCEPTS
Evolution, structure and representation
Edited by Philip Van Loocke

3. EVALUATIVE SEMANTICS
Language, cognition and ideology
Jean Pierre Malrieu

EVALUATIVE SEMANTICS

Language, Cognition and Ideology

Jean Pierre Malrieu

London and New York

First published 1999
by Routledge
11 New Fetter Lane, London EC4P 4EE

Simultaneously published in the USA and Canada
by Routledge
29 West 35th Street, New York, NY 10001

© 1999 Jean Pierre Malrieu

Typeset in Times by
MHL Typesetting, Coventry
Printed and bound in Great Britain by
St Edmundsbury Press, Bury St Edmunds, Suffolk

All rights reserved. No part of this book may be reprinted or reproduced or utilised in any form or by any electronic, mechanical, or by other means, now known or hereafter invented, including photocopying and recording, or in any information storage or retrieval system, without permission in writing from the publishers.

British Library Cataloguing in Publication Data
A catalogue record for this book is available
from the British Library

Library of Congress Cataloging in Publication Data
Malrieu, Jean Pierre, 1964–
Evaluative semantics: cognition, language, and ideology/Jean Pierre Malrieu
p.   cm.
Includes bibliographical references and index.
1. Semantics.   2. Cognition.   3. Ideology.   4. Discourse analysis.
5. Evaluation.   I. Title
P325.M28   1999
401'.4–dc21   98-33200
                                                                                   CIP

ISBN 0-415-19761-9

CONTENTS

List of figures	ix
List of tables	xi
Acknowledgements	xii

Introduction   1

1 Ideology and discourse   10

Introduction 10
1 *Theories of ideology 12*
2 *Ideology and practice 17*
3 *Ideological critique and disrepute 33*
4 *The fundamental dilemma 39*
5 *Strategic efficiency and ideological consistency 41*
6 *Types of consistency 44*
  Conclusion 49

2 Evaluation and cognition   50

Introduction 50
1 *Evaluation between affects and cognition 51*
2 *Lessons in psychoanalysis 59*
3 *Cognitive models of evaluation 65*
4 *Models of text processing 76*
5 *Modes of interpretation 80*
  Conclusion 83

3 Interpretative shortcuts   85

Introduction 85

1 Content analysis: the origins 86
2 Inferences to the context 87
3 Scientificity of textual analysis 90
4 Discourse analysis and ideology 92
5 Discourse analysis à la française 96
6 Modes of enunciation 103
7 Symbols 108
   Conclusion 112

4 Evaluative semantics   **114**

Introduction 114
1 Non-denotational approaches 115
2 Evaluation, pragmatics and semantics 122
3 Model-theoretic semantics 124
4 Compositional semantics 128
5 The nature of semantic values 131
6 Semantics of contextual modification 135
7 Opacity in evaluative semantics 139
8 Possible worlds and conflicting worlds 143
   Conclusion 147

5 Semantic networks and discourse representation   **149**

Introduction 149
1 The nature of semantic networks 150
2 Discourse representation formalisms 152
3 Underlying conceptions of discourse 155
4 The world of semantic networks 159
5 Three basic strategies of content representation 166
6 The conceptual graph model 167
7 Some critiques of the conceptual graph model 175
   Conclusion 177

6 Styled semantic networks   **179**

Introduction 179
1 A relational model 180
2 Tense 182
3 Negation 182
4 Quantification and determination 185
5 Modalities and modal aspectualization 189

6 *Interrogatives and modalities* 191
  7 *Attitude and speech act reports* 193
  8 *Representing discourse* 195
  9 *A Projection game for styled semantic networks* 197
 10 *Applications of semantic networks to content analysis* 203
 11 *Implementation* 206
     Conclusion 207

7 Dynamic semantic networks   209

Introduction 209
1 *Modelling interpretation as a dynamic process* 210
2 *Estimating ideological consistency* 212
3 *Globally asymptotically stable dynamics* 214
4 *A numerical estimation of ideological consistency* 216
5 *Nature and effects of the links* 220
   Conclusion 225

8 Setting the weights   227

Introduction 227
1 *The structure of ideologies* 228
2 *A derivation algorithm* 230
3 *Default relation settings* 231
4 *An example of ideology* 234
5 *Semantic properties* 243
   Conclusion 253

9 Evaluation and rhetorical attitudes   254

Introduction 254
1 *The text* 255
2 *Mark Antony's evaluative attitudes* 257
3 *Evaluative ambiguity* 260
4 *Rhetorical questions* 265
5 *The role of connectors* 270
6 *Irony at work* 276
7 *Application to other classes of disambiguation problems* 278
   Conclusion 279

CONTENTS

Conclusion	**280**
Appendix A	**289**
Appendix B	**293**
Notes	**295**
Bibliography	*300*
Index	*312*

FIGURES

1.1	Structure and perspective.	24
1.2	Discourse as a network.	27
1.3	The roles in Bordieu's text.	36
2.1	Brain and cognition according to Edelman.	57
2.2	Evaluation and dynamic schemata.	72
2.3	Cognitive and meta-cognitive evaluative processes.	74
2.4	Role and reputation in evaluation.	75
4.1	Two-step semantics for natural language.	125
4.2	Nonmonotonic inheritance – the Nixon diamond.	144
4.3	Pre-emption and ambiguity in nonmonotonic inheritance.	146
5.1	A network without semantics.	150
5.2	The advantage of graphs over trees in semantics.	155
5.3	The world of semantic networks.	160
5.4	Three basic types of data structure.	166
5.5	An example of a conceptual graph.	168
5.6	An example of type hierarchy.	169
6.1	Injective and non-injective projection.	200
6.2	Data structures and multiple inheritance.	207
7.1	The consistency function and a map of the evaluation state space.	211
7.2	Graphs of transform F for two values of β.	218
7.3	Mutual attraction.	221
7.4	Mutual repulsion.	221
7.5	Attraction–repulsion; Jesuit's dynamics.	222
7.6	Attraction–repulsion; Jansenist's dynamics.	223

FIGURES

8.1	The three-layer structure of ideologies.	228
8.2	Collapsed and expanded view of a context.	229
8.3	Effect of negation.	243
8.4	Effect of negation on a standard.	243
8.5	Relations sensitive to negation.	244
8.6	Relations insensitive to negation.	244
8.7	Effect of potential modality.	246
8.8	Effect of unreal modality.	247
8.9	An alternative effect of unreal modality.	247
8.10	Ranking of quantifiers.	251
8.11	Effect of passivization.	251
9.1	The global dynamics of the text.	277

TABLES

1.1	Two neo-Marxian schools.	33
4.1	Evaluation of belief fact.	142
4.2	Consistency of belief report.	143
6.1	Unification and quantification.	198
8.1	Negation and quantifiers – case (a).	249
8.2	Negation and quantifiers – case (b).	250
8.3	Negation and quantifiers – case (c).	250
9.1	Simulations – lines 3–5.	259
9.2	Simulations – lines 32–3.	260
9.3	Simulations – line 2, first reading.	262
9.4	Simulations – line 2, second reading.	262
9.5	Simulations – lines 5–6.	263
9.6	Simulations – lines 7–8.	264
9.7	Simulations – lines 9–12.	265
9.8a	Simulations – lines 16–18.	267
9.8b	Simulations of interrogatives.	267
9.9	Simulations – lines 23–5.	269
9.10	Simulations – lines 30–1.	270
9.11	Simulations – lines 13–15.	272
9.12	Simulations – lines 19–22.	273
9.13	Simulations – lines 23–7.	275
9.14	Simulations – lines 28–9.	276

ACKNOWLEDGEMENTS

This book is very much the product of the stimulating intellectual (and aesthetic) environment of the European University Institute of Florence. The four years I have spent there have been, overall, both happy and productive, thanks to interactions with remarkable professors and researchers, especially Alan Kirman, Mark Salmon, Nikos Georgantzis, Stefano Guzzini, Anna Leander, Anne Sophie Perriaux, Pascal Briois, Régine Perron, Fabrice Montebello, and Pierre Antoine Dessaux. The interdisciplinary nature of this work reflects the pluridisciplinarity of the EUI, and the diversity of its researchers.

Apart from the EUI, I am specially in debt to François Rastier, who contributed to the semantic side of this research, and to Yves-Marie Visetti and Bernard Victorri, who contributed to the connectionist side. Yves-Marie and Bernard gave me the idea of establishing mathematical convergence results and helped me to clarify my theoretical orientations.

Despite these important contributions, I must confess that the writing of this book is pretty much the history of a solitary research. I take full responsibility for its shortcomings and bold hypotheses.

This research was made possible by a Lavoisier grant from the French Foreign Affairs Ministry. The book would not exist, either, without the support of my family, especially Jean Paul and Angèle Malrieu, Marina Macchion and Pierrette Claverie. Finally, I would like to thank Claire Le Dez for her patience during intensive work periods.

INTRODUCTION

> I would like to make a movie about ideology. In this movie, ideology is a comet, and men are the Magi. Neapolitan Magi. Following the comet, men discover reality.
>
> Pier Paolo Pasolini.

In his *1984*, George Orwell imagines a language, called *Newspeak*, which forbids the utterance of deviant statements. Fortunately, no such language exists, probably because the relation between signifiers and their meaning cannot be easily controlled. As stated by Stalin – another credible expert in totalitarianism – language is not, in itself, ideological (Stalin 1951). Discourse is. But what is the nature of the frontier between what can and cannot be said in an ideology? Several answers have been given to this question. None of them, I would argue, is fully satisfying. Ideological correctness is neither a matter of logical consistency with a doctrine, nor the result of a discursive system largely similar to that of language. Nor is the line dividing what can and cannot be said according to an ideology, the same as that dividing what can and cannot be conceived of in the conceptual system of an ideology.

I propose another answer to the above question: the consistency of a discourse with an ideology depends on the compatibility between the evaluations it conveys and the system of values of the ideology. This hypothesis, I will claim, leads us to conceive of a much more flexible relation between ideology and discourse. It also permits us to reinstate language, with all its shades of grey, at the centre of this relation. In order to put this hypothesis to work and thereby assess its validity, I will attempt to estimate the consistency of a discourse with a system of values. To do so, one must possess a theory of value judgements, and, more generally, a theory of evaluation in language. The object of the book is therefore to provide a theory of evaluative meaning effects, of their social and cognitive foundations.

Despite some pioneering work by Marxian philosophers of language (Bakhtine, Volosinov), this issue has remained marginal within linguistics.

INTRODUCTION

Until recently, evaluative effects were still considered as second-rate semantic effects. On the contrary, I believe that evaluation is a fundamental semantic notion, and a genuine dimension of meaning. There are, however, good reasons why the evaluative function of language has not aroused as much interest as reference and praxis. One may indeed question whether it is reasonable to call 'semantic' a class of effects and phenomena which depend so crucially upon subjectivity (prior experiences, moods, emotions) and upon social norms. However, between the option which consists in reinforcing a narrow definition of semantics and the option which favours an opening towards cognitive science and social factors, the latter seems rapidly to gain audience within the academic community. My research is inscribed within this general movement which simultaneously tries to account for the global nature of meaning, and tries to keep with the requirements of formalization and rigour which characterize the history of semantics.

The first question to arise, in the project of constructing an evaluative semantics, is that of the type of contexts which determine the evaluative meaning of words, phrases, sentences and discourses. My proposal is to search for maximally general contexts, and to call them 'ideologies'. This may seem disconcerting to the readers who consider the process of science as necessarily going from the particular to the general. However, one of the hypotheses of this research is that there are contexts more general than what is usually called 'context' in analytical philosophy and pragmatics – i.e., roughly speaking, the situation in which the speech act takes place. Another hypothesis is that there are also contexts that are wider than what is called in political philosophy and sociology 'a discursive formation', i.e., the discourses of an apparatus (Althusser), or the discourses of a social field (Bourdieu).

We have all had, of course, the experience that our evaluation of somebody, or some idea may vary according to the people we are talking to. Everybody, I suppose, has found himself defending an opinion (regarding the quality of a movie, for example) one day, and a slightly different one the next day. These shifts tend to suggest that our evaluative beliefs do not really matter, and that they are fully determined by our desire to please, seduce, contradict, or attack our interlocutors of the moment. I believe, on the contrary, that this is too pessimistic a view. I will not try to resuscitate the traditional concepts of social psychology, and in particular, the distinction between latent attitudes and manifest variability. I just want to remark that the shifts of evaluation are not only the result of the desire to say 'white' when someone else says 'black'. It may as well be that we believe in fact something is 'grey'. But if someone says 'black', then, to suggest 'grey', we must introduce some 'white'. The question is why do we often shift from 'some white' to 'white'? The reason may be that 'white' is easier to defend than 'some white'. This is not to assume the necessary supremacy of radical positions. I do not want to suggest that radical evaluations are the only evaluations that may succeed. My point is that, if they are to succeed, that is, be efficient in the debate, my evaluations ought to be coherent in some sense. And if they are incoherent, this incoherence must be either dissimulated or acknowledged and circumscribed. What I call ideology is the most general system of guidelines, provided by culture (mainly political, but not only) to render discourses coherent.

One may object that it is not necessary, once we have acknowledged that the immediate pragmatic context is too narrow to account for all the constraints bearing on our evaluations, to extend the contexts until they become entities as comprehensive as ideologies. It may be argued that intermediate contexts, such as the social apparatuses (Althusser) or the fields (Bourdieu) to which we belong are more appropriate candidates. Remember, however, that according to Althusser, an ideology realizes itself in a multiplicity of ideological state apparatuses, and that it is characterized by the relations of unevenness–subordination between these apparatuses. There is therefore something 'above' the discursive formations tied to the apparatuses. I do believe something similar, in the sense that I do think that something is shared by the various discursive formations. However, since Bourdieu's critique of the notion of an apparatus (Bourdieu 1980a), it is no longer possible to understand ideologies as a global will operating in a deliberate manner, bringing individuals into subjection, and inculcating in them definite beliefs. Nevertheless, this does not necessarily mean that Bourdieu is right in suggesting that there is nothing above social fields, that ideologies are only perspectives on the social, and that, ultimately, they are reducible to the tensions and the strategies of distinction within and between social fields. This presentation, which insists on the relational structure within which discourses are inscribed, has the drawback of denying discourse any important status. It prevents Bourdieu from recognizing the specific contribution of discourses (not only discourse in general, but specific discourses, including their contents) in the making of this relation. In particular, Bourdieu passes silently over the fact that if we do not have a coherent discourse, our strategies are likely to fall short, not because we will not be able to act in a right way, but because we will be dominated by the discourse of our adversaries. What I call ideology is a system of evaluations which produce discourses able to support social relations in a durable way.

Despite (or because of) this clarification, the word ideology may still seem surprising. Why use such an old-fashioned, controversial term, caught within so many debates, when Foucault, for example, proposes or redefines for us a long list of concepts such as discourse, discursive formation, strategies, doctrines, creeds, world views, positivity, knowledge, science, theory, énoncé, text, archive, to mention but a few? The first reason to stick to the term ideology is that no other term indicates so clearly a normative and evaluative dimension in opposition to the dimension of knowledge (which is the almost exclusive object of the 'first' Foucault, to whom we owe all the conceptual apparatus aimed at the description of discourse). The second reason is that all these units of discourse share, to different degrees, and insofar as they are realized in linguistic forms, the effects that are the object of this research. It would be erroneous to suggest that evaluative effects depend on a precise type of discursive unit, while, on the contrary, these effects arise within all discourses that 'have not passed the threshold of formalization'. Ideology is the most general type of evaluative context that one may think of, but it permeates all types of discourse (in different ways), and it is most often apprehended within discourses that belong to 'smaller' discursive units.

One may also simply deny the existence of global, comprehensive, normative discourses in modern occidental societies. Because the reader has certainly gone through the end of history, the end of the sacred and the end of metaphysics, I will not engage, thirty years after Bell announced the end of ideologies, in another stereotyped 'end-of' debate. Let us simply remark that even if Bell was right, and if ideologies have really disappeared from the occidental world, this entails that ideologies have indeed existed and have been influential in the past. Therefore, the theory of ideological determination of discourse which I try here to elaborate may at least prove useful for historians, and more generally, for the social scientists interested in the history of ideas. In addition, since Bell wrote about the death of ideologies, the world has evolved, and some recent developments in India, Africa, ex-communist countries, and even within western democracies, have led social scientists to evoke, sometimes with fear, a 'return of the past'. The revival of ethnic and nationalist discourses may unfortunately force us to reconsider Bell's prognosis.

There is an optimistic version of the 'end of ideologies', which interprets their alleged disappearance as a progression of the individual consciousness liberated from the influence of collective thought. There is also a more pessimistic version according to which, since the crumbling of ideologies, public discourses are just a big soup and public communication one huge channel surf. A recent manifestation of this pessimism is the theme of the 'pensée unique' in French politics and media. It is assumed that genuine debates have become impossible since a softly hegemonic, consensual discourse has taken over the ideologies. Even though there is certainly something true in this portrait, politicians and journalists should perhaps remember that a discourse without opposition is often simply a dominant discourse. It has been shown, for example, that the ideology of modernization which has dominated the public discourse of the right wing since the 1960s in France, despite its claim to transcend (and, finally, abolish) the ideological oppositions, is the legitimating discourse of the ruling class in western Europe (Bourdieu and Boltanski 1976). Therefore, in the French context, these authors feel entitled to speak of the 'ideology of the end of ideologies'.

INTRODUCTION

To conclude this preliminary discussion of the word ideology, let me make clear that ideology, in the traditional sense of the term, is not the object of this research. I will not attempt to make a realistic description of ideological phenomena; I will not make hypotheses regarding the reasons, both logical and historical, explaining the success and the decline of precise ideologies; I will not try to figure out a universal model of ideologies. I doubt, in fact, that such a model exists. It is of course possible to list a certain number of abstract properties that ideologies possess or ought to possess. However, there seems to be something unique at the core of each ideology so that they hardly appear as the specification of a general model. The closer we get to the specificity of the dogmatic efficiency of an ideology, the more difficult it becomes to turn our intuitions into formal descriptions. I will therefore limit myself to a rather simple definition of ideologies as systems of values. However, some solutions allowing one to articulate conflicts of values with conflicts of ideas will be proposed. Briefly stated, it will suggest replacing the 'possible worlds' of Kripke's semantics for modal logic, by 'conflicting worlds' representing the conflicting perspectives on society. Technically, these conflicting worlds will be defined as extensions (in the sense that nonmonotomic logic gives to the term) of the doxa.

The second question to arise, in the project of an evaluative semantics, is that of the relation between utterances and contexts. To put the problem in very general terms, the wider contexts become, the more difficult it is to define the exact sense in which they continue to be contexts. When they grow so large that the persons who participate in a communicative action are not aware of them, one may wonder how these contexts can be relevant. Let me briefly mention two traditional answers given to this question, which are respectively associated to the notion of a real and of a logical determination of discourse by ideology.

The real ideological context of an utterance is made from the ideological formations within which speaker and hearers are inscribed, either by conscious adherence or because of the social formations to which they belong. Ideology, as a real phenomenon, bears on the meaning of an utterance if it brings, or has brought, the author of the utterance and its hearers into ideological subjection. I believe, with many others, that this notion of a subjection is problematic, and therefore, I attempt to propose another, less alienating, vision of the ideological influence.

The doctrinal context of an utterance is the propositional part of the ideologies which influence the speaker and the hearers. But it connects up with social formations. 'Doctrine is, permanently, the sign, the manifestation and the instrument of a prior adherence – adherence to a class, to a social or racial status, to a nationality or an interest, to a struggle, a resistance or an acceptance' (Foucault 1971: 19). Doctrines can be assimilated to contexts in that they set the boundaries between what can and cannot be said. I believe, on the contrary, that in the absence of specific inquisitorial institutions devoted to the task of enforcing the conformity of the utterances to the doctrine, utterances are not ruled in or out by a comparison with a doctrine. As Bourdieu has shown in the case of the dominant ideology in modern societies, the conformity of a statement to an ideology is not a matter of logical or conceptual compatibility with a theory. Therefore, doctrine understood as the axiomatic reconstruction of the conceptual system of an ideology, is not the object of this research, nor, I would argue, the appropriate type of context for an evaluative semantics.

Because ideologies are not tangible contexts that physically or logically surround the utterances that would exist independently of them, and to which every actor of a communicative action has equal access, context dependency is in fact the result of a process of mutual construction. The utterance depends on the ideological context, that is, on the ideological adherences of the actors involved in the communicative action. But because these adherences fluctuate depending on the communicative situations, and above all, because they are partly inferred (by other actors) from the utterances themselves, the context must be (re)constructed by the actors at the same time as they interpret the utterances. In the book, I propose a model for a simple class of such processes: the case of the evaluative interpretation of a discourse by a single actor. Evaluative interpretation will be modelled as a disambiguation process during which the receiver of a discourse attempts to situate it within the ideological space by watching out for the evaluative meaning effects it conveys.

This brings in cognition, which may seem very natural given the recent interest aroused by cognitive semantics. But remember that things have not always been that obvious, and that Foucault, for example, refused categorically to account for discourse on the basis of the subject and the human consciousness. Talking about myths, kinship systems, languages, sexuality, desire, relations of production, class struggles, he used to criticize '... that ideological use of history by which one tries to restore to man everything that has unceasingly eluded him for over a hundred years' (Foucault 1972: 14).

There is little doubt that if Foucault had witnessed the current developments of cognitive research, he would have extended this critique to cognitive science. For, in his view, the relation between ideology and science lies in the capacity of science to truncate, modify, redistribute, confirm, develop and leave aside knowledge. The way in which cognitive science operates a selection, a reformulation of the findings of social psychology, the way it passes over the theses of psychoanalysis in silence, the way it recentres social sciences around the study of mind are striking illustrations of what Foucault defines as the ideological uses of science.

On the other hand, I do not see any reason why we should share the hatred of the subject which characterizes so many French intellectuals of the 1970s.

INTRODUCTION

Discourses lodge themselves in writings, institutions, social practices, but also in the human psyche. They are made with it, and for it. Therefore, one cannot separate the study of culture from the study of mind. However, this does not imply that the study of culture can be reduced to the study of mind. I believe, on the contrary, that one of the main tasks of cognitive science should be to explain why and how mind is so dependent upon culture. We should ask why language, social representations and ideologies contribute much more to our representations of social realities than does our experience of these realities. Our models of the mind should help us understand why knowledge acquisition prevails over learning from experience. This is not an easy task as soon as one tries to go beyond the traditional rationalizations which present ready-made, cultural knowledge as pragmatically (or economically) optimal for social actors endowed with a bounded rationality.

Because the model of evaluative interpretation which is proposed in the book does not address the issue of learning, it cannot be seen as a direct contribution to this general project. However, I shall argue that Lacan, who paid attention to the relation between evaluation and symbolic order, and Edelman, who includes value-oriented processes in his theory of neural Darwinism, have both made some proposals in this direction. I shall therefore claim that evaluation is a key notion to describe the complex articulation between subjective experience and cultural knowledge.

The paradox of this articulation can be best exemplified by the case of language. On the one hand, because nobody is the repository of all the semantic relations language is made of, language, as a cultural fact, is always richer than its subjective appropriations. On the other hand, because words and expressions of language have, for all of us, deep resonances, the subjective appropriation of language is always richer than language itself. We face here two orders of complexity, that of individual memory, and that of cultural memory, which seem to be far beyond the orders of complexity currently addressed by cognitive science, history and sociology. The strategy adopted in the book is to reduce complexity by focusing on the intersection of these two orders. Subjectivity is first described as a set of filters operating on cultural knowledge. Although these filters differ from each other as much as subjects differ, they do have some common characteristics. Among the most noticeable, I submit, is permeability to evaluations. In other words, among the various semantic and conceptual components of a culture, the evaluations are those that are more likely to pass through the filter of 'ordinary' subjectivity.

One should therefore distinguish between ideologies as real, social phenomena, and mental ideological representations (not necessarily conscious). Just as with language, ideology is richer and more complex than its subjective appropriations. Ideology is not made up of evaluation only – it is not even limited to a normative doctrine – while mental ideological representations are often made of evaluations. Because ideologies are semantic contexts *qua* mental representations, we shall be concerned primarily with ideologies as mental systems of evaluation. This does not imply, however, that we need to be concerned with the ins and outs of individual memory, nor with the subtleties of the subjective processes of evaluation. First, I shall argue that it is possible to distinguish (at least in heuristic perspective) between, on one hand, cognitive evaluative processes, which range from deeply rooted, unconscious evaluative schemes to formal methods of evaluation, and, on the other, semantic evaluative processes, which are driven by language. By focusing on the latter I shall concentrate on the cognitive processes that depend most on language and normative knowledge. At that level, inter-individual variations of attitudes can be accounted for as the result of conscious and unconscious adherences to socially pre-constituted systems of values (ideologies). Secondly, ideologies aim at social diffusion. As institutionalized discourses, ideologies possess a strategic capacity. They take advantage of the nature of human cognition, of its permeability to evaluations, of the various cognitive levels at which these evaluations lodge, to pervade the mind of the subjects. Ideologies are normative and evaluative because this is the best way for them to gain an audience, and to dissimulate themselves into doxic evaluative dispositions. Finally, language itself is evaluative, both in the sense that words may have fixed, or socially determined evaluative resonances, and in the sense that syntactic and discursive compositions create evaluative semantic effects.

The last question that I wish to evoke in this introduction is the status of formalization in this research. Since many theoretical aspects of evaluative phenomena remain to be clarified, one may question whether the formalization of the evaluative properties of discourse is not premature. More fundamentally perhaps, since formal models of cognition still cannot pretend to realism, is not formalization a way to escape the underlying theoretical problems – an attitude of *fuite en avant*? In defence of formalization, I would like to argue that it possesses at the highest degree what Foucault called 'the power of affirmation', by which he did not mean a power opposed to that of negation, but 'the power of constituting domains of objects, in relation to which one can affirm or deny true or false propositions' (Foucault 1971: 27). In this research, formal instruments have no role other than to unearth the importance of evaluative meaning effects, and to constitute them as an object for further research. As a consequence, the model of evaluative interpretation proposed in the book does not lead to a *method* in the traditional sense of the term. Much more theoretical work is certainly required before the model yields a robust method of discourse analysis. A similar remark applies to the computer implementation of the model, which is not so much undertaken in order to provide software for discourse analysis, but to furnish an instrument allowing us to experiment with evaluative meaning effects. As a last consequence, I shall not attempt to apply the model to a sociological analysis of a specific ideology in a large corpus of texts. Instead, I shall make an in-depth analysis of a single text by Shakespeare, in order to show how the model performs on complex texts (throughout the book, most examples are drawn from this text, which can be found in Appendix B). I believe that this example will demonstrate that no semantic theory, or formalized method of discourse analysis other than the one defended here, is capable of coming closer to the rhetorical effects which are of interest for sociologists.

The book is organized as follows. Chapter 1 locates the research project with respect to existing theories of ideology and with respect to sociological debates concerning the relative importance of propositional and pragmatic components in social communication. Chapter 2 discusses the psychological foundations of evaluative processes. Special attention is devoted to psychoanalysis, to Edelman's theory of the mind, and to text processing. The first part of Chapter 3 reviews some influential methods of discourse analysis in order to pick up, here and there, meaning effects that ought to be integrated in the model. The second part is devoted to a methodological discussion concerning selection processes in discourse analysis. Chapter 4 introduces and discusses the fundamental notions of this research: the *evaluation* of discursive content and the *ideological consistency* of discourse. An evaluative semantics is sketched. Chapter 5 contains a brief survey of semantic networks, which aims at justifying the technical choices made in the following chapter. The second part of Chapter 5 is intended to render the reader familiar with the basic notions of conceptual graphs, and with game-theoretical semantics. Chapter 6 contains a detailed discussion of the discourse representation formalism which will be used in the two final chapters. Chapter 7 provides the model itself. Evaluative meaning effects are modelled as the dynamic modification of parts of discourse, and ideological consistency is measured by the variations of evaluation during the dynamic process. Chapter 8 explains how parameters of the dynamic systems are set, and how ideologies are structured to perform this task. Chapter 9 gives an application of the model, where it is argued that an evaluative approach can be of benefit to natural language processing.

Not all chapters are of equal importance. Chapter 4 is fundamental, as well as Chapters 7 and 8. The latter requires a prior reading of Chapter 6. Therefore, these four chapters form the core of the book. Chapter 9, which gives an idea of the potential applications and of the limits of the model, is essential too. Chapters 1 and 2 should allow the reader to grasp the broad theoretical incentives which have led to the model, as well as what is at stake. Chapters 3 and 5 are less essential, especially for the reader who is already familiar with discourse analysis and semantic networks. Nevertheless, both chapters adopt an original approach to the fields they treat.

1

IDEOLOGY AND DISCOURSE

Introduction

Althusser said that the greatest event of history to date was the encounter of the working class with Marx's theory of capital. Althusser, of course, conceived of Marxism as a science, and not as an ideology. Nevertheless, this notion of an encounter, that is, of a mutual recognition between one, or several social formations and a discourse is perhaps the best characterization of ideology. The theory of rational expectations and financial markets; Pontifical Infallibility and the Catholic Church; inferiority of the Jews and the Nazi concentration camps: an ideology is a theory of the social formations that will make it real, and therefore true.

This is one of the features by which ideology differs from science. The constitution of the field of science in Europe in the seventeenth century did not follow the social divide between bourgeoisie and aristocracy, the two social formations which dominated the period, and whose struggle would eventually change Europe (Shapin 1991; Shapin and Schaffer 1985). Science has played a part in many social formations, and, contrary to ideology, it has never been exclusively concerned with the reproduction or the transformation of the social formations that uphold it. The second main difference is certainly that ideology contains a 'doctrine' while science has no other doctrinal content than its methods of validation. Because ideological doctrines are highly resistant to innovation (Shils 1968) in contrast to scientific methods of validation which organize the progress of knowledge, ideological change tends to be exogenous while scientific change is mostly endogenous.

Despite these differences, one cannot simply assume that passing tests of scientific validation guarantees that scientific discourses are not ideological. As Foucault warned us, scientificity is not exclusive of ideology: 'By correcting itself, by rectifying its errors, by clarifying its formulations, discourse does not necessarily undo its relations with ideology. The role of ideology does not diminish as rigor increases and error is dissipated' (Foucault 1972: 186).

This may sound paradoxical. How can scientific truth be ideological? The reason is of course that science, as a real, historical discursive practice, does not equally validate, develop and acknowledge all previously existing fields of knowledge. Not all fields of knowledge pass the threshold of scientificity, and those that pass this threshold are deeply modified by this evolution.

> The hold of ideology over scientific discourse and the ideological functioning of the sciences are not articulated at the level of their ideal structure (even if they can be expressed in it in a more or less visible way), nor at the level of their technical use in a society (although that society may obtain results from it), nor at the level of the consciousness of the subjects that build it up; they are articulated where science is articulated upon (*se découpe sur*) knowledge. (Foucault 1972: 185)

It seems therefore that to avoid being ideological, science must at least make explicit its relation to knowledge. The same type of requirement applies to the scientific discourses which have passed the threshold of formalization, and which should clarify their relation to the scientific discourses upon which they draw. This research, which is a modest contribution towards a formalized, scientific theory of the relation between ideology and language, is no exception. Following Foucault's advice, I shall attempt to re-situate my vision of the relation between ideology and language within the context of the various modes of ideological critique, and their underlying theories of ideology. I hope that the methods which I employ will be articulated upon the theses of sociology and political philosophy concerning ideology. However, I cannot be exhaustive on this large topic, and I shall therefore concentrate on Foucault's methodological writings, Althusser's political philosophy and Bourdieu's sociology.

There are, however, two difficulties which render it even more difficult for a scientific theory of ideology to be ideologically neutral than it is for other scientific theories. The first of these difficulties is the apparent incompatibility between the requirements of science (for example, refutability), and the traditional practice of ideological critique. Together with psychoanalysis, ideological critique is one of the few modes of interpretation that claim to discover, within the discourses they comment upon, another meaning which the apparent meaning dissembles rather than reveals (Ricoeur 1965). The similarity of psychoanalytical interpretation and ideological critique can be illustrated by the Freudian tone adopted by Bourdieu to qualify ideological discourse:

> Expression is here [within ideological discourse] as much to mask the *primitive experiences of the social world* and the *social fantasies* which lie at its root as to unveil them; to say them, while saying in

the way it says them, that it does not say them. (Bourdieu 1982: 176)[1]

The distance which ideological critique introduces between the interpretation and the apparent content of discourse gives it its originality and equally creates the difficulty involved in this type of reading. For the defenders of the notion of ideology, this hermeneutic shift is the only solid guarantee of scientificity. For its detractors, this shift renders all the interpretations arbitrary and incapable of falsification. Given this debate, it is natural to question whether a theory of ideology and language like the one which I propose in this work is able to achieve some sort of scientificity or whether it is condemned to remain the expression of simple suspicions concerning the ideological commitments of discourse.

The second major difficulty is due to the meta-theoretical nature of the notion of ideology. The frontier between ideology and the theory of ideology is very difficult to distinguish. All major ideologies are also theories of ideology. In general, ideologies see themselves as knowledge, and other ideologies as ideologies (erroneous knowledge). A clear example of this situation is the Marxist philosophy of history. In addition theories of ideology are also ideologies because they cannot claim that they are ideologically neutral. Even the theories that disclaim the notion of ideology itself may be judged as ideological, since a refusal of ideology in general may help dissimulate an ideology in particular. All these remarks obviously apply to the theories of the relations of ideology and language, and therefore, to the theory which these preliminary discussions are directed at. I do not have pretensions to break this hermeneutic cycle. However, I must make clear the reasons why the methods of ideological critique which I will propose do not transform the cycle into a spiral of ideological relativism.

1 Theories of ideology

Since there is no universally accepted definition of the term 'ideology', Althusser's definition will serve as a start for our discussion:

> An ideology is a system (with its own logic and its own rigor) of representations (images, myths, ideas or concepts), possessing an existence and a historical role within a given society. (Althusser 1965: 238)

This definition reveals a tension between an internal characterization of ideological *systems* ('own logic and rigor') and an external characterization which emphasizes the social *function* of ideologies. The mere concept of 'symbolic action', launched by C. Geertz to account for ideological interactions (Geertz 1964), reveals a similar duality between a symbolic level and a pragmatic level. Such a tension is in fact so widespread in the literature that one may think of classifying theories of ideologies according to the importance that they give to one type of characterization against the other.

Internal theories

In the first category, one would locate Shils' description of ideologies as special belief systems, which differ from ordinary outlooks, creeds and world views due to a certain number of features, such as explicitness of formulation and comprehensiveness; authoritative and explicit promulgation of contents; integration around one or a few pre-eminent values and principles; insistence on their distinctiveness and unconnectedness with other ideologies; resistance to innovation and denial of the facts that are contradictory to the doctrine; affective overtones which accompany the acceptance of ideologies (Shils 1968). Simmel's explanation of the symmetrical rise of ideological pairs (materialism vs. idealism, etc.) is another example of a logical characterization of ideologies (Simmel 1978). Clearly other cases in point are Hirschman's studies of conservative rhetoric (Hirschman 1991) and Boltanski and Thévenot's 'grammar' of ideological discourses (Boltanski and Thévenot 1983, 1991; Boltanski 1990). Outside sociology, the autopoietic theory of law (Teubner 1987; Luhman 1988), which draws upon systems theory in order to claim that law has an internal dynamic, deserves to figure within this first class of theories. Within philosophy, we may consider Derrida's method of conceptual 'deconstruction' (Derrida 1967). The 'French' school in social psychology (Moscovici 1961), which believes in the autonomy of 'social representations' with respect to macro-sociological determinism, is at present attempting to apply its methods to the internal theory of ideologies, an undertaking which is not without difficulties. Theories which search for the structure of myths (Girard 1977) within an ideological discourse should also be included. Finally, theories that regard ideologies as dogmatic systems (Legendre 1983) – and therefore similar to religion – ought to be placed in the first category. *Goliath: the march of fascism* is an excellent example of monography describing the internal dynamics of an ideological development (Borgese 1938).

External theories

In the second approach, one would find Marx's theory of ideology, according to which representations and intellectual outputs are the direct product of material behaviours. One would also find Lenin's theory, which reduces ideologies to the instruments of class struggle. One may also wish to locate in the second stream of thought Bourdieu's analysis, according to which ideologies support domination, either directly, by their content, or indirectly, because they are the discourses used by institutions in order to reproduce themselves. Foucault has elevated the obligation to account for discourse on the basis of the social conditions which make it possible to the status of a methodological *principle of exteriority* (Foucault 1971: 22). If modern pragmatic philosophy, which regards beliefs as permeated by action, had paid more attention to ideology, it would perhaps have contributed to the external theories of ideology. Given that external theories are the dominant paradigm within sociology, listing all the influential authors (Mannheim, Pareto, etc.) who have explained collective thought by social factors would be a labourious task which I do not intend to undertake here.

Theories of this second class have often criticized those of the first. According to Marx and Engels, for example, internal characterizations of ideologies are by nature idealist, and therefore, ideological themselves. More diplomatically, Bourdieu has noted that the 'semiological approach' to ideologies (Bourdieu 1980b: 230) and 'internal readings' (Bourdieu 1982: 192) are likely to miss the crucial relationship between ideologies and institutional reproduction. Despite these authoritative warnings, my research does not belong to this second line of thought. My project, being a semantic project, cannot easily take into account non-semantic elements. This is a limitation, and I do not pretend that the formal methods that will be proposed as the outcomes of this research can reach the levels of subtlety and complexity which political philosophy achieves in ideological debates. However, I shall claim that external approaches too have their limits; that an enlarged definition of semantics may allow one to internalize some of the aspects that hold the attention of external theories; that some other aspects, left aside by external theories, can be accounted for within a semantic approach.

Concerning the critique of idealism, we may first note that a certain dose of idealism is not always detrimental in sociology. However, since this is a vexed debate, let us just sketch its epistemological dimension. Elementary observation suggests that, in the explanation of social phenomena, both 'material' and 'ideal' causes are interrelated. When a 'materialist' approach wants to disclaim an 'idealist' interpretation, it has to prove that it can explain all observed facts with its own hypotheses. This strategy is generally less adequate for 'idealist' interpretations, because the idealist 'causes' that are employed to explain phenomena are usually not raw data, but instead, data which are partially constructed by the scientist (for example beliefs, mentalities, reconstructions of discourses), and therefore less intrinsically convincing. Consequently, idealist interpretations have to adopt a less ambitious strategy than materialist interpretations. They cannot simply disclaim materialist interpretation on the basis of their own results. They usually have to show that all current materialist hypotheses are unsatisfactory (they ignore the evidence which engenders the idealist interpretation), and then propose their own explanation to fill the gap. When an idealist interpretation does not make any reference to material causes, this does not necessarily mean that the existence of this type of cause is denied. The only thing that is denied is the possibility to account for all the observed facts on the basis of materialist reasoning alone.

Cold theories

Besides these two main groups, there is a third one, which Nisbet has suggested naming 'cold theories' of beliefs (Nisbet and Ross 1980). These theories regard ideologies as providing social actors with the type of information needed to exercise a 'bounded', or 'subjective rationality' (Downs 1957; Simon 1982). According to Downs, the social actor adheres to ideologies because it is in some sense 'rational' to do so. Since it would require a costly effort to search for information and to undertake intensive reasoning on the part of a social actor to make up his mind on political and social issues, ideologies reduce this effort by proposing ready-made, simple solutions. In this 'rational' interpretation ideological biases arise from the effects of the actor's perspective, from scarcity of information and from pitfalls of analysis. Because they focus on the individual level, cold theories must account for the collective dimension of ideologies through diffusion processes. Some 'cold' thinkers consider that the diffusion of an ideology is sufficiently explained when the researcher has exhibited the ideal type of social interaction in which the ideal-type actor has some 'good reasons' to subscribe to the ideology (Boudon 1986, 1990). Some others require that the diffusion processes be more clearly articulated, and turned into genuine 'epidemiological models' (Sperber 1992, 1996). Although, in many respects, social psychology cannot be called a 'cold' discipline, some social psychologists have intensively studied the individual level of diffusion processes and have proposed several models of attitude change (Festinger 1957; Bem 1967).

I fear that cold theories are better suited to knowledge and ordinary beliefs than to ideological beliefs. People who are ideologically involved do not relate to their own ideology, nor to that of others, in a 'cold' way. Inversely, ideologies neither expect from their members 'cold' membership nor 'cold' manifestations of this membership. According to Althusser's formula 'ideology *interpellates* the individuals', and 'prescribes material practices regulated by material rituals'. As noted by Shils (whose stance is totally different from Althusser's), complete individual subservience is often required from the members of ideologically oriented groups; it is also often necessary that the conduct of all members be entirely permeated by their ideology.

In the paradigm of 'bounded rationality' (read 'economic rationality') ideologies are totalizations which free social actors from the obligation of searching for costly, rare, and complex information concerning their environment. This description does not seem very accurate. Marxist ideology for example is not a simple theory, and its members have to make intensive intellectual investments to participate in it. Consider also the case of Islamic fundamentalism, which in occidental societies, is almost as much an ideology as a religion given the range of social and political issues it deals with. In France, for example, Islamic proselytizers do not try to convince the underprivileged youth of Arab origin by providing him or her with a simple, universal discourse. On the contrary, Islamic religion is presented as something deep and complex, which, like science, requires a lifetime of involvement. Khaled Kelkal, the young 'Islamic terrorist' shot by police in 1995, explained to the sociologist Dietmar Loch, in 1992:

> I was with a Muslim in a cell. There I learned Arabic. And I also learned my religion: Islam. I learned it well. I learned a great openness of mind through knowing Islam. My perspectives broadened. And I see my life... *not simpler*, but more coherent.[2]

In providing this example, my intention is neither to associate terrorism and ideology, nor to contest the rationality of religious and ideological commitments. It may well be that learning a new language in jail is more rational that doing nothing. The only point I want to make is that a strategy which requires, in order to change one's vision of the world, a new language to be learned, is certainly not the result of a wish to minimize costs. Therefore the argument of low costs does not seem to hold. The other (related) argument of simplicity, is explicitly rejected by Kelkal himself.[3]

There are, of course, popularizations of Marxism, of Islam, and of all ideologies. The capacity to address audiences with various levels of complexity is certainly an important factor in the success of ideologies. For cold theories the rational adherence to popularizations is the result of the simplicity of the messages and of the moral and scientific reputation of the theories that are popularized. I shall claim that 'popularization' does not only happen through a simplification of the ideological statements, but also through the superposition of two logics of unequal complexity: the logic of knowledge and the logic of evaluation.

We may enlarge these objections to cold theories and note that ideology is perhaps one of the applications of rational choice theory which best reveals the limits of this paradigm. Applying 'rational' explanations to the most fanatic behaviours, including those which lead to collective crime, genocide or suicide sheds a new light on the nature of these explanations. It is precisely when a type of explanation works everywhere in the same way, and allegedly with the same success, that we start doubting its validity. The success of cold theories is largely due to the fact that they are not easily falsifiable. In other words, they are just *ex post* theoretical hypotheses which cannot be tested. Simplicity is their only comparative advantage over more complex models which are based on less narrow visions of man and society. I believe that this advantage is strongly counterbalanced by the fact that these simple models are often tautological. The only kind of models inspired by cold theories which makes genuine predictions and which could be systematically tested are epidemiological models. But, to date, there has been no substantial contribution of epidemiological models to the sociology of ideas (Scubla 1992).

2 Ideology and practice

In order to circumscribe the kind of contribution that internal approaches can make to the theory of ideology, I shall first examine the limits of purely pragmatic theories of ideology.

External theories are all based on the idea that if ideologies have to be accounted for by 'real' phenomena (read 'material'), this is because they are in some sense, 'real' themselves. The first way to understand this materiality is to assume that 'thought' itself is material. This assumption is traditionally associated with Marxism. With the metaphor of the 'camera obscura', in *German Ideology*, Marx has indeed sketched a 'cognitive' theory of ideology, according to which the material alienation of man mechanically produces his erroneous beliefs. This ambitious project has not been taken up, even by recent Marxist theory. As stated by Boudon, 'No one has ever succeeded in producing any hypothesis concerning the nature of what would be, within the ideological process, the analogy of the optic nerve or the eye in the process of vision' (Boudon 1986: 66).

Althusser was perfectly aware of the difficulties raised by the analogy of the 'camera obscura' and the naive thesis concerning the 'materiality of thought' which it contains. He rejected it as an error of the 'young Marx'. Whatever sense the word 'representation' may take, it is not true, Althusser said, that ideologies are the representation of man's conditions of existence.

> It is not their real conditions of existence, their real world, which are 'represented' by 'men' in the ideology, but it is mainly their relation to these conditions of existence which is represented to them. It is in this relation that the 'cause' which must account for the imaginary deformation of the ideological representation of the real world, is contained. ... it is the *imaginary nature of this relation* which supports all the imaginary deformations that one can observe (provided one does not live within its truth) in every ideology. (Althusser 1970: 10)

It is not clear, however, how a representation of the conditions of existence can avoid being simultaneously a representation of one's relation to these conditions... In fact, the shift from the 'representation of the conditions of existence' to the 'representation of the imaginary relation of individuals with their conditions of existence' simply re-introduces imagination (a form of thought, mainly unconscious) as a key element in the ideological process. This allows Althusser to avoid the positivism of the young Marx, while allegedly bridging Althusser's theory of ideology with Freud's theory of unconsciousness.

This fragile solution is only slightly compatible with the main response that neo-Marxist (and Althusser's) theory has given to the problems raised by the analogy of the camera obscura. In essence, the mechanical dependency of ideas upon conditions of existence becomes a false problem as soon as one realizes that 'ideologies are not made up of ideas but of practices' (Pêcheux 1978: 98). For Althusser,

> We shall say, considering a single individual, that the existence of the ideas of his belief is material, in this that his ideas are material acts entangled within material practices, which, in turn, are regulated by material rituals.... (Althusser 1970: 28)

Althusser's insistence on rituals may seem a little bit exaggerated in the context of modern democracies. To speak of 'rituals' precludes taking into account the specific type of 'regularities' and 'predictability' of our democratic political practices, and the specific types of articulation between the private and public sphere that characterize the media. In any case, after Habermas' careful study of 'communicative actions' (Habermas 1984) and of the 'public sphere' in modern societies (Habermas 1978), it is no longer possible to assume that the binding force of discourse operates today exactly as it used to in traditional societies.

Bourdieu provides us with more subtle versions of the relation between beliefs and practice. First, ideas can be the result of *habitus*, that is, of practices embodied as a system of dispositions. Secondly, ideas can be seen as the instruments which allow social actors to defend the fields in which they operate with respect to other fields, and also as the instruments by which social actors position themselves within the interplay of forces which characterizes a given field. The concept of habitus allows us to consider ideas as tied to practice, while the concept of social field allows us to consider ideas as serving the purposes of action. However illuminating this double thesis may seem, it faces a certain number of objections. If I mention some of them here, it is not so much with the aim of making a genuine contribution to these difficult matters, but in order to help the reader gain a clearer idea of the kind of ideological phenomena that inspire this research. Many statements I will make in this section will neither be discussed nor supported by evidence. However, some of them will be developed in the next chapter.

Ideology and habitus

Although the concept of habitus has proved useful in explaining the adherence of social actors to the established order, it is also well known that the habitus is not an excellent predictor of ideological adherence. The same habitus – or, at least, the same practices and the same conditions of existence – can produce completely different political opinions. As an illustration of this variability, one may think of the recent and massive shift from a communist vote to a vote in favour of the extreme right in the French industrial working class. Bourdieu is of course aware of this variability:

> The same dispositions can engender very different opinions, sometimes even opposed opinions, for example in the religious and political domain, depending on the state of the field (and sometimes within a single life, as is witnessed by numerous ethical and political conversions). (Bourdieu 1992: 12)

One must therefore distinguish between the ideologies, which are devoted to the legitimation of a social organization, and the habitus which are representations and practices deeply interiorized and embodied by the social actors sharing the same social conditioning. Ideologies are the result of a deliberate intention to justify the social order, while habitus are unconscious, or unquestioned systems of disposition. This distinction is more or less equivalent to the distinction between ideologies and, respectively, social representations in the French school of social psychology and attitudes in American social psychology (Doise 1990: 153).

As an extreme case, the representations seem completely absorbed within the social order. This is the case, in traditional societies, when the divisions which constitute a social order take the form of the 'doxa', that is, of 'tacit theses posited on the hither side of all enquiry'. As noted by Bourdieu himself, in modern societies, the domain of doxa is not coextensive with reality, and is therefore complemented by the domain of opinion, that is, 'implying awareness and recognition of the possibility of different or antagonistic beliefs'. Despite all their efforts to disguise themselves within the realm of doxa, ideologies are condemned to remain explicit, and therefore contradicted and contested. Ideologies do not stand as close to the habitus as doxic theses do. They are not, even in Bourdieu's theory, exclusively a matter of habitus. In particular, they depend upon the strategic behaviours of the actors within the social fields to which they belong.

Discourses of legitimation (the ideologies) always legitimate domination. They justify social divisions and the division of labour. But the discourses of legitimation are not simply the instruments of domination. Because discourses of legitimation are made up of transposed, misrecognizable forms of the social divisions, the real nature of these discourses is often hidden even to those who use them. 'Dominants are dominated by their instruments of domination.' By this formula, Bourdieu refers either to the fact that the representations dominate the subject because they are rooted in the social order which produces its habitus, or to the fact that the subject exercises domination at the cost of having to preserve the very structure of the field which renders this domination possible. There are therefore two kinds of subjections. The subjection of the dominated is the interiorization of the discourse of the dominants. The subjection of the dominants is both a subjection to the habitus of the dominants, and subjection to the established order, to the divisions which underpin it, and to its institutions.

Bourdieu, for political reasons, never fully developed the idea of a subjection of the dominants to the instruments which bring the dominated into subjection. Pushing the research in this direction would have compelled him to recognize that these instruments are intrinsically valuable in some sense. This would have been completely opposed to Bourdieu's project, which is to denounce domination by the denunciation of the arbitrariness and the artificial character of its instruments. I concede that no other author has paid as much attention as Bourdieu to the 'value' of discourse. But, according to him, this value is entirely 'social'. The value of discourse is the value of its social use. In other words, discourse has no intrinsic value. There is no room, in Bourdieu's theory, for any intrinsic and 'positive' features of discourses which would render them more or less suitable for the production of social uses of distinction.

I propose the hypothesis that there is a third type of subjection to the instruments of domination, which is neither the result of the habitus of the dominants nor the product of a social organization. This subjection is a subjection to discourse itself. More precisely, it is a submission to the necessity of preserving the efficiency of discourse. This efficiency has at least two dimensions. In one respect, there is the capacity to produce profound adherence to the social order through the reinforcement of the habitus of the dominants and the persuasion of the dominated. In another respect there is the capacity of discourse to oppose other discourses and to defend economic and political interests. In the articulation of habitus and discourse, of dispositions and language, evaluation plays a central role. Because I do not want to engage in a thorough discussion of the psychological and cognitive aspects of evaluation, I shall postpone to the next chapter some more detailed arguments in favour of this thesis. For the moment, I shall simply assume that the efficiency of discourse, as far as it operates through the creation and mobilization of deep adherence, lies in its capacity to convey compatible values.

I shall turn now to more theoretical objections to the description of ideologies in terms of habitus. Even if the social distribution of the habitus could predict the social distribution of ideological adherences, this would not solve all the theoretical difficulties. The mere concept of habitus, conceived to be the centre of a theory of practice, is intrinsically problematic for the 'objectivist' mode of thought. On Bourdieu's own admission:

> As with all 'dispositional' concepts, the concept of 'habitus', which has been used historically in a way that enables it to refer to acquired, permanent, generative dispositions, is valuable principally due to the false problems and the false solutions it eliminates, to the questions it helps to reformulate and solve, and to *the scientific difficulties it raises*. (Bourdieu 1980b: 89)

The habitus leads us into uncharted territory where the explanatory and the explained coincide. Practice is the product of habitus and habitus is the product of practice, and so on. The habitus is not only the embodiment of individual history, but also the embodiment (by a mimesis which is never simply the imitation of one particular person by another) of the history of previous generations, and so on. Therefore the concept of habitus leads us into yet more unknown territory where individual and inter-generational history coincide. In addition, the concept of habitus is indissolubly linked to Bourdieu's own intellectual habitus, which consists in shifting the semantic categories (agent, patient, object) through the permutation of active and passive voices, of present and past participle forms, of verbal and nominal forms, in formulae such as 'structured structures functioning as structuring structures', 'possessed by his possessions', 'dominated dominant', etc.

My reluctance to accept the circularity that the concept of habitus introduces within sociological theory is perhaps the result of an undue objectivism on my part. Nevertheless, I would argue that in the general system of conformities to which this concept refers, some articulations are insufficiently detailed. A cognitive and psychoanalytic theory of embodiment is still missing in Bourdieu's theory. In particular, no attention is paid to the emotional and evaluative constitution of identity which underpins the construction of identity which is due to practice. In other words, the emphasis put on the terms 'practice' and 'embodiment' leads one to underestimate the evaluative, or moral nature of human beings. Besides the 'empire of value', one may claim that Bourdieu also underestimates the 'empire of truth'. With his descriptions of language as a social practice, with the emphasis he places on speech at the expense of language structure, Bourdieu transforms into habitus both the capacity and the desire for language. His perspective has the advantage of providing a theoretical framework for the explanation of the social variations of linguistic competence. But this does not help us to understand the psychological foundations of social learning. Finally, the concept of habitus is supposed to apply to all sorts of societies. This postulate seems contradicted by the evidence which suggests that social learning differs depending on religious, legal and political traditions.[4]

With reference to the present work, these professions of faith lead me to propose that the study of the dependency of ideological representations upon practice be complemented by a study of the dependency of ideological representations upon values and the way these values are interiorized by the subjects.

Ideology and perspective

If, according to Bourdieu, the social origin and the habitus are not sufficient to explain the ideological adherences, this is because these habitus must be replaced within the context of the social fields in which they are inscribed. Sociology is therefore the science of the *relation between habitus and social fields* (Bourdieu 1992: 124).

The concept of field is a reaction to the concept of apparatus. Athusser, in a famous paper entitled *Ideology and Ideological State Apparatuses* (Althusser 1970) proposed to distinguish between repressive state apparatuses, which rely on violence and physical constraints to impose a social order, and ideological state apparatuses, which, without resorting to violence, create the ideological conditions of the reproduction–transformation of the relations of production. Examples of such ideological state apparatuses are religion, the education system, trade unions, art and culture. These apparatuses, are, according to Althusser, the arenas in which the social classes struggle for domination. An ideology is then defined as a system of relations of contradiction–unevenness–subordination between the ideological state apparatuses. For example, in modern capitalist societies the education system is dominant, while in pre-capitalist occidental societies, the religious apparatus was dominant. Although neither Althusser nor his followers, like Balibar, conceive of the social classes as existing prior to the spaces and the instruments of their struggle, they regard class struggle as the motor of history, and the relations of production as what is at stake within this struggle.

This intellectual construction has today almost totally vanished. There has been a consensus (both political and theoretical) to banish the monolithic notion of social classes struggling for their necessarily antagonistic interests. Bourdieu's paper *Le mort saisit le vif* (Bourdieu 1980a), which is implicitly angled at Althusserism, attacks the concept of ideological state apparatus. In the first part of this paper, Bourdieu claims that the concept of apparatus implies a mechanical and teleological view, in which the operations of inculcation of the ideology are the product of deliberate class intentions. On the contrary, according to Bourdieu, the inculcation of ideas matters less than the learning and the embodiment of social identity and attached social ambitions by individuals. Furthermore, the concept of 'apparatus' does not allow us to take into account the very contribution of the dominated to their own domination. As a consequence, Bourdieu proposes to replace the concept of apparatus by the concept of field, which he grants with a finer texture and a greater autonomy with respect to the other fields. Examples of fields studied by Bourdieu are philosophy, journalism, sport and fashion. Theoretically, a field is defined as an interplay of forces within the institutional heritage endowed by its history. It does not imply consciousness, nor manipulation, nor functional aggregation of wills and behaviour. The unity of the field is the result of the adherence of social actors to the mere principle of that field, which guarantees their social position. Members of the field (belonging to different sides) derive advantage from the field, and consequently do not usually wish to leave it. They may even unite against others when conflict arises between fields.

The concept of field, in Bourdieu's sociological theory, allows three types of metaphors: that of the spectrum of forces, that of the landscape, and that of the market (Silber 1995). In society, as in physics, space is less important than the lines of forces that operate through it. However, in society, the forces are not as much objective forces as power, that is, the advantages gained in history, and reified as privileged positions. Thus the spectrum of forces (the domination of age, sex, wealth, status, culture) is reified, naturalized and institutionalized into a topography (a landscape) of society. The spectrum/landscape duality is the semantic *raison d'être* of the concept of 'field'. It allows the unification of, on one hand, society as a space of domination and, on the other, society as a space of points of view. Ideology, within this theory, is a point, or a region of the social landscape, that is, both a point of conflict and domination, and a perspective on the social. Finally, there is a third metaphor, that of the field as a market. The field can be characterized as a 'law of value', which gives the 'price' which may be attributed to each discourse in each point of that field. This law of value is interiorized by the members of the field in the form of 'tastes' – like the 'philosophical taste' in the philosophical field (Bourdieu 1992).

All this remains metaphorical, and hence simultaneously illuminating and unsatisfactory. On the one hand, it is clear that we are within society, and not outside. Therefore, our beliefs depend on 'where we are', and our discourses depend on 'where we speak from'. On the other hand, society is not a landscape, and our representations of society are not a matter of vision. Society is represented and conceived rather than perceived. Strictly speaking, discursive relations are not the mercantile relations implied by the metaphor of the 'law of value' either. Why, then, does Bourdieu make such a heavy use of these metaphors? The reason is clearly that in order to denounce the logic of fields for which he has no particular sympathy (economics, religion, physics) Bourdieu needs to express himself with their language. This strategy may also be a scientific handicap. Strictly speaking, for example, the metaphor of society as a space of points of view presupposes either that there is a real landscape which imposes the

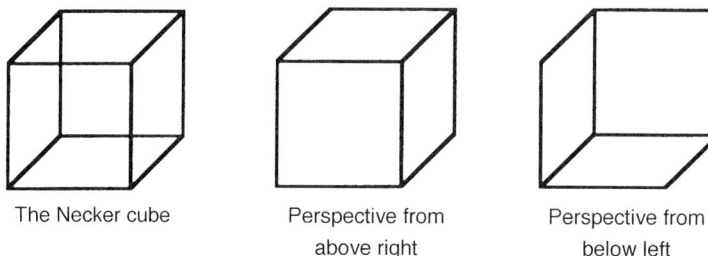

| The Necker cube | Perspective from above right | Perspective from below left |

Figure 1.1 Structure and perspective.

distribution of the perspectives, or that the 'landscape' is totally constructed out of the social distribution of the points of view. The purpose of metaphor is precisely to avoid the need for this kind of clarification.

The metaphor of society as a space of points of view would perhaps become more interesting if it illustrated the constraints which are put on 'how we see' by 'what is conceived'. It is not difficult to provide simple cases in which a structure imposes a choice between several alternative 'perceptions'. Consider, for example, in Figure 1.1, one 'conceptual' representation on a cube. Given this representation, there are only two different possible perceptions of the cube: one in which the beholder is above and on the right of the cube, and one in which the beholder is below and on the left of the cube. In other words, it may happen that a conceptual reality offers only a few remarkable angles upon itself.

I shall argue below, and throughout this work, that society too, and in particular, its representations in discourse, may constrain the space of possible perspectives which one can take upon it. The social perspectives which sociology studies are not only the results of social differentiation, because social differentiation itself requires the existence of these perspectives in order to happen.

To spin out this argument in less metaphorical terms, we may also object that there is one noticeable absence from the sociological theory of fields, that is, the *substance of discourse*. In other words, there is a recurrent postulate according to which the substance of the discursive means of interaction, and the substantial ideological conditions of domination, do not matter as much as the forms of interaction and the social contexts in which they take place. First, the power of language does not lie within language, but arises from the institutional contexts in which speech acts take place (Bourdieu 1982).[5] Secondly, the discursive content of a social interaction is either irrelevant, or totally reducible to the structure of the interaction (who interacts, where, when, what social profits are at stake). Given the irrelevance of discourse content, the task of sociology is to get rid of it whenever this seems possible:

> Many historical debates, especially but not exclusively concerning the arts would be enlightened, or more simply, *annulled*, if one could bring to light, in each case, the complete universe of distinct (sometimes opposed) significations which the concepts at stake, 'realism', 'social art', 'idealism', 'art for art's sake', have in the social struggles within the whole field ..., or within the sub-fields of those who use such concepts as signs of adherence ... (Bourdieu 1992: 113)

I would prefer to subscribe to the project of 'enlightening' rather than to that of 'annulling' debates as important as those concerned with realism in art history. Sociology cannot afford to annul discourses, because they are as much the source of social struggles and social distinctions as their product. I do not intend, however, to engage in a chicken and egg debate: although it is my conviction that representations can be at the origin of social reality, I shall not attempt to demonstrate it here. I shall simply argue, as outlined below, that even if one adopts Bourdieu's economic view of discourse, there is, besides the scarcity of discourse which is produced by its social appropriation, another type of scarcity, which cannot simply be explained by this appropriation.

The scarcity of discourse

I assume that every reader has experienced the 'desire for an idea', that is, the need to invent something, to solve a problem, to find an argument which has the power to convince others and change one's environment. Sadly, neither great ideas nor convincing discourses appear at will. This is partly a consequence of our limited intellectual capacities and of the complexity of the world. But this is perhaps not the only reason. One should also take into account that we are always already immersed into more or less coherent representations of society which do not let themselves be easily modified given the relations which unite them. These relations forbid us to modify one representation without modifying the consistency of our world views, a consistency which is our best guarantee against the arguments of our contradictors.

Let me give an example. A politically committed individual may deplore the hegemony of free-market ideology. The inability to present a coherent alternative to this economic discourse may be partly the result of the actor's limitations. But one must admit that this is not only a matter of individual limits. At the global level too, since the historical collapse of Marxism made many Marxist concepts taboo, no such theory is available. There is no discursive formation capable, at one and the same time, of applying its general principles in a straightforward way to concrete issues, of exercising a large number of unquestioned truths, of making people feel that each and every single statement is underpinned by scientifically guaranteed presuppositions, of making objections to every alternative view, and of drawing practical recommendations which conform to its theory. The hegemony of free-market ideology is, to a certain extent, an indication that the social need for an alternative has diminished. However, one cannot reasonably interpret every ideological hegemonic position as a lack of need or a lack of will to find an alternative. It is much simpler to concede that whatever social wills there may be, they cannot be transformed into collective action until a coherent discourse emerges, one which will confront the dominant discourse. If this is not the case, social action is either inefficient or efficient only to the extent that it can exploit discursive rights (traditional or legal conventions for negotiations) obtained in periods when the actors had stronger discourses.

This example suggests that there is a scarcity of discourse. According to Foucault, this scarcity is the result of three types of procedures of rarefaction. External procedures consist of rules of exclusion organized around the divisions between permission and prohibition, reason and insanity, truth and falsity. These rules reveal that discourse is not only the instrument, but also the object of power and desire. Internal procedures consist of the categories that regulate textual production: commentary, authorship, work, disciplines, doctrines, etc. Finally, there are also some conditions which bear upon people's access to discourse, its exercise and its appropriation. However,

> the existence of systems of rarefaction does not imply that over and beyond them lie great vistas of limitless discourse, continuous and silent, repressed and driven back, making it our task to abolish them and to restore it to speech. ... Discourse must be treated as a discontinuous activity, its different manifestations sometimes coming together, but just as easily unaware of, or excluding each other. (Foucault 1971: 22)

In this passage, the fundamental scarcity of discourse is simply the specificity of the historical existence of (possibly) interrelated discursive practices. In other words, one can only conceive of the profusion of discourses on the grounds of the multiplicity of human subjects and individual experiences of the world. For Foucault, however, discourse is neither the product of the subjects nor the reflection of their experiences of the world. The scarcity and the discontinuity of discourse become unquestionable as soon as the individual level is recognized as irrelevant for the description of discourse. This may be correct, but it is nevertheless a postulate. I would like to suggest that in the case of ideologies, that is, in the case of discourses which are both aware of each other and exclude each other, it is possible to propose another argument in favour of scarcity and discontinuity.

This argument is neo-Darwinian, and maintains that in a *competitive* environment, only the 'best' discourses can survive. The word 'competitive' does not refer here to natural competition, but to social competition, that is, to the very will of differentiation and domination. This differentiation is realized by the appropriation and the integration of symbolic resources. Therefore, the state of development and the potentiality of the symbolic order influence the process of differentiation. This does not mean that there is, strictly speaking, a symbolic scarcity. The struggle for the appropriation of symbolic resources is not the consequence of an intrinsic limitation of the symbolic order. The rules bearing on the combination of signifiers do not significantly limit the generative capacity of this order. It is only when the purely symbolic constraints (grammatical, logical and argumentative rules for language and discourse) combine with the constraint of differentiation and conflictual opposition that one can talk of a discursive scarcity.

More concretely, suppose that the dominant discourse upon the social is a network of propositions, entities and values, as in Figure 1.2. Suppose also that the truth value of the propositions and the 'favourability' of entities and values is either −1 or 1. Suppose further that the edges represent the logical implications (i.e. contradiction) between propositions, the causal relations between entities and the axiological solidarities (i.e. incompatibilities) between values.

Assume finally that there is a social consensus upon the structure of the network, and that the only things that can be discussed in public debate are what correspond to the 'values' of the vertices of the network, and the 'signs'

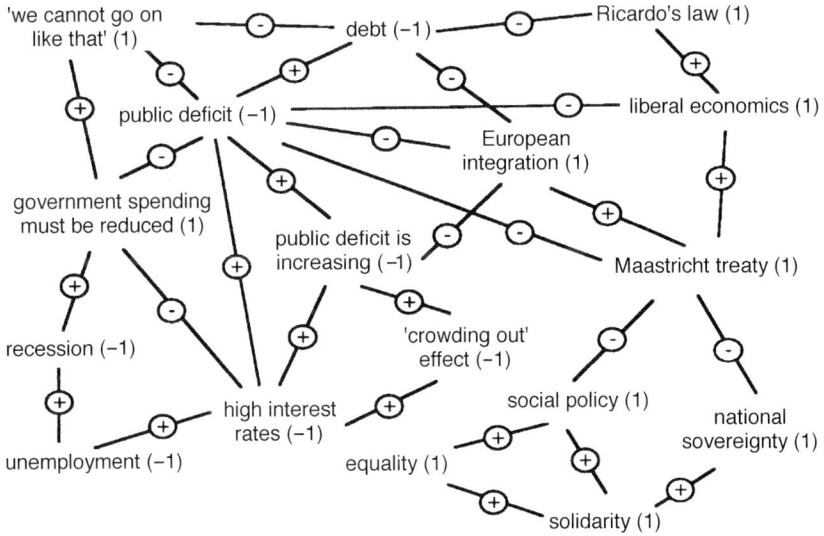

Figure 1.2 Discourse as a network.

of the edges. This assumption reflects the fact that the domain of opinion is surrounded by the universe of doxa, which assigns boundaries and skeleton to it. This assumption may also be justified by the social will for differentiation. Because comparing two states of the same network is easier than comparing two different networks, proposing another discourse which would be totally distinct from previously existing ones does not facilitate the confrontation with these discourses, and therefore, does not facilitate differentiation.

The network above represents, in a highly schematic way, a right-wing position about the problem of public deficits. The network is consistent in the sense that most positive edges connect a vertice to another which has the same polarity, while most negative edges connect a vertice to another with opposed polarity. There are, nevertheless, three main points of inconsistency, which reflect the traditional weak points of discourses favourable to economic rigour and economic integration: the fact that cutting government spending in periods of low demand may create recession, the opposition between Maastricht treaty and national sovereignty, and the low profile of the Maastricht treaty regarding social policies.

If I want to contest this discourse on a single, or a small subset of these values and weights, I shall certainly fail to make a strong claim. If the area of the network I contest is highly connected with the rest of the network (for example, I may wish to claim, contrary to the dominant opinion, that public deficits are useful), it will be easy for my adversaries to show that I decrease the consistency of the network. If the area I contest is only loosely connected with the rest of the network (for example, if I claim that Ricardo's theorem is wrong), my adversaries will argue that my contest is only marginal, and that fundamentally, I am saying the same thing as them. In both cases, my attempt to confront the dominant discourse will have failed.

I may be more successful if I change large parts of the network by criticizing, altogether, the European construction, liberal political economy, and by emphasizing the priority of social policy and solidarity. Ideologies behave similarly when they search for general principles which can shift, at one and the same time, the polarity of all vertices of a discourse. This is the case, for example, of the Marxist critique of idealist statements and values. More generally, ideologies try to occupy one of the coherent positions which arise from an historical state of the doxa (consensus).

Neural network theory shows that when networks similar to the one I have sketched above are endowed with specific dynamics and learning algorithms, they can 'learn' a pattern of weights enabling them to select, for all inputs, the stable state of the network (an attractor) which is the closest to the input. These networks learn a small number of stable 'equilibria' reflecting the categories under which inputs may be subsumed. I believe that the long-term dynamics of public discourse are similar in some sense to the learning dynamics of these physical and computational systems. The first analogy which inspires the formal proposals of this research is therefore the analogy between the social dynamics of discursive differentiation and the learning dynamics of certain neural networks. Ideology can be seen as an attempt to 'carve up' doxa in such a way that each statement, each local state of the public debate converges towards an equilibrium, that is, one of the ideologies which make up public discourse. An ideology struggles to impose the discursive relations between notions, propositions and values that enable it to classify utterances as belonging to its own discourse or to the discourse of one of its rivals. The classification of the statements must reflect (a) the doxa, (b) the interests defended by the ideology, (c) the consistency of the statements with the ideology under which they are classified. More generally, an ideology can be seen as a system which associates a degree of consistency to each possible ideology.

The social debates which modify the ideologies are complex and very sensitive to external factors, such as strategic behaviours and interests. There are therefore clear limits to the analogy I proposed above, and which would have us believe that everything happens within the boundaries of discourse. In addition, the social processes of differentiation are clearly not regulated by mechanical learning algorithms. Note, however, that at each moment of these social debates, each time someone argues about the ideological nature of a statement, and each time someone is persuaded or sceptical regarding this ideological nature, someone makes an 'ideological interpretation' of this statement. As the outcome of this interpretation, the statement is found consistent (or inconsistent) with an ideology. I believe that the individuals who make these interpretations are 'ideologically trained'. In other words, they have (at least in part) interiorized the results of long-term ideological differentiation. There is therefore a second analogy between the cognitive processes which allow a social actor to position a discourse with respect to a set of ideologies and the dynamics of relaxation of certain neural networks. I shall develop this point in the next chapter.

I said above that the efficiency of discourse and its capacity to influence or convince people, lies, to a large extent, in its ability to convey evaluations. In this subsection, I have focused on another type of efficiency, that which consists of the capacity of one discourse to confront another, to adapt to polemical situations and to defend specific interests. This second type of efficiency requires that discourse be able to develop itself, to multiply itself, to produce itself and to differentiate itself. But discourse must not lose its unity in these operations. Discourse must simultaneously benefit from its generative capacities (that of language, that of argumentation, that of rhetoric) and from the normative efficiency of its central theses and values. Each ideology has its own way to deal with this dialectic of centrality and marginality, of integration and diversification. Each ideology has its own definition of universality and each has its own procedures to validate new statements from the periphery. Despite this diversity, all ideologies express themselves through language, and therefore, must all control in some sense the generative capacity of language in order to be certain that their statements are in harmony.

One way to guarantee coherence is to ensure a logical consistency with all previously accepted statements, or with a core of statements (a doctrine). This solution has the drawback of being extremely rigid. As we will see in the last section of this chapter, Bourdieu has convincingly argued that neither ideologies nor discursive formations are characterized by a logical consistency.

Another way to guarantee coherence could be to intervene in the generative capacity itself, by defining an 'ideological language'. Foucault, however, kept repeating that discourse is not the same thing as language. 'From the kind of analysis I have undertaken, words are as deliberately absent as things themselves; any description of vocabulary is as lacking as any reference to the living plenitude of experience' (Foucault 1972: 48). And he concluded from his research on the fields of knowledge that the unity of discursive formation is not the result of a specific language. Similar conclusions have been drawn by Pêcheux concerning the unity of 'ideologies'. After important debates, which will be evoked in the third chapter of this book, the notion that language and ideology belong to different levels has finally prevailed.

The third way to enforce consistency is to set up specific institutions devoted to the control of the utterances (the Inquisition in the Catholic Church, media censorship during the MacCarthy era for example). This is a costly strategy, which can never be applied on a large scale without drifting towards totalitarianism.

The most flexible way to guarantee coherence, and that which will draw my attention in this work, is to make sure that new statements fit the evaluations of the ideology. This flexibility is due to the fact that an evaluative control operates, so to speak, 'at the surface' of language. It is due to the fact that this control is sensitive to the slightest change at this surface, but at the same time, flexibility is ensured by the fact that this evaluative control remains 'at a distance' from language itself. In particular, the evaluative control is not required to fully reconstruct the contextual meaning of an utterance, nor to guess the meaning that the author intended to convey. The flexibility of the evaluative control is the result of the paradoxical status of evaluation, which is both a genuine semantic dimension, and a dimension which is so special and autonomous with respect to the other dimensions that it can give birth to specific interpretative modes.

The fields and the media society

Let us end the discussion of the relation between ideology and practice with an inspection of the state of this relationship in the context of modern society. I contend that although many ideological beliefs still offer direct guidance to individuals in their social actions, many other beliefs have little, if any, contact with concrete decisions and behaviours.

Several authors have defended the notion that representations have an autonomy with respect to practice. Michel Serres, for example, in a series of books entitled *Hermes I* to *VI*, develops the thesis of a generalized circulation of themes, representations and discourses between fields. This philosophical work suggests that, if there are still ideologies in modern democracies, they take the form of systems of representations which operate across our fields of practice.

The most radical critique of the full determination of belief by practice is certainly that of Baudrillard, who argues that the movement of modern society towards virtuality and simulation results from the subordination of the logic of practice to the logic of signs (Baudrillard 1993). Although I do not adhere to Baudrillard's ultimate conclusions, such as the disappearance of reality itself, I concede that he drew attention to dimensions of modern society that had been overlooked by the objectivism of sociology. I shall borrow from Baudrillard the idea that, in modern democracies, the conditions have been fulfilled for a relative autonomy of beliefs with respect to practice.

The evidence which upholds this idea can be briefly outlined as follows: the evolution of modern society, characterized by the decreasing involvement of individuals in politics, and the parallel growth of available information (from distant places in the world or concerning events which, despite their proximity, are beyond reach given the segmentation of society and powers) generates many situations in which individuals cannot act in response to incoming flows of news. The range of issues which are presented for our intellectual and emotional appreciation, but which have, nonetheless, no concrete relevance for us – in the sense that we have no conceivable means of modifying them or of modifying our life in relation to them – is expanding. We acquire a wide range of beliefs and attitudes which never demand any decision from us, which are of no 'practical' interest to us, and which do not contribute to strategies of social recognition or social distinction. The frequency of such situations may create indifference or, alternatively, emotional relations to the world.

Similar arguments have been developed by theorists who insist on the relation between 'sensitivization' and moralization (Greimas and Fontanille 1991), and theorists who depict ethical judgements as rooted in 'evaluative emotions' (Livet and Thévenot 1993). There are, according to these authors, several basic 'orders of judgement' which are 'determined by the type of interplay of evaluative emotions, before any genuine judgement of value'. These theories insist on the continuum between emotion, judgement, formation of evaluative beliefs, emotion-sharing through communication, and finally, action. Boltanski, for example, details several predefined modes (which he calls 'topiques') of 'socialization' of the emotions created by the spectacle of distant suffering: denunciation, sentimental empathy, and aesthetization. These cultural resources, which regulate people's preconceptual recognition and coordination naturally connect up with ideologies.

> The term 'topique' must be understood in the sense it had in ancient rhetorics, that is, it must be put in relation, simultaneously, with an argumentative and an affective dimension. Speech is here an affected speech, and it is through emotions that we can conceive of the coordination of the beholders – who are also actors – and, consequently, of the transformation of individual concerns and individual speech into collective commitment. To turn these topiques into political ideologies, liable, in particular, to be distributed on a left–right axis, we must fill in, by means of precise descriptions, the system of places which constitutes the general framework of these 'topiques'. (Boltanski 1993: 10)

If we believe Boltanski, besides the traditional chain of causalities (a) below,
we should also consider the chain (b).

(a) *practice* $\rightarrow$ *habitus* $\rightarrow$ *ideology* $\rightarrow$ *action*
(b) *emotion* $\rightarrow$ *evaluation* $\rightarrow$ *topique* $\rightarrow$ *ideology* $\rightarrow$ *action*

From this perspective, ideologies can no longer simply be understood as strategies of justification and instruments of distinctions, but have to be understood also as the result of empathetic relations to realities to which social actors can only gain access through the media. Ideologies depend on these evaluative reactions, and conversely, these reactions depend on ideologies.

To conclude this brief discussion of the relations between ideology and practice, one must acknowledge the importance of socio-pragmatic studies, and particularly, their achievements in the field of the sociology of taste. However, I do not believe that nationalism, racism, liberalism or Marxism, can be accounted for in terms of habitus. I do not believe, either, that the only things that matter in discursive exchanges are the side-effects of these exchanges. In the production of discourse, there are some constraints which go beyond the constraints attached to its immediate social uses.

Despite my critique of pragmatic theories of ideology, I share most of Bourdieu's critique of objectivism. I even believe that the theoretical mode of thinking has the same reasons to underscore the importance of evaluation as it has to underscore pragmatic reasoning. In December 1995, the French government, led by Prime Minister Alain Juppé, proposed to change the system of health insurance. An important movement of protest almost paralyzed France for three weeks. A survey revealed that among the people who where against the reform 80 per cent were unable to mention one of Juppé's proposals. The result of this survey was broadcast and used against the movement by journalists and politicians who claimed that it revealed the irrationality of the opposition to the reform. Of course, the only thing that the survey proved was that evaluative reasoning does not necessarily allow people to remember the detail of the information they have used to make up their mind on a given issue. This example shows that cognitive foundations of evaluative reasoning must be clarified if we want to avoid political exploitation and biased sociological interpretations.

I shall now return to the opposition between internal and external theories. As we shall see, this distinction is not as clear-cut and as simple as it may at first seem.

3 Ideological critique and disrepute

We can discern, in contemporary French neo-Marxism, at least two main schools. It may be convenient to summarize their differences in the form of a table (Table 1.1).

The first school is located within the field of political philosophy and is associated with the work of Althusser. It draws upon Marxist-Leninism and regards class struggle as the motor of history (much less emphasis is placed upon technological progress than in *Capital*). It focuses on material and ideological domination, it rejects the young Marx and it has abandoned the interpretation of beliefs as transposed practices. The second school is located within the field of sociology, and is associated with the work of Bourdieu. This school has abandoned the interpretation of history and action by the means of class struggle. Instead, it concentrates on 'symbolic domination'. It is directly inspired by the young Marx and it takes up Marx's project of a theory of practice. Both schools are legitimate interpretations of Marx. The Althusserian school represents more or less the orthodox reading of Marx, while the second is inspired by Marx's satirical vein (particularly apparent in *The German Ideology* and *The Holy Family*).

Table 1.1 Two neo-Marxian schools

Key figure	Althusser	Bourdieu
Discipline	Political philosophy	Sociology
Adherence	Marxism-Leninism	Left
Father	Second Marx	Young Marx
Nature of domination	Material, ideological	Symbolic
Beliefs and practice	Ritualistic articulation	Habitus
Class struggle	Motor of history	A mode of struggle among others

In his early works, Marx devotes much effort to show that the discourses he analyses can be reproduced within his own conceptual framework. Instead of truly *explaining* a discourse by its material and social causes, Marx shows that he is able to capture its vocabulary, its style and its modes of reasoning, and correlate them with social positions. Marx suggests that other discourses (for example philosophy and political economy) are either empty or endlessly repeating themselves. In any case, Marxian theory encompasses them. This type of analysis, I would argue, is intended as much to discredit other discourses as to explain them by their social causes, and discuss their truth or falsity.

Marx's talent for caricaturing pedantic discourses has found, in Pierre Bourdieu, both a continuator and a theoretician. Bourdieu has shown how accent, pronunciation, tone, corporal hexis, the correctness of language and the propriety of discourse (all elements previously neglected by semiotic studies) are major factors in creating an impression of legitimacy. The legitimacy is never as strong as when it is simultaneously recognized and misrecognized, in the sense that the receiver becomes aware of the symbolic authority of the speaker, though he remains unaware of the mechanisms that create this feeling. Bourdieu argues finally that the accumulation and reproduction of symbolic power are similar to those of wealth. Cultural capital helps its inheritors make their way in the educational system, and to gain access to positions of authority where they can produce more symbolic capital and impose it on a larger scale.

Besides the careful application of this general framework to various social fields, Bourdieu has provided us with several analyses of the procedures of self-justification that characterize the discursive genres. He has largely directed his comments towards political discourse (Bourdieu and Boltanski 1976), artistic discourse (Bourdieu 1992), and philosophical discourse (Bourdieu 1982) – with special attention to Heidegger and Sartre. But perhaps, the most revealing example of the strength and the limits of Bourdieu's method is to be found in the last chapter of *Ce que parler veut dire* (1982) which first appeared as an article in *Les Actes de la Recherche*.

On one hand, these pages appear as an ordinary comment, as an additional step in the natural progress of hermeneutics. In this article, Bourdieu comments upon a text by Balibar (the French Marxist political philosopher), which is in turn a comment on a comment, still by Balibar, on *Capital*. Furthermore, the text is organized in such a way that Balibar's article is juxtaposed with comments by Marx himself, selected by Bourdieu from *The German Ideology*. In this way, it seems as if Bourdieu, in a move which is traditional in the hermeneutic game, tried to re-establish an authentic Marxist spirit where Balibar had betrayed it. On the other hand, the very title of the chapter – 'Le discours d'importance. Quelques réflexions sociologiques sur "Quelques remarques critiques à propos de 'Lire *le Capital*' " ' – should warn us that we are faced with a text which wants to break, by means of excess and parody, the chain of self-legitimating comments. This change of tone is reinforced by the textual layout, which includes cartoon portraits of Marx in the margins with his quotations contained in comic-book speech balloons.

The text, supported by a complex set of mirror relations, is balanced upon these two contradictory foundations. In this construction, each element has its counterpart. Bourdieu criticizes the misappropriation of Marx by Balibar, but in the same way as Balibar employs Marx against deviant interpretations, Bourdieu uses Marx against Balibar. Bourdieu criticizes Balibar's efforts to present himself as Marx's heir by suggesting that Balibar is retrospectively disowned by Marx. The logic of appropriation and inheritance is therefore simultaneously denounced and employed. Lastly, Bourdieu attacks the self-legitimation of Balibar's discursive genre, but he borrows stylistic and iconic elements from other genres which are the traditional duals of political philosophy: parody and satire. The meta-discourse of Bourdieu's text can be summarized by saying that to a *legitimation from above*, which is attributed to Balibar, Bourdieu opposes an implicit *legitimation from below*.

The symmetry between 'upward' and 'downward' legitimation does not imply that Balibar's and Bourdieu's texts are equivalent. On the contrary, Bourdieu's critical operations of reversal are consistent with the conviction that in communicative actions, content is less important than form; what is said is less important than how it is said. In this view, not all genres have equal status, not all strategies of self-legitimation are equally acceptable. I do not believe, however, that the genre of ideological critique is, by itself, a guarantee of respectability. The pages by Lenin on Kautsky in *State and Revolution*, for example, are more akin to insult than discussion. The sociological critique *à la Bourdieu* is no more valuable *as a genre*. If we focus on the formal level we discover that Bourdieu's text can be characterized by the reversal of a set of *generative schemes*, of both theoretical and practical nature, which oppose

- consecrated/de-consecrated (Marx)
- distant/intimate (in relation to Marx)
- name/icon (signs)
- reference/presence (semiotic ontology)
- typewritten text/handwriting in balloons (materiality of the signifier and attached conventions)
- text/speech (type of discourse)
- quotation/facsimile (status of reported text)
- sentence and paragraph boundaries/physical cuts in the montage of the facsimile (units of meaning)
- writing/circling by hand, underlining, drawing arrows (practice)
- political philosophy/comics used for popularization and satire (genre)
- formal/authentic (style)

For many of these pairings it is unclear why the second term of the opposition should necessarily be preferable to the first. For some of them, like that concerning the status of the reported text or that concerning the units of discourse, the first may even seem preferable. There is indeed something violent in treating someone else's text as a 'physical entity' and cutting it as Bourdieu does regardless of its natural, meaningful units. There is something unfair in making a montage which suggests that there is no substance at all in a text. More fundamentally, reversing the generative schemes leaves them unquestioned. This leads Bourdieu to use formal instruments that are similar to those of the genres which he denounces. We are still far from Bourdieu's aim of establishing a relation between the subject and culture or political debate which would be 'something other than a relation of distinction' (Bourdieu 1990: 31).

One could claim, however, that the reversal of the generative schemes is valuable in that it allows a 'democratization of the hermeneutic stance' (Bourdieu 1993: 923). It is doubtful whether this 'political' or 'sociological' justification of discourse will lead very far. That sort of characterization does not offer a firm foundation for the process of hermeneutics. To illustrate this point, I shall develop further my remarks concerning the pragmatics of Bourdieu's text. To this end, I present, in the form of a diagram (Figure 1.3), the three stances, the three voices of the text (Balibar, Marx, Bourdieu).

In this scene, the actors play different parts. Balibar is the 'usurper' (Bourdieu 1982: 219), who struts about; Marx – the betrayed king – in ironical stage-whispers, makes the comments; unfortunately these comments remain 'often a little bit polemical' (Bourdieu 1982: 209); Bourdieu – the director – possesses the theoretical knowledge which allows him fully to understand Balibar's acting, and to go beyond the polemical level.

My intention, in presenting things this way, is not to disparage Bourdieu's text. On the contrary I believe that this is a rather successful piece of

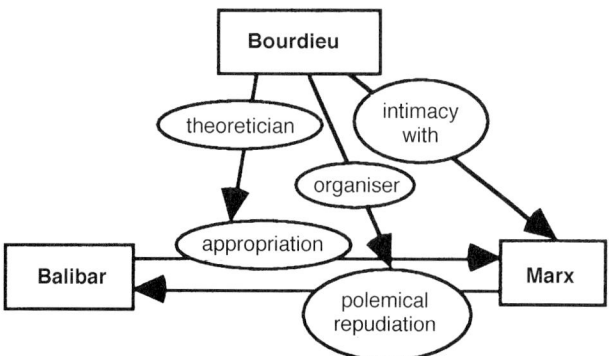

Figure 1.3 The roles in Bordieu's texts.

sociological critique, containing interesting theoretical proposals, and moreover, pleasant to read. My intention is simply to show that no form, no genre, no mode of enunciation, no social position, no stance is ever exempt from the effects of tautological self-legitimation. To enlarge upon this argument, I shall locate our discussion in relation to a recent debate raised by Bourdieu's methodological text in *La misère du monde*.

In his latest writings, Bourdieu claims that it is the sociologist who is, amongst all scientific practitioners, the most aware of the pluralities of perspectives on the social and most aware of his own perspective. Consequently, the sociologist is also the most capable of seeing (and even experiencing) the world as non-sociologists do. This difficult exercise, similar in some sense to the self-awareness required by the exercise of psychoanalysis, has provoked the interest of certain philosophers (Karsenti 1995), while some others have insisted on the general contradictions of this founding notion (Monod 1995). It has been shown by the latter that the critique of the 'positions of enunciation' held by the rivals of sociology cannot constitute a foundation for sociology. I share this opinion, and I believe that it is illusory to attempt to escape from relativism by resorting to a 'sociologically correct' position of enunciation. More generally, it is likely that the validity of discourse will never be guaranteed by its form, nor by its authors' position of enunciation. 'Who you are' and 'where you speak from' are neither necessary nor sufficient conditions for the validity of discourse.

Textual analysis (of sociological inspiration) that limits its ambitions to unveiling the discursive devices that generate effects of legitimation often makes use of similar devices to bring the texts and their authors into disrepute. The confusion here between science and polemic is no accident. Such is the nature of the ideological critique that highlighting an effect of self-legitimation tends to cancel this effect. This remark renders it possible to struggle against (formal) domination with theoretical instruments, and inspires most of Bourdieu's scientific and political programme. Unfortunately (or fortunately, depending on the perspective) the theoretical critique not only cancels the legitimating effects, but may also produce an effect of de-legitimation. The sociological critique, in addition to defusing the effect of self-legitimation, often devalues the position of an author who employs this self-legitimating trickery. Often this devaluation is more than proportional to the amount of legitimation the author expects to gain. This is the first reason why science and polemic cannot fully be distinguished within the ideological critique.

I believe that this confusion will remain as long as the scientific critique has no other methods to highlight a legitimation effect, other than to reproduce it by linguistic means (paraphrasing this effect in a way that makes it yet more salient, so much so that it becomes excessive and self-annulling). Confusions will arise until we discover a way to model the linguistic effects of legitimation, or at least some related effects of a cognitive nature that form the basis of these effects. This model should be capable of incorporating *the strength* of a justification effect. Altogether, these requirements suggest the need to endow sociology with a genuine semantic theory which permits the comparison between the evaluative effects arising from different formulations and different modes of enunciation.

The main (theoretical) reason why I propose to go beyond the denunciation of the formal artefacts which uphold symbolic domination is that I regard as illusory the hope of distinguishing, on an objective basis, between the effects of justification that are produced by rhetorical tricks, those that arise from the coherence of discourse, and those that accompany even the simplest speech act. Accepting these distinctions would imply a reification of the traditional distinction between *form* and *content*, a reification which would be contradictory to the very idea of semantics. Another strategy to justify the alleged distinction between the various effects of legitimation is to assume a distinction between 'discourse' and 'discourse about discourse'.

> Discourse contains a discourse about discourse that has no other function than to signify the intellectual and political importance of that discourse and of the person who holds it (cf. 'important', 'fundamental problem', 'this conclusive point', 'more fundamental and having more consequences', 'much deeper', 'this point is of a fundamental political importance', 'there, we are broaching something much deeper'). (Bourdieu 1982: 208)

Is it true, however, as Bourdieu would have us believe, that the discourse about discourse has no other function than emphasizing the importance of discourse? Does it not allow for the construction of a hierarchy of arguments? Does it not help the reader to orient himself within the text? Does it not convey the author's impressions about his own discourse? Does it not express the author's value judgements concerning the arguments? This meta-discourse may reach an excessive level of reader orientation and a ridiculous level of pretension. But are there many ways to stress the political importance of a point, other than to declare that 'this point is of a fundamental political importance'? Why should the author employ a less affirmative turn of phrase if he is convinced of this political importance? In addition, it is not possible fully to distinguish between discourse and meta-discourse, because meta-discourse pervades the meaning of discourse. Stating that a point is important not only refers to a discursive importance, but also to the importance (social, causal) of what this point refers to. In other words, both discourse and meta-discourse contribute, indivisibly, to the sense of discourse. Conversely, there is no discourse without an implicit meta-discourse. This is of course one of the main theses of the analytical philosophy of language. But this idea is also widely accepted in French pragmatic linguistics. According to Ducrot for example: 'Every statement, albeit seemingly "objective" (*The Earth is round*) hints at its enunciation: as soon as one speaks, one speaks about one's own speech' (Ducrot 1980: 40).

I shall not reiterate the arguments which support this widely accepted position. I shall stress only one of its consequences, that is, the fact that ideological critique should not focus exclusively on a hypothetical meta-discourse distinct from discourse. More generally, a model of linguistic justification should not pick up a few significant features in a text, and then base its conclusions on these features alone (the assessment of the various strategies of selection is the theme of the third chapter of this book). The scope of this model should be broadened to include the effects of legitimation that arise from the ordinary uses of language. This would allow us to treat, in an integrated framework, the explicit claims to legitimacy, those claims that are dissimulated, and those that are contained in every act of enunciation.

4 The fundamental dilemma

Bourdieu distinguishes between two forms of discursive legitimation. The first one is a direct legitimation, where a discourse supports the vested interests of a social class. For example, arguments of feasibility and optimality are the traditional form of direct legitimation of social and economic policies employed by those who govern. The second type of legitimation concerns the various ways in which discourse can be used as an instrument of social distinction. Bourdieu has devoted much attention to the social uses of language and on many occasions he has claimed that the second type of legitimation is more important than the first one.

> The conception which imputes the effects of legitimation to actions intentionally oriented towards the legitimation of the established order does not even hold in the case of highly differentiated societies, where the most efficient actions of legitimation are left to institutions, like the educational system, and to mechanisms, like those which guarantee the hereditary transmission of the cultural capital. (Bourdieu 1980b: 3)

In other words, it does not matter what children learn at school. The task of the education system is not to inculcate erroneous beliefs (although that may happen). The ideological function of the education system is not to be found in the content of education but in the reinforcement of the distinction between, on the one hand, the legitimate (standard) language and the legitimate culture, and on the other, its popular foil. One must therefore distinguish the content of education from the 'discourse' of the educational system, a discourse which aims at the justification of the selection process and of the relation between qualification and career. In other words, the sociologist must distinguish between discourses as the raw material both produced and consumed by institutions and the discourse (often implicit) of the institutions upon their discourse. This conviction has led Bourdieu to criticize, on various occasions, methods of discourse analysis, 'abstractors of textual quintessence', semantic analysis of discourse, and more generally, all the approaches focusing on the content of discourse, approaches which have never succeeded in isolating and making explicit the discourse on discourse (Bourdieu and Boltanski 1976: 2).

Bourdieu also distrusts content-oriented descriptions because they may produce an illusion of substantiality, thereby implicitly presenting what *is said* as what *ought to be said*, and by extension, what *is* as what *ought to be*. All content-oriented analyses are either suspected of being assimilated to a heterodox point of view which reinforces, despite its critical stance, the status of orthodoxy and legitimacy of the discourses upon which it comments (Bourdieu 1977: 159), or guilty of supporting these discourses by the very fact of giving a them new shape. Indeed, this change of form not only eliminates the legitimation effects produced by the original form, but is also much more deeply misleading because it suggests that the content of discourse can be separated from its form and its uses. This double critique, which goes far beyond the simple critique of idealism, is sometimes termed by Bourdieu as 'sociologism', an expression which reveals how closely the perverse effects of legitimation are linked with the practice of social sciences.

I would like to think that I share Bourdieu's prudence. But I have to admit that this insistent focus on language forms (norms of standardization) and on language performance (accent, corporal hexis during speech acts), is to the detriment of other language functions and also plays a function in Bourdieu's own theory. Neglecting the informational and referential functions of language allows Bourdieu to invalidate all the claims to legitimacy that are based on competence, on technical capacities, on intelligence and on the capacity to tell the truth. This invalidation is often rather successful, but it never reaches the point where the reader can no longer ask himself 'But isn't that true, after all?'. A similar doubt may haunt the reader when confronted with Bourdieu's postulate that domination effects are arbitrary. The question always tends to re-emerge in its most abrupt and basic form: 'Isn't domination natural after all?' In other words, Bourdieu's external critique of dominant discourses leaves their claims to legitimacy almost completely intact.

In this, we are facing a dilemma. If we want to criticize discourses from the inside, we are condemned to take what they say too seriously and to miss the point, that is, their social effects. We then find ourselves in the trap of idealist rhetorics. But if we concentrate on their social function only, then we cannot criticize them from the inside, and we cannot contest the core of their claim to legitimacy.

Throughout this research, I shall look for a way out of this dilemma. My intuition is that the content of discourse matters more than Bourdieu is prepared to admit although not as much as, nor exactly in the way, that defenders of the dominant discourse would have us believe.

5 Strategic efficiency and ideological consistency

Consider a piece of discourse which, because of the social position of its author, former president of France Valery Giscard D'Estaing, naturally belongs to the dominant discourse.

> One should not be liberal because one is against state interventionism. One should be liberal because this is the most modern and the most complete theory of growth that exists.[6]

Interestingly, in this statement, there is no reference to truth, nor to empirical validation, nor to social utility, nor even to practical efficiency. The only thing that seems to matter is that the discourse has some comparative advantages over other discourses. The first advantage is that 'liberalism' is more modern, that it has the appearance of being ahead of other discourses when they are ranked on the universal scale of evaluation which opposes past and future. The second advantage is that liberalism, *as a theory*, is more 'complete'. I interpret this argument as the fact that liberalism (allegedly) offers the best compromise between thoroughness, integration of its concepts, and scope.[7] In other words, liberalism is, in the order of knowledge and in the order of discourse, *strategically superior* to its rivals.

I believe that this is the extent of the commitment of ideologues towards the content of the discourses they produce and diffuse. They are not concerned with the principles of empiricism, nor with the careful methods of the historian, nor with the rules of hermeneutics. They care neither about truth nor about efficiency. All they expect of a discourse is that it should compete favourably with other discourses on a wide range of issues. The requirements of ideologues regarding the properties of their discourses do not reflect the nature of things, the empire of truth, or the continuous progress of spirit. They simply reflect the necessity of being *strategically efficient* in the competition of discourses within the public sphere.

This is, however, a very demanding requirement, and few people are capable of fulfilling it in an inventive way, that is, by creating or developing a new mode of justification. For most politicians, experts and academics, the obligation to be strategically efficient imposes a strict loyalty to a pre-fabricated discourse. The advantage of pre-fabricated discourse over spontaneous discourse is that it has been extensively 'tested' on a large scale, on a wide range of issues, and that it has survived the confrontation with antagonistic discourses. Ideologies are the best example of preconstituted discourses. Social actors who are ideologically committed benefit from the coherence of their own discourse with that of others who also adhere to this ideology. They also benefit from the coherence of their discourse with the discourses that they have previously held. When there is a doctrinal break, there is a collective management of this change. The ideology provides the instruments for minimizing the inconsistencies (modes of conversion).

No ideological representation of the world is fully consistent. The complexity of the social universe soon imposes modesty on any world view, however; when the real world does not work as the ideological world predicts, the ideology creates some special categories to handle the exceptions. These include the categories of 'perverse effect', 'counter-intuitive results', 'paradoxes' and 'folly of youth'. They are sometimes present in discourse itself, although they sometimes need to be inferred from linguistic markers such as connectors (but, although, etc.). Most of these categories tend either to circumscribe or to minimize the inconsistency of a given situation with an ideological representation of the world.

What makes a discourse efficient? Are not scientificity and truth the best guarantees of discursive competitiveness? I propose the hypothesis that the strategic efficiency of discourse depends, not on the careful procedures of science and hermeneutics, but on the *ideological consistency* of discourse. This expression should not be taken in a logical sense; it does not refer to the deductive relations that may exist between the various ideological statements. It refers to the integration of values, descriptions of the world and changes that can be made to it, into a coherent system. Ideological consistency is a harmony of values, objects and actions. It expresses the hope and the wish that desirability, truth and possibility (feasibility) can be reconciled.

In this attempt to enforce an axiological solidarity between these dimensions, ideologies can follow several strategies. In general, they assign the responsibility of each dimension to a different ideological function. Traditionally, values are the domain of politicians, theory is the work of intellectuals, scientists and academics, and action is the domain of political militants and trade unionists. Each ideology adopts a different ranking of these functions, according to their perceived importance. In modern occidental societies, the dominant ideology assumes that the logic of feasibility must be submitted to the logic of scientific management. On the contrary, for left-wing ideologies and despite the fact that, after its historical failure, the Marxist model has not been replaced, there is still a need for the invention of the future through social struggle and political action (the masses must decide on the possible).

Class interests, field interests and institutional interests are supported by political decisions, and the justification of these decisions makes heavy use of arguments of feasibility. Thus, the dialectic of reality and possibility seems to be the prevailing domain in which ideologies must achieve persuasive force. This insistence on the practical function of ideologies has the drawback of identifying ideologies with discourses of government. This reduction may be judged excessive. Not all ideologies are dominant, not all need to justify policies. Moreover, many dominant ideologies do not limit themselves to selecting, from among the conclusions of the technocrats, those that correspond to their interests. More importantly perhaps, with the exception of purely economic interests, concerning which the ruling class possesses a superior degree of consciousness, interests are pursued according to the way they are represented and perceived. The perception of interests is therefore influenced by values and considerations of desirability. Modern Marxist theorists, who distinguish between the *reproduction–transformation of the relations of production* (through legal decisions and state policies) and the *ideological conditions* of this reproduction–transformation, are perfectly aware that direct justifications in terms of feasibility and optimality rely on a much broader justification of the established order which operates through an adherence to shared values.

These remarks lead us to the second fundamental hypothesis of this work: *that ideological consistency depends on the compatibility*[8] *of values*. This hypothesis presupposes that considerations of value prevail upon purely theoretical considerations, as well as upon issues of feasibility. To make this claim less audacious I shall, from hereon, avoid the term value, and talk about *evaluations*. In my view, evaluation encompasses truth and feasibility. To put it another way, truth and feasibility are special cases of desirability. Although this conception is not widely accepted, it is not a new one. Grice was aiming at something similar when he wrote

> I have some suspicions that the most fruitful idea [in the characterization of what it is to be a rational being] is the idea that a rational creature is a creature which *evaluates*, and that the other possible characterizations may turn out to be coextensive with this, although in some sense less leading. (Grice 1989: 298)

There are, however, several ways in which one semantic dimension can encompass another. Encompassing may mean being able to predict the results of the latter on the basis of the former's logic.[9] It may also mean reflecting the latter's logic. It is in this last sense that evaluation encompasses truth and possibility. Therefore, far from claiming that considerations of evaluation can substitute considerations of truth and possibility, I shall assume only that evaluation has the facility to reflect them. Ideologies can be seen as systems that minimize delays and discrepancies during the process of reflection. As an illustration, one may consider the fate of 'idealist' values in Marxist ideology or that of 'humanist' values in postmodern philosophy. Viewed simultaneously as being based on erroneous assumptions, as impossible and as 'abstract', these values have either been devalued or have simply ceased to be values. These examples show that ideology tends to 'systematize' evaluations in a way that reflects both the ideological vision of the world and the plans to change it.

6 Types of consistency

One could think of types of consistency other than evaluative consistency to describe the unity of the discursive formations which make up ideologies. I shall examine the consistency of the 'dominant ideology', the existence of global ideological patterns and their relationship with evaluative patterns.

The dominant ideology

The simplest way to conceive of the unity of a discursive formation is to identify it with a 'doctrine'. From this perspective, statements of doctrine are either presuppositions which back new statements, axioms from which new statements are deduced, or general principles which orient the production of new statements. This description of ideologies as doctrine is convenient in the sense that it allows the conceptual reconstruction of an ideology in a purely rational and logical way. This description is never as successful as when ideology presents itself as a scientific doctrine.

One should not confuse ideology and the scientific discourses which legitimate it. As a political or managerial discourse, ideology never proceeds as scientific discourse does. This is the first feature that struck Bourdieu in his research on the 'dominant ideology' in France in the 1970s.

> It may be that the most important property of [the discourse of the ruling class in modern occidental societies] is to allow itself, given the market in which this discourse is supplied, to leave implicit pre-suppositions and logical relations. (Bourdieu and Boltanski 1976: 5)

As we have seen above, according to Bourdieu the sociologist should be concerned with neither the reconstruction nor the deconstruction of a hypothetical conceptual apparatus. The mere substitution of the anarchic succession of themes and variations with a chain of arguments organized in a seemingly deductive order would make the specific characteristics of these discourses disappear. But then, what is the cement of this 'disjoint discourse' which can 'do without proof and logical control'? Bourdieu proposes several related answers to this question. First, ideological statements group together because of the practical objectives they pursue. The identity of the productions of the dominant ideology derives from the specific linguistic market in which they are supplied.

> The norms of propriety, which exclude concepts which are too obscure and reasoning which is too complex, in brief, everything that 'smells intellectual', bring to light the objective law of this linguistic market which, within a discourse of power, in other words, a discourse oriented toward action, retains the elements which may predict action, that is, the adoption of positions. (Bourdieu and Boltanski 1976: 6)

The function of this discourse is not so much to convince and to justify as to maintain the cohesion of the executives through the ritual reaffirmation of necessity and the legitimacy of its action, and the faith of the group in this necessity.

This first description has the drawback of being valid for discourses of government and management only. It cannot be extended to other types of ideological discourse, like the anti-Semitism of the French extreme right for example. In the contemporary context, and given the apparatus of legal constraints bearing on the expression of racism, modern anti-Semitism is not a discourse oriented towards action. It seldom produces decisions or political proposals against the Jews. Nevertheless, anti-Semitism clearly inspires the discourses of the extreme right, which accuses the Jews of being unpatriotic, downgrades their culture, and trivializes their historical suffering. There is therefore a clear consistency in this discourse despite the fact that it can seldom translate itself into action. This is why I believe that Bourdieu is wrong in assuming that political discourses 'pass over globalization'. Like anti-Semitism, and in addition to their practical function, political and managerial discourses have an evaluative consistency, which acts as their underlying totalization.

The second answer given by Bourdieu to the problem of the identity of the managerial discourse is to present it as the product of the discontinuous application of a small number of generative schemes.

> The dominant discourse on the social owes its practical coherence to the fact that it is produced by a small number of generative schemes which let themselves be reduced to the opposition between the past (out-of-date), and the future, or in more fuzzy and seemingly more conceptual terms, between the traditional and the modern. ... Whatever field it is applied to, the scheme produces two opposed and hierarchical terms, and hence, the relation that holds between them, that is, the process of evolution (or involution) leading from one to the other (for example small, grand, and growth). Each of these fundamental oppositions evoke, more or less directly, all the others. (Bourdieu and Boltanski 1976: 39)

Generative schemes are abstract topoi which facilitate discursive entailments. This is particularly true of the schemes that are 'lexicalized' in the form of pairs (old/new, compromise/conflict, etc.). But they are more than simple topo also, since they organize the dialectics of the political discourse. This is the case with 'methodological' generative schemes, such as the scheme of 'supersession of extremes' which allocates a third term to allow one to escape the sterile opposition of two 'extreme positions' (for example, liberalism as a solution to the alternative between fascism and communism). In both senses, the mere notion of evaluative schemes presupposes that social discourse proceeds by the subsumption of facts and issues under social distinctions. These distinctions are clearly evaluative implications. Generative schemes can therefore be adequately described as simple, abstract, ideological patterns producing evaluative patterns.

Ideological patterns

It may be claimed that the concept of generative schemes is too general to account for ideological discourse. As Bourdieu himself notes

> It would not be difficult to provide examples of the application of dominant schemes beyond the limits that political divisions ascribe to them, and the political polemic takes delight in these discrepancies between the expressions of the habitus and the conscious and controlled manifestations of the political competence. If this happens, it is because the institutional barriers that are raised by the politically constituted units ... introduce discontinuities in the continuity of the habitus. (Bourdieu and Boltanski 1976: 42)

In this passage, Bourdieu locates the generative schemes in relation to the 'opinions produced by the habitus'. He acknowledges that the concept of generative schemes is not adequate to characterize the political divisions. All generative schemes are almost homologous and all political discourses use more or less the same generative schemes. The difference and the conflicts between discourses cannot be accounted for on the basis of different and conflicting generative schemes. Political differences arise from the very mechanism of political differentiation, which is essentially structural – 'political classification tends to generate discontinuity out of continuity (like language, which produces distinctive phonemes out of a sonorous continuum)'. Political conflicts express themselves through the reversed application of the same generative schemes; depending on the discourse, controversial social realities shift from one side of the opposition to the other (for example, 'small enterprises are out-of-date', 'small enterprises are the future').

As always in Bourdieu's sociological theory, the symbolic and discursive dimensions do not play any genuine role in the formation of political and ideological divisions. They are merely the instruments of the processes of distinction. A discursive opposition helps the formation of a social distinction, but essentially, any such opposition would suffice. Generative schemes are no exception. They are so versatile that they can apply to any reality and be used within all discourses. As purely dialectic tricks, they make no real contribution to the content of discourse. It is only in institutional contexts, like political science exams in high schools, that the most methodological of these schemes transform themselves into strong constraints bearing on discourse.

Several authors have proposed more elaborate ideological patterns. Boltanski and Thévenot, for example, in their study of the major types of discursive justification have addressed the problem of summarizing several typical expressions of these discourses. They selected six books, each one being representative of one type of justification, and laid out the following programme.

> Our objective was to isolate, extract and gather in an easily accessible form the main elements that one should make use of to recompose the original text if, perchance, the original version be lost of destroyed, or to invent new statements that could be inserted into it without marring it. (Boltanski and Thévenot 1991: 198)

It soon became clear that this could not be done simply with generative schemes, and that more complex generative patterns had to be used. Boltanski and Thévenot ended up with a set of interrelated categories that can be interpreted as grammatical categories of the discourses of justification. It is worth noting that these categories are the same for the six discourses they study, and which correspond to the world of inspiration (1), the domestic world (2), the world of opinion (3), the civic world (4), the mercantile world (5) and the industrial world (6). I shall briefly summarize these categories, without going into the details of the lexical items that can be associated with them in each world.

> *Common superior principle.* Beings are compared and evaluated with respect to their capacity to conform or to behave according to this principle. *e.g.* inspiration (1), tradition (2), competition (5), efficiency (6).
> *State of grandeur.* Ideal state of superiority which determines the various, ranked states of grandeur. *e.g.* genius (1), fame (3), representativity (4), desirability (5).
> *State of smallness.* State of inferiority, decay. *e.g.* returned to earth (1), slovenly ways (2), indifference and banality (3), division (4).
> *Dignity.* Quality shared by all persons (human nature) allowing their participation in the economy of grandeur. *e.g.* common sense (2), interest (5).

Grand and small subjects. Superiors and inferiors. *e.g.* father, king, ancestors, parents, family, chief, *versus* egoistic self, bachelor, stranger, woman, child, dogs, cats (2).
Objects. Status symbols and environments in which grandeur is made objective. *e.g.* dream, body, unconscious, drugs (1), good manners (2), laws (4), wealth (5), means of production (6).
Investment. Sacrifice by which subjects acquire grandeur. *e.g.* renouncement of habits (1), of egotism (2), of privacy (3).
Relations of grandeur. The way in which grand beings comprehend, express, realize small beings, the way in which small beings participate in this relationship. *e.g.* responsibility of the grand beings towards the small beings and respect of the small beings for the grand beings (2), fascination and identification (3).
Relations. Natural relations between subjects and objects, subjects and subjects, objects and objects, which are regulated by their respective grandeur. *e.g.* persuade (3), unite for collective action (4), buy and sell (5).
Figures. Contexts which are likely to produce optimal distributions of the states of grandeur. *e.g.* imagination (1), home (2), market (5), organization (6).
Tests. Passing tests gives access to grandeur. *e.g.* family ceremony (2), demonstration (3), voting (4), business transaction (5).
Judgement. Expression of the outcome of the test. *e.g.* trust (2), verdict of the polls (4), price (5).
Evidence. Type of evidence supporting judgement. *e.g.* intuition (1), exemplary anecdote (2), audience (3), money (5), measure (6).

Consider how uncomfortable it would be if one could not rely on some kind of regularity, or relation, between the different components of the world. It would be disturbing indeed if 'grand' actors for example, performed more 'small' actions than 'small' actors. It would be puzzling if 'good' policies had 'bad' consequences, or if 'good' phenomena systematically entailed 'bad' ones. An ideology is a system of evaluation of concepts that ensures the existence of regularities in the discursive composition of concepts. Boltanski and Thévenot provide us with the social categories that underlie this desire for consistency. Their 'grammatical categories' suggest that the consistency of an ideology may be analysed and modelled as the existence of a set of stable relations between categories of ideological grammar. These stable relations (for example, '*grand* persons are able to pass *tests*' or 'persons experiencing a *state of grandeur* are *grand persons*') can be called 'ideological patterns'. The evaluative consistency of an ideology could then be conceived of as semantic patterns of evaluation which fulfil the constraints arising from these relations. In other words, in an ideology, the evaluative patterns (the distribution of evaluations) have to reflect the ideological patterns (the typical relations between the fundamental categories).

Conclusion

The production and reception of discourse are influenced by their ideological context. According to pragmatic theories of ideology, reality (interests and social distinctions) exerts a one-way influence on beliefs and discourses. From a pragmatic perspective, whoever attempts to grant beliefs with an autonomy with respect to material reality is guilty of idealism. I have been arguing against the purely pragmatic theories of ideology, and in favour of an internal theory that would escape from the critique of idealism by focusing on the evaluative level. Indeed, recognizing that a discourse is evaluatively coherent does not entail that one adheres to its content. In addition, evaluative statements are often closer to interests than ordinary statements. Far from losing touch with reality, focusing on the evaluative level brings us back to reality. Evaluations are the semantic reflexes of ideological perspectives upon reality. Therefore, focusing on the evaluative part of meaning allows one to express these perspectives in semantic terms.

In contemporary political life, ideologies have become rather fuzzy. Thus, one may wonder whether ideologies still have any sort of coherence besides the pragmatic interests they serve. Because it is often difficult to perceive the global consistency of political discourse, one may assume that there is in fact no such thing as ideological consistency, and, maybe, no such thing as ideology. However, the absence of clear logical boundaries between modern political discourses is not conclusive evidence of the end of ideology. Ideological consistency lies in evaluative ideological patterns rather than in logic. Modern ideologies have little to do with doctrines and principles. They promote their central values (e.g. 'private property') through the promotion of evaluative patterns (systems of relations) which resemble the system of language. This is why ideology is still a matter of structure despite its current tendency towards fuzziness. However, we need some new theoretical concepts to accommodate this type of fast-evolving, multi-state structure. One of the hypotheses of this work is that the connectionist models used in cognitive science offer such concepts. In other words, to understand the very nature of ideology and ideological discourse, one must study the way in which they exist in the human mind. The next chapter addresses the issue of the status of evaluative phenomena in cognition and text processing.

2
EVALUATION AND COGNITION

Introduction

My intentions, as stated in the introduction to this book, are not to deal with cognitive evaluative processes in general, but to concentrate on those which are driven by language. More specifically, I also focus on semantic evaluative processes that depend more on cultural systems of evaluation (social representations, ideologies) than on narrow pragmatic contexts or personal factors. Nonetheless, as interpretative processes, semantic evaluative processes do not exist outside cognition. They are indissolubly semantic and cognitive. It is therefore useful to discuss the status of evaluation within cognition.

Evaluation must first be situated with respect to affects and cognition. Drawing upon Edelman's Neural Darwinism and upon some recent connections made between emotion theory and evaluation theory, I argue that most research in the field of social cognition remains tied to a narrow cognitive perspective. I shall therefore call for another balance of interest, in the theory of value, between the affective and the cognitive level. However, does this mean that the affective level must be conceived of as an autonomous, independent basis for evaluation? Psychoanalysis teaches us that human desire is deeply modified by social censorship. Evaluation is precisely one of the ways in which culture gives a shape to our affects and it should therefore be perceived as a point of articulation between affects and cognition.

The cognitive models of evaluation will briefly be reviewed in order to list the most basic features of evaluative processes. It is indeed likely that these features are shared by semantic evaluative processes. To home in on the object of this research (the interpretation of social discourse), I shall evoke text processing models. Their functionalism, I would argue, renders them inadequate in accounting for evaluative interpretative processes. I shall therefore draw upon more phenomenological descriptions of evaluation in order to answer the following questions. What are the possible relationships of a social actor to a text, when the scope of the reading covers its social environment? If an intentionality specific to the act of reading 'with social issues in mind' exists, how could it be formalized?

1 Evaluation between affects and cognition

Western philosophy traditionally opposes theory and practice. At least since Kant, the notion of value is supposed to belong to the practical sphere rather than to the theoretical sphere. For Kant, there is no superiority of theory over practice. However, it is certainly fair to say that in the history of modern thought, the objectivist mode of thinking has become so dominant that little room has been left for values. According to Grice, something has been left out in this evolution of modern philosophy: 'What has been left out has been left out because it is what everybody regards with horror, at least when in a theoretical frame of mind: the notion of value' (Grice 1989: 297).

I shall not try to explain why theoretical descriptions of human thought have prevailed upon more comprehensive and accurate descriptions, and on this subject, I refer the interested reader to Bourdieu's analysis of the social function of objectivism. I shall only stress the consequence of this 'bad evaluation' of the notion of value. The notion of value is associated with subjectivity, affectivity, morality, contingency, irrationality, and opposed to objectivity, science, truth, stability and reason. Values take place on the 'wrong' side within the system of oppositions which structure our philosophy.

The mere term 'evaluation' reveals an attempt to shift the notion of value toward the theoretical sphere. The morpheme 'eval', almost verbal, suggests action, and the morpheme 'tion' suggest duration. As most terms constructed with the morpheme 'tion' the term 'evaluation' refers both to a process and to the result of this process. Together, these two morphemes suggest an evaluative work consisting in combining various reactions to the multiple aspects of the object to be evaluated.

Within a differential perspective, we would say that the sememe 'evaluation' is opposed to the sememe 'value' by the specific seme/ objective. In practice, the very word 'evaluation' acts as a marker of theoretical or managerial discourse. It either refers to a cognitive appraisal of a phenomenon, or to the cognitive theory of processes of evaluation involving both cognitive and affective aspects. To conclude this semantic overview, evaluation is situated between affects and cognition, though closer to the latter.

Cognitivism and social psychology

In the various sub-disciplines of contemporary psychology, the question of evaluation has had something of a chequered history. Since Thomas and Znaniecky's founding paper in 1918, social psychology has viewed evaluation as a psychological disposition. To distinguish between general dispositions (moods, affects, and moral or ethical stances, for example) and dispositions towards specific objects and representations, social psychology has used the word 'attitudes'. Most research in social psychology concerns the various factors which influence attitude formation and changes. In the last two decades, cognitive science and cognitive psychology have attempted to propose more precise hypotheses concerning the cognitive mechanisms underpinning attitudes. Even in the area of social judgement, recent research chooses to label itself 'social cognition' in order to stress the attention now paid to the 'processes' underlying judgement. But the evolution towards a cognitively-based psychology does not consider all themes of psychology. Everything takes place, in this evolution including a number of vocabulary changes; in particular, the abandonment of the word 'attitude' in order for the new disciplines (namely cognitive science and cognitive psychology) to appear different from social psychology which they view as an old (outdated) discipline.

In philosophical psychology and cognitive science, evaluative phenomena have never been a major concern. In 1989, George Mandler wrote 'Psychology in general is still valueless (though, of course, not value free)'. For most authors, values are too cognitive to deserve a specific reflection. They reappear, from time to time, as components within the theories which intend to propose 'cognitive' models of emotions (De Sousa 1987). Some other authors believe that evaluation is too cognitive to be useful within emotion theory. It is interesting to note that the attention paid to evaluative and emotional phenomena has long been one of the main divisions between, on one hand, social psychology, and, on the other, psychology and cognitive science. As a consequence of the contemporary 'cognitivization' of psychology and social psychology, evaluative phenomena are relegated to the margins of the debate. On the contrary, emotional phenomena arouse growing interest among cognitive scientists due to their eventual integration within a general project of neuro-bio-chemistry theories of emotions.

I hesitate to counter this evolution, but I remain attached to the concept of evaluation, which, from a cognitive perspective, may appear rather sketchy. I am aware that the reluctance to add 'evaluation' to the core of fundamental cognitive notions is not simply the result of strategies of disciplinary distinction. Some aspects of this notion do indeed render it difficult to incorporate within the cognitive paradigm. However, I do not think that the major cognitive proposals made to date are any more clear. In addition, there are perhaps other good reasons to keep with the notion of evaluation. In order to argue in this direction, let me briefly sketch the central perspectives on evaluation, and describe the difficulties arising from each approach.

At first glance the panorama of the academic community dealing with evaluative phenomena appears as a perfect illustration of what Bourdieu calls a social field, that is, a system of positions which, despite their respective strategies of distinction, share the same basic presuppositions. The distinction between affects and cognition is one of the most basic of this field. The location of evaluative phenomena with respect to these two tenets shows that every possible position is occupied, and that each possible opposition is emphasized. Some authors argue that evaluative processes are affective, some argue that they are cognitive, and still others claim that they are both cognitive and affective. It is worth noting that these positions are more or less the same in social and cognitive psychology. The 'law of value' assessing discourses within these fields rewards the quest for empirical evidence allegedly supporting the hypotheses more than the theoretical clarification of the very notions of affects and cognition. Finally, both social psychology and social cognition carefully ignore Freud's theses regarding the relation between affects and culture.

1 *Evaluation belongs to the affective sphere*. This does not entail that evaluative responses are never cognitively mediated, but simply that affective evaluations (feelings, likes and dislikes, pleasantness judgements) follow an autonomous logic. Within social psychology, this position is defended by the authors who believe in the existence of clear-cut distinctions between affective, cognitive and behavioural components of attitudes (Ostrom 1969; Breckler 1984; Breckler and Fried 1993). This position is defended, in the field of cognitive psychology, by scientists such as Zajong who argue that cognitive and affective responses to stimuli are produced by two independent functioning systems (Zajong 1980; Zajong and Markus 1984). In Zajong's model, affective reports are mediated by familiarity with the stimuli. Affects are triggered by the holistic grasp of 'preferenda' (in opposition to features detected and used by cognition, which he calls 'discriminanda'). Most empirical evidence in favour of Zajong's model concerns the relation between exposure to stimuli and affective evaluation.

2 *Evaluation belongs to the cognitive sphere*. Stated otherwise, a theory of cognitive preferences can ignore affective processes. Some influential social psychologists conceive of no other possible cause for attitude change but cognitive information processing (Fishbein and Ajzen 1975; Ajzen 1974). Some cognitive scientists prefer to integrate evaluation into cognition, assuming for example that attitudes contain 'evaluative components' residing in memory, and stored with knowledge about objects (Pratkanis and Greenwald 1989). Some impression formation specialists use the term 'evaluative concept' to refer to 'evaluative components' concerning persons (Wyer and Srull 1989).

The hypothesis which separates affective and cognitive processes is clearly not without problems. The relation between affects and cognition, now minimized, is fundamentally left unexplained. Hence the number of scientific contributions (based on experiments) exploring the circumstances in which affective processes dominate judgement, and those in which cognitive processes tend to regain control.

3 *Evaluation is indissolubly cognitive and affective.* This idea is defended by social psychologists supporting the unity of attitude, according to which the distinction between its affective, cognitive and behavioural components is seen more as a heuristic framework than as the affirmation of separate realities (Olson and Zana 1993). This approach may seem much more reasonable with regard to the plentiful evidence suggesting that affects and cognition function in a synergetic manner (Eagly and Chaiken 1993). Yet, there are very few models showing the interaction between affective and cognitive aspects of evaluation. The main reason for this is that affects are not easily modelled, and that, traditionally, cognitive scientists are much more comfortable with symbolic than with non-symbolic processes. As a consequence, most research concerns categories which help us identify our affects, and not the affects themselves. Narrowly defined cognitive theories of affects assume that representations of affects are normal concepts, functioning in the same way as ordinary concepts. This opinion presupposes that we carry on the same type of relation to the external world and to our internal states. On the contrary, several authors emphasize the difference between ordinary concepts and emotion concepts, and suggest using the term 'endocept' to refer to the latter (Ariety 1976). Despite these attempts to take into account the specificity of encoding affects in memory, no fully satisfying theory of the relation between emotions and affects *as states* and emotions and affects *as categories* has emerged. Affective and evaluative dispositions are still understood and modelled after the representation of objects.

Certain authors do not feel comfortable within this narrowly cognitive orientation. Ortony for example, does not believe that internal representations of our emotional dispositions are dispositions and criticizes the widespread practice of treating likeableness ratings as surrogates for liking ratings.

> The problem is that the general concept of likeableness is nothing more than a very general trait. Although it might on occasion be the underlying representation for dispositional liking, it is not always so, and quite possibly is not even normally so. (Ortony 1991: 343)

For Ortony, purely cognitive approaches can only predict, or make expectation (concerning liking dispositions) conditional on likeableness. But because predictions can be wrong, and because there are many examples of inconsistencies between likeableness and liking judgements, Ortony suggests making additional hypotheses concerning affective dispositions themselves, and their relations with our direct experiences. I will return to his proposals in section 4.

Evaluation and emotional development

In order to understand more precisely the interplay of emotion and cognition in the making of evaluative psychological processes, it may be useful to evoke briefly the child's emotional and cognitive development. The evaluative skills of the adult involve the awareness of the object as a distinct, external entity, the awareness of the self, and the awareness of the fact that others may have different evaluations of the same object. These elements are not yet available to the young child during its first years. The evaluative judgements of the adult progressively arise out of more primitive forms of evaluation. However, this evolution does not take the form of a continuous, linear progress. The infant comes across several phases of disequilibrium which are resolved by new forms of regulation. This history, which gives shape to the adult's elaborate judgements, is essentially social, in the sense that it mainly depends on the child's relations with its human environment.

In the first weeks after his birth, the child's vision is much less developed than his auditory capacities. The infant emotionally reacts to the human voice before reacting to visual stimuli (Wallon 1949: 242). This chronology partly explains why speech, and later language, is so important in our development, as is witnessed by the fact that deafness is a much more serious handicap than blindness from a developmental point of view. From one to six months, the response to human verbal communication keeps improving and becomes an exchange, in which the child plays an active part despite its very limited linguistic resources. At the beginning, the infant tends to respond positively to all communicative behaviour, and negatively to indifference. Around the fifth month, he is capable of understanding the evaluative tonality of a verbal communication. This does not entail that he understands the meaning of words. But he distinguishes the prosody associated with approving and scolding messages (Fernald 1989; Papousek *et al.* 1990).

It is in relation to his mother that the child reaches a first level of symbolization. From two to five months, there is an emotional symbiosis between the child and the mother, who are not yet differentiated. After six months, the child realizes that his mother is only a part of the world, and not the whole world. His attachment to the mother becomes a specific attachment, and around eight months, the child starts to express a 'fear of strangers', that will influence his relational behaviour for several years. This 'objectal' period (Spitz 1983) lays the basis, at the affective level, for the cognitive notion of an object (Gouin-Décarié 1962). As child and mother become separated, their relation needs more 'tuning' (Stern 1989). In the attempts of the child and the mother to share (and influence) their affective states, the child discovers that there are several ways of expressing them. According to Stern (1989), this emotional tuning, which often resorts to evaluative expressions, lies somewhere between imitation and symbolization. The first semantic space acquired by the child is therefore affective.

The mother often uses the affective tuning to achieve educational purposes. The illocutionary and expressive components of educative speech acts are perhaps more important than their actual content in the early stages of a child's development.[1] However, praise and admonishment conveyed by tone of voice and expressive accents are always linked with basic language expressions and dichotomies (yes/no, do/don't, nice/nasty, good boy/bad boy, clean/dirty, etc.). It is therefore reasonable to believe that the first semantic dimensions constituted within a child's cognition are evaluative.

Studies in early lexical development seem to support this hypothesis. Early vocalizations function as direct expressions of the child's internal affect states (Barrett 1996: 364). In addition, Dore (1985), has suggested that idiosyncratic affect expressions are acquired before any other word type. Some other case studies indicate that this not a typical pattern of development (Dromi 1987; Harris et al. 1988). However, the evaluative dimension is not exclusively expressed by means of idiosyncratic expressions, and therefore, their absence does not entail that the affective or evaluative dimensions are absent. A child may possess much more referential words than expressive words, and yet, make much more use of the latter than of the former ones. Therefore, the studies of the child's early vocabulary by no means contradict the importance of the evaluative semantic dimension during the first stages of cognitive development.

Biological foundations

Another important contribution from a completely different field of research deals with the role of value in the biological foundations of cognition. Edelman's Neural Darwinism may appear as incidental to our discussion, but it nevertheless provides us with many new insights concerning the nature of value.

Edelman's model is far too complex to be succinctly summarized. Without going into details regarding the various levels of neuronal organization and neuronal selection contained in this model, I shall make a few comments on the global organization of the brain upon which Edelman's theories rest. The easiest way to get acquainted with this model is to consider the very diagram used by Edelman to summarize it in his book *Bright Air, Brilliant Fire* (1992).

As is evident from Figure 2.1, Edelman distinguishes between two main sources of information: internal states and external signals (including proprioceptive signals). Different subsystems of the brain manage these sources. The limbic-brain stem system is the part of the brain dealing with internal states. The thalamo-cortical system is a complex system of neural maps, massively re-entrant, dealing with external signals. Internal states and

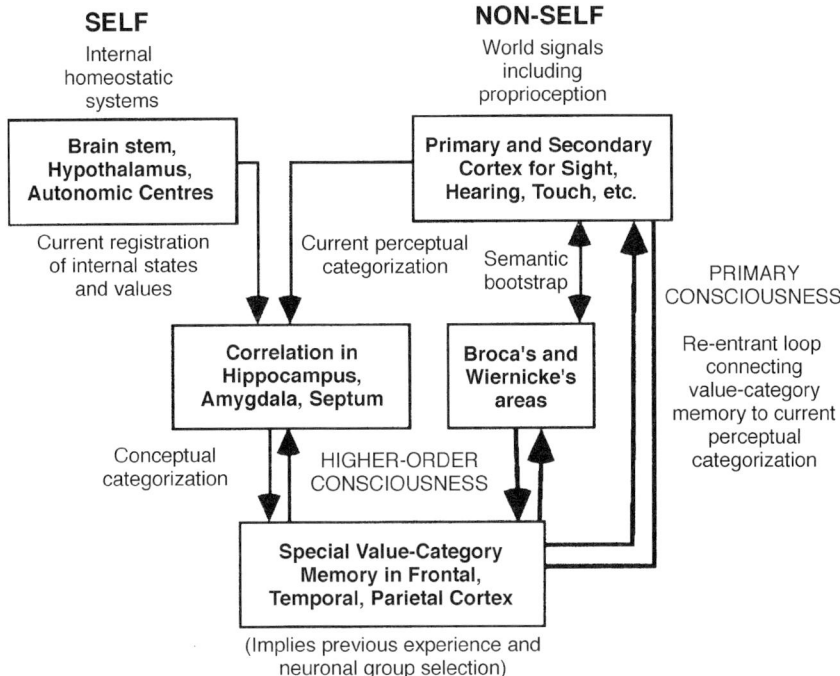

Figure 2.1 Brain and cognition according to Edelman.

perceptions are correlated through a 'system of values' reflecting the various 'preferences' of the living organism with regard to each perceptual modality. These 'preferences' are largely innate, and correspond to the main hedonic interests of the species (heat, nutrition, reproduction, etc.). By categorizing the association between perceptual categories and values, the cortex is able to form special 'value-categories'. A re-entrant loop connecting these value categories to current categorical perceptions allows the brain to coordinate various perceptions into a 'scene', thereby producing what Edelman calls primary consciousness. Higher-order consciousness involves the association of symbols with value-categories and perceptual categories, the coordination of symbols into syntax, and the categorization of the relations between perceptual categories and value categories.

This model yields certain insights concerning the notion of value and its various (interrelated) levels of application.

At a basic level, we encounter the values correlated with perceptual modalities. The role of these values is to guide our perception and our behaviour in order to satisfy both the hedonist system (pleasure, well-being) and the interest of the species (safety, reproduction). Of course, the satisfaction associated with our internal states tends to reflect the interests of the species. But they need not coincide. It is therefore necessary to distinguish between the satisfaction produced by our internal states and the system of value which regulates our relation to the world. Edelman is not always very explicit on this point, especially when he depicts the system of value as serving hedonistic purposes. I believe, however, that one of the main interests of his model is precisely to emphasize the autonomy of the value system. The second interest is perhaps to give biological foundations to the value system as an interface between the registration of our internal states and the perceptual categories. Contrary to what has often been assumed in the literature on evaluation, at the most basic level, the evaluative disposition towards an object is neither the internal states induced by the object, nor the perception of these states. In fact, except in the case of objects which directly modify our internal states, this modification itself depends on the value system.

One of Edelman's main theses is that the acquisition of our perceptual categories is value-driven. In fact, for Edelman, perceiving is categorizing, and categorizing is a global behavioural response, involving instantaneous and continuous reorientation of our perception. Our value system exercises remote control over our perceptual behaviour.

At the next level, special areas of the cortex categorize associations between perceptual categories and values. The value-categories resulting from this categorization are still value-laden, and thus, our pre-linguistic concepts are by their very nature 'evaluative'. Pre-linguistic concepts do not categorize things of the world, then associate them with values. Instead, they categorize the relation between classes of perceptual categories and values. They are not 'files' with a value component and a perceptive component, but, at the same time, value *and* perception. As a consequence, our pre-linguistic concept of sexual differences for example, involves evaluations. In addition, these evaluations are not made by the basic values of our value system, but categorize associations of basic values. This means, for example, that our conceptual system and our limbic system do not necessarily deal with conflicting values exactly in the same way. Moreover, evaluations cannot be separated from concepts, and concepts are the result of personal history, which includes a very complex succession of associations of experiences, internal states and values. Thus, evaluations depart from genetic determinism.

At a third level, evaluations are involved in our linguistic concepts. Edelman goes into much less detail concerning this level than with the other two. It has even been argued that his model is not articulated with existing models of linguistic competence and logical reasoning (Clancey 1993). I shall not attempt to fill the gap between value-laden, pre-linguistic categories and linguistic categories, but consider only two specific modes of articulation between them. The first, evoked in the next section, concerns the capacity of culturally defined linguistic categories to modify and repress value-categories. The second, which is the very object of this research, concerns the importance and the function of values in linguistic reasoning itself.

2 Lessons in psychoanalysis

If values are situated somewhere between affects and cognition, this does not imply that the affective and cognitive poles are symmetrical, nor that they make equal contributions. Perhaps no other theory of the unequal relation between affects and cognition is as illuminating as Freudian theory.

Social evaluations and the repression of affects

According to Freud, affects result from the satisfaction and frustration of our basic sexual drives, and, more generally, of our desires. Since these drives and these desires, especially in their incestuous and aggressive forms, are not compatible with social life, they undergo a cultural censorship. Parents reproduce within the family sphere the prohibitions (and corresponding evaluations) of their culture. Parents trade their love and care against the repression of unacceptable affects. The result of this early education is the repression of an affective, subjective order by an evaluative, social one. The values placed on behaviour, which are socially and culturally determined, regulate affective dispositions. These values are, at first, more normative than cognitive. They are nonetheless cognitive in the sense that they are always conveyed or accompanied by speech acts. The role of culture is to articulate basic evaluations more elaborately to encompass principles such as morality, truth, efficiency and reciprocation.

There is a strong conflict between social prescriptions and the child's drives. This conflict is not due to the strength and the obstinacy of a child's drives, but to the child's 'polymorphous perversity'. It is not the rigidity of desires which causes problems, but their fluctuating nature. Some commentators have emphasized the interdependency of drives and prohibitions (Legendre 1985). They argue that the unconscious permanently changes its investments, that it is dedicated to the task of displacing, identifying, recombining. In other words, there is no such thing as a natural human desire. Human desire grows parallel to and thanks to censorship.

Freud's most important thesis is perhaps that social censorship does not exercise itself in a simple and straightforward way. The repression of unacceptable drives is the result of a complex unconscious mechanism. Social censorship is internalized by the subject in the form of several interrelated unconscious topiques (id, ego, super-ego) at the occasion of key psychological evolutions, like the resolution of Oedipal complex. I shall not reiterate Freud's conclusions concerning the unconscious foundations of social censorship. But it is important to remember that in his theory, unconscious learning is much more complex than learning through experience. Thus we find a basic opposition between Freudian psychology and some recent research trends in cognitive linguistics, which describe morality as 'experiential', that is, acquired through direct experiences of pain and pleasure (Lakoff 1995).

What is the exact nature and role of evaluations conveyed by language within Freudian psychology? In his various models of the psychological apparatus Freud pays little attention to language. Often relating consciousness with structured perception, he does not emphasize the role of language in the unconscious either. One may wish to infer from these models that there is an unconscious constitution of identity underpinning the constitution of the self, the learning of language, and the exercise of cognition. This would not imply that evaluations conveyed by speech acts and discourse are unimportant. However, one may wish to argue that these evaluations' efficiency (what makes them normative and binding) lies below conscious cognition.

Other arguments in favour of the pre-linguistic nature of evaluation can be found in the psychological studies of the young child. Melanie Klein, for example, has shown that our sense of value is rooted in very primitive experiences of 'good and bad objects'. She claims that relations to objects (like ingestion or rejection during the oral stage) evolve during the child's development, ultimately producing the evaluative attitudes of the adult. Yet she also recognizes the importance of parental speech and she admits that access to enunciation is a key threshold in the child's development.

Though not considered in his models of the psychological apparatus, elsewhere Freud himself emphasizes the relation between cognition, affects and language. One of the best examples of the way in which Freud articulates these various levels of the psychological system is perhaps found in his famous analysis of the 'fort-da' game. In this case study outlined in *Beyond the Pleasure Principle* (1920), Freud observes a child playing with a wooden reel tied to a piece of string. The child's game consists in throwing the reel over the edge of his curtained cot, so that it disappears into it, while uttering an expressive 'o-o-o'. He then pulls the reel back to his view, with a joyful 'a-a-a'. Freud's hypothesis that these 'o-o-o' and 'a-a-a' correspond to the German words 'fort' ['gone'] and 'da' ['there'] is confirmed by the parents, who are more familiar with their child's limited language. Freud's interpretation of the game shows it to be a reproduction of the child's renunciation of instinctual satisfaction when he allowed his mother to leave without protesting. The reel is therefore a substitute for the mother, and the true object of the game is the absence and the presence of the child's mother. This example shows that basic phonemic distinctions, basic indexical words, basic spatial semantic categories (which are the object of so much attention on the part of cognitive scientists today), and motor skills are acquired simultaneously by the child with the repetition of traumatic or pleasant experiences. However Freud refuses to consider that the benefits derived from the compulsion to repeat compensate for the pain it creates. This leads him to propose yet another psychological principle: the death principle.

The supremacy of social evaluations

It is this aspect of Freud's work – by far the most daring – that Lacan has chosen to focus on (Derrida 1996). His attempt to make sense out of Freud's notion of the death principle led him to conceive of the unconscious as 'structured like a language'. In this version of psychoanalytical theory, repression substitutes experiences and desires with signifiers borrowed from the 'symbolic order'. Although these signifiers do not necessarily belong to language, most are indeed linguistic signifiers. The compulsion to repeat is thus explained as the unconscious repetition of a 'sentence', that is, of a chain of signifiers. The important figures in the subject's development, such as the father, the phallus, and even the subject himself are bound within this sentence as signifiers. This enables Lacan to speak of a symbolic determination of the subject. This theory is supported by empirical evidence concerning the importance of 'names', 'numbers' and 'words' in the unconscious productions (dreams, myths, tales). Such evidence addresses the phenomenon of 'double bind', or the overdetermination of certain signifiers (or of their noticeable absence) which, aside from their ordinary meaning, also play a part in unconscious processes. The second source of evidence in favour of symbolic determination is the clinical evidence concerning physical symptoms, which, particularly in the case of hysteria, allegedly exhibit the structure of a language.

Lacan's thesis of symbolic determination is rather speculative. Even if Lacan provides us with some of its fundamental categories, no one has ever succeeded in grammatically defining the language of the unconscious. In addition, several axes of Lacan's research have never been fully articulated. Several theoretical differences, (and perhaps contradictions) do exist between (a) the syntax of the unconscious (in *Séminaire sur la lettre volée*), (b) the rhetoric of the unconscious (in *L'instance de la lettre dans l'inconscient*), (c) the pragmatics of the unconscious (for example in *Subversion du sujet et dialectique du désir*). Despite the lack of articulation of these different levels, Lacan's thesis of the symbolic determination remains one of the major conjectures of psychology.

Even if this conjecture proved to be false, and if the unconscious were unrelated to language, several of Lacan's notions may deserve the attention of current research on evaluative phenomena. Let us consider briefly the three main axes along which Lacan develops his theory of the unconscious.

(a) *The syntax of the unconscious*. By this expression, I refer to Lacan's attempt to characterize the internal logic of the chain of signifiers. In this part of his work, Lacan looks to reconcile the linearity of the signifier and the memory of the signifier. There is indeed a contradiction between Lacan's thesis that the unconscious talks, and Freud's idea that the unconscious is timeless. For Lacan, this contradiction is resolved by the fact that the unconscious repeats itself. In order to discover the reasons behind this compulsion to repeat, Lacan attempts to unmask the rules governing the succession of signifiers in the unconscious. However, because he does not believe the determination of the subject by the signifiers to be a real one, his solution consists in reversing the problem. He suggests that even if the succession of signifiers is arbitrary, the potential parses that can be made of the chain of signifiers are not. To illustrate this point, he considers a random chain of positive and negative evaluations. He then considers some sequences of evaluations, and shows that as soon as they overlap, their arbitrary nature is lost. The various ways of parsing the chain are inter-related. They partly 'memorize' each other, in the sense that observing a sequence necessarily informs us about the preceding one. The relation between short parses produces a short-term memory and repetition, while longer parses produce long-term memory and repetition.

Lacan's formal example should be considered as an analogy rather than as a concrete fragment of the language of the unconscious. Through this example, Lacan intends to emphasize the self-organizing power of symbols. He suggests that there would be no possibility of repression, and therefore, no unconscious at all, if the symbolic order did not possess this combinatorial capacity, this capacity to be born of randomness. Indeed, if the unconscious is capable of repressing our experiences of reality, it does so because it has the capacity of treating elements of this reality as symbols, and imposing its combinatory rules on these elements. If repression exists, it is because the symbolic order is able to develop parallel to our experiences and, somehow, to cope with their diversity and their novelty. In the unconscious, the signifiers 'cover' experiential reality in the same way as the signifiers of language 'cover' the signified. But no symbolic structure exists without constraints. In the expression 'symbolic order', the word 'order' needs to be understood in a literal way, that is, not only as a vague synonym for 'domain' but as a reference to a structured domain, one which is bound by constraints.

How are these very general considerations relevant to our discussion on the nature of evaluation? Let us assume with Freud that there is indeed a repression of affects. Lacan assumes in addition that repression works through the substitution of value-signifiers for affects. More precisely, a system of value-signifiers substitute our affective experiences. As I said above, the signifiers of the unconscious, although not restricted to linguistic signifiers, are mainly borrowed from language. Therefore, one may wish to distinguish two statuses of the same signifier: that of the signifier in language, and that of the signifier in the unconscious. The signifier, in the unconscious, is in fact a value-signifier. The relations which hold between the signifier and other signifiers are evaluative. In other words, the signifiers, in the unconscious, have a 'semantics' which is primarily based on value. This 'semantics' partially corresponds to the semantics of the language from which it is borrowed. This 'value-sharing' between the two levels is what ensures that repression occurs under the control of culture, that it obeys the cultural norms embedded in language. Of course, the value of the signifier in the unconscious and its value in the system of language need not be exactly the same. However, it is likely that the evaluative system of language signifiers is largely reproduced within the unconscious. In other words, culture is the main provider of signifiers for the unconscious. The evaluative semantics of the unconscious language is largely determined by the semantics of language itself. The unconscious takes benefit from the symbolic resources and the symbolic creativity of culture. Evaluation is therefore at the very intersection between the subjective, private order, and the cultural, public order.

(b) *The rhetoric of the unconscious*. By this expression, Lacanian psychoanalysts refer to the thesis by which operations of the dream, and more generally all manifestations of the unconscious, are in fact metaphors and metonymies. This part of Lacan's theory allows us to understand how, despite the fact that the unconscious symbolic order mainly reproduces normative prescriptions of a culture, its manifestations tend to transgress these prescriptions. This transgression is rendered possible by the 'sliding of the signified under the signifier'. The unconscious thwarts censorship by allowing signifiers to mean something other than what they ordinarily mean. This is what happens when several chains of signifiers (conscious and unconscious) intersect.

(c) *The pragmatics of the unconscious*. This expression may seem strange to those who are familiar with Lacan's remark that the subject of the unconscious talks *without realizing*. How, under such conditions, is it possible to assume that the subject of the unconscious is the author of speech acts? Lacan has so systematically pointed out the relationship between his theory and structuralist linguistics that little room has been left for pragmatics. This constant reference to structural linguistics dissimulates the importance of pragmatics in Lacan's theory, and the influence of pragmatic considerations can be identified on three different levels:

1. Lacan's constant attempt to infer the structure of the unconscious from the pragmatics of the analytical therapy (transfer) and the pragmatics of certain games reflecting the relational structure of the unconscious.
2. Lacan's reinterpretation of all classical categories of psychoanalytical theory (pleasure, reality and death principles, Oedipal complex, castration, etc.) in pragmatic terms. This new interpretation involves specifying the actors of the unconscious scene, attributing them with discourses, and allowing the subject of the unconscious to 'identify' with these various actors. Roughly speaking, the actors of Lacan's pragmatic theory of the unconscious are the traditional actors of the psychoanalytical descriptions (father, mother, phallus, etc.) in addition with certain meta-actors, like the other and the 'Other'. Mental illness,

neurosis and perversion can be described as special biases in the unconscious 'beliefs' of the subject concerning the pragmatics of the unconscious scene (who talks, who demands, who desires).
3   All statements such as 'the unconscious is the discourse of the Other', which are explicitly pragmatic.

One may be surprised that despite evidence concerning the role of pragmatic components in Lacan's theory, the importance of pragmatics has been so underscored by commentators. One of the reasons is perhaps that Lacan always recycles pragmatic components as signifiers. In Lacan's writings, the unconscious beliefs of the subject are systematically rephrased in terms of confusion and substitution (metaphor, metonymy) between signifiers. However, this very general direction of Lacan's demonstrations should not lead us to underestimate his theory's debt to pragmatics. I would argue that Lacan's texts would be much more difficult to read and understand if we could not rely on our intuition concerning the pragmatic elements involved. Even if we reject Lacan's most speculative theses, we can still understand those which concern the pragmatics of the unconscious, because they are also a phenomenological description of our intimate relation to the unconscious and to language. I shall now briefly consider two of these theses which are relevant for our discussion of evaluative phenomena.

In Lacanian psychoanalysis, the subjection to the symbolic order is often illustrated by the fact that subjects are inscribed as signifiers (their name and other referent expressions, such as pronouns) within discourse. In phenomenological terms, this means that we cannot have a holistic grasp on discourse. Our only means of exploring discourse is to talk, to follow its argumentative paths. But we cannot handle it like a finite object. This remark joins a more general and slightly different one, according to which the subject of enunciation is *within* language and not situated *without*. From a phenomenological perspective, this means that language is available to us from a specific point of access, with a specific semantic perspective. It is impossible for us both to perceive language from a global perspective and simultaneously grasp its details. Even if we start from a certain word, we cannot consider all the relations of this word with the others in the system of language. Therefore, language and discourse are somehow incommensurable with our capacity of conception.[2] Contrary to what Althusser would have us believe, the subject does not have the feeling that he is the source of meaning. The subject may be unaware of the ideological determinations bearing on his discourses, but he knows that he does not 'possess' language, since he receives it from others. Language's alterity partially explains that we do not feel entitled to modify the semantics of language. Evaluative relations, which connect remote parts of the system of language, are no exception. They inherit from language this obviousness rooted in the massive presence of the whole linguistic system. We are broaching here the question of the consistency of the symbolic system.

The second of Lacan's theses, closely related to the first, is stated in its canonical form as 'The unconscious is the discourse of the Other'. This statement allows both the readings 'the discourse about the Other' and 'the discourse pronounced by the Other'. The Other, in Lacan's conceptual apparatus, is the 'treasure of the signifier', the system of (unconscious) language, a place of total knowledge. For the subject of the unconscious, everything takes place as if the Other had the possibility of speaking and desiring. According to Lacan, this unconscious belief explains most features of human desire (in particular, the quest for the unrestricted, the unconditional). In addition, this belief explains why social discourse is so prevalent in the formation of individuals' social categories and social judgements. The discourse of the father, the discourse of the others, and finally, social discourse itself tend to appear as the discourse of the Other. In many respects, Lacan's concept of the Other has no function other than allowing us to conceive of a pragmatic unconscious scene. Note, however, that the subject of enunciation need not be aware that the real pragmatic contexts of enunciation of social discourses are associated, at the unconscious level, with another (fictional) pragmatic context which tends to give social discourses a status of authority not necessarily possessed on their own.

As we shall see in the next chapter, discourse analysis has been deeply influenced by Lacan's ideas. Social psychology has been much less receptive to them. Cognitive science should perhaps reconsider Lacan's theories. They could certainly contribute to the development of 'weak views of subjectivity' to accompany 'strong views of subjectivity' which are currently fashionable. By 'weak views of subjectivity', I refer to conceptions of the subject which emphasize the role of culture both in the evolution of the subject's desires during his life, and in the learning processes which uphold cognition. Such 'weak views of subjectivity' are required if we are to develop a theory of evaluation which takes psychoanalysis into account.

3 Cognitive models of evaluation

I will now briefly review some influential models of evaluation, in order to determine which proposals should be integrated into a model of semantic evaluative processes. I will not attempt to assess these cognitive models on the basis of empirical evidence. My impression is that despite academic practices which would have us believe that cognitive psychology has reached a stage in its development in which it is capable of modelling itself after physical sciences, this discipline still cannot play by Popperian rules. This does not mean, of course, that any reference to empirical evidence should be abandoned, though the obsession of experimental validation also has drawbacks. The primary drawback is the models' lack of biological realism. Indeed, such are the objects and the methods of social psychology that the primary evidence against which models are judged necessarily imposes a type of modelling which is essentially unrealistic. The scientific nature of social psychology allegedly rests on the results of experimental tests. After more than fifty years of work, these results are now comprehensive both in scope and in detail. In addition, they concern high-level psychological phenomena which are deeply influenced by social and cultural factors. There is therefore a gap between current 'realistic' descriptions of the mind in cognitive science (for example, that of Edelman) and the corpus of evidence which has been made available by social psychology. Cognitive social psychology has to resort to unrealistic models because 'realistic' descriptions of the mind do not allow for any predictions about the phenomena that interest social psychology. Classical computational representations of the mind are the only models which allow social psychologists to 'account for' the experimental data. Though they are of course aware that these models are not realistic, they assume that as soon as computational models of the mind are labelled 'metaphorical', their lack of realism becomes acceptable. This view is no longer supported by a large part of the academic community, now aware of how misleading the computational metaphor can be. In particular, the traditional distinction between long-term memory and working memory has been put into question by much recent work (Rosenfield 1992, Dennet 1992, Edelman 1992). In this context I question whether the 'cognitivization' of social psychology is not premature.

Realism and the computational metaphor

The computational metaphor is also largely dominant in cognitive theory of evaluative phenomena. Almost all models follow classic computational distinctions between (a) the structure of representations in memory, (b) access to this information, and (c) the processing of information in evaluative judgements.

(a) Most models make assumptions regarding the number and nature of various components of representations. Such models usually distinguish between a factual component (putative knowledge concerning the object, for example, knowledge about a person's behaviours), a trait component (semantic description of the object, for example, a person's 'generosity'), and an evaluative component, based on the most salient elements of the previous components. Much effort has been devoted to defining precisely the types of elements on which the evaluative component is based. Additional assumptions are made regarding the relationship between these components, and in particular, regarding the strategies for maximizing inter-component consistency.

(b) Modelling access to information involves specifying, in each context and for each type of evaluative task, which kind of information is used. Some models attempt to explain the association between evaluative tasks and the choice of a type of information as the result of the subject's strategy. Access to information is supposed to have a cost (inferred from response times), and the task is supposed to set some standards regarding the reliability of conclusions which may be drawn from the information. The subject's strategy is then described as the minimization of costs under specific task constraints. The cognitive modelling of information access is therefore deeply influenced by economic models of information.

(c) Most models of evaluative information processing may be classified either as descendants of Anderson's Linear Information Integration model (Anderson 1981), or as category-based models. In Anderson's model, which is often called 'piecemeal processing', subjects evaluating an object first consider the evaluative implications of each piece of information they possess. They then average these evaluations, assigning a weight to each that corresponds to its relative importance. On the contrary, category-based judgements of value proceed by subsumption under categories. Prototype-based theories of categories lead to models in which objects are judged in terms of the prototypes which are relevant for their evaluation (Bodenhausen and Lichtenstein 1987). Dual processing models make hypotheses regarding the factors which induce piecemeal processing and category-based judgements (Fiske and Pavelchak 1986; Brewer 1988). Finally, certain models emphasize the role of exemplars in evaluative processes (Smith 1992).

The foregoing summary does not, of course, give a fair account of research in social cognition. Nevertheless, it reveals that these models view memory as segmented in independent, localized components, which is largely incompatible with recent theories of memory such as re-categorization (Rosenfield, Dennet, Edelman). Similarly, one may wonder whether 'economic' theories of access to information are adequate. Indeed, much recent work on the brain reveals that both information and instruments of categorization are highly redundant. This redundancy suggests that many phenomena formerly interpreted in terms of whether or not certain information had been 'accessed' may otherwise be explained by the fact that some items of information dominate others in the global processes of categorization. A similar doubt applies to the models of information processing. Are flow-charts adequate representations of real cognitive processes? Why use diagrams with conditional tests (IF-THEN) if we never observe bifurcation points, but just some dominant effects?

These three objections amount to a single one: the sharp distinction between representations, access and processing is certainly misleading. One of the strengths of connectionist modelling of cognition is precisely to avoid the distinction between information, mode of access and inference. Indeed, in connectionist networks, the information is spread in the overall pattern of weights allowing it to associate input with attractors. Stated otherwise, information is access. In addition, access is categorization, and categorization is also inference, since it involves complementing missing parts of the data. Similar views inspire Edelman's modelling. For Edelman, information is just a capacity of categorization, which is distributed in a highly redundant way. In addition, evaluative processes, like all other cognitive processes, are not procedural. Technically, they are never exactly the same because they never repeat the same selections of neural groups and neural maps. Evaluative processes are global re-categorization processes which involve, each time they occur, complete re-affectation of neural resources.

More fundamentally perhaps, one may wonder whether the computational metaphor allows us to take into account the relation between local and global determinations of cognitive processes. Within computationalist views of the mind, the global level is the 'program' used for a given task, whereas the local level refers to information in memory. In cognitive modelling, this leads to an accumulation of propositions such as the following:

> For this type of task, search for information of that type and process it that way. If no information of that type is available, then search for information of another type and process it in another way.

This kind of cognitive modelling rests on the existence of a small number of data types in memory (the components of representations). This rules out the possibility that information could be encoded in a redundant way – in as many ways, perhaps, as there are modes of categorization, or at least, in as many ways as have already been categorized. The small number of representational components and their alleged separation perhaps reflects the small number of processing objectives which are imposed on subjects during experiments.

The evaluative synthesis

This critique of the computational metaphor invalidates neither the experimental observations nor the general hypotheses supported by these observations.

The most general of these hypotheses, and that which is perhaps the most widely accepted in the field, is that evaluation processes 'synthesize'. Evaluative reasoning puts together various pieces of information, resulting in evaluative judgements and descriptions which are simpler than their non-evaluative counterparts. All models reflect this synthetic power of evaluation. The piecemeal model is in itself a model of evaluative synthesis. In other models, this synthesis is presented as a process of selection of salient information. Whether or not models view an object's evaluative representation as a good surrogate of the 'true' (exhaustive) representation, they all acknowledge the 'unifying' capacity of evaluation.

It will not be contested here that even if the affective side is set aside, and if exclusive attention is paid to the cognitive level, there are still several different axes along which evaluation may be performed: efficiency, justice, morality, truth, praiseworthiness, etc. (Ortony *et al.* 1988). Such a multiplicity of principles would not be disturbing for a 'multiple' theory of evaluation if each principle applied to different types of realities. Theories, for example, would be placed on the axis of truth, acts would be placed on the axis of justice, persons would be placed on the axis of morality, and phenomena would be placed on the axis of utility. The work of the expert in cognitive science would be to rebuild, beyond linguistic confusion, an ordered semantic world where all types of realities and corresponding mental processes could be clearly distinguished.

Unfortunately, this is far too optimistic a hope. Representations cannot be cast into a strict ontology. They are often simultaneously understood from several points of view, triggering conflicting evaluations. Ideas may be true and yet have dangerous consequences, projects may be ethically perfect and nevertheless unfeasible, a person may be good at one thing and bad at another, etc. This seems to suggest that evaluation is a multi-dimensional phenomenon, though everything takes place as if we could never accept that various dimensions of evaluation are independent. As I argued in the first chapter, ideologies are precisely global representations which attempt to reconcile these various dimensions. But besides the ideological solutions, there are many other well-known ways to deal with these evaluative conflicts. One way consists in using schemes of inconsistency circumscription. The dialectics between heart and reason ('I know he is great but I just cannot stand him') is one such socially determined scheme. A second way of dealing with evaluative inconsistencies is to suspend judgement ('I cannot make up my mind on this issue'). A third way may consist of adopting a specific perspective on the object to be evaluated. By narrowing the context of evaluation, we are almost always capable of solving evaluative dilemma.

To conclude, evaluation is indeed multi-dimensional, though we behave as if uni-dimensionality were the rule and true multi-dimensionality the exception. I shall argue in Chapter 4 that the attempt to enforce uni-dimensionality of evaluation is especially noticeable in language.

There is no doubt that emotions influence evaluative processes. Love generally leads to indulgence; envy distorts our appreciation; sadness, euphoria, pride ... most emotions modify our evaluations (Forgas 1991). Ortony has recently added another domain of application to the cognitive power of synthesis of evaluation. Drawing upon his previous research on emotions, Ortony claims that there are 'relatively undifferentiated emotions of momentary liking or disliking', which he calls 'attraction emotions'. In addition, Ortony suggests considering, besides a fact component, a trait component and a value component, that representations also have an affective component.

> What I am proposing is that the affective experience component [of a person's representation] contains a summary record of the liking and disliking experiences that the target person has induced in us, in the form of something like a frequency distribution of positive and negative feelings of different intensity. This is not a record of the particular emotions induced, but only a record of the magnitude and sign of the undifferentiated affect (Ortony 1991: 346).

If we keep in mind that in the article we have quoted, Ortony intends to develop a theory of value-integrating emotions, it becomes evident that Ortony believes affective evaluations are a synthesis of emotional experiences. Combining this idea and the previous one according to which evaluation is a synthesis of cognitive appraisals, the end result is the idea that evaluation does not only depend on affects and cognition, but also acts as a bridge between them. The theoretical argument supporting this hypothesis is that affective processes and cognitive processes, viewed as (though not limited to) evaluation processes, share a fundamental structure. Both can be summarized by an orientation and an intensity. As such, they are obvious candidates in support of interpretative shortcuts and synthetic reports. I believe that this structural identity allows for confrontation of both sides of evaluation and, therefore, that evaluation may be seen as a bridge between objective and subjective reasoning.

A general framework for cognitive modelling

How does evaluative synthesis work? When we evaluate an action, for example, we consider its actors, means, purpose, outcome, location, time, etc. These components are the elements which define the schema for the action. Therefore, evaluation is based on the existence, or the dynamic construction of schemata. It is reasonable to believe that existing schemata possess their own global evaluations. On the contrary, dynamically assembled schemata allow us to combine the evaluations attached to fragments of representation. The dynamic construction of a schema is probably a rather complex phenomenon, much more complex than the simple addition of all the elements of the schema. This dynamic schema construction certainly relies upon the existence of abstract schemata.

The complex architecture and global nature of schemata render it unlikely that the piecemeal model is appropriate for evaluative tasks other than the aggregation of evaluations which are independent from one another, and make independent contributions to the global evaluation. In other words, the piecemeal model is valid only for marginal cases in which the evaluation of a fragment of representation can be considered outside the context of the representation. In almost all cases, to perform the evaluation, several fragments of the representation must be considered simultaneously, and in relation to one another. To illustrate this point, let us consider the example of a person who knocks out another individual. Both from the point of view of the intention and the outcome of the action, this may be judged a bad action. However, if we situate this action in a boxing ring, it may be judged quite successful. I will return to the context-dependency of evaluation in Chapter 4, when I discuss the nature of evaluative meaning functions in evaluative semantics.

Assuming evaluation is driven by schemata, how should it be modelled? Despite some advances in connectionist schema theory (Smolensky 1986, for example), current research is still far from proposing artificial networks capable of simulating cognitive processes as complex as evaluative processes. A general direction can nevertheless be sketched for the connectionist modelling of structured representations (Visetti 1990). Categories can be modelled as stable states (attractors) of neuronal dynamics, and schemata and schemata-based inferences as sequences of attractors. The benefits of this approach are twofold. First, on account of the neuronal analogy, connectionist models are slightly more realistic than computational models. Secondly, connectionist models address the problem of learning. Yet, there is also a drawback, since connectionist models often remain relatively impenetrable. To compensate for this problem, one may use connectionist models in which the dynamics are in some way 'intuitive'. This can be achieved through 'energy functions' which measure the system's consistency. In Hopfield networks, for example, the categorization of the input is carried out by finding a local maximum of a function of coherence.

If we consider evaluative processes in this framework, we must first assume that the object to be evaluated takes the form of a list of representational features. The activation of these features in turn activates the schemata which are relevant for the interpretation of the object. These schemata are associated with global evaluations. In other words, there is a global evaluation corresponding to each stable state (attractor) of the neuronal system implementing the schema. Alternatively, the representational features activate memory traces, which are associated with low-level evaluations. These memory traces are dynamically assembled into context-sensitive schemata (cf. Figure 2.2). The way in which dynamic schemata are assembled determines the manner in which they are evaluated. In the evaluative processes, the elements around which schemata are constructed are much more important than the peripheral elements. Returning to our previous example, let us consider the case of a boxer

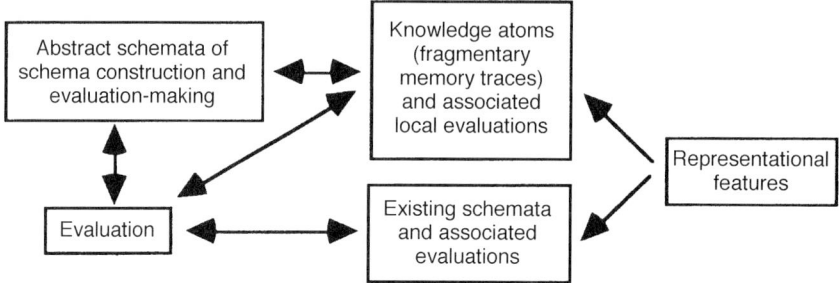

Figure 2.2 Evaluation and dynamic schemata.

who has been knocked out in a ring, and lies unconscious on the floor. Witnessing this, I may begin worrying about him. I will perhaps imagine his death, or a permanent handicap. My evaluation of the overall event may also change. Just a moment ago, I thought the uppercut was perfect, but now I realize someone has been harmed. This shift of evaluation comes from the fact that I have built a schema centred around the consequences of the knock-out. The evaluation of the situation is informed by the way schemata are assembled.

In consistency-driven models, activation spreading maximizes the coherence of the system. It selects (or builds up) schemata that are maximally consistent with representational features. When I first evaluated the event, the representational features included, along with situational features, the perception of the gesture, the boxer's fall, and his adversary's satisfaction. The corresponding schemata for uppercut, knock-out and victory are activated as a result of consistency maximization. Then, as the boxer lies in the ring, my expectations that he will recover are not fulfilled. To accommodate these new representational features, which are not consistent with my conceptual states, I have to activate, or build new schemata.

This raises an important point. Consistency maximization allows us to make inferences concerning the global evaluation of schemata. Therefore, we may wish to say that each schema is associated with a global evaluation function. This terminology should not mislead. When we evaluate a situation by framing it within a schema, we do not simply derive a global evaluation. We also modify the evaluation of parts of the schema. That is, the global evaluation has an impact on local evaluations. It is easy to give an example of this feedback effect: assume that at the beginning of a boxing match I have a poor opinion of a boxer. If this boxer is injured in the ring, my compassion may completely alter my feelings towards him. It is never just a whole event which is evaluated, but also the parts of this event. Therefore, as in neural networks terminology, the term 'function' in the expression 'evaluation function' does not refer to a 'function' in the classical mathematical sense of the word. It is simply a way of characterizing the *dynamics of evaluation*. One of the main difficulties in cognitive modelling of evaluation (and in cognitive modelling, in general) is to make these dynamics complex enough to reflect the subtleties of evaluative processes, while still achieving simple functional properties for these dynamics.

To this general framework of cognitive modelling, one may wish to add another type of evaluative effects, which has been described by George Mandler. Mandler conceives of value as a sort of side-effect of schema-based categorization. Roughly speaking, likes are produced by successful categorization (conformity of stimuli with existing schema), whereas dislikes are produced by unsuccessful categorization (schema discrepancy). The intensity of values is determined by the 'efforts' which are made to achieve categorization. Categorization requiring no effort produces zero intensity values; categorization requiring only slight assimilation produces low-intensity values; categorization involving assimilation to an alternative schema produces high-intensity values; categorization requiring changes to be made in an existing schema produce the highest intensity values.

This model raises a fundamental objection. We possess, or are capable of producing, schemata for badly evaluated objects and situations. As Ortony points out, we may be fully capable of identifying that we are being burgled, and yet, feel quite upset in front of an armed burglar (Ortony 1991: 340). The satisfaction which we achieve in being able to categorize situations does not necessarily counterbalance the dissatisfaction they may produce.

Despite this problem, Mandler's model leads us to ask whether value is a cognitive or a meta-cognitive notion. Research on impression formation seems to suggest that evaluation is a purely cognitive notion (a notion on which cognition operates). However, as Mandler suggests, there is a relation between the notion of value and consistency, the latter of which is a meta-cognitive notion. Consistency-driven modelling allows us to formalize Mandler's evaluative effect. Indeed, the 'success' of categorization, which, according to Mandler's theory, determines the valency of the evaluation, can be formalized as the consistency achieved by the system. The 'effort' which determines the evaluation's intensity can be formalized as the variations in consistency. If consistency increases continuously during the evaluation process, this means that the schemata which have been selected or assembled fit the representational features reasonably well. On the contrary, if consistency stops increasing at some point, this means that the schemata which were first assembled have not allowed us to achieve satisfying levels of consistency. Our initially drawn inferences are discarded. To achieve higher levels of consistency, the subject may modify representational features (discard some information, search for more information), or dynamically assemble new schemata. In either case, the overall consistency of the system fluctuates before stabilizing. The magnitude of this fluctuation indicates the strength of the 'Mandler effect'.

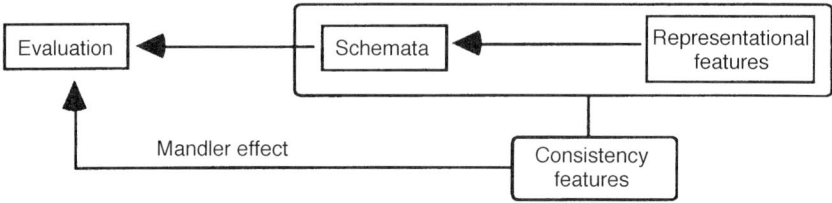

Figure 2.3 Cognitive and meta-cognitive evaluative processes.

As Figure 2.3 illustrates, it is possible to model the Mandler effect as a kind of meta-cognitive bootstrapping. I turn now to some evaluative effects which are not easily modelled within the simple framework of consistency-driven, schemata-based inferences.

Jansenists, Jesuits and evaluative attitudes

Some schemata and prototypes, rather than simply reflecting what reality *is*, prescribe what reality *should be*. These are the norms, or the standards imposed on social reality. While often explicit, they need not necessarily be so. It would be very difficult, for example, to make a clear-cut distinction between expectations and social norms. In addition, neither norms nor expectations must always be stated in the positive. Norms can define what reality should *not* be, and negative expectations exist (nationalism, for example, often has negative expectations concerning the behaviour of a nation's 'enemies').

When a situation is understood in relation to a normative expectation, what matters is the difference between the situation and the expectation. When a situation is evaluated by comparing it to a standard, what matters is the deviation from this standard, implying that the subject must have a perception of this deviation. This point has been overlooked by much research in cognitive science, a discipline which has always been more concerned with the perception of similarity than with the perception of difference. I believe, on the contrary, that evaluative processes involve, aside from the assimilation of some data to a schema or a prototype, the perception of contrasts.

Consider, for example, the evaluation of a social action involving a social actor and his behaviour. Assume that in the context of the action, the actor has a predefined social role. This role sets some standards concerning his behaviour. Let us also assume that this actor has a certain personal reputation, which defines additional expectations concerning his behaviour. We may evoke the case of Bernard Tapie, the French businessman and politician, who has been found guilty, among other things, of fiscal fraud. This fraud may appear especially scandalous if we take into account the probity expected from a member of the parliament. Yet, this fraud may also

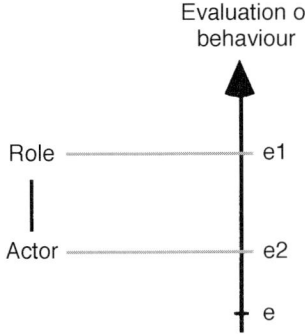

The evaluation of the action depends on the deviation of its actor's behaviour from the standards associated, on the one hand, with the actor's role and, on the other, with the actor's reputation:

$E(\text{action}) = f(e - e1, e - e2)$.

One may assume that these two effects are independent:

$E(\text{action}) = f(e - e1) + g(e - e2)$.

Figure 2.4 Role and reputation in evaluation.

appear rather benign if we compare it to Tapie's other supposed wrongdoings (fixing football matches, misappropriation of funds, etc.). Therefore, the evaluation of action also depends upon the reputation of the actor (Figure 2.4).

The relative importance given to social norms and to reputation define two evaluative stances. The first, which I propose to call the Jansenist attitude, emphasizes the role of social norms. The second, which I would call the Jesuit attitude, is more concerned with social reputation than with moral obligations and with duties imposed by social roles. In Chapter 7, I will further discuss how these two attitudes are also relevant on a semantic level, and in particular, how they help in modelling the evaluative behaviour of connectors.

I believe that the triangular relation between norms, expectations and facts allows us to describe the internal structure of most *evaluative attitudes*. By this expression, I refer to a subset of culturally identified (and defined) emotional attitudes which regulates our evaluative judgements. Examples of such evaluative attitudes are indulgence, comprehensiveness, pity, indifference, resignation. Some of these evaluative attitudes are also rhetorical attitudes: indignation, irony, concession, reproach, accusation, etc. Identifying the evaluative attitude of a speaker is a key element in the evaluative interpretation of his discourse. If, talking about a friend of mine, I say 'This bastard won at the lottery' this sentence is evaluatively inconsistent unless it becomes clear that I am expressing envy and not hate.

Until now, AI and NLP have paid little attention to evaluative attitudes and rhetorical attitudes. This may be one of the reasons why NLP faces so many problems in the automatic understanding of discourse. Adopting an evaluative perspective may help to solve some of the difficulties. There is no better way to detect irony, for example, than to discover an evaluative inconsistency in discourse. I will come back to this issue in Chapter 9.

4 Models of text processing

Models of impression formation and social judgement form the bulk of research on evaluative phenomena. In comparison, little work has been done in the field of text processing to address the issue. Nevertheless, because the object of this research is the evaluative interpretation of texts, it is necessary to situate this object within the context of the cognitive models of text processing.

The processing tasks

In literature on text processing, it is usually assumed that a subject may treat a text in different ways, depending on the purposes underlying his reading. Therefore, cognitive sciences conceive of the act of reading as a specific *task*. Within the context of a given task, a subject can be regarded as a system (more or less integrated) which processes some input and produces some output. In particular, the relation between input and output can be studied via measures of performances, constituting one of cognitive sciences' major sources of empirical evidence. The three main tasks usually assigned to subjects are understanding, retention and summarizing, specific tests being associated with each.

From which of these tasks are evaluative processes born? More precisely, is evaluative reading a form of understanding, a form of retention, or a form of summary? The answer, I would argue, is 'none'.

(a) *Evaluation and understanding*. Understanding, to begin with, is not the goal of evaluative reading. There is of course no reading without understanding, and evaluation itself is a form of understanding. However, evaluating is a simple form of understanding which allows us to avoid more demanding forms. There is thus a conflict between evaluative understanding and what is usually called understanding. To illustrate this difference, let us consider the following statement from a computer magazine:

> New Macintoshes with a PCI bus are faster than old NU-BUS Macs, and this speed difference will become more and more noticeable as new cards hit the market.

For someone who knows neither what the bus of a computer is, nor what computer cards are for, this statement is rather difficult to understand. Nevertheless, from an evaluative standpoint, the statement is quite clear. It means, by and large, 'new Macs are better than old Macs because of something called a PCI bus, whatever that is'. This example shows that an evaluative reading allows us to make sense of a statement without truly understanding it. Evaluative reading not only allows us to follow when we are unable to really understand, but also frees us from the necessity of understanding when we are capable, but prefer not to.

(b) *Evaluation and retention.* Similar remarks can be made concerning retention. Evaluative reading discards most of the information it uses to derive evaluations. Even when remembered, information is no longer accessible for recall. It can only be retrieved for evaluative purposes, in the context of an evaluative appraisal. For example, after we have read a newspaper, if we are asked about its content, we often have a difficult time replying. We can remember nothing, or only a small part of what we have read.[3] This does not mean we have forgotten everything, but simply that our reading is evaluative, and not geared to enabling us to answer the question 'What is in the newspaper this morning?'. Later in the day, if someone mentions a topic, we may be able to say 'There is an article on such-and-such a subject in the newspaper today'. We may even be able to give details about what we have read. The fact that we were able to recall several hours later what we could not recall immediately following our reading, simply shows that memory is, as Edelman claims, a process of re-categorization. Moreover, evaluative categorizations are not necessarily accessible and re-usable by other kinds of categorizing processes.

The difference between evaluation and retention has been studied by social psychology. It has been shown, for example, that judgements about persons are more greatly influenced by the first information acquired than by subsequent information, whereas recall performs best with more recently acquired information (Dreben *et al.* 1979). This provides definitive proof that evaluation and retention are two very different cognitive attitudes.

(c) *Evaluation and summarizing.* Summarizing holds particular importance in cognitive research on text understanding. Indeed, one of the most influential models of text processing, namely Van Dijk and Kintsch's model (1983), is supported mainly by evidence drawn from experiments in which subjects are asked to summarize texts. According to this model, subjects first construct a 'text base', that is, a semantic representation of the content of the text. This first step is modelled by propositional analysis (a method of content representation based on simple logical formalism). Subjects then make inferences and couple this semantic information with prior knowledge, thereby constructing or updating a 'situation model'. This idea has found its technical realization with the notion of frame (or schema). Formally, a frame is a data structure with empty slots which are filled in during reading. The frames incorporate the reader's expectations as well as his prior knowledge, and correspond to the typical information linked with a situation. Frames are thought to exist prior to, and to guide the act of reading. Thus, the use of frames and schemata usually reveals a top-down model of text comprehension. Schank himself has stated this very confidently:

> We would claim that in natural language understanding, a simple rule is followed. Analysis proceeds in a top-down predictive

manner. Understanding is expectation based. It is only when the expectations are useless or wrong that bottom-up processing begins.

In Kintsch and Van Dijk's traditional psycholinguistic model, top-down processing is modelled as the integration of the information yield by propositional analysis into a frame, or schema, representing the mental representation of the situation evoked by the text.

There have been many variations on this model. However, the basic intuition underpinning various versions is perhaps that neither in a text, nor in the mental representation of its content, are all elements of equal importance. At the textual level, the *macrostructure* indicates the salient elements. At the cognitive level, the salient elements are assumed to be located at the top of the conceptual structure representing the text content. In short, such fundamental elements are the text's topic, or theme. Then, secondary elements, like facts and argumentative developments, are attached to the prior ones, and so on as their importance decreases. Therefore, the fundamental organization of both texts and mental representations of texts is viewed as hierarchical.

The Kintsch and Van Dijk model, born in the 1970s, is now outdated. Kintsch himself has abandoned it, and now works with bottom-up models of text processing. Linguists concerned with textuality, such as Rastier, have convincingly argued that the Kintsch and Van Dijk model is, in fact, only valid as a model of summarizing, and not as a model of text interpretation.

> The experimental results allegedly supporting the model are artificial: starting from the principle that understanding is summarizing, students are asked to summarize texts, and it can be remarked that their summaries do not significantly differ from the macrostructure as it is elaborated (and formatted) by the scientist during Propositional Analysis. From this, it is concluded that the model is valid. But summary itself is a genre, which conventionally selects what is generally called important information. A summary does not represent a text, it is rather a rewriting in another textual genre, which corresponds with the postulate that texts are means of conveying information. (Rastier *et al.* 1994: 173)

Understanding is not summarizing, but can evaluating be considered a form of summary? Some researchers in social psychology use the term 'evaluative summary' to refer to the evaluative component of representations (Fazio 1990). I have emphasized the synthetic power of evaluation. I concede that it is very likely that the global evaluation of text content is indeed influenced by the textual macrostructure (above all if this macrostructure is apparent in the form of titles and headlines). But the purpose of an evaluative reading is not the elaboration of a comprehensive, hierarchically structured, and fully accessible representation. In such a case, evaluation would serve to retain information, a hypothesis contradicted by much empirical research.

Evaluation as a non-purposive action

Evaluation is neither a matter of understanding or retention, nor of summarizing. Does this imply that we should conceive of evaluation as a specific task? Although it may seem reasonable to consider all acts of reading as tasks, the hypothesis becomes problematic as soon as one realizes that most acts of reading taking place in the non-professional social sphere are ill-defined with respect to their goals. In particular, reading a newspaper often corresponds to imprecise motivations, expressed in vague formulas such as 'staying informed'. Cognitive sciences are not unaware that such loosely defined practices of reading exist, but they regard them as being at the limit of all possible understanding.

> It is totally unrealistic to describe the processes implemented by a subject in situations as vague and non-constraining as tasks where the subject is asked to 'read for the sake of reading'. (Denhiere and Rossi 1992: 10)

As the reader will have noticed, what is unrealistic is not that someone could 'read for the sake of reading', but that such an activity could become a scientific object. Since in most mediated communicative actions such as newspaper reading, the actor has no defined objective, one may view the object of sociological text analysis as an 'unrealistic' scientific object. The problem is in fact one of the non-purposiveness of reading.

Many scientific disciplines have faced the problem of modelling non-purposive actions. It is the importance of non-purposive actions which has led sociology to reject the strong assumption (originally made by Max Weber) according to which 'understanding' an action meant understanding the actor's conscious motives for undertaking it. More recently, in the field of Artificial Intelligence, a leading researcher has suggested that some of the shortcomings of robotics, for example, could be due to the fact that robots are assigned overly specific tasks (Winograd 1992). Both in sociology and Artificial Intelligence, it has been proposed to adopt a vision of action inspired by phenomenology. Habermas, for example, has borrowed the concept of the *lifeworld* from Husserl, and thus refers to the fundamental orientation towards the surrounding world which precedes and renders intentional actions possible. Winograd has suggested we draw our inspiration from Heidegger, and endow computer systems with an openness to the world similar to the Heideggerian *Sorge*.

These references to phenomenology are aimed at describing the orientation of the subject towards his surrounding world. Several aspects of this orientation must be emphasized: (a) This orientation cannot be 'turned off'. (b) It is beyond the will of the subject and corresponds to something deeper in his nature than any conscious, intentional activity. (c) It has no specific, immediate purposes. (d) Society as a whole is merely the broadest manifestation of this surrounding world. (e) Although this orientation is pre-conceptual, it is not simply a matter of perception or direct experience. Our conceptions (acquired through narratives, for example) are just another form of openness to the world, and thus remain tied to pre-conceptual forms. This is what makes us social beings, spontaneously entering into interpersonal exchanges and building representations of our social world through story-telling.

It is in phenomenological terms that evaluation is best described. Evaluating is almost as basic to human cognition as awareness. It is a form of vigilance, of watchfulness, which operates, so to speak, in the background of our consciousness. I would even suggest that it is the evaluative stance which gives our relation to the world the taint of worry which Heidegger expresses through his concept of *Sorge*. And it is perhaps when the evaluative perspective tends to dominate our perception of the world, thereby producing anxiety and anguish, that the Da-sein is capable of becoming aware of the ontological difference.[4] Without pushing the parallel with Heidegger's phenomenology any further, I have only intended to clarify that we do not read *in order to* evaluate. We read *and* we evaluate because evaluation is a fundamental component of attention.

This does not entail, of course, that there is only one mode of attention and, in the case of text processing, only one mode of interpretation. In some cases, the evaluative processes are conscious, and tightly linked to other cognitive processes. In other cases, they work in a more autonomous fashion.

5 Modes of interpretation

I distinguish between five modes of evaluative interpretation, not so much to establish a typology, but rather to show how the different levels of complexity are articulated. To label the first two levels, I borrow from Bakhtine the notion of *responsiveness*. For the Russian philosopher of language, every act of reception is also an act of response, a virtual dialogue:

> The listener who receives and understands the (linguistic) signification of a discourse adopts simultaneously, towards this discourse, an active and responsive attitude: he agrees or disagrees (totally or partially), he completes, he adapts, he prepares to execute, etc. ... The understanding of a living speech, of a living utterance, is always accompanied by an active responsiveness

(although the degree of this activity may vary) (Bakhtine 1984: 174).

However, mediated communication is not always very 'alive', and the degree of response to the messages we receive, especially those which are not directed at us, may be quite low. This is why I propose to consider simple evaluative responsiveness as the lowest possible degree of response, distinct from active responsiveness.

1 *Simple evaluative responsiveness* is the cognitive response to semantic evaluative effects. In this type of interpretation, the subject lends himself to the evaluative effects contained in the message. The subject calculates a global evaluation 'as the message would have him do so'. Of course, the subject's system of values interferes with evaluations conveyed by the message. But in evaluative responsiveness, there is no awareness of a potential conflict between these two sources of information. This absence of conflict is due to the fact that in evaluative responsiveness, it is not the message itself which is evaluated, but only the content of the message. Evaluative responsiveness may lead us to change our system of values. This is what happens when, without having any established critical stance towards the discourses we receive, we slowly adapt our values and our beliefs in relation to it. Moreover, we need not be aware of this evolution. When we hear that someone is frequently praised, or an idea frequently defended, we tend, in the long run, to internalize a positive opinion of the person or subscribe to the given idea. Responsiveness is the source of internalization of social representations, which are upheld by their obvious nature and by social consensus.

2 *Active responsiveness* consists in confronting the beliefs and the values a discourse conveys with our own beliefs and values. As Bakhtine puts it, we agree or disagree, we feel close to or far from a discourse. When we do so, we intend to situate the discourse with respect to our own personal standpoint. Contrary to the previous mode of interpretation, active responsiveness implies that we do not only evaluate the content of discourse, but also the discourse itself. If the discourse is consistent with our normative beliefs, we tend to agree with it. If it is inconsistent, we disagree with it, and reject it. Alternatively, we can just ignore a discourse which is inconsistent with our value system. In this last case, we do not explicitly disagree – we may even agree – but we simply avoid modifying beliefs which are inconsistent with what we have just accepted. This type of interpretation is responsible for the 'imperviousness to information' which social psychologists diagnose in 'naive thought' (Moscovici 1986). Active responsiveness also accounts for the fact that subjects strongly involved in an ideology tend to underestimate the differences between the opinions which differ from their own opinion. Their ideological commitment decreases their perception of the ideological contrast with that of others (Sherif 1973).

3 *Ideological categorization* consists in locating a discourse within the polemic realm. There are at least three important ways in which ideological categorization can be carried out:

(a) *Inferential categorization.* In this type of interpretation, the receiver starts from one or more propositions in a text and makes inferences until he derives a proposition which is clearly ideologically connoted. The prototypical sequence for such reasoning is, 'From text T, one can infer a proposition q, q belongs to the doctrine of ideology I, therefore T is inspired by I'. Although this type of interpretation may help determine an ideological adherence, it is probably more useful and successful when applied to social controversies (local ideological conflicts).

(b) *Recognition of ideological patterns.* I argued, at the end of the previous chapter, that ideological discourses can be defined in terms of ideological patterns, which characterize the 'way of thinking' inherent in an ideology. In the case of Marxist ideology, for example, two such fundamental patterns could be that of an 'idealist argument' or of a 'capitalist'. Recognizing ideological patterns generally requires identifying discursive entities (such as that of 'idealist argument'). It also often requires typecasting elements of discourse (substituting the type 'capitalist' for the type 'person', for example).

(c) *Ideological perception.* This type of interpretation is a bottom-up, ideological disambiguation of a text. Several ideological hypotheses compete with one another. During the process of reading, some hypotheses dominate others. Ideological hypotheses tend to be validated if they render the text consistent, and otherwise tend to be invalidated. Of course, ideological disambiguation of a text requires one to identify, or at least, to make hypotheses regarding the evaluative attitudes of its author.

I shall focus, in the book, on ideological perception. This is not to say that the two other modes of ideological categorization are less important. However, I believe that the analogy between perceptual categorization and ideological categorization deserves to be studied. First, it has been shown that social categories are prototypical (Dahlgren 1985, 1988), and therefore close to perceptual categories. Social experiments, such as social categorization games, have largely confirmed psychological findings (Boltanski and Thévenot 1983). Secondly, many ideological categories cannot be easily expressed in rational terms. To illustrate this point, let us consider the case of political life in France, which has been structured (for more than a hundred and fifty years) by the division between left wing and right wing. This dichotomy is the basis of the perception of political discourse. Interestingly enough, most political scientists admit that despite all ideological changes, the opposition between left and right continues to 'work'. In other words, the antagonism between left and right remains useful in order to interpret political discourses and predict political decisions. Most political scientists and French citizens are capable of recognizing a left-wing from a right-wing discourse. However, they would be often hard pressed to justify their analysis. Ideological adhesion can be robustly identified, although the processes of identification remain largely unclear. Thirdly, the notion of ideological perception is connected to that of lexical perception, proposed by the field of semantics (Rastier 1991, Ch. 8).

Above all, the notion that ideological categorization functions as bottom-up disambiguation is the only one in accordance with phenomenological descriptions of evaluative processes. This notion allows us to conceive of ideological categorization as working in the background of cognitive interpretation processes, but nevertheless, as following them very closely. The analogy with perception points out that ideological categorization functions in very much the same way as evaluative processes. This similarity reflects the fact that active responsiveness and ideological categorization are evaluative processes themselves, having discourses as their object.

The semantic evaluative processes triggered by a text and the evaluation of the text are phenomenologically similar but nonetheless distinct. One of the main goals of this research is to define the latter in terms of the former. I shall model ideological perception as the perception of the evaluative processes themselves. More precisely, ideological categorization will be based on the perception of texts' ideological consistency. And this consistency will be estimated by virtue of the perception of evaluative processes, themselves.

Conclusion

I have argued that the importance of evaluative processes stems from the primacy of the affective level during the first years of a child's development. Indeed, evaluative processes progressively arise out of affective dispositions. But these affective dispositions are not natural. They are social, or at least relational. Studies in emotional development teach us that our affective disposition is derived from two basic relational experiences: love (of the mother), and fear (of the stranger). The conquest of autonomy, which is realized by means of auto-stimulation, and body control, is the third fundamental axis of the child's emotional development (Malrieu 1952). This small number of basic affective dispositions explains why the more elaborate evaluative processes of the adult tend to be synthetic.

Evaluative processes are rooted within affective processes. But how exactly? One simple hypothesis would be that we learn to call good what appeals to our desires. However, psychoanalysis teaches us that the notion of desire alone does not offer firm ground for the understanding of evaluative processes. Human desire is originally perverse and polymorphous, and is shaped by its conflicts with cultural norms, partially conveyed by linguistic means. One must therefore conceive of evaluation as a bridge, or as a point of articulation between affects and cognition. Edelman has taken this idea one step forward in the direction of biological foundations. However, his Neural Darwinism remains to be articulated with models of reasoning. At the level of cognitive modelling of evaluative processes, almost every area remains open to research. No satisfactory model will be available until we know how to solve the general question concerning the connectionist modelling of complex schemata. In addition, some meta-cognitive effects must be taken into account, as well as global evaluative attitudes which also influence evaluative processes.

The biological distinction between limbic system and cortex, as well as the existence of specific areas devoted to the correlation of the two systems, is the fundamental physiological evidence supporting the hypothesis of a relative autonomy of evaluation with respect to cognition. Phenomenological observations of the evaluative dimension of discourse understanding also suggest that evaluative processes must be given relative autonomy with respect to other cognitive processes. There is no reason to believe that evaluative processes are totally similar to and determined by cognitive processes. In particular, selecting salient elements and placing information into hierarchical structures may not be as important, nor function in the same way in evaluative processes as in summarizing. This calls into question the traditional selection strategies of discourse analysis, assessed in the next chapter.

3

INTERPRETATIVE SHORTCUTS

Introduction

The need to cope with large amounts of textual materials is not specific to modernity. According to editors of the Renaissance, law for example was already presented as an *ocean* of texts.[1] Ten centuries before the advances of information science, canon law used highly sophisticated techniques of compilation, classification, and reproduction of texts. All these techniques were used as a support for a fundamental process: interpretation. Archival techniques allowed one to pick up texts which were relevant for the problem at hand. The rules of hermeneutics defined how to use relatively small parts of texts (a sentence, a word sometimes) as an impulse to thought, as a source of comments.

In the middle of this century, with the advent of content analysis, some methods of textual manipulation have ceased to serve the purpose of interpretation. Instead of stabilizing the procedures by which texts produce more texts, content analysis has devoted all its efforts in systematically replacing texts by fewer texts. By comparison with the sequence of operations involved in ordinary interpretation (accessing texts, reading them, confronting them, commenting on them) the methods of content analysis appear as a collection of shortcuts. Operations of selection, counting, coding, summarizing, subsuming under categories and aggregating the results of prior operations are all shortcuts around the demanding task of interpretation.

It may be useful to discuss the intellectual project of content analysis. Its origin and its conditions of emergence may help further the understanding of the scientific status of textual analysis. To put it simply, the development of content analysis has had three different triggers, which will be evoked successively: wartime propaganda analysis (section 1); the belief that the statistical distributions of words within discourses are correlated with non-discursive realities (section 2); an outdated conception of the 'scientificity' of the social sciences (section 3).

Theoreticians of content analysis have elaborated a coherent theory of their methods. However, consistency does not entail validity, and content analysis has been intensively criticized from all sides. All these critiques amount to a single, massive one, which is that content analysis does not take into account the meaning of texts. Quantitative social scientists are indeed lifting message components out of their various dramatic and symbolic contexts, thereby statistically combining fragments of content that are essentially not comparable. Because of this taint of indifference to the contextual nature of meaning, there is a large consensus within the academic community to minimize the use of content analysis methods and to propose alternative ones. Since the 1960s, numerous methodologies have shown up to replace the purely quantitative methods of content analysis. Most of them are hybrid methods, which associate the expertise and the skills of the human interpretation with tight protocols ensuring that the results are replicable. This cluster of methods is today referred to by the generic expression 'discourse analysis'. Within these methods of textual analysis, two main paradigms must be distinguished: the Anglo-American discourse analysis (section 4) and the French *analyse du discours* (section 5). These paradigms neither pay the same attention to ideological phenomena, nor have the same apprehension of ideology. Yet, they share the belief that ideological significance can be 'read off' from certain classes of linguistic items in the texts.

Insofar as it has produced valuable methods of ideological identification, this belief is a source of inspiration for the research undertaken here. In order to include them as semantic effects within the model proposed in the following chapters, the linguistic devices that discourse analysis regards as capable of conveying ideological meanings must first be listed and described. However, this inclusion within a semantic model with broader scope changes the status of these devices and of their semantic interpretation. Instead of appearing as the core, they appear as the limit-cases of a much more general interaction between ideology and language. This change of perspective, by which what was considered as the rule becomes a particular case (however important it may be) leads me to cast doubt upon the usual practice of pointing out a few linguistic items within the text. Although the 'interpretative shortcuts' of discourse analysis are a great improvement over the 'non-interpretative shortcuts' of content analysis, they are still 'shortcuts' in the sense that they *select* relevant components of the texts before basing the interpretation on these components. I will discuss successively two forms of selection: focusing on illocutionary components (section 6), and on symbols (section 7).

1 Content Analysis: the origins

In this brief discussion of content analysis, I will draw upon a classical presentation by Krippendorff (1980). Drawing upon some previous research by George (1959), this popular textbook argues that it is the wartime propaganda analysis that has been the fundamental impulse towards content analysis. Let us briefly comment upon these historical elements.

The orientation of propaganda analysis towards the forecast of an enemy's strategic decisions has strongly influenced content analysis in the direction of prediction making. Content analysis has also some roots in the ideological normativity of the MacCarthy period, when it was sought to identify 'scientifically' pro-Russian newspapers and authors. This historical origin reveals that ideology is indeed the major concern of content analysis, and that its first practitioners conceived of content analysis as an instrument of ideological struggle.

There is however one fundamental problem with the claim to prediction. The predictive successes of propaganda analysis were rendered possible only by the existence of the propaganda being studied. In the absence of a highly centralized and goal-oriented source of the messages, planned actions do not necessarily follow the conditioning of the public. Since such conditions are seldom fulfilled in modern occidental societies, the claim to reliable predictions is more often hollow.

More fundamentally, propaganda analysis brought with it a tendency to look at the messages as cryptic. In this orientation, a text is no longer regarded as a text but as a code that has to be translated to reveal its real meaning; the hidden intentions of its senders. Such an approach denies to its object the status of ordinary speech, or of an ordinary message. The object of propaganda analysis is the 'speech of the enemy', a kind of speech which tries to condition us, which is not a speech in its full dignity. Propaganda analysis replaces the authors of the messages by forces of manipulation, dissimulated behind their discourses. The receiver is also portrayed as being necessarily fooled by the sender. Although human practices demonstrate that speech, and more generally, communication, is often instrumentalist, such preconceptions are certainly not a universal starting point to describe communicative situations. However, as we shall see, these preconceptions have deeply influenced content analysis, which – if we believe Krippendorff – has always been more concerned with the relation between what people say and what they are going to do than with the relation between what people say and what they think.

2 Inferences to the context

The instrumentalist nature of propaganda analysis reflects itself within most of the case studies presented by Krippendorff. But there are also echoes of this conception within the theoretical discussion which occupies the first part of Krippendorff's textbook. Even if the author seems extremely self-confident and does not explicitly consider any fundamental objections to content analysis, the strength of his presentation is that it implicitly take into account the major critiques. To put it in metaphorical terms, Krippendorff carefully elaborates a theoretical niche where content analysis will be protected from most attacks. Although he often moves away from this niche, he never strays very far from it. Here is how Krippendorff first presents content analysis: 'Content analysis is a technique for making replicable and valid inferences from data to their context' (1980: 21). To make more explicit what this author means by 'context', let us quote him again:

> The vicarious nature of symbolic communications is what forces a receiver to make specific inferences from sensory data to portions of his empirical environment. This empirical environment is what we refer to as the *context of the data*. (1980: 23)

This precision constrains the context of the data to be the empirical environment, strictly speaking. This does not include *representations* of the empirical environment formed by the receiver. It entails that the aim of content analysis is not to discover social representations, but the objective social reality – all concrete examples given by Krippendorff, in fact, concern inferences to the objective context of the data.

Krippendorff's presentation is the only coherent one. If he had claimed that the results of content analysis concern social representations, he would have raised a fundamental objection: to analyse representations, one must treat them as representations, that is, *structured, meaningful entities* designed to be *produced and interpreted* by social actors. Krippendorff is perfectly aware that content analysis does not easily manipulate highly structured data[2] (for example relational data, or syntactic constructs) and that its procedures differ so much from cognitive processes of interpretation that it can make no claim to model the production and the appropriation of social representations by social actors.

This strategy is defensive, and therefore difficult to attack. Still, there is one obvious objection to this programme: very few theoretical arguments can be given in favour of a strong correlation between the results of lexicometric studies and the state of society. Lexicometric studies can reveal a few things concerning the discourses about society, but not about society itself. The only reason why one can argue that symbolic data are correlated with reality is to assume that these data represent, or refer to their environment. Again, this implies that these data must be treated as representations, and therefore that the inferences drawn from them must be close to the processes of so-called 'natural inference' by which we understand discourse.

To circumvent the notion of meaning, Krippendorff needs to justify the elimination of interpretation and cognition from the theoretical universe of content analysis. His argument goes like this: both the layman and the social scientist deal with symbolic data; the layman is not interested in a reflexive knowledge on his own cognitive processes, all he seeks is information concerning his environment; *similarly*, the social scientist involved in content analysis *should be* more interested by the context of the data than by these cognitive processes.

This argumentation is based on a confusion between two different contexts of the data: that of the original receivers and that of the content analyst viewed as a receiver. Indeed, the data collected by the analyst are no longer 'live' data taken in their original communicative context. In particular, the information conveyed by the data is not pragmatically relevant for the analyst, as it might have been for the original receiver. Therefore, from the point of view of the analyst, the context of the data cannot be simply the receiver's empirical environment or the analyst's empirical environment narrowly defined. It should primarily include the original senders and receivers. The object of the analyst's inferences should be the data-making process, and the data interpretation process by the receiver.

However, this is not what Krippendorff recommends.

> Although content analysis may concern itself *with making the kind of inferences that are made by some receiver when attempting to understand symbolic communications*, the technique has been generalised and is probably more successful when applied to non-linguistic forms of communication where patterns in data are interpreted as *indices and symptoms* of which untrained communicators may no longer be aware. (1980: 23)

Krippendorff does not forbid the emulation of natural inference – he ventures out of his niche. But since he knows perfectly well that this cannot be done in a satisfying way with content analysis methods, Krippendorff does not recommend it either – he goes back into his niche. His claim that content analysis techniques 'generalize' the processes of natural inference is merely rhetorical.

If Krippendorff accepts the assimilation of the analyst to the original actor of the communication, it is only to the extent that this assimilation legitimizes the restriction of the notion of 'context'. Apart from this, the analyst and the communicative actor are not supposed to draw the same kinds of inferences. The sole insistence with which Krippendorff suggests an incommensurability between the normal practices of interpretation and the scientific inferences (with the list of oppositions routine/careful, informal/procedural, untrained/expert), would be conclusive. In fact, Krippendorff argues in favour of the analyst's autonomy with regard to the normal practices of interpretation. The whole argumentation aims at justifying the elimination of the communicator as an interface between the data and its context.

3 Scientificity of textual analysis

Standard interpretation processes start from a text, and develop its meaning by coupling the explicit information with background knowledge. Thus, cultural studies need cultural knowledge to explain cultural productions. Moreover, interpretations are convincing if and only if the interpreter and his reader share the same knowledge. The validity of such a consensus is not maintained by content analysis. On the contrary, cultural knowledge is seen as dependent on the communicative actions that produce and reproduce it. According to content analysis, the rules of scientific empiricism should be the only criteria for the acceptation or rejection of an hypothesis concerning the content of a text.

There is no claim to scientificity without a representation of science. The representation of science which supports content analysis is not very original. It includes a methodological doubt concerning the validity of cultural knowledge, an identification of the human interpretation with 'subjectivity', the belief that truth is accessible only through quantity. There are, in the history of science, other moments characterized by the same vision. Consider, for example, the early developments of British eugenics, and, more precisely, biometrics. Galton and Pearson, for example, were in search of the causes of intelligence. To this end, they used to perform large amounts of correlation calculus between physical characteristics (including the size of the feet for example) and the results of intelligence tests. Their method may seem strange to modern readers. Why did they have to test these non-plausible hypotheses? The reason is that biometricians located their own scientificity precisely in the fact that they would not *a priori* neglect any hypothesis, even the oddest one. Science is here conceived as deliberate naïveté. The rejection of intuition and of common sense is elevated to the dignity of a scientific principle. The fundamental metaphor of this conception of science is the *tabula rasa* of all prior knowledge.

A similar representation of science upholds content analysis. In this discipline too, evidence acquired through human perception and simple reasoning is neglected in favour of evidence acquired through statistical tools. Objectivity is supposed to arise mechanically from the elimination of subjectivity. There is also a fascination for the gigantic, de-cerebrated chains of words, which lexicometrics scrutinizes. This fascination appears as a confirmation of Michel Foucault's hypothesis according to which societies attempt to 'evade the ponderous, awesome materiality [of discourse]' Foucault 1971: 8). Indeed, the attention paid to the materiality of signifiers allows content analysis to evade the materiality of discourse. The methods of content analysis are in accordance with the 'sovereignty of the signifier', by which 'western thought has seen to it that discourse be permitted as little room as possible between thought and words' (Foucault 1971: 20).

Could textual analysis comply to another idea, hopefully less primitive, of science? One may distinguish, within textual analysis, between the concepts and methods that it borrows from other disciplines, and the methods of sociological inference that it builds upon these elements. All textual analyses have at least two levels. A low level makes use of notions inherited from linguistics, psycho-linguistics, semantics or pragmatics to describe and pre-process the textual material, and a high level processes the data yielded by the first.

The high level is mainly a matter of statistical hypothesis testing, dimensional analysis and classification. All these methods have been intensively discussed from the epistemological point of view. Most researchers admit that the Popperian epistemological framework is adequate to define and assess their scientificity. This view will also be the guideline of our work. It will be assumed than truth is the capacity to pass refutation tests against nature. Within textual analysis, nature is a set of texts processed by the low level, and the high level of any textual analysis is a particular kind of refutation test or discovery method.

Since any textual analysis must draw upon the concepts of other disciplines, the degree of scientificity of these disciplines sets a kind of upper limit for the scientificity of textual analysis. Because they partially rely on linguistics, socio-linguistic studies and studies inspired by the theoretical work of Bourdieu, for example, cannot be more scientific than linguistics itself. For the same reason, the studies that try to identify the genre of texts from the analysis of their modes of enunciation cannot be more scientific than pragmatics. And sociological studies that test hypotheses concerning the content of texts cannot be more scientific than semantics. But textual analysis should take the best out of these disciplines. It should be as scientific as these disciplines can be.

I return briefly, in the next section of this chapter, to the specific methodological difficulties raised by pragmatic analysis. From an epistemological point of view, among linguistics and semantics, semantics is certainly the most problematic discipline. Semantics describes meanings, or meaning effects, which are not observable entities. Meanings are nothing else than what is made objective by a semantic theory. This circle can be broken by confronting the meaning constructed in a certain way with meanings of a different sort (constructed by another theory, or simply expressed within natural language). But it would be illusory to think that we can directly relate meanings with things of the external world or psychological states, because we only have access to them through intentional processes, which, in turn, let themselves be apprehended by meanings alone.

This does not entail that semantics is condemned to stay out of the Popperian paradigm. As Barwise pointed out, semantic theories can be falsified: 'This is the primary evidence with which we judge a semantic theory; do the inferences declared valid by the model theory square with the pretheoretic judgements of native speakers of the language' (Barwise 1988: 12).

There is therefore a basic strategy that allows us to test the validity of hypotheses regarding the content or the nature of a text. It involves first judging the underlying semantic theory along the lines defined by Barwise. It also implies validating or rejecting the results of the overall hypothesis by means of statistical evidence yielded by asking a sample of subjects to read the text, and by interrogating them about its content or nature.

Interestingly, the total automatization of the meaning construction from the linguistic form is not a direct guarantee of scientificity. Lexicometric tables and plots are the result of totally automatic tools. This alone renders them neither meaningful, nor scientific. Furthermore, even if it yields expressive semantic representations, automatic meaning construction can be biased. It is not enough for a meaning construction procedure to perform in a perfectly deterministic way to be free from preconceptions.

On the other hand, the absence of an algorithm which would allow the translation from the linguistic form into a semantic representation does not invalidate a semantic theory. To illustrate this point, let us consider the case of mathematics. Spoken and written mathematics, as they appear in education or in publications, are far from being completely formalized. However, any (correct) piece of mathematics can be fully formalized by translating it into the language of sets theory for example. Mathematicians (at least those who are specialized in logical formalization) know how to make the translation, though they would be unable to give an algorithm performing the translation. The analogy with natural language ends here. While mathematicians can rely on some theoretical results about the possibility of formalizing mathematics, we do not possess similar results for natural languages, except for small subsets of some of them. In any case, even if designing an algorithm of meaning construction is valuable *per se*, and constitutes an interesting means of validation of a semantic theory, the existence of such an algorithm is not a necessary condition for the validity of this theory.

Concerning textual analysis, it is often more crucial to rely on a very expressive semantic representation than on the automatization of the translation process. In practice, there is often a trade-off between expressivity and automatization. Since automatization decreases the costs of the analysis and expressivity increases scientificity, this trade-off ultimately reduces to a trade-off between costs and scientificity.

4 Discourse analysis and ideology

The Anglo-American *discourse analysis* is traditionally opposed to the French *analyse du discours*. The former comes from anthropology; it pays a great deal of attention to oral language and conversation; it aims at the description of communication and of the uses of language; it borrows its methods from interactionism and social psychology; its objects are 'immanent'. The latter comes from linguistics; it focuses on written material produced in institutional or doctrinal contexts; it aims at the construction of typologies of textual genres based on the analysis of language registers; it borrows its methods from linguistics and history; its objects are 'constructed' (Maingueneau 1987: 10).

The two paradigms are also opposed in their treatment of ideology. It is worth noting that the word ideology is absent from one of the classical English textbooks on discourse analysis (Brown and Yule 1983), while it is recurrent within the main French textbook on the subject (Maingueneau 1984). With the exception of a few important authors – such as Kress, Hodge, Trew, Fowler, Seidel – to whom I will come back, the theme of ideology is not central within discourse analysis. In contrast, the French analyse du discours in the 1970s may appear as a golden age of the research on ideology and language. I will briefly discuss the respective conceptions of the relation between language and ideology in the Anglo-American discourse analysis and in the French analyse du discours, without going into the details of the analytical methods that can be derived from these conceptions.

The starting point of all research concerning language and social representations is Saussure's idea that the system of language segments reality into conceptual chunks, thereby imposing categories by which we perceive and understand the world. As a consequence, two different languages structure reality in different ways. These arguments have been taken a step forward by Whorf through his studies of the Amerindian languages, which show how world views emerge as the aggregation of conceptualizations tied to specific linguistic forms (Whorf 1971).

The thesis of a strict correspondence between the system of language and the perception of the world has been thrown into question by much recent work.[3] It has been remarked that languages such as English and French, despite a certain number of acknowledged differences, do not manage to 'carve up' reality in different ways – even where they would be expected to do so given the difference of their lexicon and grammar. More fundamentally perhaps, it has been argued that the categories of human thought exhibit a complex structure – involving, for example, spatial and kinesthetic image schemas – which differs from the set of structural relations which constitutes the Saussurian 'value' of a term (Lakoff 1987). This does not entail, of course, that cognition and language are unrelated, but rather that this relation is better exemplified at the level of metaphors, which are linguistic reflexes of the cognitive processes by which an object domain helps conceptualize another object domain (Lakoff and Johnson 1980). World views are then understood as the product of the state of the metaphorical system of a language, within a given culture, at a given moment of its history.

Although ideologies reveal a tendency to create their own vocabulary, the fact that several ideologies can coexist within the same linguistic environment proves that language cannot explain ideological variation. This suggests that the Saussurian framework is better suited for world views and social representations than for ideologies. If the whole set of linguistic resources does not produce ideologies, where do ideologies come from? The traditional answer to this question is to assume that ideologies are produced by the *selections* made within the resources of the category system and of the metaphorical system (Lakoff 1995).

Within this general framework, debates have focused on the issue which generates most controversies: gender. Certain feminist studies claim that the pervasive ideology that depreciates and excludes women operates through specific linguistic practices (Lakoff R. 1975), while others argue that the structure of language itself is incriminated (Coffey 1984).

I will not take sides in this debate. My position, much closer to that of Bourdieu, is that the term 'ideology' is improper to qualify the meaning relations that reflect and support masculine domination (Bourdieu 1990: 3). As stated in the first chapter, one must distinguish between the ideologies, which are discursive formations devoted to the legitimation of the social order, and the habitus which are representations and practices deeply interiorized and embodied by the social actors sharing the same social conditioning. Ideologies are the result of a conscious intention to justify, while habitus are unconscious, or unquestioned systems of dispositions. This distinction can also be rephrased in terms of doxa and opinion.

> When there is a quasi perfect correspondence between the objective order and the subjective principles of organization (as in ancient societies) the natural and social world appear as self-evident. This experience we shall call doxa, so as to distinguish it from an orthodox or heterodox belief implying awareness and recognition of the possibility of different or antagonistic beliefs. (Bourdieu 1977: 164)

Because the opposition between male and female is 'naturalized' within an extensive set of homologous oppositions which constitute the most basic habitus of many cultures (Bourdieu 1990), gender does not belong to ideology (as I understand it). Or, to put it in another way, my understanding of ideology is not directly inspired by evidence concerning gender.

The fact that the male–female distinction is, to a large extent, still doxal in modern societies may seem to justify the attempts to modify the linguistic practices that go mostly unnoticed and unquestioned, such as the systematic use of masculine determiners to express general categories including both male and female members. However, this should not lead us to adopt the naïve belief which inspires political correctness, namely, the belief that once language gets rid of this discriminatory practice, it will be neutral with respect to gender. More generally, the idea that ideologies reflect themselves within a subset of the whole set of linguistic resources and practices may suggest that once these linguistic biases are identified and eliminated, language may recover its innocence. If, as I would argue, ideological effects within language are not limited to a subset of language, but are coextensive with language, then, the whole project of political correctness appears, at best, as limited, and at worst, as ideological itself, in the sense that it tends to dissimulate the bulk of ideological effect mediated by language.

Despite the supremacy of gender and race studies in Anglo-American discourse analysis, there is a more marginal, but well-established tradition which takes ideology as its object. This stream of research devotes its efforts to show how, in a given sentence, the choice of a syntactic form (in particular, choices regarding themes, nominalization, passivization and aspectualization) can be triggered by ideological purposes (Kress 1983, 1981; Kress and Hodge 1979). The emblematic example of such studies is Trew's comparative analysis of English newspapers' coverage of African events (Trew 1979a, 1979b). It is shown that categorization (the use of the word *riot* vs. the word *demonstration* in the headlines, for example) defines the whole mental model which is implicit in the report. The author shows also that syntactic forms, like passivization and nominalization, help dissimulate the responsibility of some actors in the events.

This case study and some others (Seidel 1985) contain, either implicitly or explicitly, a set of propositions concerning the semantic effects of some syntactic forms. For example, it is assumed that passivization diminishes agentivity. It is also assumed that the use of definite determiners, of nominalization, and of some marks of aspect can make information appear as 'given' instead of 'new' (Halliday 1979), a semantic effect which connects directly with the phenomenon of ideological presupposition.

Some objections can be made to this kind of semantic postulate. It may be claimed that syntactic choices must be re-located within the context of the various registers to which they belong. It is well known that *Le Monde*, for example, writes down things in a much more prudent way than many other French newspapers. Given its low-tone register, some statements that would only be slight critiques if they appeared in another newspaper, appear as strong critiques when they are read in *Le Monde*. Readers are usually aware of these choices of expressivity, and perfectly able to decode them. However, this objection does not totally invalidate the semantic postulates of discourse analysis, which are, in general, simple and intuitive. I regard the formalization of the semantic effects corresponding to these postulates (in particular, those concerning degrees of agentivity and neutralization through presupposition) as one of the main requirements bearing on the formal model that will be developed as we proceed.

There are also, in Trew's or Seidel's analyses, certain methods which I will not attempt to formalize mathematically. This is the case with all the descriptions, much less semantic by nature, of the transformations occurring at the different stages of the press coverage of an event. This diachronic perspective, which obeys Foucault's advice to pay attention to the series and the breaks in the production of discourse, is not directly relevant for our research. It shows, however, that some authors like Seidel, have drawn their inspiration from both the Anglo-American and the French schools of discourse analysis.

There has been, during the 1990s, a revival of ideologically-oriented discourse studies, under the label critical discourse analysis. CDA's programme is to study how specific discourse structures are deployed in the reproduction of social dominance (Fairclough 1995). The final aim of CDA is to expose, understand, and resist social inequality (Van Dijk 1998b). Despite the unity of this critical programme, CDA is a very multidisciplinary trend of research, which does not have a well-defined methodology. The attempt to merge in a single theoretical framework the findings of classical discourse analysis and the psycholinguistic models of text and speech processing has neither solved all theoretical difficulties nor generated new, original methods. In Van Dijk's own admission 'Despite a large number of empirical studies on discourse and power, the details of the multidisciplinary theory of CDA that should relate discourse and action with cognition and society are still on the agenda' (Van Dijk 1999).

This book may be viewed both as a contribution and as an alternative to CDA. It is a contribution in the sense that I subscribe to CDA's general programme and to most of its theoretical foundations. However, it is also an alternative, in the sense that both concerning the status of ideology and nature of cognition, the views developed here differ significantly from those which inspire CDA's. These differences have clearly appeared in the discussions contained in the first and second chapter of this book, and will not be restated here.

5 Discourse analysis *à la Française*

French discourse analysis is not simply an academic discipline. It is a political project, launched in 1963 by J. Dubois and Pêcheux, blessed by the Central Committee of the French Communist Party, and overtly dominated by the political thought of Althusser (Maldidier 1989). In its first decade, this project involved many influential French linguists, among whom were Pêcheux, Culioli, Fuchs and Slakta. Since the middle of the 1980s, *l'analyse du discours* has become a discipline rather than a project. Its capacity to bring together scientists of the various disciplines of social science has decreased. Linguistics has ceased to be the leading discipline, and current research is much less innovative than it used to be.

French discourse analysis has developed along three main axes: 'lexicometrics', Pêcheux's 'Analyse Automatique du Discours' and the sociolinguistics of registers. Lexicometrics (textual statistics) applies Benzecri's correspondence analysis and automatic classification to textual material (Lebart and Salem 1990). The AAD attempts to define a materialist theory of discourse (Pêcheux 1969, 1982). The sociolinguistics of registers draws upon Culioli's theory of indexicality to study the relation between registers and genres (Achard 1995a). These three axes are distinct, but not unrelated. All trends of French discourse analysis share the same hostility towards semantics. Semantics is viewed as a linguistic idealism. Therefore linguistics cannot tell what meaning is. Meaning is the object of ideology theory, not of linguistics. However, as I said above, French DA involved many linguists. In fact, its instruments and methods are linguistic in the traditional sense of the term. In order to resolve this contradiction, French DA uses two main theoretical tricks. The first is to distinguish between text and discourse. Text is studied by means of linguistic theories and discourse is described by ideology theory. In other words, there is no room left, in French DA, for a linguistic semantics. The analysis goes directly from linguistic features to political interpretations. The second trick is to distinguish between registers and genres. It is assumed that registers are purely linguistic, while genres are purely sociological. Thus the 'analyse du discours' has made few contributions to the semantic theory of textual genres. More generally perhaps, one may argue that in the French version of discourse analysis little room is left for cultural studies between linguistics (narrowly defined) and politics or sociology.

'Automatic analysis of discourse'

Pêcheux's project can be summarized as an attempt to discover whether a discourse can be seen as a paraphrase of another discourse from the same discursive formation. Discourses are represented as graphs. An edge represents a 'predicate' and its arguments. Vertices represent the relations of subordination between phrases, the relation of complementation of the noun, the relations of conjunction. The method is based on local comparisons of the graph (comparing binary relations with binary relations). Not surprisingly, the method has practical shortcomings. In particular, Pêcheux's method is not workable for texts that have not been produced as paraphrases of each other: the analysis either fails to discover the relations of similarity between discourses or discovers paraphrases where there are in fact no relations of that kind.

One may judge that the local comparison of the graphs lacks reliability and is today rather obsolete in the view of the modern instruments of matching between graphs. We should remember that in the 1970s, the technological constraints did not allow the computationally expensive algorithms required by matching operations. But above all, we should not forget that Pêcheux's project, which remains Harrissian in essence, is not aiming at the recognition of 'patterns', but at the identification of the typical discursive 'environments' of the expressions. Pêcheux is interested in what an ideology prescribes *at each point of the enunciation*, as the natural 'complementation' of what has just been said. He does not believe, though, that a subject prescribes a verb or that a verb prescribes a subject. The control of ideology over language is not that tight. However, Pêcheux believes that the complementation of the noun and the subordination of propositions, for example, are often regulated by ideologies.

To illustrate this point, consider the sentence 'I think that we must reduce public deficit'. Pêcheux would interpret it as the result of two successive operations of 'embedding' and 'articulation'. He would assume that the preconstruct 'the public budget is in deficit' belongs to the *transverse discourse* of 'we must reduce debts'. This makes possible an 'embedding' of the first preconstruct, in the form of 'we must reduce the public deficit'. Then, Pêcheux would interpret 'we must reduce public deficit' as belonging to the transverse discourse of 'I think'. This allows one to make an 'articulation' of the two phrases, and to generate the final sentence.

For Pêcheux, discursive formations do not differ by their language (*langue*) since they use the same operation of syntagmatization (embedding and articulation). But, at the semantic level, discursive formations differ, since they assign different 'transverse discourses' to the same expressions. This is why linguistics cannot say what meaning is. Beyond the linguistic constraints bearing on discourse, there are ideological constraints, which contribute to the full meaning (Slakta 1971).

Pêcheux conceives of discursive formations as ceaselessly repeating the same things. Except for the variety introduced by the genres in which discursive formations express themselves, an ideology uses the same expressions, the same arguments, the same modes of enunciation. Pêcheux's project is to investigate the local relations (due to routine, to reflex) that render it possible for discourse to generate itself along the lines defined by the ideology. He therefore conceives of semantics as a crossing of preconstructs. He extends to the domain of discourse Jakobson's idea of the crossing of the paradigmatic and syntagmatic axes.

At this point, I put forward another hypothesis to explain this dichotomy between, on one side, a space of preconstructs structured by relations of 'transversality' and, on the other side, the operations of syntagmatization which allow the combination of preconstructs to make discourse. It seems to me that Pêcheux's thought is dominated by the metaphor of material production. There is indeed a striking similarity, and an explicit analogy, between the chains

$$\text{raw material} \rightarrow \text{transformation} \rightarrow \text{appropriation of the surplus value}$$
$$\text{preconstructs} \rightarrow \text{syntagmatization} \rightarrow \text{enunciation}$$

Remember that Pêcheux, drawing upon Althusser's formula 'Ideology interpellates individuals as subjects', conceives of enunciation as the illusion by which individuals believe themselves to be the source of meaning. As capitalists dissimulate to themselves (and to workers) that they make no contribution to the production of value, speaking subjects, by means of enunciation, dissimulate to themselves that they make no contribution to discourse. This illusion is the most basic of all ideological illusions.

How would we evaluate, today, the theory that has just been sketched? There are, in my opinion, at least two negative points and two positive points.

The first negative point concerns the theory of articulation and subjectivity. Although one may still wish, today, to get rid of the idealism of Austinian theories of enunciation, this does not imply that the subject must be described as completely alienated by ideology. Pêcheux's theory of articulation has had the same destiny as Althusser's theory of subjectivity: it has simply disappeared from current academic debates. I shall not try to resuscitate it. I believe in fact that Althusser and Pêcheux's attempts to combine Marxism and psychoanalysis are based on a misinterpretation of Lacan. As argued in the previous chapter, Lacan's theory contains implicit phenomenological descriptions of our unconscious relation to language. Contrary to what Althusser and Pêcheux would have us believe, these descriptions do not support the idea that the subject is the source and the origin of meaning. In Lacan's theory, the autonomy of the self is an illusion based on the subject's imaginary constitution, not on its relation with language (this is especially clear in *Le stade du miroir*). More generally perhaps, for Lacan, the subjective foundations of ideology lie in the *imago*, not in the enunciation (on this subject, see *Propos sur la causalité psychique*). Althusser and Pêcheux's reading of Lacan is therefore not in line with the main streams of Lacan's thought.

The second negative point concerns the hold of ideology upon discourse. Although Pêcheux has always emphasized the real dimension of discursive formations (their relation with the reproduction of social relations), it is useful to concentrate on the purely discursive aspects of his theory. I would argue that his focus on paraphrase led him to consider discursive formations as the transitive closure of a paraphrase relation between preconstructs. To use another mathematical metaphor, everything takes place as if Pêcheux conceived of discursive formations as a fixed-point of a discourse generation process. 'What can and cannot be said' is determined by the *syntactic* transformations and concatenation of a set of preconstructs.

The general feeling is that things do not work according to the syntactic determinism evoked by Pêcheux. It is indeed dubious that at each moment of the enunciation, the discursive formation proposes a class of paraphrases which constitute the 'transverse discourse' of what has just been said, and which can be combined with it. In addition, discursive formations evolve in time, and are therefore endowed with a domain of memory, a domain of actuality and a domain of anticipation (Courtine 1981); there is no strict and stable frontier between one discursive formation and another (Courtine and Marandin 1981; Achard 1995b); not all discursive formations oppose each other in the same way and with the same intensity (Maingueneau 1987: 85); discursive formations are based on abstract generative schemes (Bourdieu and Boltanski 1976) and ideological patterns (Boltanski and Thévenot 1991) instead of on atomic, elementary statements and their rules of combination. More fundamentally perhaps, discourse does not develop mechanically by routine associations between statements. Cognitive structures, non-linguistic knowledge about the world, and value systems trigger complex associations. There is therefore another logic behind the statistical correlation between units of discourse. This logic is that of meaning itself, of meaning in a social environment.

To conclude these critiques, I would argue that despite many remarkable achievements, Pêcheux's theory is not a genuine theory of discourse. I concede that Pêcheux clearly distinguishes between language and ideology. But in reality, his theory of discourse remains modelled after the theory of language, since it transposes the structure of language (that of Jakobson, of Harris) to the field of discourse. The theoretical shortcomings of Pêcheux's model are largely due to the lack of new hypotheses concerning the structures of discourse itself.

There are also, in Pêcheux's work, some insights and some proposals which continue (or deserve) to inspire current research in the field. The most illuminating of Pêcheux's ideas is perhaps that meaning is a phenomenon of interdiscourse. I fully subscribe to Pêcheux's fundamental thesis, which states that

> Words, expressions propositions, etc., change their meanings according to the positions held by those who use them, which signifies that they find their meaning by reference to the ideological formations in which those positions are inscribed. (Pêcheux, 1982)

Pêcheux is certainly right when he claims that the 'meaning' of an expression is its position within the 'interdiscourse', that is, the relations with the ideologies it emanates from and which it contradicts. He may be wrong, however, when he pretends that these relations are necessarily dissimulated from the subject.

The second positive point is Pêcheux's theory of ideological ambiguity. His famous paper on the 'Mansholt report' (Pêcheux *et al.* 1979), has in fact launched a series of applied and theoretical research on this topic. It has recently been shown, for example, that the French word *qualification* has been neither used nor understood in the same way by employers and employees – employers use it indifferently for tasks and persons, while employees use it for persons exclusively (Boutet 1994). Examples of this kind are so numerous that many socio-linguists, like Pierre Achard, consider ambiguities as the main instrument of discursive compromise between social actors (Achard 1995a: 12). This thesis is not contradictory with some recent empirical work by French social psychologists, who argue that in the processes of discursive interactions, social actors, instead of researching a consensus, want their points to be made without restriction and compromise – regardless of the uses which, given their ambiguity, their opponents can make of these points (Moscovici and Doise 1994).

As stated in the previous chapter, one of the purposes of this research is to model the cognitive processes of ideological disambiguation (the mechanisms by which a receiver tries to identify the ideological allegiance of the message it decodes). This does not mean, of course, that no attention is paid to ambiguity. Indeed, whoever possesses a theory of disambiguation will almost necessarily possess a theory of ambiguity too.[4] The notion of *ideological consistency* not only lays the foundations for a modelling of ideological disambiguation processes. It also opens the way to a theory of ideological ambiguity, since the ideological ambiguity of a discourse can be modelled as the simultaneous consistency of discourse with several antagonistic ideologies.

Categorization in French discourse analysis

Besides his influential theory of enunciation and indexicality, Culioli has made another important contribution to discourse analysis. Together with Fuchs, Culioli has developed a linguistic model which allows one to typecast notions on the basis of paraphrase criteria. For example, the model can determine whether, within a set of utterances, the notion 'masses' or 'women' can be typed as 'inanimate' on the basis of a series of tests (Pêcheux 1978, Fuchs and Leonard 1979). The basic idea is obviously to check whether utterances 'talk' about the masses in the same way that they talk about inanimate entities. The originality and the strength of the model lies in the number of linguistic features involved in the tests.

Several objections can be made to this model. First, one may wonder why Culioli and Fuch's ontology is relevant. In other words, it is not clear why the dichotomy animate/inanimate, or the dichotomy state/process should be more basic and more relevant for linguistics than the dichotomy of gender, or the dichotomy of number. In my view, these studies are unduly objectivist. They systematically assume that social distinctions are secondary with respect to 'natural' distinctions. Secondly, the method is based on tests of acceptability upon which even native speakers of a language can scarcely reach an agreement. Thirdly, a confusion arises, in the application of the model, between the picture that an author makes of the place of women in a society, for example, and the author's moral or political judgement on this state of things. In a classical study drawing upon Culioli and Fuchs' method, Bourdieu, Godelier and Clastres are reproached with their mode of writing about women (Michard-Marshall and Ribéry 1982). Roughly speaking, it is claimed that they write about women as if women belonged to the category 'inanimate'. This critique is particularly surprising when one reads, in another paper by Bourdieu, that 'Women enter within the dialectics of pretension and distinction as objects rather than as subjects' (Bourdieu 1990: 31).

Even if Bourdieu's mode of writing about women reflects the relations between men and women in the society he describes, this may be a consequence of the intermingled relation between form and content. An author naturally adapts his style, through a certain degree of mimesis, in order to give a more accurate view of his objects. This does not necessarily mean that the author is blind to the presuppositions involved in his style. This example demonstrates that it is almost as difficult, for a sociological analysis, to escape from 'sociologism',[5] as it is to escape from the critique of 'sociologism'.

Despite these objections, some features of Culioli and Fuchs' model deserve to draw our attention. This is the case, for example, concerning the asymmetry that these authors discover, within the linguistic comparisons ('as ... as', 'more ... than', etc.), between the term that is the focus of the enunciation, and the term that acts as a reference in the comparison. It is claimed that the semantic effect of these linguistic constructions is to make the reference mark appear as the norm. I will develop this idea in subsequent parts of this work. It will be argued that the comparison with a standard is a basic cognitive process, which gives birth to several semantic dynamics, and that these dynamics, far from being limited to the explicit comparison, underlie a wide range of meaning effects.

After this brief evocation of the two main schools in discourse analysis, I will enlarge my argument, and consider current research from a more general point of view. It may be argued that within communicative actions, not everything is necessarily relevant for social science's purposes, and that the relevant part consists of a stable core, expressed by specific linguistic ways. If that were true, it would be legitimate to select the relevant elements within discourse, by focusing on the appropriate linguistic components.

The above hypothesis can take various forms and lead to various strategies: the search for ideological drives within discourse, the search for embedded values, the search for normative contents in general, the search for world views and beliefs, the search for the exercise of a symbolic power, etc. Under such strategies, it is assumed either that a matrix (social knowledge and norms) is conditioning the everyday communicative actions, or that communicative actions produce consensus-based knowledge and norms. In both approaches the discursive diversity mobilized in communicative actions is doubled by a much more restricted, coherent and binding level, the description of which is the aim of the analysis.

In the last two sections of this chapter, I will ask whether it is possible to individuate within linguistic communications some elements that would stand out as having a special social relevance *per se*. The question is whether such a class of linguistic components exists, and if so, how to differentiate it from the rest of the elements. In other words, are there some linguistic markers of socially relevant components? I will pay attention to two possible strategies: focusing on the modes of enunciation, and focusing on symbols.

6 Modes of enunciation

The dominant practice within discourse analysis consists in studying the relation between linguistic *registers* and *genres*. It is assumed that social roles are associated with specific language registers, which in turn impose some constraints onto the linguistic markers of enunciation. Obeying these constraints helps other social actors to recognize language registers, thereby reinforcing the legitimacy of social roles. It is also assumed that these constraints mainly concern indexical and illocutionary elements. Most studies focus on markers of aspect, gender and person, such as pronouns, possessives and the tenses of the verbs. Indexical and illocutionary components are indeed a major source of sociological induction concerning the self-perception of social groups and categories. French discourse analysis relies heavily on Culioli's linguistic theory of enunciation, for example (Achard 1995a).

Since the meaning of indexical components depends on the context of the speech acts, their study must necessarily refer to this context. In addition, even in a given context, the same pronoun, for example 'we', may have several alternative uses. Describing the range of possible uses (inclusive? exclusive? nature of the membership? etc.) and identifying the use of each occurrence requires a clear conceptual layout and a careful analysis. In any case, the mapping of the social actors, (both individual and collective), onto the pronominal system is always complex. This type of analysis, which requires all the skills of an expert in pragmatics, receives only little support from lexicometric analysis. Within publications that combine both approaches, there is often a gap between the trivial indications yielded by lexicometrics, and the subtle discussions which arise from the lengthy analysis of a few significant occurrences.[6]

There is an important exception to the obligation of interpreting indexical components with respect to the communicative context. It may happen that the speaker makes explicit reference to another, similar situation of the past (be it real or fictitious) in reference to which he wishes that the present situation be understood. The study of such cases has lead Maingueneau to propose a distinction between *discursive deixis* (who speaks to whom, where, when) and *founding deixis* (the protagonists and the situation evoked by the speaker) (Maingueneau 1987: 29).

What are the limits of these methods? To be fair to them, one must admit that these limits come from the complexity of their object rather than from their intrinsic weakness. As recognized by many authors, the context which determines the meaning of indexical components is not a simple catalogue of referents. It involves fictitious collective or monumental subjects (e.g. the nation), and, more generally, a cultural knowledge about the type of situation. Thus, the 'situation' is always a mix of the actual situation and of ideal, culturally-defined situations. However, it is not enough to show how, by the mutual respect and the consensual acceptance of constraints concerning the modes of enunciation, a communicative situation is categorized.

First, society does not propose a model for each possible communication situation. It is well known that social roles are to a certain extent ambiguous, and that they may induce conflicting obligations (Boudon 1982). In addition, it is not always clear which role and sub-role a social actor fulfils at the time and place of the communication situation. Facing these difficulties, the expert in discourse analysis may object that since there is no clear social setting for these non-prototypical situations, they are not associated with precise registers and roles. On the contrary, I believe that these cases, far from being marginal, represent the bulk of communication situations. Most of the times, the communication situation does not fit the standard roles, registers and modes of enunciation. As a consequence, actors must adapt and invent adequate modes of enunciation or accept that the specificity of the communication situation be eliminated. In this second case, the actors experience a 'forcing', which makes them adopt communicative attitudes that are not really satisfying. They say 'what they think has to be said, in the way they think it has to be said'. They may or may not be conscious of the inadequacy between the situation and the cultural resources. But in any case, in order to describe a communicative situation, the sociologist often needs to put the actual communicative situation in relation to a set of cultural models which are not intrinsically appropriate. I return below to the exact nature of this 'inadequacy'.

Secondly, for several types of reasons, the members of a communication situation need not have the same model in mind. It may happen, due to the unequal distribution of cultural knowledge, that they do not agree on the nature of the communication situation (Boutet 1994). It may also happen that their respective interests make them wish to shape the communicative actions in different ways. Because the social roles are partly defined by the modes of enunciation, entering a communicative action is often the occasion of redefining these roles, or of changing temporarily from one role to another. Because not all players of a communicative game will have the same 'pay-off' depending on the way the situation is set up, conflicts may arise concerning the very nature of the situation. These conflicts are sometimes explicit. Most of the time, social actors try to modify the nature of the communication situation by 'pulling' it towards a specific model during the communicative action. This is usually done by successive shifts of enunciation, which tend to amount to a change in the corresponding functions of enunciation.

Finally, it may be argued that even in the case of standard, ritualized situations of communication, the binding force and the normative impact of the discourses, rather than arising from the rigid definition of their functions of enunciation, are due to the implicit mobilization of other, much more authoritative functions of enunciation. It is indeed reasonable to think that if the audience of a communicative action had a clear consciousness concerning its nature and its mechanism, then this audience could systematically keep a critical stance towards what is said. People would be able to distinguish between the different components of the speech act. They would rationally assess the content of discourse, and rationally assess the compatibility between the expressive and illocutionary components and the nature of the speech act. But in no way would this assessment produce the kind of indiscriminate persuasion effects, identification phenomena, and fascination, which are still very much present in modern communication.

In Durkheim's vocabulary, we may say that the profane communicative situations of modern societies still base their efficiency on an implicit reference to the sacred. Obviously, in today's occidental societies, the sacred is not what it used to be, and it is not possible to call it in its old forms. But as Durkheim pointed out, in the economy of the normative system, the forms of the sacred are not as important as the mere idea of a dividing line, of a frontier, of a division between the sacred and the profane. In modern communication, this division is no longer a religious, or pseudo-religious division. Nevertheless, one may claim that each time a difference of status is installed in a communication situation, it is the very division which founds any power that manifests itself. According to this view, the principle of authority precedes and undergoes any act of discursive authority. This authority is never just the authority attached to a social role, it is always a piece of Authority itself. And, if we believe Lacan, Authority itself is nothing. Although it may have a lot of mythological representations, its foundation and its efficacy lie in the fact of its alterity, in the fact that it cannot be reached. This implies that communicative actions which have a social impact – and which therefore interest social scientists – are never self-contained. They point to an ill-circumscribed entity, something which is beyond.

This process, which allows a communicator to benefit from structural authority, is even more efficient when this transfer of 'force' is dissimulated. Bourdieu has insisted on this necessary absence of transparency, showing that there is no recognition without misrecognition. Another author claims that this dissimulation, at the scale of modern occidental societies, takes the form of a denial. Although current ideologies pretend that symbolic imposition has disappeared from industrial societies, the generalized use of dogmatic procedures could very well be the blind spot of our societies (Legendre 1988).

As striking evidence of this denial, Pierre Legendre has reported the frequency of some 'reversed illocutionary transfers'. These are modes of illocution which tend to abolish the distance between the speaker and his audience. Their aim is to locate the speaker within the general discourse of 'authenticity' and 'transparency' of communication. The speaker is credited with the wish to abolish the old, authoritarian, modes of speaking to the public, precisely while he makes use of the kind of dogmatic effects which he seems to abolish. Legendre has noted that the political rhetoric which systematically replaces the address 'Français' by 'Françaises, Français' is hypocritical in the sense that it tries to dissimulate the power of public speech to summon the whole *demos*. He also vigorously criticized the habit of television and commercials of systematically personalizing the addresses (referring to a product or to the television program as *mine* for example, or when a French journalist addressed a colonel of the FORPRONU saying 'mon colonel').

> These practices, that invoke the subject of the enunciation for the sake of benevolent love have the opposite effect of crushing the subjects, and deny them any space for speech; and thus constitute the beginning of a gigantic fraud. (Legendre 1982: 234)

The existence of such reversed illocutionary transfers just reveals how important 'normal illocutionary transfers' are. By this expression, I refer to the way in which illocutionary components borrowed from a certain type of speech act can endow another type of speech act with a normative efficiency that it would not have on its own.

The above discussion strongly supports the strategy of discourse analysis to focus on indexical and illocutionary components. But focusing on pragmatic components should not be an exclusive strategy. Many authors, including Foucault, have therefore proposed other theoretical frameworks besides pragmatics to guide the analysis of discourse.

According to Bourdieu, for example, a social actor who undertakes a communicative action needs, in order to make symbolic earnings, to master language as a whole, not only the constraints concerning enunciation. More precisely, he has to produce the kind of language that has a high value on the particular linguistic market in which he is competing. This involves making choices concerning the vocabulary and the syntax being used, as well as adopting the right accent, and more generally, having the adequate corporal 'hexis'.

Some other authors have directly insisted on the theoretical need to extend the study of social discourse beyond the analysis of its pragmatic dimension.

In his study of the *linguistification of the sacred*, Habermas has questioned the respective contribution of pragmatic and assertoric components to the efficiency of discourse. It appears that, from a sociological perspective, these classes of components cannot be studied separately:

> As we have seen, in grammatical speech, propositional components are joined with illocutionary and expressive components in such a way that semantic contents can fluctuate among them. Whatever can be said at all, can also be expressed in assertoric form. With this basic feature of language in mind, we can make clear what it means for religious worldviews to connect up with communicative actions. Background knowledge enters into the situation definition of goal-oriented actors who regulate their cooperation in a consensual manner; the result of such interpretative accomplishments are stored in worldviews. As semantic contents of sacred and profane origin fluctuate freely in the medium of language, there is a fusion of meanings; moral practical and expressive contents are combined with cognitive instrumental contents in the form of cultural knowledge. (Habermas 1984: 88)

If I interpret this passage aright, Habermas regards as fundamental the capacity of language to express illocutionary and expressive components in assertoric form. Indeed, sacred speech seems to be characterized by the strength of its illocutionary and expressive components, that is, by the components that build up the semantic contents in relation to the ritualistic situation and to the speaker. Explaining the 'linguistification of the sacred' consists in describing how the normative contents survive the change from a ritual situation to a cooperative situation. In the second type of situation, normative contents can no longer be conveyed by illocutionary and expressive components alone. Therefore, the capacity of transferring the illocutionary to the assertoric enables the reintroduction of normative elements as background knowledge within non-normative situations. A part of this background knowledge is embodied within the semantics of the language, and is activated by semantic triggers. Finally, the illocutionary components of profane grammatical speech, which are in theory reduced, as far as their binding force is concerned, to consensus, can inherit, via the 'fluctuations' above mentioned, a part of the normative power of sacred speech.

In conclusion to this section, although indexical and illocutionary components are some privileged objects of sociological discourse analysis, they are never independent of the content of discourse. Whenever a social scientist wants to give a non-referential reading of a pronoun (when, instead of presupposing a clear assignment of the pronoun to an objective participant of the communication situation, he claims either that the pronoun refers to a fictitious, socially constructed entity, or that its referent is by nature ambiguous) he must justify his particular interpretation of the pronoun by the semantic components which surround it, showing, for example, that the properties which are attributed to the pronoun do not fit any of its possible 'objective' referents. This type of inductive interpretation, close to literary criticism, is often fragile from the methodological point of view. This is not to assume that they are incorrect. On the contrary, they reveal that the rigorous methods of discourse analysis are still incapable of integrating the most illuminating modes of interpretation.

7 Symbols

Instead of describing a method or a cluster of practices, I will discuss in this section the notion of 'symbol'. Since Leibniz, this notion has been associated with the idea of a 'shortcut' by the philosophical tradition. Indeed, a symbol (Leibniz is mainly thinking about mathematical symbols, but remember that his project is that of a *Characteristica Universalis*) replaces the idea in the human mind, precisely to free it from the burden of manipulating the idea itself.

In addition, it is no accident that both the concept of symbol and the concept of *unconsciousness* made their appearance simultaneously within occidental philosophy. By introducing both concepts in a related way, Leibniz was contesting Descartes' foundation of subjectivity into consciousness. Descartes' philosophy made little room for a symbolic contribution to thought, (that is, the contribution of language). With Leibniz, both thought and subjectivity change metaphysical status. Such changes do not concern this discussion except in one consequence: as far as symbols are involved, and contrary to Descartes' philosophy, the subject is in a relation of unavailability to himself.

In the social sciences, 'symbol' and 'symbolic' have almost become synonyms for non-material influences upon people, that is, the kind of influences which are not based on threats or on bargains. Ruling classes exercise on popular classes a 'symbolic imposition', thereby accumulating a 'symbolic capital'; class domination is upheld by 'symbolic power' (Bourdieu); psychoanalysts explain the influence of culture over individuals by the primacy of the 'symbolic order' over the imaginary re-elaborations of experience it represses (Lacan); the discourses of public action have their own logic, which is the logic of 'symbolic action' (Geertz); the exchange of goods is fake, and its real nature is to be a 'symbolic exchange' (Baudrillard); anthropologists study the 'symbolic function' which organizes primitive societies, etc. Textual analysis also makes a heavy use of this notion. Quoting again from Krippendorff,

> Intuitively, content analysis could be characterised as a method of inquiry into the *symbolic meaning* of messages.[7] (1980: 22)

By the word *symbol*, Krippendorff means a *sign* regardless of its peculiar nature (phonetic, scriptural, visual...).[8] Nevertheless, this legitimate attempt to generality raises some problems. Indeed, the category of 'symbol' is a much less general semiotic category than the category of sign. Contrary to a conventional sign, a symbol relates to what it symbolizes by a certain identity of nature. As stated by Hegel,

> the symbol is not just an arbitrary sign, but a sign which, as it is external, already contains the content of the representation it wants to evoke. But at the same time, what it wants to bring to consciousness is not itself as a concrete and individual object, but the general quality of which it is supposed to be the symbol.[9]

What does it mean, then, for a linguistic sign, to be a symbol? Simply that in the use of a linguistic symbol, the signification rebounds on the proper meaning of the sign, towards another, wider meaning. Because symbolizing implies that a signified points towards another signified, Saussure's strict distinction between signifier and signified is somehow abolished. As a consequence, a symbol appears to be a word which has a stand-alone value. In particular, this value is assumed to be almost independent of its linguistic environment. This property may be a justification for a general shortcut strategy which consists in deliberately neglecting the syntactic and argumentative context of the signifiers which are true symbols.[10]

In this second sense, symbols are in fact tropes. For example, the symbolism of the word *Hiroshima* does not lie in the link between the signifier *Hiroshima* and its referent. Hiroshima is a symbol because the signified of this word (the town) stands for the nuclear explosion, and because in turn, this event may stand for another signified, say, the threats of atomic weapons, or nuclear apocalypse. In the technical vocabulary of the theory of tropes, the last linguistic device would be called an antonomasis: an event or an individual (usually a proper noun at the linguistic level) stands for the category to which it belongs, or for an abstract property it possesses. On the opposite, *greenhouse effect* would be called an analogy, based on the fact that sun rays, atmosphere and earth stands in a relation similar to the one that exists between sun rays, a greenhouse and the piece of earth it covers. Finally, the ability of the attaché case (and other status symbols) to symbolize economic power can be interpreted as metonymy.

Thus there are clearly two meanings (at least) of the word symbol. In the first sense a symbol is simply a sign, while in the second, a symbol is a trope. From the first meaning, the notion of 'symbol' inherits the idea of a 'system of language'. It seems therefore possible to establish, between symbols, the kind of stable and yet complex relations that exist between the signifiers of the system of language. From its first meaning, the notion of symbols also inherits the idea that within communication, 'everything' is symbolic. From the second meaning, the notion of symbol inherits the property of having a stand-alone meaning, which, in addition, is socially significant.

To what extent is this confusion of meanings acceptable? In particular, is it true that, in the narrow acceptation of the term, symbols form a symbolic system? In order to answer this question, we must go deeper into the analysis of what exactly symbols are.

According to Freud the symbolic over-determination of certain linguistic signs is not a process whose dynamics are contemporary to any speech act, nor to the recent history of any culture. As Freud writes in his *Introductory lectures on Psychoanalysis*, '[The] comparisons that are at the basis of the dream's symbol are made once and for all, and are always ready for use'.[11]

If, as Freud maintains, symbols have 'fixed' translations, where do they come from, and how is it possible to discover their meaning? The answer to this question is given as follows.

> This knowledge [about the meaning of the symbols] comes from very different sources, from tales and myths, from jokes, from folklore, that is, from the study of manners, customs, proverbs and songs of different peoples, from poetic and common language.[12]

It seems therefore that it is not the dream's work that produces the symbols, but the culture's work.

Surprised that Freud himself did not push these insights to their ultimate conclusions, Ricoeur has proposed to distinguish between three levels of symbolic creativity (Ricoeur 1965). The first one is the level of sediment-symbols, which are the symbols that one can find in the old tales, or as material for dreams. At the second level, are the symbols which play a role in the institutional representation of a society, and which are studied by structural anthropology. The third level is that of *prospective symbols*, that is, symbols whose meaning are *in status nascendi*. The study of the uses of sediment symbols and institutional symbols within communication has an intrinsic interest. Nevertheless, since most of these symbols are listed within dictionaries of symbols, their quantitative analysis is not very innovative. Discourse analysis is much more concerned with the third type of symbol, which reveals how culture and history contribute to the changing semantics of a given society.

The birth of a symbol requires several levels. First a small number of personalities, historical references and values overcrowd public discourse. Secondly, one of those entities becomes emblematic. Thirdly, the linguistic sign which refers to this entity is used to refer to a category, or a general property. Very often, this constitutes an antonomasis, that is, the designation of a quality by a proper name.

Several remarks can be made concerning the status of a symbol. First, if symbols arise in this way, there is little probability that they constitute a 'system' similar to the 'symbolic systems' studied by structural anthropology or to the 'system of language'. In particular, it is not clear why there should be a closure of the set of symbols. The second remark is that one can make sure that a sign is also a symbol only if one can demonstrate a trope. In the absence of a trope, a symbol is also a word, and there are no criteria allowing us to discriminate between this word as a genuine symbol, and this word as a simple word. To put it another way, it is not enough for a term to occur repeatedly in discourse to become a symbol in the full sense of the term. Generally speaking, regularities within the content of discourse do not systematically generate an adequate counterpart at the semantic or the linguistic level. Therefore, frequency counts do not count symbols, but simply words.

Let us finally consider another aspect of symbols, which might provide other reasons to hunt for them within discourse. Symbols might be relevant for social science because they are supposed to be in charge of conveying the values in which the social order is rooted. Apart from evidence coming from the analysis of rituals (political, religious, or, in our times, mass media rituals) there are also some theoretical reasons for the uses of symbols in the sphere of value representation. It has long been noted by Hegel that symbols are never completely adequate to their signification. According to the German philosopher, symbolism is a lesser achievement among artistic expressions because the idea is somehow brutally predominant within a symbol. A symbol, so to speak, forces a concrete existing form to represent a concept. For example, in Hegel's view, symbols are mainly used to evoke the sublime. This is why symbols cannot but create in their spectator's mind the feeling of an incommensurability. Symbols contain an attempt to abolish the difference between signifier and signified. But when they fail to do so (and this is inevitable), the signified is reinforced by the failure itself. It appears to be distant, intangible, irreducible to concrete representations: sublime.

Values, and especially those used in complex modern dogma, are not always easily defined nor easily exemplified. Then, the symbol points towards an ill-circumscribed entity. Some authors would even maintain that by definition, and for the sake of dogmatic efficiency, the reference of the symbol is in fact most often an empty space.[13] Whatever assumption is made about the substantial reality of the referent of symbols, it follows from the above arguments that symbols, far from being primitive tools of value representation, are adequate to create a feeling of value within their receiver's mind.

Defining value-symbols in this way raises another methodological problem. Concepts too are in a sense inadequate to their object, and used to refer to values. One may even claim that values are by essence concepts, and not symbols. For example, shall we say that *the market* is a symbol? If we do so, almost all concepts become symbols, a clearly undesirable consequence. On the other hand, no one really knows what *the market* is, though this notion has certainly become one of the major ideological elements of modern discourse and is often used as a value *per se*. Thus, an expression such as *the market* has all the characteristics of a value-symbol. In conclusion, it seems that no clear distinction can be made between purely value-dedicated signifiers and others. Therefore, using the term symbol to subsume the (ill-defined) class of value-dedicated signifiers is certainly misleading.

In conclusion, it seems that within discourse analysis, there is a widespread confusion between two meanings of the word 'symbol'. On one hand, a symbol is a linguistic signifier, and, on the other, a trope. This confusion is seldom clarified because one can then transfer all the advantageous properties of each meaning to the other. However, this ambiguity cannot be justified, and discourse analysis should make explicit which meaning it refers to whenever it claims to manipulate or to discover symbols.

Conclusion

I regard as natural and legitimate the tendency of social science to try to define behind linguistic expressions a core of relatively shared beliefs, either cognitive or normative. Although some linguistic devices are the privileged reflexes of these beliefs, these devices do not make sense out of their immediate linguistic and discursive context. The success of discourse analysis methods which focus on these devices must not be misleading: this success is due, to a large extent, to the fact that the contribution of the whole range of textual semantic effects is controlled, and thus implicitly taken into account by the analyst. In the perspective of automated procedures of discourse analysis, there would be no assumption more misleading than to focus on one type of linguistic element to the exclusion of the others.

Even if some elements of linguistic communication are indeed more relevant than others for sociology, I do not believe that these relevant elements can be picked-up on the basis of purely linguistic criteria, that is, among certain classes of linguistic components. This leads me to stipulate (a) that the analysis be undertaken at a semantic level and (b) that the semantic level be coextensive with the linguistic data as a whole.

At first sight, these requirements may seem rather obvious. In reality, they go counter to the usual practice and the theoretical foundations of most existing discourse analysis methods, and, especially, to French discourse analysis, which is notoriously allergic to semantics. I have attempted to find the causes of this strange pathology, both in the political history of discourse analysis, in its conception of illocution and of symbolism. I have also proposed some remedies, which tend, in one way or another, to reinstate within linguistics, and in particular, within semantics, some discursive components, such as evaluations, that were viewed as non-linguistic.

If we subscribe to the above requirements, the task of discourse analysis can be defined as involving two separate steps. First, a semantic representation must be inferred from the linguistic data. Such inference processes must be closely related to 'natural inference', that is, to the kind of mental operations involved in story-listening and story-telling. Secondly, the semantic data obtained in the first step must be subsumed under relevant categories. The methods of categorization should pass Popperian-style tests to be regarded as valid. In the rest of this book, these categories will be the ideologies. The methods of categorization will be falsifiable (as Popper recommends) because they will be based on a mathematical estimation of consistency, an estimation that can be (statistically) rejected by native speakers of a language. However, to carry on this programme, we need a semantic theory of evaluation, which is the object of the next chapter.

4

EVALUATIVE SEMANTICS

Introduction

Multiple kinds of semantics have been proposed since scientists from various disciplines first tried to formalize the notion of 'meaning'. These semantics compete with each other on the basis of different convictions about what needs to be accounted for in Natural Language. Ultimately, these differences amount to different presuppositions about the nature of 'meaning' itself.

Despite this variety of approaches, very little attention has been paid to evaluation in language. The reason is twofold. There is, on one hand, the distinction between semantics and pragmatics in the analytical philosophy of language, and, on the other, the dichotomy between denotation and connotation in the European tradition of semantics. If the notion of evaluation has had so little echo in semantics, this is largely due to the fact that, in Anglo-American formal philosophy, evaluative accents have been treated as pragmatic components, and therefore excluded from semantics. In the continental tradition, most linguists drawing upon Saussure have conceived of evaluative accents as connotations, and have been reluctant to take into account connotative semes.[1]

There are, however, two important exceptions to this general indifference: markedness theory and the theory of argumentation within language (AWL). Besides these approaches, one may also question whether the recent developments of cognitive semantics can be of benefit to a semantics of evaluation. Finally, one may wonder whether the post-Saussurian tradition has reached a point of development that allows it to re-integrate connotative semes into its conceptual apparatus. The first section of this chapter is therefore devoted to the assessment of non-denotational approaches from the point of view of their potential contribution to the development of an evaluative semantics.

Despite all the critiques it has faced, the denotational paradigm remains one of the main sources of inspiration for semantic research. The concepts and principles of truth-conditional semantics (compositionality, systematicity) remain useful guidelines for semantic modelling. Truth-conditional semantics has also provided more formal instruments than any other type of semantics. The purpose of this chapter is therefore to determine to what extent evaluative semantics could be modelled according to truth-conditional semantics.

This requires us first to discuss the nature of semantic evaluations. I argue that in evaluative semantics, the semantic values of expressions have a much simpler structure than in truth-conditional semantics. I then discuss the notions of compositionality and systematicity of semantic functions. The conclusions of these discussions lead me to propose another type of semantics, which I call a semantics of contextual modification. The problems of semantic opacity in evaluative semantics are examined. Not surprisingly, these problems can be solved by considering intensional evaluative semantics. However, another solution exists, which requires another notion to be defined: the ideological consistency of a statement.

The last part of the chapter is devoted to general considerations concerning the modelling of ideologies in model theory. I sketch some formal solutions for the representation of ideologies as global, partial models. These general proposals allow us to understand how the evaluative description of ideology relate to the assertional descriptions of ideologies. In particular, they allow us to understand how conflicts of evaluations are related with assertional conflicts (contradictory theses).

1 Non-denotational approaches

The label 'non-denotational' covers semantic paradigms which are rather distinct from each other. They are therefore discussed almost independently.

Markedness theory

If we exclude some early work in 'impressive phonology' (Grammont 1933) and the Russian philosophy of language (Bakhtine 1984, 1977), markedness theory (Andrews 1990; Batistella 1990) is perhaps the first important linguistic theory dealing with evaluative phenomena. According to the traditional Prague School definition of the difference marked–unmarked, 'The terms of opposition at any level of language are not mere opposite, but rather, they show an evaluative non-equivalence that is imposed on all oppositions'. In what concerns semantic markedness strictly speaking, markedness theory claims language reveals, both in its forms and its uses, the primacy of positive evaluation over negative evaluation. This primacy is especially noticeable in:

- The fact that the negatively evaluated morphemes are 'marked' (derived from positively evaluated morphemes by the adjunction of a mark). For

example, *un*-happy derived from happy. Note that there are many exceptions, such as *in*-nocence.
- Phenomena of so-called 'contrast-neutralization'. Stated otherwise, non-evaluative uses are reserved to the morphemes that can also be used in a positive way. According to the classical example given in the literature, 'how tall is Harry?' does not suggest anything about Harry's size, whereas 'How short is Harry?' does so. Note that the social causes of these uses (norms of politeness) are not taken into account.

However enlightening markedness theory may be, markedness is only a very specific aspect of the linguistic and semantic manifestations of evaluative phenomena. Markedness theory focuses on phonology, and, as far as evaluative issues are concerned, is mainly concerned with lexicon. Thus, it gives little clue, if any, on evaluation at the level of phrases, sentences and discourse. In addition, the recent convergence between markedness theory and cognitive linguistics has somehow diminished the amount of attention paid to evaluative phenomena in favour of phenomena of prototypicality. Despite its early focus on evaluation, markedness theory tends to assimilate evaluative neutrality, generality and prototypicality.

The findings of markedness theory concerning the unmarkedness of positively evaluated linguistic items are difficult to interpret. Is this a purely linguistic phenomenon, or does it have cognitive implications? According to several psycholinguistic studies, the early semantics of the child is 'naturally positive' too. It has been shown, for example, that the young child learns the correct meaning of the word 'more' before that of the word 'less' – which is often used as a synonym for 'more' (Clark 1973). This 'positiveness' of semantics raises arduous philosophical questions concerning the respective status of being and non-being. In any case, it would be hazardous to assume that this primacy of positive evaluation is due to the primacy of pleasure over pain, for example. There is no doubt that body control and successful actions (from self-stimulation to games) are very rewarding for the child (Malrieu 1952). However, in line with many philosophers, like Heidegger, certain influential psychologists believe that the child first comes to an autonomous existence by experiencing frustration and abandonment and not satisfaction (Wallon 1949). From an emotional point of view, pain has no primacy over pleasure. In fact, pain is so basic in our emotional experiences that it is often reflected, at the linguistic level, by grammatical markers and specific morphemes (negative marks, for example). Therefore, the 'positiveness' of semantics is largely counterbalanced by the fact that negative evaluation is conveyed by closed-class[2] forms and expressive components.

More generally, it is not sure that markedness theory and cognitive linguistics are fully compatible. According to one of the basic theses of markedness theory, positively oriented linguistic items tend to be unmarked, while negatively oriented items tend to be derived from positive items by means of specific marks. This entails that positively oriented items seem to be cognitively more basic than negatively oriented ones. From there, one may wish to deduce that positive evaluation is somehow cognitively prior to negative evaluation. However, for cognitive linguistics, the use of closed-class forms tends to reveal more basic cognitive notions that open-class forms. Since negative orientation is often conveyed by closed-class forms, should not we conclude that it is more basic than positive orientation? In fact, I doubt that markedness theory and cognitive linguistics really agree on the status of linguistic marks.

Theory of argumentation within language

The second approach which has largely contributed to the analysis of evaluative phenomena is the theory of argumentation within language (Ducrot 1980; Anscombre and Ducrot 1988). This theory, due to Oswald Ducrot, studies the argumentative entailments from a linguistic point of view. It regards the meaning of a proposition as the set of all possible argumentative entailments that can be made from it. In AWL, these entailments rest on topoi (doxal associations between predicates) of the form 'the more P, the more Q'. AWL has shown that many argumentative entailments are triggered by evaluative factors. In addition, AWL has brought to light the evaluative behaviour of many connectors.

I borrow from AWL many fundamental principles. The first one is *semantic graduality*. This principle states that in language, every predicate has a degree of semantic 'realization'. The strength of this semantic realization is determined by the linguistic and argumentative contexts. Applying this idea to evaluation, I assume that each predicate in language receives from its linguistic context the intensity of its evaluation.

The second principle is *non-informativity*. This principle states that if the 'information' contained in a sentence is understood narrowly to be the objective, factual description of the sentence content, the information is not relevant for argumentation. This is perhaps best exemplified by the case of the French adverbs 'presque' (almost) and 'à peine' (only slightly). Consider the sentences

(a) Pierre est presque en retard (Peter is almost late).[3]
(b) Pierre est à peine en retard (Peter is only slightly late).

From an informational point of view, in (a), Peter is not late, while in (b), he is indeed late. However, (a) argues against Pierre, while (b) argues in favour of him. Therefore, the argumentative orientation (which is here also an evaluative orientation) does not depend on the informational content.

In the context of our research, non-informativity takes the form of *evaluative relativity*. Consider a proposition P and a proposition Q about the same person A. The model presented later in the book will allow us to derive $E(A,P)$, the evaluation of A in the context of P and $E(A,Q)$, the evaluation of A in the context of Q. These evaluations do not have any autonomous signification. All that is required from the model is that if there is a consensus among the speakers of the language to declare that P argues in a stronger way than Q in favour of A, then $E(A,P)$ should be superior to $E(A,Q)$.

AWL has recently tried to go beyond the propositional level, and to become a lexical semantics. However, it has not yet produced a semantic theory of the composition of words into phrases and sentences. In addition, in choosing to formalize background knowledge as topoi, AWL has restricted its expressive capacities. Topoï become nothing more than monotonous relations between argumentative scales. Although this is a rather simplistic form of reasoning, some AWL linguists claim that argumentation, conceived as a linguistic phenomenon, makes no use of more sophisticated entailments (Raccah 1993). However, this thesis seems to be contradicted by the fact that the notion of topos cannot account for the semantic behaviour of adverbs such as *trop* (Carel 1995). The case of *trop* reveals a more general shortcoming concerning the notion of topos. Using topoi renders it impossible to formalize the comparison with a standard or norm. There are indeed, among the norms attached to a social role, prescriptions which require from the actors a fixed behaviour, and which sanction any deviations from this norm. Formalizing these obligations would force us to consider more complex structures than simple covariations between evaluative scales. At least, one needs to structure these scales, by assigning them an origin, thresholds and regions. It is also necessary to consider the interaction between more than two scales. In fact, one has to consider the evaluative relations (mutual reinforcement, inversion, expectation) between the components of schemata. However, if we admit that schemata play a role in argumentation, it is no longer possible to assume that argumentation is *within* language. In drawing this conclusion, we are just following Ducrot himself, who has recently changed his mind on this issue, and now claims that argumentation is *not* within language.

Cognitive semantics

The recent developments of cognitive semantics have not modified the fragile status of evaluation in the field of semantics. Unlike spatiality and force dynamics, evaluation is not viewed as a fundamental semantic category. As far as I am aware of it, the only important contribution of cognitive semantics to the theory of linguistic evaluative phenomena is Lakoff's research on the metaphors by which we conceive of morality (Lakoff 1995).

I have one problem with Lakoff's attempt to find in metaphors the cognitive foundations of our most basic categories. This undertaking tends to suggest that the object domains which are the target of metaphors are cognitively more basic than the source domains. Let me borrow from Lakoff an example which seems to contradict this idea. Studying the moral conceptual system, Lakoff discovers that 'bookkeeping' is one of the most widespread metaphors by which we understand morality. There is indeed a lot of evidence showing that we proceed, in everyday conversation, by the means of moral accounting (we have moral 'debts', we want to make someone 'pay' for what they have done to us, etc.). However, it seems rather surprising to suggest that book accounting is cognitively more basic than morality itself. It is more likely that the primitive categories of good and bad are acquired long before the sense of bookkeeping. One may even wish to argue that conversely, it is the various target domains of moral metaphors (wealth, nurturance, etc.) which are pervaded by moral meanings. The same remarks could be made concerning evaluation. The mere notion of value seems to be rooted both in the metaphors of value as wealth and value as health (etymologically, 'value' comes from the Latin verb *valere*, which means 'to be in good health'). However, is it reasonable to believe that there is no primitive sense of value underpinning these metaphors? I do not want to underestimate the importance of analogy in cognition. But like cognitive scientists when they assume that the sense of spatiality is more basic than that of dance for example, I would rather assume that the sense of value is more basic than that of bookkeeping. This puts into question the practice of discovering basic cognitive categories by chasing metaphors.

Studying metaphors for evaluation is nevertheless useful and perhaps necessary because these metaphors are prototypical manifestations of evaluative connotations. Spatial metaphors of value (value as height, as deepness, as superiority, as movement), also inform us about the cognitive schemes allowing reasoning on values (Hare 1964). In this perspective, the metaphors for morality studied by Lakoff represent an important sub-domain of metaphors for evaluation.

Differential semantics

If cognitive semantics has not done much yet in favour of the notion of value, we can perhaps expect more from the differential paradigm in semantics (Breal 1897; Saussure 1972; Greimas 1966; Pottier 1974). Drawing upon Saussure's notion of value, differential semantics conceives of the meaning of a signifier as its linguistic signified. The linguistic signified must be confused neither with the reference of the signifier, nor with the psychological, or conceptual reality with which the signifier may be associated. The signified of a morpheme (also called sememe), is made of the relations of the sememe with other sememes (relations which are called semes). One of the purposes of differential semantics is to classify these relations of similarity and difference according to their nature and their degree of generality, thereby structuring the system of language in classes.

Despite the necessary clarification and the useful practical suggestions it has provided us with, I do not believe that differential semantics is the ultimate theoretical framework for working on evaluation in language. First, differential semantics is not properly articulated with syntax and logic. There is no theory of the impact of syntactic construction, negation and modalities on isotopies. This means we cannot conceive of evaluative compositionality in the differential framework, an undertaking which seems absolutely necessary for a semantics of evaluation. Secondly, evaluation is not a purely linguistic phenomenon. Most discourses refer to a situation in the world through indexical components and proper names. The evaluation of these components is not a matter of language. It depends on the reality they refer to. And thirdly, differential semantics does not allow us to account for the variations of evaluation which are due to different ideological perspectives. With respect to this problem, Eagleton's critique still seems to hold true:

> Language cannot be, for Saussure, as it is for Volosinov and Bakhtine, a terrain of ideological struggle. Such a recognition would involve, precisely, the displacement and rearticulation of formal linguistic difference at the level of other theoretical practices. If the dictionary informs us that the opposite of capitalism is totalitarianism, we will need more than the *Course of General Linguistics* to illuminate that particular diacritical formulation. (Eagleton, 1980: 165)

The variations of evaluation of a sememe like 'capitalism' could be explained and modelled if each possible evaluation corresponded to a 'sociolect'. This would postulate the existence of ideological languages. Discourse analysis has hosted extensive debates on this issue. As stated in the previous chapter, the opinion which has rightfully prevailed is that ideologies cannot be characterized by a language. Therefore, the hold of ideology upon meanings cannot be adequately described with the notion of sociolect.

Interpretative semantics

From an evaluative point of view, differential semantics is perhaps more interesting as a linguistic basis for interpretative semantics (Rastier 1987). The purpose of this semantics is to describe the cognitive processes starting from the text and ending up with a referential impression. This referential impression depends on the type of isotopies which are realized during interpretation. The classification of isotopies rests on the nature of their semes (generic vs. specific, inherent vs. afferent). Inherent semes are relations between sememes which hold in the system of language whereas afferent semes are relations which depend on social norms. Inherent semes are activated by the very occurrence of a sememe, whereas afferent semes are activated by the linguistic context. By proposing to take into account afferent semes, interpretative semantics opens the way for a semantics of evaluation. Indeed, it makes frequent use of evaluative semes like /euphoric/ (Rastier 1987: 35). The contextual activation of evaluative semes may result in an evaluative isotopy. The specific contribution of evaluative isotopies to referential impression has not yet been studied.

I have one problem with the distinction between inherent and afferent semes. I concede that this distinction is rather intuitive when we consider the difference between a morpheme marking aspect ('ing' for example) and a word like 'capitalism'. It is clear that in the first case, the seme /duration/ belongs to the system of language, whereas in the second case, the seme /opposite of totalitarianism/ belongs to socially determined semantic norms. But from a sociological perspective the distinction between system of language and semantic norms is far from obvious. Consider the case of the word *caviar*. Simple empirical research has shown that when subjects are asked to list the semantic traits associated with this word, the trait /luxurious/ comes up as often as the trait /fish/ (Rastier 1987: 63). Therefore, there is no reason to decide that /fish/ is inherent and /luxurious/ afferent other than through the implicit assumption according to which the system of language reflects a natural, material, scientific ontology. However, as a sociologist, I am not ready to make that sort of assumption. The attempt to found the distinction language/sociolect on the distinction nature/society is no longer acceptable as soon as we realize that nature is a social construction too. As a consequence, we should perhaps abandon the distinctions system of language/sociolect, and inherent/afferent semes. I prefer to distinguish, within an *occurrence* of a sememe,[4] between the semes that it inherits from its *type*, and the semes that are activated in context. The type of an occurrence depends on the type of discourse it appears in. In science for example, /black/ is a seme inherited by default from its type by any occurrence of 'raven'. In poetry, both /black/ and /death/ are inherited from its type by an occurrence of 'raven'.

Interpretative semantics is close to Halliday's social-semiotic perspective on language (Halliday and Hassan 1985). In both paradigms, meaning and meaning effects depend on socially defined genres and text typologies. At a higher level, these genres and types belong to discourses (political, medical, etc.), disciplines (political philosophy, AI, etc.), discursive formations (discourse of the Church, eugenics discourse, etc.), and social fields (sport, fashion, media, etc.). These various contexts orient interpretation processes. Some of these contexts are institutionalized, and are therefore endowed with strategic capacities. Disciplines for example, attempt to stabilize the meaning of the concepts they use.

> A concept is a constructed sememe whose definition is settled by the norms of a discipline in such a way that its occurrences are identical to its type. The conventional validity of these disciplinary norms allows the translation of the concepts, which are therefore free from the diversity of contexts and independent from the variety of languages. (Rastier 1991: 126)

In other words, by using concepts, disciplines try to reduce the dependency of meaning upon linguistic and external contexts.

This definition is particularly useful for our purpose since one may regard ideologies as the equivalent of Rastier's disciplines. Indeed, an ideology sets some permanent values (in the sociological sense of the term), and hence, it tends to ensure that the evaluation of concepts does not fluctuate too much depending on their context. This is true at least of the concepts that belong to the dogmatic core of an ideology. Other concepts, such as those which acquire their value only syntagmatically, derive their evaluation in context from the stable evaluations of the concepts of the core. The evaluation of the concept of 'control' for example, immediately raises the question: control of what? If the linguistic context is 'control of public expenditure', the evaluation of the phrase depends on the evaluation of the concept of 'public expenditure', that may belong to the core of the ideology.

Rastier's definition can therefore be amended as follows. *A core-concept is a constructed sememe whose definition is settled by an ideology in such a way that the evaluation of its occurrences conforms to the evaluation of its type*. The formal developments that follow try to model how, in real discourses, the evaluation of the occurrences dynamically deviates from the evaluation of their type.

2 Evaluation, pragmatics and semantics

Semantics is the branch of language theory concerned with the study of the designata of expressions. Rudolph Carnap defined its position within the whole science of language as follows:

> If, in an investigation, explicit reference is made to the speaker, or to put it in more general terms, to the user of the language, then we assign it to the field of pragmatics. ... If we abstract from the user of the language and analyse only the expression and the designata, we are in the field of semantics. And if, finally, we abstract from the designata also and analyse only the relations between the expressions, we are in syntax. (Carnap 1942)

Traditionally, in the philosophy of language, evaluative accents have been treated as expressive components, and therefore excluded from semantics. This view has never been questioned by social scientists, who have paid exclusive attention to pragmatics – Habermas' theory of communicative action for example, heavily relies on speech act theory (Habermas 1984). And indeed, since sociologists are interested in linguistic communication as a social action, it was natural to regard the meaning of a proposition as depending on the context of its utterance (the communication situation). Because it is fascinated by the binding force of language, by its capacity to give form to society, sociology expected from semiotics an explanation of the effects of language. Speech act theory, with its distinction between a literal content and an 'illocutionary force', was therefore naturally appealing for social scientists.

I have no doubts concerning the close relationship of pragmatics with sociology except for the fact that this relationship has excessively diminished the interest of sociologists in semantics itself. This chapter calls for a new balance of interest in sociological theory, between the different disciplines of semiotics. Viewed from the other side, it is in favour of an enlargement of semantics to the phenomenon of social evaluation.

The reason for shifting our attention away from pragmatics is that beyond the local conditioning of a communicative action, there are other determinants. Ideologies for example, or world views, do have a bearing on the meaning of communicative actions. But they need not be accounted for at the pragmatic level, since they tend to transcend the peculiarity of the communication situation. The purpose of this chapter is to ask whether such general determinants of meaning can be formalized at the semantic level, and what happens to the very notion of semantics when we try to do so.

As stated above, the object of semantics is the relation of expressions to their designata. In practice, most semantic theories allow for a comparison of the meaning of different expressions. That is, semantic theories may ask whether two different expressions have the same meaning, or if one meaning can be deduced from another. Semantic theory is primarily concerned with formalizing these 'inferences'.

Formalizing need not mean simply giving some rules of inferences. More fundamentally, it entails establishing general results about their properties. The first general question that may come to mind is whether every expression has one meaning or several. When the 'meanings' that are considered are 'truth-values', this issue turns out to be one of consistency. If, for example, an inconsistency is introduced in a theory, one may wish to know whether this inconsistency contaminates all expressions of the language, or if it remains 'localized'.

If, besides a theory of truth, the language is also provided with a theory of proof, one may wish to obtain general results about the relation of truth to provability. For example, given a proof system and a theory of truth, it may be regarded as a valuable result to know that everything true is also provable. The converse of this, ensuring that everything proved is also true, may represent a general assessment of the proof system. The existence of such general results suggests what the *raison d'être* of semantic theory is: it allows us to know what we can expect from a language.

In the domain of natural language, the incentive for neat semantics is to represent meanings in a more satisfying way than natural language itself. In particular, it aims at eliminating the ambiguity that often affects natural language expressions. For each possible 'reading' of an expression, a good semantic theory will use a different representation.

The relations of inference that may exist between the constructs of semantic theory are another key reason for its superiority over natural language. It is often impossible to draw fully reliable inferences using ordinary linguistic devices. Nevertheless, the inferential power of natural language is impressive in scope and flexibility. Emulating this power, or simply understanding it more completely remains a major goal of semantic research. Therefore, the goal of linguistic semantic theory is to formalize natural inference as much as possible given the constraint of being absolutely reliable.

That capacity of drawing correct inferences can also be considered as a way of coping with the redundancy of natural language, a desirable property that explains why information retrieval and database theory relies highly on semantic theory. Finally, some applied linguistics, such as automatic language translation, regard the predicative structures ordinarily used in semantic theory as the universal structures able to bridge the different languages.

The mere notion of inference suggests that 'truth' is the underlying concept of semantic theory. The meaning of a sentence may then be regarded as the conditions that the world must fulfil in order to make the sentence true. Such a paradigm has been highly dominant in the discipline, and is known as 'truth conditional semantics'. Since this has produced most of the insights of modern, formal semantics, I will consider exclusively truth-conditional semantics in what follows.

3 Model-theoretic semantics

Set-theoretic encoding of meaning

The traditional way of providing neat semantics to a natural language consists in exhibiting a translation of this language into a formal language that has semantics. Usually, the target language of the translation is one of the numerous predicate logics, and the semantics of this logic is a form of model theory (see Figure 4.1).

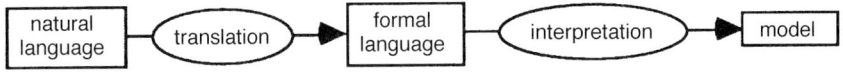

Figure 4.1 Two-step semantics for natural language.

Model theory links the expressions of predicate logic with their 'semantic values', that is, their meaning. Most expressions have either 'true' or 'false', as their meaning. Some expressions, such as factual statements, are true in a single or a few models, while others, such as the universal theorems of logic, hold in all models. Validity (truth in all models) should therefore be distinguished from 'truth in a model'.

Intuitively, a model represents 'reality'. But in a sense, does not the subset of language containing all true expressions represent reality? The reader may then wonder why we look for an extra-linguistic way of representing reality. If we were able to isolate a subset of expressions (possibly infinite) that could, via a set of rules, generate all true expressions, we could do without the very idea of a model. This last approach is known as 'proof-theoretic' instead of 'model-theoretic'. Despite a number of important results about the relation between the two approaches, it remains impossible to unify them fully.

What are the respective advantages and drawbacks of proof-theoretic and model-theoretic approaches? The former is more or less equivalent to the definition of a system of automated deduction. Not surprisingly, it leads to almost direct computer implementations. On the other hand, as complexity grows with the set of deduction rules, the 'formal demonstrator' often tends to function as a black-box. On the contrary, despite a relative indifference to the problems of computational efficiency,[5] the model-theoretic approach often remains more intuitive than its rival. Let us mention finally a third approach to semantics, called 'game-theoretic', which may appear as a hybrid of the two traditional approaches. Indeed, it retains the notion of a model, but it formalizes the interpretation of the expressions as a game. This game may be regarded as a simple demonstrator. In this chapter, because it is rather dominant in the field of natural language semantics, I will focus on the model-theoretic stream of thought.

The idea that inspires model theory is that reality itself could be organized in a way that would simplify its comparison with linguistic expressions. In particular, in a way that would avoid any redundancy in the information about the world contained in the model. It naturally leads to a fictitious reality, suitably organized to allow a correspondence with formal languages.

The implicit ontology behind model theory is that the world consists of *individuals* and of the *properties* that affect them. Individuals correspond to the *constants*, while properties correspond to the *predicates* of the formal languages. Besides these two fundamental categories, model theory may also include properties of properties, up to an arbitrary level of abstraction. Finally, a model is provided with truth values (usually 'true' and 'false').

Within a model, individuals are formally represented by a set of 'atoms'. This set is also sometimes called the 'universe of discourse'. Intuitively, it contains all entities whose meaning is self-contained. To put it in another way, the meaning of the constant 'Paul' is the atom 'Paul#1467', a particular individual. The atoms are what the discourse is about. Note that the distinction between individuals and properties is largely a matter of convention. Natural language does not, in this respect, make assumptions as strong as the ontological distinction of semantic theory.

How are properties represented? Let us begin with a property corresponding to a one-place predicate, such as 'is a cat'. Such a property may be represented by the subset of the universe of discourse that verifies it. In this case, it would be the subset of all cats. Since a set may be represented by a characteristic function, our property might as well be represented by a function ranging from the set of atoms into the set of truth values. This function would map the cats into 'true' and the other atoms into 'false'.

Consider now a property corresponding to a two-place predicate, such as 'like'. This property is satisfied by all pairs of individuals where the first likes the second. Therefore, it is natural to represent it by a set of pairs, that is, by a subset of all possible pairs of individuals. Again using the equivalence between sets and functions, we might also represent the 'like' property as a characteristic function ranging over the set of all possible pairs.

Taking a step further, the reader may have understood that since properties may be represented by sets, properties of properties may in turn be represented by sets of sets. And indeed, the main achievement of model theory is that the meaning of arbitrarily abstract and complex properties may be expressed by the sole 'universe of discourse' provided with set-theoretic operations.

Besides the simple attribution of a property, most languages possess more elaborated meanings, such as the so-called universal or existential statements. These statements do not attribute a property to a given individual but instead, affirm that the property holds for all individuals, or for at least one of them (possibly unknown). The meaning of such statements should also be represented in the model. Since these statements are genuine judgements about the world, they either hold or do not. Therefore, their meaning, or semantic value, may be regarded as being either 'true' or 'false'.

The application of a quantifier to a predicate containing variables cannot be dealt with in a similar way to the application of a predicate to another predicate. Indeed, the meaning of a quantified expression does not depend only on the meaning of the so-called 'open formula' that results from the removal of the quantifier. Instead, it depends on the meaning of the open formula given different 'assignments' of its unbound variables to beings of the universe of discourse. Tarski found a way out of this problem by defining the *satisfaction of an expression in a model*, a more general notion than the notion of truth, valid for all kind of expressions, and on the basis of which truth itself is defined (Tarski 1952). The impact of this elegant solution has been so strong that very few modern semantics do without the so-called 'Tarskian semantics'.

In standard first-order logic, the variables may be instantiated to members of the universe of discourse only. Such a constraint may be relaxed, and variables may be allowed to instantiate to propositions. Such a logic is then known as a 'second-order logic'. With the introduction of appropriate tools such as those of Lambda Calculus, one may also think of variables directly applying to arguments, and instantiating to predicate functors or other types of expressions. All these more elaborate tools have proved useful, if not necessary, for the advanced developments of formal semantics.

Partial models

Most research in model theory has attempted to reduce the complexity and the size of models by focusing just on a few parts of them. Making models partial first implied the rejection of the 'closed-world assumption' (Hintikka 1973). When this assumption holds, a model contains all the elements needed to establish anything that is true. Propositions that cannot be found true are therefore false. On the contrary, in a so-called 'open world', not all true propositions may be established. In addition, truth and falsity become symmetrical. It is not enough to fail to derive a proposition to ensure its falsity, since some non-derivable propositions are possibly true.

Once we have rejected the closed-world assumption, it becomes possible to focus on 'partial models'. Most of the work in this direction sought to determine how one partial world could embed another. In particular, much attention has been paid to the problems arising from the enlargement of a partial model by an increase of information. As the limiting case, the conditions that the partial models must fulfil if they are to converge towards a total model have been explored.

Since discourse unfolds in a diachronic way by adding pieces of information, the semantics of discourse, such as discourse representation theory, make heavy use of the notion of a partial model (Kamp 1981). The most radical proposals in the direction of partiality come from so-called situation semantics, which, as their name suggests, derive the meaning of a proposition from its content and the circumstances that the 'situation' defines (Barwise and Perry 1983).

Since social knowledge is always partial, value-oriented semantics should also reject the closed-world assumption. But if open worlds are the correct framework for the achievement of partial models, this framework does not really help us concretely to design these worlds. Very often, there is a lack of guidelines in the operation of making models partial. This is because 'situations' have often been thought of as a way of formalizing the dependency of meaning upon the concrete conditions of utterances. And partial models have been mainly intended at formalizing the instantaneous state of a discursive development. They both refer to a local semantic level.

This chapter claims that too little attention has been paid to the social dimension of knowledge as a way of achieving meaningful partiality. Beyond the local effect on meaning, beyond the temporal reception of discourse, there may be some relatively stable perspectives about society. Such world views transcend the particularity of concrete situations. It is therefore possible to conceive of partial models of a high semantic level.

Models reflecting ideological perspectives are more easily made partial than models of reality because the way the world should be is simpler to model than the way it is. To convince ourselves of this difference, let us consider the sentence 'the police killed a student during a demonstration'. In truth-conditional semantics, the fact that the police killed a student in a demonstration, for example, will be true only if the model contains such information. If the police kill a child, for example, it will have to be specified too. By contrast, one should be able to deduce that both events are to be deplored just because it is bad to do something bad (killing) to beings which, unless specified, are not bad (students and children). Similarly, if an action is good, for example, it will certainly be regarded as a good thing that someone recommends it, or urges it to be done. If an actor performs a good action, then it is likely that he will be found good for that reason. These examples reveal that evaluative reasoning is much more economical (in terms of information) than matter-of-fact reasoning. Where truth-oriented semantics needs detailed information about the world, value-oriented-semantics needs only to know some general characteristics of the world.

4 Compositional semantics

Compositionality

The economy of means achieved by the set-theoretic representation of meanings is not pursued for the pure sake of elegance. Let us try to rephrase the expression 'sets of sets' used above. Since sets are meanings, could not we speak of 'meanings of meanings' instead? If we trust semantic theory, this sounds correct. Therefore, it seems that semantics allows meanings to combine with each other. More precisely, meanings apply to, or affect other meanings, as sets may have sets as their elements, or equivalently, as functions apply to functions in the traditional sense of mathematical function composition.

In the expression 'meaning of meanings', the composite nature of 'meaning' is clearly apparent. Therefore, despite the fact that an expression acquires its meaning only as a whole, this meaning depends on the meaning of the sub-expressions. Such a formal achievement, highly desirable in itself, has a deeper justification in the human uses of natural language. The capacity of understanding new (never heard) sentences is indeed a striking feature of the human mind. Such a capacity of endlessly renewed linguistic interpretation could not be explained if the meaning of a new sentence did not depend in some sense on something given. But what could this be except the parts of the sentence, and, ultimately, the words that it contains? Such an intuition was cast by Frege in the so-called 'compositionality principle': *the meaning of a sentence is a function of the meaning of its parts and of their mode of combination* (Frege 1952).

Not only are human beings able to understand new sentences, they are also potentially able to create and understand an infinite number of them. On the other hand, one has to admit that the linguistic equipment of the human psyche is finite. This paradox spells out the recursivity principle: sentences are understood or generated by the application of a *finite set of rules which may be applied in an iterative manner.*

One should not be misled by the fact that, within model theoretic semantics, the decomposition of a complex meaning proceeds, through iteration, to the nested levels of embedded meanings. Of course, it is true that given the rigid individual/property ontology, the decomposition reaches an end at the atomic level. But at that bottom level, no information whatsoever is encoded! To capture the information according to which the police killed a student, the function representing the predicate 'kill' must yield 'true' when applied to the pair (police, student). Therefore, the information is stored in the definition of the predicate and not at the atomic level. And the same argument may be employed at any level of abstraction of the properties. In short, a model must contain nothing less than all the information available about the world. The set-theoretic (or equivalently, the function-theoretic) representation of this information offers no simplification in this respect.

Zadrozny's theorem

One may then remark that compositionality is achieved in a rather artificial way. Indeed, in Fregean and Montagovian semantics, though the meaning of a sentence does depend on the meaning of its parts, it is only because some parts of the sentences (typically, the verb) are given a 'meaning' which is close to the meaning of the sentence itself. Therefore one may wish to view the various compositional semantics as theoretical frameworks devoted to the task of transferring the meaning of complex expressions into the meaning of their elements. Although this process may require very sophisticated mathematical tools, one is entitled to regard it as a kind of formal trick. Roughly speaking, set-theoretical compositional semantics does not *create* the meaning of a complex expression out of the simpler meanings of its parts. It just duplicates the meaning of a complex expression out of the meaning of one of its elements, which is as complex as the meaning of the expression itself.

This critique does not concern the whole of Montague's programme. In particular, the treatment of determiners in Montague's Grammar is a fundamental contribution to semantics (Montague 1973; Dowty *et al.* 1981). More generally, one may wish to say that the most interesting parts of Montague's Grammar concern all the elements that do not have a clear meaning in componential semantics (determiners, modalities, auxiliaries). Instead, when looking at ordinary predicates such as 'eat' one may find that compositionality does not guarantee the relevance of a semantic theory. It might be that Montague himself shared this view when he decided to entitled its main contribution 'The proper treatment of quantification in ordinary English'. In any case, as we will see in the following paragraphs, other theoreticians have been aware of the limits of the notion of compositionality.

Hirst first pointed out that however tortuous a predicate may be in the way its meaning depends on the meaning of its arguments, it was always possible to design a meaning function tortuous enough to represent it (Hirst 1987). As a limiting case, even a predicate whose meaning was an absolutely random function of the meaning of its argument could still be represented and inserted into compositional semantics. But would it not be too odd a behaviour to be still called 'meaning'? Usually regarded as a strength of semantics, such an unlimited flexibility of the formalization of meaning has begun to be viewed as a weakness.

Hirst's remark has recently found a formal counterpart. According to a theorem by Zadrozny, any semantics for a given language can be made compositional (Zadrozny 1992). It means that the compositionality requirement is formally vacuous. The conclusion to draw from this theorem is not that one should do without compositionality, but instead that its definition should be made more binding. Choosing the meaning functions within certain classes of functions for example, restores a meaningful compositionality. Following Hirst's terminology, semantics that comply to such an obligation are said to be 'systematic'. In more intuitive terms, one may wish to judge the quality of a semantic theory by the fact that its elementary meanings are genuinely elementary. To put it in another way, a good semantic theory should not define the meaning of its elements (words) with the only objective of constructing the meaning of phrases. It should primarily pay attention to the substantial meaning of words, such as the ones contained in dictionaries. And it should complement this 'local' information with 'global' information concerning the syntactic and casual structure of phrases. But there is no good reason to re-integrate artificially global information within local information, especially at the expense of genuinely local information.

5 The nature of semantic values

How many dimensions?

The developments of the so-called 'multivalued logics' show that the opposition between truth and falsity appears in some cases to be too rigid. Some intermediate levels of truth have therefore been thought of. Pushing the idea to its ultimate consequences, fuzzy logics have pictured truth as having 'degrees'.

Analogously, although it is difficult to exhibit anything that has no social repercussions, there may be some persons, events or facts which are irrelevant to social issues. It therefore seems that, much more acutely than in the case of truth, the semantics of evaluation needs to incorporate, besides the extremes of 'good' and 'evil', the possibility of neutrality. Furthermore, it is doubtful that neither actions nor actors that do have a social or moral impact would easily let themselves be labelled under the strong dichotomy of 'good' and 'evil'. Whatever the perspective may be, the 'moral' nature of most of them will certainly lie in-between.

If most of the objects of social discourse are in fact a mix of good and evil, the corresponding semantics should be based on a scale of evaluation rather than on a pure dichotomy. Whether this scale should be discrete or continuous, numerical or qualitative, are secondary questions. The main problem is whether there is a unique dimension in this scale. At this point, it is the very question of the nature of the 'good' which is raised.

It seems clear that unlike truth checking, evaluation may be carried out in several directions. To name just a few, one may assess a phenomenon from the point of view of pleasantness, utility, efficiency, morality, beauty, feasibility, etc. The assessment of discourse from the point of view of truth may even appear as a particular form of evaluation. The multiplicity of the axes of evaluation and their relative independence may be clearly exemplified by cases of conflicts between them. A crime for example, may be useful. A strategy may be efficient but unfair. A theory may be true but immoral. An act may be moral in its intentions, but immoral in its consequences, and therefore unfair, etc.

As stated in the second chapter, such a multiplicity of principles would not be disturbing if each principle applied to different types of realities. Theories for example, would be placed on the axis of truth, acts would be placed on the axis of justice, persons would be placed on the axis of morality, and phenomena would be placed on the axis of utility. The work of the expert in semantics would be to rebuild, beyond linguistic confusion, an ordered semantic world where all types of realities could be clearly distinguished.

Unfortunately, it is doubtful that the diversity of principles of evaluation define a similar division of reality. Take the case of values such as 'freedom' or 'democracy' for example. In one sense they are phenomena, states of the society. But in another one, they are shared ideas about some desirable states of society. As such, they often involve a unique claim to justice, morality, utility and truth. It is the essence of a value to realize this fusion. Therefore the objective of value-oriented semantics may be to take this synthetic operation into account, rather than trying to decompose it.

In the process of language, we discover that the different axes of evaluations are continually mixed up. Theories are 'dangerous', persons are 'negative' or 'wrong', phenomena are 'criminal' (unemployment for example), etc. Looking at argumentative processes too, we detect constant transfers of evaluation between actors and their actions, working in both directions (Plantin 1990). Instead of projecting this linguistic and argumentative spontaneity back onto a hypothetical universe where the different axes of evaluation would be independent, it may be more relevant to model precisely that capacity of combination and rotation of the evaluative axes which is so striking within discourse.

We may also remark that besides some axes that let themselves be identified, the bulk of qualifications can be used in almost all axes. Adjectives such as 'marvellous' or 'perfect' for example, possess an important capacity of adaptation to any reality. As further evidence of this, let us mention the adjectives such as 'horrible', or 'nice', which were originally non-aesthetic, but have come to denote aesthetic evaluations. Both types of adjectives refer to the idea of evaluation itself, without presupposing any particular principle.

In language, uni-dimensionality of evaluation is the norm, and multi-dimensionality the exception. This is specially apparent from the fact that when two evaluations are conflicting, they must be articulated by a connector. Consider the two sentences:

(a) I like him. He has stolen my car.
(b) I like him, but he has stolen my car.

Out of the blue, (a) is surprising. It forces us to wonder whether the first part of (a) is an antiphrasis, or whether there is something we ignore which stops us from understanding the connection between the two sentences. On the contrary, (b) sounds perfectly normal. This simple example shows that ordinary linguistic practice does not favour the simple concatenation of statements which are evaluatively conflicting. Language tends to articulate evaluative conflicts. When it does not, the perception of the conflict is reinforced. We immediately guess that this lack of articulation has a purpose. The author intends either to be ironical, or to point out an exception.

In French, the connector *mais* is one of the main instruments of discursive articulation. In the literature on the argumentative behaviour of connectors, *mais* is often opposed to *pourtant* by the fact that '*P mais Q*' tends to resolve the contradiction between P and Q, whereas '*P pourtant Q*' leaves the contradiction unsolved. In addition *mais* often suggests a subjective, evaluative articulation, while *pourtant* is more objective and non-evaluative. It is interesting to remark that the evaluative connector 'resolves conflicts', while the non-evaluative connector leaves them unsolved. There is other linguistic evidence suggesting that evaluation is synthetic in essence.

More fundamentally perhaps, if we want to express a conflict of evaluation, we have to distribute these evaluations in different parts of discourse (like two different words, or two occurrences of the same word). Otherwise, our discourse becomes evaluatively *ambiguous*. From the point of view of semantic modelling, this remark is crucial. It entails that each elementary piece of discourse tends to be either evaluatively univocal or ambiguous. In both cases, there is no need to consider complex evaluations. Ambiguity corresponds to the fact that two different evaluations of the same element render discourse equally coherent. Conflicts arise from two different evaluations 'located' at different places in discourse. But in each discursive place, the evaluation tends to be simple. This is of course an important difference between cognitive processes and semantic processes. If I had to model the former, I would have to take into account the complex structure of evaluation. But because I concentrate on the latter, I can rest on a rather minimal structure for evaluations. This makes me prefer the third of the following solutions:

(1) A radical solution to account for the correlation between all the evaluative axes would be to lump them together. One may easily gather strong empirical evidence in favour of this strategy. For example, most dimensional analyses concerning social judgement reveal the existence of an evaluative factor which massively contributes to the explanation of the data (Beauvois 1976; Beauvois and Deschamp 1990: 7).

(2) Another obvious solution would be to define a partial ordering on the set of evaluations. For example, we may consider that evaluations take their values within an n-dimensional space. This would certainly be preferable to the first solution, but it would also have a cost: the evaluative 'spill-over' effects would not be automatic. The problem is that the fine tuning of these effects is anything but simple. Most people have difficulties mastering these effects within their everyday reasoning.

(3) In order to account for both the multiplicity and the unity of evaluation, one can assume that values are totally ordered, but also that these values always correspond to the evaluation of something of a given *type*, playing a given *role*, in given *situation*. Thus, it must be distinguished between the evaluation of France as an economic power in the GATT negotiations from the evaluation of France as a football team in the European championship. Both evaluations are real numbers ranging from -1 to $+1$. But it is clear from the situation (i.e. the kind of realities and the role they fulfil) which kind of evaluation is actually at hand.

The distinction between types (e.g. NATION), role (e.g. NEGOTIATION-MEMBER) and situation (e.g. URUGUAY ROUND) is rather intuitive. However, it is often tempting to have a unique concept for constructs such as A NATION AS A NEGOTIATING MEMBER IN THE URUGUAY ROUND. In artificial intelligence such constructs are sometimes labelled types, and sometimes labelled roles. The purpose of so-called terminological languages is to control the formation and the relationship between such terms. From now on, I shall use the word 'type' to refer to the more complex term 'type in a role in a situation'.

Evaluation and ideological consistency

Besides the structure of evaluation, one may also question whether all syntactic types of expressions have an evaluation. It is clear that nouns, verbs and adjectives do not differ in this respect. Similarly, it is difficult to conceive of any phrase that would be evaluation-free. In context, even adverbs and complements such as 'always' and 'with a knife' have an evaluation. If fact, it is always possible to define the evaluation of a linguistic expression as its contribution to the global evaluation of the sentence in which it occurs. For example, in the sentence 'He always makes mistakes' the adverb 'always' has a negative value since it reinforces the negative evaluation of the sentence.

I nevertheless distinguish between two basic types of evaluations: the evaluation of the content of discourse and the evaluation of discourse itself. I call the latter the *ideological consistency* of discourse. Evaluation of discourse is the appreciation of its content in terms of morality, social utility, desirability, feasibility, etc. Ideological consistency of discourse is the appreciation of discourse in terms of truth, persuasiveness, logical consistency, compatibility of values, etc. Throughout the book, I focus on ideological consistency as compatibility of values. I have argued, in the first chapter, that this choice is rendered legitimate by the fact that ideologies tend to propose values reflecting truth and persuasiveness.

The distinction between evaluation and ideological consistency is not as clear-cut at it may seem at first glance. First, evaluative consistency is a kind of evaluation. Secondly, like evaluation, ideological consistency concerns all types of expressions. It is well known that some words are not ideologically neutral, and that their mere use is a reliable index of ideological adherence (Perriaux and Varro 1991). Therefore, even words have an intrinsic consistency with an ideology. In addition, many syntactic constructions involve hidden predications. For example, although the expression 'the Islamic terrorists' is not a sentence, it nevertheless contains a relation between 'Islamic' and 'terrorists' which renders it unlikely to be used by Islamic proselytizers. Therefore, as soon as an expression combines words, we can assign to it a degree of ideological consistency. Thirdly, ideological consistency is involved in the evaluation of discourse's content. One may indeed argue that the evaluation of discourse has an impact on the evaluation of discourse content. In particular, the discursive benefits that we derive from an event may change the evaluation of an event. For example, we usually consider an 'increase of unemployment' as deplorable. However, suppose I am a politician, and that I can use this increase of unemployment as an argument against my political adversaries in the government. This may change my appreciation of the event. I may start thinking that, at least momentarily, this increase of unemployment is not a bad thing. Therefore, because ideological consistency reflects the uses that I can make of discourse, and because these uses influence the way I think about the content of discourse, my evaluation is skewed by the pull of ideological consistency.

Despite the complex relation existing between the two notions, the distinction between discourse and discourse's content is rather intuitive. Furthermore, if predicting the evaluation of discourse's content is difficult, predicting the discursive uses that can be made of a piece of discourse's content seems almost impossible. For these reasons, I attempt in Chapter 7 to define ideological consistency in terms of evaluation, though I do not try to define evaluation in terms of ideological consistency.

6 Semantics of contextual modification

As stated above, compositionality and systematicity are desirable semantic properties, but they are achieved in a rather artificial way, which prevents us from distinguishing between the meaning of words and the modes of organization of these meanings into phrases and sentences. This is why I propose to consider, instead of a compositional semantics, a semantics of contextual modification. This type of semantics is based on the classical distinction between sense and signification. Sense is the meaning of a word in the system of language, while signification is its meaning in linguistic context. Similarly, I distinguish between the *default evaluation* of an expression and the *contextual evaluation* of the same expression. As stated in the previous section, there is no evaluation without a type. Therefore, default evaluation is the evaluation of an expression of a given type. Contextual evaluation is the evaluation of an expression of a type, *which participates in other predications*. This approach will not surprise the experts in semantics. Semantics always starts from meanings in local, restricted contexts, and tries to derive meanings in larger contexts. Here, the restricted context is the type, whereas the enlarged context is the discursive context itself.

Evaluative semantics is a semantics of discourse, and evaluative meaning effects are not bound to the limits of the sentence. Although it is reasonable to believe that each rule of syntactic composition corresponds to a class of evaluative meaning effect, some of these effects, such as the effects of isotopy, are independent from syntax. Contrary to the belief which inspired Montague's programme, from an evaluative perspective, semantics and syntax are not homomorphic. However, for expository purposes, I assume in this chapter that evaluative semantics are driven by syntax.

Recent work on head-driven phrase structure grammar (HPSG) has developed the idea that within any (well-formed) linguistic expression, components can be hierarchized, and that a lexical head can be identified in each phrase (Pollard and Sag 1994). This remark suggests that the meaning of a phrase is the meaning of its head in the context of the phrase. From an evaluative perspective, this entails that once the evaluation of a phrase's head has been modified by the other elements in the phrase, the evaluation of the head summarizes the evaluation of the whole phrase.

Let us suppose that we possess a language and a context-free, head-driven grammar for this language. Let us call *Head(e)* and *Daughters(e)* the lexical head and the list of daughters of an expression *e*. Let us note [*e*] the default evaluation of an expression *e*. Assume that when [*e*] is not defined by the semantic theory, then [*e*] = [*head(e)*]. Let us choose [[*e*]] as the notation for the contextual evaluation of an expression *e*. I define the contextual evaluation of an expression as the evaluation of its syntactic head at the end of the process of contextual modification. Let us admit that the evaluation of a list is the list of evaluations of its members. The operator '±' (read 'modified by') represents the contextual modification process. Contextual evaluation can then be defined recursively by

$$[[e]] = [Head(e)] \pm [[Daughters(e)]] \qquad (4.1)$$

If semantic theory assigns a default evaluation to all the words of a lexicon, then contextual evaluation is necessarily computable since after a finite number of recursions, one necessarily encounters expressions which have a default evaluation. In Chapter 7, the '±' operator will be generalized to encompass the reciprocal modification of heads and daughters of a phrase, and more generally, the mutual modification of any parts of a discourse.

In contextual modification semantics, the '±' operator is the equivalent of the meaning functions of compositional semantics. One can indeed define '±'([*e*]) as a function of the daughters of *e*, and taking its values in the set of possible evaluation.

$$E^{card(daughters(e))} \xrightarrow{\text{'}\pm\text{'}([e])} E$$

The meaning functions of an evaluative semantics arbitrate between several aspects of a situation. They weigh the different features (possibly conflicting) of a situation, to determine whether or not the positive ones dominate the negative ones. For example, an action usually has an agent, an object, an intention, some means, and some consequences which may differ from the intention. All these parameters influence the final evaluation of the action. In general, the good reputation of an actor influences positively the evaluation of his actions (Plantin 1990). So does the nature of his intentions, and the consequences of his action. This example suggests that meaning functions may depend on each parameter in a stable way. However, systematicity of evaluative semantics cannot be achieved by requiring that meaning functions be monotonous in each argument.[6] To illustrate this point, consider again the case of an action. As stated above, the global evaluation for an action seems to depend positively on the evaluation of its actor. However, suppose that the actor has a good reputation. If the act is reprehensible, this good reputation may be detrimental to the actor. We judge the act more severely because we would not expect it from an actor with such a good reputation. In that case, the evaluation of the actor influences negatively the evaluation of the action. This example shows that the partial derivatives of evaluative meaning functions are not constant. In other words, these meaning functions are not monotonous in each argument.

The second advantage of contextual modification semantics over compositional semantics is to allow for a straightforward modelling of ideological consistency. To argue in this direction, let us briefly review the main principles of ideological consistency.

- A discourse is ideologically consistent if the evaluation of the actors it mentions squares with the evaluation of the behaviours and the properties it attributes to them (for example, good people behave well).
- A discourse is ideologically consistent if the evaluation of the actors it mentions squares with the consistency of the beliefs and the declarations it attributes to them (for example, good people have ideologically consistent beliefs).
- A discourse is ideologically consistent if it credits an actor with beliefs and speech acts which are consistent with the actor's ideology (for example, people believe in their own ideology and defend it).
- A discourse is ideologically consistent if it recommends actions which are positively evaluated, and beliefs which are ideologically consistent.
- A discourse is ideologically consistent if the evaluation of phenomena squares with the evaluation of their consequences, and if the ideological consistency of ideas squares with that of their implications.

The purpose of this research is to generalize these principles to encompass the interplay of various types of semantic relations (CAUSE, MANNER, GOAL, IMPLICATION, AGENT, OBJECT, etc.).

In the principles listed above, the use of the verb 'to square' may appear rather sketchy. It should not be understood as a vague synonym for 'being equal'. In contextual modification semantics, the expression 'A squares with B' means that A's default evaluation is not deeply modified by that of B during the process of contextual modification. To illustrate this point, let us consider the simple sentence 'Communists are dangerous'. Assume that *dangerous* is negatively evaluated. If the default evaluation of *communists* is positive, then this evaluation will be strongly affected by the predicative adjective *dangerous*. Evaluations do not square. On the contrary, if the default evaluation of *communists* is negative, then it is likely that this default evaluation will not be very much modified by the adjective. Evaluations square. In Chapter 7, a precise definition of operator ± will be given in order to reflect this semantic behaviour. For the moment, let us simply assume that we possess an operator of contextual modification such that the modification of an expression by another is inversely proportional to the extent that they 'square'. Under these conditions, the ideological consistency of an expression can be defined and estimated as the variation of evaluation affecting the different parts of the expression. The more evaluations vary during the process of contextual evaluation, the less the expression is consistent.

By analogy with the notations of intensional logic, let us write $^\wedge e$ the expression denoting the expression e. Because the ideological consistency of an expression e is the evaluation of e as an expression, it is written $[\![^\wedge e]\!]$. The basic intuition which inspires this research can be expressed by the following formula.

Let e be an expression such that

$Daughters(e) = <e_1, ..., e_n>$

then

$$[\![^\wedge e]\!] = F((\![e_1]\!] \pm [\![Head(e)]\!]) - [\![e_1]\!], ..., ([\![e_n]\!] \pm [\![Head(e)]\!]) - [\![e_n]\!]) \quad (4.2a)$$

The ideological consistency of an expression e depends on the variation of evaluation of its daughters. More precisely, the ideological consistency of e is estimated on the basis of the difference between the default evaluation of its daughters (modified by their head) and their contextual evaluation. The greater this difference is, the lower the ideological consistency or the expression is. As I will show in Chapter 7, for some adequate definitions of function F and of operator ±, rule (4.2a) can be put to work on a wide range of expressions.

As stated above, a discourse is also consistent if it recommends actions and states of things which are positively evaluated. This leads to a second rule for consistency evaluation.

Let e be an expression such that

$Head(e)$ has optative modality

then

$$[\![^\wedge e]\!] = [\![e]\!] \quad (4.2b)$$

This rule could not be simpler. Ideological consistency is here the same thing as evaluation.

7 Opacity in evaluative semantics

Truth conditional semantics cannot treat intentional verbs and modalities exactly in the same way as other verbal predicates. To convince ourselves of this impossibility, let us try naïvely to represent intentional verbs as normal verbs. The meaning of 'believe', for example, would be a function ranging from the set of pairs composed of an individual and a denotation of a proposition, and taking its values in the set of truth values. One fundamental reason renders it impossible to proceed in this way. Namely, compositional semantics proceed by composing denotations. Since the denotation of a proposition is a truth value, this denotation contains almost no information about the proposition, except whether or not the proposition is true. The problem lies in the fact that at the end of the compositional process, the meaning of expressions somehow collapse into true or false when the composition reaches the level of the sentence. Thus, our naïve semantic theory would have to take a decision concerning the truth or falsity of the sentence 'A believes P.' without knowing anything about the proposition P except its truth or falsity. This is clearly not enough information. The solution to this problem is to introduce a new class of expressions, which denote expressions. Intentional verbs can then be treated as applying to meta-expressions denoting propositions.

Intentional verbs in fact have more formal properties than simple predicates. For example, if someone *knows* something, then this something is true. To incorporate these inferential properties into semantic theory, standard logic may be enlarged with 'modal operators' such as 'possible', 'believed by x', or 'known by x', 'written in the Koran', thus becoming a 'modal logic'. The problems raised by the intentional nature of some modal operators (in particular the epistemic operators concerning knowledge and belief) remain the same. But in the context and vocabulary of modal logic, they are stated in a slightly different way. Within most textbooks on modal logic, it is written that modal operators lack one highly desirable feature: they are not, like logical connectors, 'truth functional'. This brings us back to our previous discussion concerning intentional verbs. The truth value of a modal proposition is not a function of the non-modal proposition affected by the modality. As we have noted above, it is not enough to know that a proposition is true (or false) to conclude that a given person believes it. The modal operator representing belief, like most modal operators, is therefore said to introduce 'opaque contexts'. It is important to understand that the so-called 'opacity' of modal operators comes from a comparison with logical operators, and not from a comparison with ordinary predicates. Intentional verbs and modal operators are in fact much less 'opaque' than ordinary verbs.

To provide modal logic with neat semantics, Kripke proposed to enlarge the definition of a model to include, besides the real world, an infinity of 'possible worlds' (Kripke 1963). Intuitively, a possible world, as its name indicates, represents a state of things that is just possible, or exists in someone's mind or desire. The model is also provided with 'accessibility relations' (one for each modal operator) between worlds. To each property of the accessibility relation (e.g. transitivity), there corresponds one axiom describing the inferential behaviour of the corresponding modal operator. In 'possible worlds semantics' (the usual name of Kripkean semantics for modal logics) the truth value of the sentence 'It is possible that P' depends on whether there is a possible world in which P is true. Similarly, the truth value of the sentence 'X believes that P' depends on whether P is true in the 'world' of X's beliefs. Krikpe's solution can therefore be applied to the problems of opacity raised by certain intentional verbs. Drawing upon Kripke's semantics for modal logic, Montague defined the intension of an expression as a function ranging from the set of possible worlds and taking its values in the set of possible denotations of the expression. Switching over to intensions solves opacity problems while retaining true compositionality.

In evaluative semantics, intentional verbs are not necessarily opaque. For example, intentional verbs implying a commitment of their agent towards their object are not opaque. *To wish, to want, to have to, to recommend*, are not opaque, nor are the auxiliaries *must* and *may*. This is one of the main advantages of evaluative semantics over truth conditional semantics. However, epistemic verbs (*to believe, to think*, etc.) are opaque. They are in fact doubly opaque since one must consider both opacity affecting evaluation and opacity affecting ideological consistency.

Opacity of evaluation

Let us consider the phenomena of evaluative opacity resulting from the use of an epistemic word, as in the case of a belief report 'X believes that P'. It is necessary to distinguish among

> the belief report: the proposition 'X believes that P'
> the fact: the fact that X believes in P
> the belief: the proposition P
> the belief's content: what P is about.

In order to be more concrete, let us consider the sentence 'The government believes that high wages cause inflation.' The evaluation of the fact clearly does not depend on the evaluation of the belief's content. Stated otherwise, one cannot predict the evaluation of the fact (government's believing) from the evaluation of the causality between high wages and inflation. If something seems to matter here, it is whether this causality is real or not. In other words what matters is whether the belief is true or false. However, in evaluative semantics, it is not necessary to resort to the notion of truth, because the evaluation of the belief fact depends on the ideological consistency of the belief: we generally consider it a bad thing that incoherent beliefs exist, and a good thing that coherent beliefs exist. Therefore the evaluation of a fact depends positively on the ideological consistency of the belief.

In some specific cases, we may appreciate the existence of incoherent beliefs, or the absence of coherent beliefs. This could happen if we have a bad opinion of the believer and we hope that his erroneous belief is detrimental to him. Returning to our example, assume that we believe there is no influence of high wages upon inflation. From our point of view, the belief is inconsistent. If the government bases its economic policy on this inconsistent belief, this policy is likely to be unsuccessful. Because of this, the government may become unpopular, a consequence which we may judge positive if we are unfavourable to this government. Therefore, there are some cases in which we may value positively the fact that a negatively evaluated actor has an inconsistent belief. However, this is the exception rather than the rule. Assume that we have a bad opinion of the government, and that we do not believe high wages cause inflation. If we read the sentence 'the government believes that high wages cause inflation', we spontaneously evaluate the act of belief negatively. If the author wants to be sure of inducing the opposite interpretation, he would have to suggest discourses such as:

- Fortunately for us, the government believes that high wages cause inflation.
- The government believes that high wages cause inflation. Let us not undeceive them.

This example demonstrates that the pragmatic evaluation of belief act can override its evaluation in terms of the belief's ideological consistency. Nevertheless, evaluation based on ideological consistency remains the rule. This leads us to the second rule of contextual evaluation.

Let e be an expression such that

(i) $Head(e)$ is an opaque, epistemic intentional verb
(ii) $Daughters(e) = <e_1, \ldots, e_n>$ and e_1 is the belief,

then

$$[\![^\wedge e]\!] = [Head(e)] \pm < [\![^\wedge e_1]\!], [\![e_2]\!], \ldots, [\![e_n]\!] > \qquad (4.3)$$

Similarly to intensional logic in which considering intensions allows us to 'see through' opaque contexts, in evaluative semantics, considering evaluative consistency allows us to solve problems of evaluative opacity.

Opacity of ideological consistency

The ideological consistency of a belief report does not depend on the evaluation of the belief's content. Thus epistemic intentional verbs introduce opaque contexts. Returning to our example, it is clear that the ideological consistency of the sentence 'the government believes that high wages cause inflation' does not depend on the evaluation of the effect of high wages upon inflation. As stated in the previous section, the ideological consistency of a belief report can be evaluated on two different bases.

First, one can simply assume that good people have ideologically consistent beliefs. In that case, ideological consistency of belief reports no longer raises specific problems of opacity. To evaluate the consistency of a belief report, we simply need to apply successively formula (4.3) and formula (4.2). If we restrict ourselves to a dichotomy of values (+ and −), possible results can be summarized by Tables 4.1 and 4.2.

Secondly, another solution consists in assuming that a belief report 'X believes that P' is ideologically consistent if P is consistent with I, the ideology of X. Let us denote by I(x) the ideology of an actor X, and by $[\![^\wedge e]\!]_I$ the consistency of the expression e with the ideology I. These notations lead directly to another rule of consistency evaluation for belief reports.

Let e be an expression such that

(i) *Head*(e) is an evaluatively opaque epistemic verb
(ii) *Daughters*(e) = <a, b >, a is the actor, b is the belief,

then

$$[\![^\wedge e]\!] = [\![^\wedge b]\!]_{I(a)} \qquad (4.4)$$

Both rule (4.4) and the successive application of rule (4.3) and (4.2) hold for epistemic, evaluatively opaque, intensional verbs. In practice, it can be

Table 4.1 Evaluation of belief fact

		Consistency of belief	
		+	−
Actor's evaluation	+	+	−
	−	+ or −	+ or −

Table 4.2 Consistency of belief report

		Consistency of belief	
		+	−
Actor's evaluation	+	+	−
	−	+ or −	+ or −

interesting to combine the two approaches, since they are both psychologically plausible. When we interpret attitude and speech act reports, we indeed take into account both aspects of consistency.

8 Possible worlds and conflicting worlds

The evaluative semantics as sketched above could be compared with the figure of a fair judge unaware of any contingency. It has been implicitly supposed that anybody would agree with evaluations. But besides a core of evaluations that might convince everyone, most ideas, most phenomena, most social events are judged differently depending on the perspective of the one who judges. 'Communism' for example, is evil for conservatives, but good for communists. Evaluative semantics accounts for such relativism by postulating the existence of a set of 'ideologies' reflecting different perspectives on society. Therefore, instead of evaluation *per se*, we must talk of an evaluation in an ideology. Similarly, instead of ideological consistency *per se*, we must talk of the consistency of an expression with an ideology. The consistency of a discourse with an ideology measures whether or not this ideology is inclined to utter and defend this discourse. It refers to the degree to which an ideology is ready to accept the evaluative content of a proposition, the degree to which that particular proposition could fit within the world's discourse. Or, to put it differently, the probability that spontaneously, an ideology would generate the proposition. Focusing on values, the consistency of a discourse with an ideology measures the disturbance which the discourse introduces within the ideology's evaluations, the modifications that should be made to these evaluations if the discourse were to be appropriated by the ideology.

In evaluative semantics, ideologies are the equivalent of possible worlds in Kripkean semantics. But unlike possible world semantics, evaluative semantics has no such thing as a 'real' world. All ideologies are at the same level, and no view of the world is ideologically neutral. Furthermore, each ideology has its own view of other ideologies. There is therefore a complex set of mirror relations between ideologies. In most cases, the relationships among ideologies are not friendly. The second difference between possible worlds and ideologies is therefore that possible worlds are relatively indifferent to each other (if we except accessibility relations) whereas ideologies conflict with each other.

One of the main challenges of evaluative semantics is to account for the conflicts between ideologies. These conflicts are both global conflicts between value systems and specific controversies on social issues. Both types of conflicts are related. Polemical conflicts on concrete issues induce changes in value systems, and value systems set constraints on polemical attitudes. We should therefore attempt to model how evaluative conflicts are articulated with assertoric conflicts.

Ideologies as extensions

To my knowledge, the main contribution to the formalization of inconsistencies between worlds is nonmonotonic logic. The idea is to look at possible worlds as extensions of a partial world which acts as a matrix for all of them (Stein 1991). An extension is defined as an unambiguous, consistent world state that has been built up from a partial, ambiguous world. More precisely, given a set of premises and a set of inference rules, an extension is a fixed point of the inferential process. Let us give the traditional example of the Nixon diamond (Figure 4.2).

This diagram (a typical 'IS A – IS NOT A' network) summarizes a partial model according to which Nixon is a Quaker and a republican; Quakers are pacifists; republicans are not pacifists. A path is either a concatenation of ISA links or a concatenation of ISA links terminated by an IS NOT A link. The inferential rule is the 'concatenation' of paths. I shall discuss below the methods of concatenation. For the time being, let us just note that there are two extensions of this partial model. One according to which Nixon is a pacifist, and one according to which Nixon is not a pacifist.

It is tempting to describe ideological conflicts as arising from such ambiguous configurations. One may indeed think of defining an ideology as an extension. This extension would reflect the ideological preferences about possible states of the world. For example, the extension in which Nixon is a

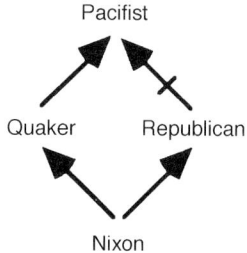

Figure 4.2 Nonmonotonic inheritance – the Nixon diamond.

pacifist may reflect the preference of the 'Quaker ideology'. More precisely, given a nonmonotonic logic and a set of elementary propositions reflecting opinions, an ideology I could be defined as possessing three components:

1   A partial order on the set of extensions: I's preferences.
2   A 'real' extension: the state of the world according to I.
3   A set of ideologies: other ideologies as conceived of by I.

Obviously, since ideological perspectives can be biased, I's vision of other ideologies need not coincide with the definition that these ideologies would give of themselves, and I's real world need not be the real world of other ideologies.

Another solution would be to define an ideology as a single preferred extension. The only necessary modification would be to interpret the partial model giving birth to extensions as a set of normative statements instead of statements about reality. If we agree upon reading the previous diagram as stating 'republicans should not be pacifists', and 'Quakers should be pacifists', then an ideology may be seen as defining priorities between normative statements. For example, the Quaker ideology may assume that Nixon can perfectly well be both a Quaker and a republican, but that the religious commitment is more binding that the political one, and therefore, that Nixon should be a pacifist.

Evaluation and inheritance

Inheritance networks are perhaps the most successful application of nonmonotonic logic. Inheritance hierarchies provides us with a straightforward articulation between evaluations and statements. Let us consider evaluations as attribute values. If a category A subsumes a category B, then B inherits from A its evaluation. Ideological controversies concerning subsumption of categories immediately translate into controversies concerning evaluations. For example, the evaluation of hunters may depend on whether or not we classify them as criminal. If we do consider them as criminals, they inherit their evaluation from that of criminals. If we consider them as a type of sportsmen, they inherit their evaluation from that, much more positive, of sportsmen.

In the case which concerns us, inheritance raises a special question: which type of inheritance is suitable for evaluation? There is considerable evidence that the social evaluation of individuals for example, depends on their social roles. Thus, individuals inherit the evaluation of their roles. In addition, the evaluation of the roles, for example, the evaluation of being a professor, may depend on more general categories, for example on the category of 'white collar' or 'intellectual'. On the other hand, it is perfectly possible to hold intellectuals in contempt, while, at the same time respecting professors. As this example shows, the inheritance of evaluative properties is subject to

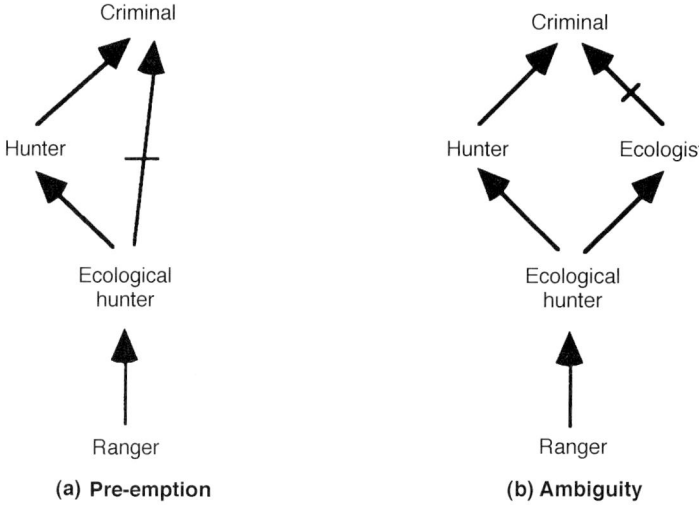

Figure 4.3 Pre-emption and ambiguity in nonmonotonic inheritance.

many exceptions, and should therefore be 'defeasible'. In practice, exceptions are handled by a mechanism of pre-emption. This notion refers to the fact that the information attached to specific categories overrides the information attached to more general ones. In the example (see Figure 4.3), hunters are considered criminals, except the ecological hunters who hunt only to restore ecological equilibrium (e.g. national parks rangers, hunting only the predators of endangered species, are ecological hunters). From the first diagram in Figure 4.3, one cannot infer that rangers are criminals, because this view of hunters is pre-empted by the fact that ecological hunters, who form a more specific category, are not criminal.

Within the formal theories of path-based subsumption, there is a distinction between two forms of inheritance. *Decoupled inheritance*, which rests on an inference mechanism called 'upward concatenation' (of paths), is tractable, whereas *coupled inheritance*, which rests on downward concatenation of paths, is not. As its name indicates, in decoupled inheritance, there is no coupling between the properties of a class and the properties of its superclasses. On the opposite, *coupled inheritance* ensures that a class possesses all the properties (that are not pre-empted) of its superclasses. To illustrate this point, consider case (b) in Figure 4.3. This network is ambiguous and possesses at least two possible extensions: one in which ecological hunters are criminal, and one in which they are not. But the surprising fact, with decoupled inheritance, is that we can perfectly well end up with rangers being criminals while ecological hunters are not. This situation is a valid extension of the network when paths are constructed by upward concatenation.

Does this rather counter-intuitive situation make a strong case in favour of coupled inheritance? Not really. The first reason is that although the above situation may happen, it does not need to happen. Indeed, there is also an extension in which both rangers and ecological hunters are (or are not) criminals. As stated above ideologies may be formalized as preferred extensions. In our case, an ideology will have at least one decision to make. It will have to say whether ecological hunters are criminals or not. To put it in another way, the ideology will have to say whether their status of ecologist makes the fact that they are hunters acceptable. Then, why not make another decision concerning rangers? In fact, decoupled inheritance is both more flexible and more tractable than coupled inheritance.

Let us not be unduly optimistic. Evaluation is always the evaluation of something of a given type, and these types are complex (category, role, situation). This requires that inheritance networks for evaluation should at least be terminological languages allowing for subsumption of complex types. Networks with roles and relations could be good candidates (Thomason Touretsky and 1991). However, though simple forms of defeasible inheritance are tractable, this is not the case for monotonic inheritance networks with roles (Guerreiro *et al.* 1990). Therefore, if we combine the computational complexity arising from subsumption in non-trivial terminological networks with that arising from nonmonotonicity, we should certainly give up any hope of tractability.

Conclusion

The strategy adopted throughout this chapter was aimed at drawing maximum benefit from the results obtained by semantic theory. This is not only a matter of intellectual economy. It makes it more likely that evaluation-oriented semantics, if ever achieved, will couple more easily with truth-conditional semantics. However, our tour of existing semantic theories has revealed that, on one hand, denotational semantics has not paid a lot of attention to evaluative issues – because they were viewed as belonging to pragmatics – and, on the other, non-denotational semantics have remained, as far as evaluation is concerned, at the lexical level. Therefore, taking into account evaluative meaning effect at the level of phrases, sentences and discourse was an unsolved problem.

It has been proposed to address this problem by means of a semantics of contextual modification, in which the *default evaluation* of an expression is transformed into a *contextual evaluation* under the influence of its linguistic context. Processes of contextual modification are not limited to the scope of the sentence. They also take place at the discursive level. More importantly perhaps, the interaction between linguistic units is not syntax-driven (in the traditional sense of the term). The contextual modification works in all directions within the various elements of discourse. In particular, the lexical head of an expression is modified by its daughters as much as daughters are modified by the head, and as much as daughters modify each other. Therefore, a semantics of contextual modification is not compositional (again, in the narrow sense of the term). As a multi-directional interaction between linguistic units, evaluative semantics lends itself to connectionist modelling.

Default evaluations and their interactions in linguistic context depend on a wider context, that I call *conflicting worlds*, or *ideologies*. Thus, one should never talk of an evaluation in itself, but of an evaluation within a specific ideological context. Ideological contexts are like the partial models of denotational semantic theory. However, ideologies have several advantages over partial models. The most important of these advantages is that they are much more economical in terms of information. Conflicting worlds are simpler than Kripke's possible worlds because social norms are simpler than reality. Stated otherwise, normative judgements are generally easier[7] to make than matter-of-fact judgements. This advantage of evaluation over truth justifies the elaboration of an evaluative semantics.

I have distinguished, in this chapter, between the *evaluation* of an expression and its *ideological consistency*. These are the fundamental notions of the book, and, I would argue, of future semantics of evaluation. While the evaluation of an expression is the evaluation of its *content,* the consistency of an expression is its evaluation *as an expression*. The latter reflects the compatibility of the expression with a given ideology. As in the case of evaluation, there is no such thing as an ideological consistency *per se*. Ideological consistency is always the consistency of an expression with a specific ideology. An expression which is weakly consistent under an ideological hypothesis may be highly consistent under another. However, the ideological consistency of an expression is not indexed by an infinity of possible worlds, but by a finite number of ideologies, that is, of socially defined descriptions and prescriptions.

I want to stress in conclusion that the distinction between evaluation and ideological consistency is analogous in some ways to the distinction between denotation and sense in truth-oriented semantics. Therefore, it is not surprising that ideological consistency, like intension, can help to solve difficult problems of semantic opacity. However, the notion of consistency has an advantage over that of intension (or sense): it can be approximated as the compatibility of the evaluations it contains. In a semantics of contextual modification, the compatibility of evaluations can be measured by the intensity of the reciprocal modification. This is the fundamental idea of the book, and it will be put to work in a mathematical manner within the following chapters.

5

SEMANTIC NETWORKS AND DISCOURSE REPRESENTATION

Introduction

Semantic networks (SNs), widely used in artificial intelligence for knowledge representation and natural language processing, are an appealing solution for social scientists working on textual data. Along with the representation of factual statements, they allow the representation of attitude reports like beliefs and states of knowledge of social actors. They also offer the possibility of representing abstract statements like theoretical assertions and more generally, ideas. In addition, semantic networks couple these expressive abilities with an inferential retrieval of the coded content.

I first discuss, in this chapter, the epistemological status of semantic networks. It is recalled that SNs are the result of at least three main scientific paradigms (section 2). SNs are then placed within the more narrow context of discourse representation and compared with other types of formalisms (section 3). However, the diversity of epistemological foundations and the tight relations with other classes of formalisms should not hide the fact that representing discourse by the means of SNs necessarily involves presuppositions concerning the nature of discourse itself. Rastier's comprehensive theory of discourse is used as a conceptual framework to assess the capacities of SNs at the various levels of discursive organization (section 4). In the second part of this chapter, the major types of SNs are described (section 5). The purpose of this discussion is not so much to make a survey of the field as to locate the networks which are developed in the next chapters with respect to existing classes of SNs. Because these networks are largely inspired from Sowa's Conceptual Structures, the last part of the chapter is devoted to a more detailed discussion of conceptual graphs (sections 6 and 7). The fundamental notions (some of which are intensively used in following chapters) are presented. A generalization to the case of modal graphs of Sowa's game-theoretical semantics for first-order graphs is proposed. The chapter ends with a series of critiques of the conceptual graph model (section 8).

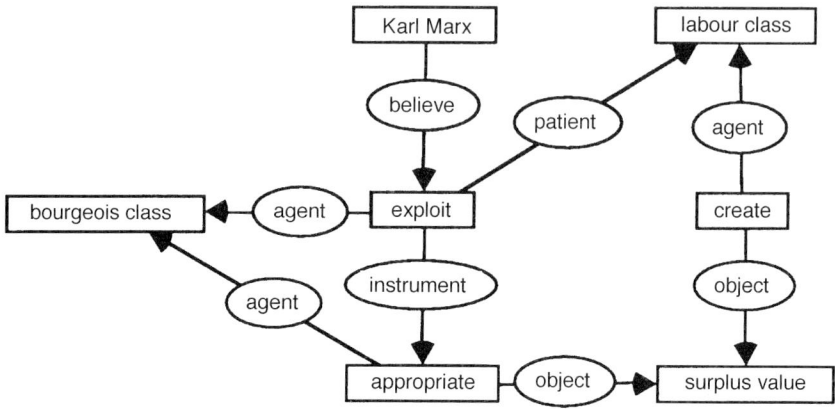

Figure 5.1 A network without semantics.

1 The nature of semantic networks

One may wonder what is exactly represented when a text is said to be 'represented by a semantic network', and what kind of 'content' is at stake when it is claimed that a semantic network represents the content of a text. More generally, what is the exact nature of semantic networks used for the purpose of discourse representation?

Semantic networks consist of a set of relations which hold between concepts. More precisely, semantic networks are directed graphs labelled on both arcs and edges. This definition is rather loose. Consider, for example, the sentence 'Karl Marx believes that the bourgeois class exploits the labour class by appropriating the surplus value created by the labour class.' There are many possible representations of this sentence using directed, labelled graphs. One such possible representations could be that of Figure 5.1.

Although this representation is, to a certain extent, intuitive, it is not clear in what sense this is a 'representation'. Loosely defined representations immediately raise a certain number of questions. Why should this representation be preferred to others? What can we do with it? Is this representation in any respect more convenient than the original sentence itself?

Part of the difficulty concerning the nature of graph-based representations arises from the fact that semantic nets can model things as different as chained causalities, narratives, sentences, expert knowledge, and semantic constraints bearing on a lexicon (Findler 1979). These various uses have greatly enhanced the formal and expressive properties of graph-based representations. However, this polymorphism raises questions over the epistemological status of semantic networks (Brachman 1979). I follow Rastier's distinction of three underlying paradigms: connectionism, classical computationalism and linguistics (Rastier 1991).

The *connectionist* approach in AI and cognitive science assumes that computers should mimic the brain, and thereby help to understand it. From a connectionist point of view, the conceptual structures of semantic networks are the artificial analogs of the neural structures which support thought. Therefore the epistemological object of semantic nets in the connectionist paradigm are the semantic associations in the brain. In practice, the connectionist paradigm has suggested a lot of very interesting methods. Semantic neural networks have been used to solve problems of syntactic and semantic disambiguation (Waltz and Pollack 1985), and for question answering (Shastri 1992). In some frameworks, the architecture is connectionist, but not sub-symbolic, because each unit encodes symbolic information (a concept, a relation, an attribute value). In others, the symbolic information is spread over the whole pattern of weights (Hinton 1989; Derthick 1987).

Classical computationalism (as, e.g., Chomsky, Fodor, Pylyshyn), assumes that computer operations should be based on the mind's symbolic calculations. The mind's operations are in turn best modelled by logical inferences. In this approach, the semantic nets represent the conceptual level, that is, mental representations. The meaning of such structures is viewed as their denotation, that is, the states of the external world they refer to.

Within AI, the computational paradigm insists on the fact that semantic nets should not simply be graph grammars without denotation. From a proof-theoretic viewpoint, this means that the inferences drawn on the expressions of these graph grammars must be perfectly controlled. From the model-theoretic viewpoint, this means that the denotation of any semantic graph must be computable. When an abstract grammar such as a semantic net syntax is provided with a denotation, it is said to have proper 'semantics'. Providing a semantics to a given kind of semantic net is generally achieved by providing it with a function that maps any graph onto a logic formula. Since it is easy to provide standard forms of logic with neat semantics, the semantic network will have the semantics of the logic it maps onto. Therefore, in the computational paradigm, the semantic nets are seen as a front-end to logic, or a bridge between natural language and logic.

The *linguistic* approach believes that the main interest of semantic networks lies in their ability to define a semantic proximity between concepts. As recognized by Brachman, in the expression 'semantic networks' the adjective 'semantic' is taken in a linguistic sense (Brachman 1979). The networks are said to be 'semantic' because they borrow their labels from natural language. There is, however, a debate about the relation between words and conceptual structures of the semantic level. The prevailing opinion takes it to be the relation between signifier and signified, the latter being understood as an idea, that is, a mental entity. This approach cannot really be distinguished from the computational paradigm in cognitive science.

A more marginal school in linguistics interprets Saussure's notion of the signified as a purely linguistic notion. That is, the signified of a word is not so much a mental image of its referent, as a situation of the word in the whole system of language. This structural view is the basis of the so-called 'differential approach' in linguistics (Rastier 1991), which regards linguistic units as standing in opposition to other linguistic units. According to differential semantics, the semantic nets represent nothing else than these relations of oppositions, either directly, when a link of antinomy relates two nodes, or via the closely related nodes of a given node, understood as the differentiating characteristics of the latter. As a consequence, the conceptual structures of the semantic nets are not universal, they depend on the particular language from which the labels of the nodes are borrowed.

J. Sowa's Conceptual Graphs are a good example of the hybrid nature of semantic nets. On one hand Sowa claims to draw on the connectionist approach, and the entity-relationship model of relational databases. On the other hand, his graphs map onto logic, and he gives, for the standard first-order subset of conceptual graphs, game-theoretical semantics that can easily be generalized to the modal case. Finally, his more recent works have focused on the use of conceptual graphs for the implementation of a semantic analyser of English (Sowa and Way 1986).

2 Discourse representation formalisms

Semantic networks are not the only kind of formalism available for the representation of discourse. Text grammars and story grammars, semantic grammars, frame languages, discourse representation structures, textual macro structures, and rhetorical structures are all well-known alternatives to graph-based representations. Because semantic networks historically developed after most of the formalisms listed above, they have often been designed as a remedy for their shortcomings. However, it is not always possible to encompass previous formalisms, and semantic networks are not the synthesis of all prior intuitions concerning the nature of discourse.

Story grammars and texts grammars (Rumelhart 1975; Thorndyke 1977), are good examples of the kind of formalisms that have not survived the confrontation with real discourses. Since Rumelhart launched them in the 1970s, these grammars, which cast into recursive rewriting rules the intuitions of literary criticism about the components of narration, have led to very few successful applications. They are, today, almost abandoned. The fundamental reason for the failure of text grammars is that they retain the idea of a 'parse' where each element of the discursive chain is assigned a *unique* function. To put it in another way, discourse grammars retain the idea of a 'linearity' of the signifier. This extremely strong hypothesis has proved workable in syntax, but not in the field of discourse. The conclusion of the whole debate about text grammars is that recursive rules are not an appropriate tool for pattern recognition, as soon as the 'patterns' are not as clear-cut and as functional as syntactic categories. This conclusion leads to a secondary one, which is that concerning the constraints bearing on discourse, it may be preferable to speak of *norms* rather than of *rules*.

Semantic grammars (Franzosi 1989) are much less ambitious. All they attempt is to provide a convenient tool to code event reports. But the 'functionally relevant' semantic categories of such grammars fell short of modelling natural language expressions centred on properties of actors or properties of actions. Neither could they follow natural language in its functional permutations (the fact that an action is considered as an actor for example). Besides these limitations, there are also theoretical reasons to doubt the intrinsic interests of these formalisms. With the recent development of unification grammars, it has became clear that even complex grammars can be expressed by recursive 'frames', such as typed feature structures (Carpenter 1992). Feature structures fully encompass semantic grammars, offering a lot of additional interesting properties, such as subsumption of sorts and of structures, unification of structures and constraints checking. Feature structures are also fully implemented, for example, in ALE (attribute logic engine).

Semantic networks took over the 'frames', previously used in AI, because they proved to be less rigid and more transposable from one situation to another. The strength of semantic networks is that contrary to frames, they do not presuppose a fixed number of 'slots' to be filled in. A semantic network is a flexible structure that may grow dynamically to incorporate new information. Any new piece of information is considered as another 'aspect' of the fact to be represented. In the AI jargon, it is therefore said that semantic networks are 'aspectualized' representations (Wilensky 1991). The other advantage of semantic networks over frames is that they do not separate the representation of knowledge from the process of inference. Instead of juxtaposing a set of data structures with an inference engine based on a set of rules, semantic networks build their inferential properties on the very structure of the net. This is especially true of parallel networks. But it is true also of deduction and induction operations based on graph-matching operations.

Since the development of recursive frame languages, the distinction between frames and semantic networks is no longer clear-cut. Feature structures, which possess the so-called 'sharing' of values, are genuine acyclic graphs. They also permit some induction operations, like subsumption and unification. Thus, they are very close to semantic networks, which are generally cyclic graphs supporting projection and matching.

Some other formalisms compete favourably with semantic networks on a certain number of points. This is the case, for example, for the main alternative to semantic networks, Kamp's Discourse Representation Theory

(Kamp 1981). Because it has been developed for this purpose, DRT has several advantages over graph-based representation when dealing with discourse. In particular, it captures the unfolding dimension of a narration, and the higher level structure of an argumentation. But this superiority has a drawback in terms of information retrieval.

> Kamp's discourse representation theory violates the compositionality principle to a certain extent. Kamp's treatment fails to give us a way of recovering the knowledge of the parts from the knowledge of the whole and of the mode of construction. (Gochet and Thayse 1989: 158)

Because Kamp wanted to treat properly the kind of sentences which receive their meaning from the discursive context, in his formalism, it is often impossible to disentangle this information from its context. For discourse analysis purposes, this is a real handicap.

Among the theories of discourse structures, rhetorical structure theory (Mann and Thompson 1987) deserves a special mention. RST argues that in most coherent discourse, consecutive discourse elements are related by a small set of rhetorical relations. RST distinguishes between two types of relation: subject matter and presentational relations.

> Subject matter relations are those whose intended effect is that the reader recognize the relation in question; presentational relations are those whose intended effect is to increase some inclination in the reader. (Mann & Thompson 1987: 18)

Subject matter relations are informational relations (for example, VOLITIONAL CAUSE), very similar to the standard relational primitives used in semantic networks. On the contrary, presentational relations (for example, EVIDENCE) are intentional relations which are the real novelty of this model. Because RST relies on a relational model, presentational relations can easily be expressed within semantic networks, by means of specific relational primitives.

Several objections have been made to RST. It has been claimed, for example, that it underspecifies the intentional structure of texts (Grosz and Snider 1986). Other authors have questioned whether (as RST would have us believe) one and only one type of rhetorical relation exists at the same time between two elements of discourse (Moore and Pollack 1992). I would like to add a more general critique. From a semiotic perspective, it is not clear whether textual genres can be defined by a selection of a few types of universal rhetorical relations. It might be that there are no such things as universal presentational primitives and that each type of text defines its own, coherent set of rhetorical relations. If this proved true (as

SEMANTIC NETWORKS AND DISCOURSE REPRESENTATION

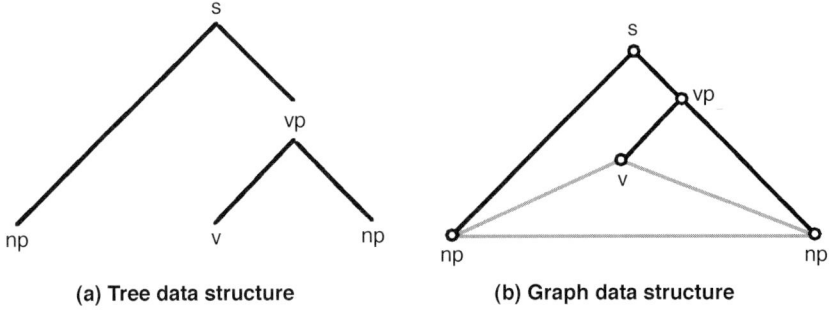

Figure 5.2 The advantage of graphs over trees in semantics.

is likely), one could not simply pick up presentational primitives from the Mann and Thompson catalogue and apply them to the discourse at hand. One would need to proceed the other way around, starting from the discursive genres, and defining in an integrated manner the presentational strategies of each genre.

This rapid evocation of discourse representation formalisms shows that despite a fast technical evolution, firm traditions have already been established. To remain at the technical level, graph-based representations have the advantage of generality over all more restrictive solutions. Acyclic graphs are more general than trees, and cyclic graphs are more general than acyclic graphs. Adopting general data structures frees us from making restrictive assumptions regarding the nature of semantics. In particular, because graphs are not algebraic structures, semantics based on graphs need not be compositional in the traditional sense of the term. To illustrate this point, consider the simplest syntactic structure, np-v-np and its corresponding parse (case (a) in Figure 5.2).

Assume that our semantics is compositional and isomorphic to syntax. The use of this sort of data structure means we cannot to take into account any direct semantic relation which may exist between the two noun phrases, for example. On the contrary, graph-based data structures (case (b) in Figure 5.2) can easily incorporate, in a unique framework, additional semantic relations such as relations of isotopy and casual semantic relations. This example shows that the objections that can be made to traditional compositional semantics have a correlate, at the technical level, in the objections that can be made to the use of trees as semantic structures.

3 Underlying conceptions of discourse

Although there is no strict mapping between technical solutions (data structures and algorithms) and epistemological orientations, most formalisms have underlying conceptions regarding the nature of discourse. I attempt, in this section, to contrast the preconceptions which inspire the representation of discourse by semantic networks with the preconceptions inspiring other formalisms.

Many hypotheses have been made regarding the ultimate nature of 'discursivity' and 'textuality'. Many authors have tried to define the ties which bind together parts of discourse, and the absence of which leads to desultory discourses. I follow Rastier's framework, which comprises four levels of descriptions of discourse content: thematical, dialectical, dialogical and tactical (Rastier *et al.* 1994). Each level corresponds to a level of coherence of the discourse.

1 *Thematics* deals with the selections that a discourse makes within the semantic universe. Thematics distinguishes between several sorts of semantic units at different levels. Roughly speaking, it studies the textual 'vocabulary'.
2 *Dialectics* deals with representation of time and aspect. It describes the constraints bearing on the temporality of states and events reported by the text.
3 *Dialogics* deals with modalities. It concerns both epistemic modalities (are statements asserted, possible, necessary, or impossible?) and modalities of enunciation.
4 *Tactics* deals with the sequential disposition of the signified, and with the order in which the various semantic units are produced and interpreted.

As we will see, not all formalisms pay equal attention to all these levels of description. In particular, let us try to clarify the commitments of semantic network-based representations of discourse towards each level.

1 *Thematics*. For all formalisms based on hierarchical data structures, the topic of the discourse is the top of the hierarchy. Because frames cannot easily be combined, these approaches face serious difficulties as soon as several data structures are mobilized to describe the content of the text.

To overcome these difficulties, one influential theory of discourse comprehension has been proposed by Van Dijk and Kintsch (1983) to distinguish between the *micro* and *macro*-structure of a text. The microstructure is the list of propositions 'contained in' (in fact, 'reconstructed from') the text. The macrostructure is the set of general and salient propositions that summarize the text. The topic of the text is then the top of the macrostructure, or what remains when all peripheral elements have been eliminated.

This model has been intensively criticized, both at the theoretical level and at the empirical level. Van Dijk himself admits that the propositional translation is *ad hoc*, and many authors emphasize the primitive nature of the propositional language, and in particular, the important loss of information which occurs during the translation process (Brow and Yule 1983). Despite all its weak points, the Van Dijk and Kintsch model has an important strength: it shows how thematics and tactics are related. To put it in another way, the model shows how textual organization (title, headings, distribution of information within sections and paragraph) helps the reader make his own way through the microstructure, and isolate the topic of the text. Drawing upon this model, Van Dijk and many others have proposed interesting descriptions of the expository constraints bearing on specific genres (financial reports, weather reports, news agency wires, etc.).

I concede that some functional discourses have a fixed form, and unfold in a pre-defined way. But this is not true of less institutionalized discourses. Even within the boundaries of a genre, no hierarchical structure is able to capture the variability of discursive strategies. A similar doubt inspires all theories which, instead of presupposing some structures of discourse, study rhetorical transitions (RST) and argumentative entailments (Perelman and Olbrechst-Tyteca 1988; Ducrot 1984). In these dynamic approaches, structural considerations are neglected in favour of the study of local relations. More fundamentally perhaps, argumentation theory claims that discourse itself is dialogical. Stated otherwise, discourse always presupposes a fictional pragmatic scene, involves heterogeneous pieces of content, which must be referred to several implicit sources of enunciation. These phenomena are often summarized by the notion of discursive *polyphony* (Nølke 1993). Phenomena of polyphony reveal that the structure of argumentative texts is deeply influenced by the structure of conversation. This is an important cause of disorder and variability within textual macrostructures.

Associative networks are, at the global level, loosely structured systems. Their strength is to give a fair account of the local semantic relations. The global organization is, in associative networks, an emergent organization, not a pre-defined structure. The first emergent property of semantic networks is *connexity*. Because this notion and a few others are a very natural counterpart, at the formal level, to the coherence of discourse (Heidrich *et al.* 1989), the concepts and methods of graph theory can help formalize thematics. Three main methods are available.

1   Decomposition in *strongly connected components* allows one to isolate the parts of discourse. If, in addition, these components are genuine *blocks*, one can infer a series of properties concerning the existence of cycles and paths. In particular, in a block, given three concepts, there is a path from one to another that does not pass through the third. The existence of blocks is a very strong indication of coherence, and can help discovering recurrent semantic nuclei.
2   It may be interesting to know whether a concept, or a proposition, is an *articulation point*, that is, a point that, if removed, increases the number of strongly connected components (i.e., breaks up a strongly connected component into several smaller strongly connected components).

Although there is no general method to find all the articulation points of a graph other than to remove each point and calculate the number of strongly connected components, a theorem by Harary eliminates, on the basis of trivial matrix calculation, a large number of 'bad candidates', which cannot be articulation points (Hage 1979). This theorem makes the structural analysis of graphs computationally more affordable.

3   Simple *measures of centrality* may help in solving, or at least, bring formal confirmations at the preliminary step of every discourse analysis: determining whether a concept or a proposition is the topic of the discourse.

The other main concern of thematics is the study of isotopies. As explained at the end the previous section, graph-based data structures lend themselves to the representations of non-syntactic relations. This is a clear advantage over other formalisms (and, in particular, over propositional formalisms) when the problem at hand is the representation of isotopies. Nevertheless, the model that I propose in the next two chapters adopts a double strategy concerning the issue of isotopy. In the next chapter, I exclude from the model all the relations of isotopy. The fundamental reason for this choice is that, up until now, there has been no satisfying theory of the influence of syntax, negation, quantification and modalities on isotopies. In Chapter 7, I try to develop one such theory for a certain class of isotopies: evaluative isotopies.

2 Dialectics. There has always been indecision, in semantic networks, concerning the representation of time and aspect. Sometimes, temporal indications are treated in the same way as ordinary information is treated. Sometimes, specific inferences related to time and aspect are taken into consideration, and time is treated as a modality. Because semantic networks do not generally support modal reasoning, the representation of time and aspect is one of their weakest points. The networks that I propose in the next chapter are no exception. I shall not try to equip them with a temporal modal engine.

Contrary to semantic networks, discourse representation theory has made many contributions to the field of dialectics. In the design of DRT, Kamp had one main goal in mind. He intended to propose a theory of temporal reference. Therefore, his theory aims at giving the meaning of time and aspect in terms of truth conditions. Although it is reasonable to believe that the evaluative dimension of linguistic temporal markers is not unrelated to their interpretation in terms of truth conditions, there is also strong evidence that a purely informative approach is not sufficient. I have shown in the previous chapter with the case of the French adverbs 'à peine' et 'presque' that the evaluative behaviour of aspect markers cannot be fully depicted within a referential framework. As this example demonstrates, evaluative dialectics cannot be reduced to referential dialectics.

3 Dialogics. The same kind of remarks apply to this level of description. Because semantic networks usually support simple subsets of first-order logic, both alethic and epistemic modalities have never been fully integrated. In addition, indexicality and modes of enunciation are almost absent in semantic networks. On the contrary, DRT has made some important contributions to the field of dialogics, and to the way it interacts with tactics (cf. the study of the anaphoric properties of attitude verbs in Asher 1986). However, semantic networks do also offer some interesting possibilities in the domain of modal representations. I argue, in the next chapter, that semantic networks allow us to aspectualize alethic modalities. In addition, epistemic modalities and speech act reports can easily be represented, within a network syntax, as embedded graphs.

4 Tactics. At first sight, semantic networks seem at odds with tactics. Indeed, while the flow of signifiers in natural language is linear, graphs are in essence, non-linear representations. On the contrary, DRT, for example, pays a lot of attention to the order in which discursive elements are cast, and hopes that this order is an important clue for the efficient treatment of anaphora. However, taking a closer look at graph operations, it becomes easier to understand why many psycho-linguists and cognitive scientists have used semantic networks to model the sequential processes of text understanding.

- Definition and thematization can be represented as node expansion and node contraction.
- The integration of a new sentence to the previously interpreted sentences can be modelled by operations of joins between graphs.
- Coreference and anaphora can be represented either by special links, or by node elimination.
- Connectors and rhetorical relations can be represented by relational primitives.

Despite these solutions, some difficulties persist. Most graph operations, such as the search of the maximal joins of two graphs, are computationally intractable. And they cannot take into account complex argumentative entailments, like the entailments based on topoi.

4 The world of semantic networks

I do not intend to give here a detailed presentation of the numerous types of semantic networks that have been developed for various purposes. The interested reader is referred to the articles 'Semantic Networks' and 'Inheritance Hierarchies' (by Sowa and Touretsky respectively) in the *Encyclopaedia of Artificial Intelligence*. A special issue of the review *Computers and Mathematics with Applications* contains many interesting contributions, as well as a comprehensive survey of the field (Lehmann

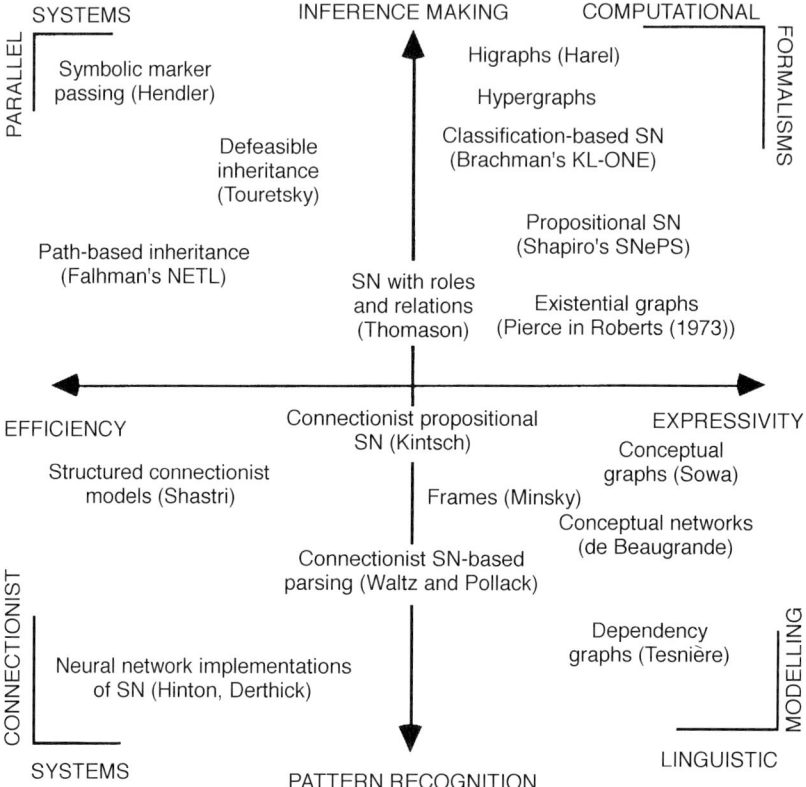

Figure 5.3 The world of semantic networks.

1992). The proceedings of the Catilina workshop, published under the title *Principle of Semantic Networks* is an unmissable collection of papers by the leading scientists of the field (Sowa 1991).

I choose to present the world of semantic networks as being organized around two main axes (see Figure 5.3). One axis corresponds to the trade-off between expressivity and computational efficiency. The second axis corresponds to the opposition between symbolic inference making and sub-symbolic pattern recognition. These axes define four main zones: parallel systems, computational formalisms, connectionist systems, linguistic modelling.

Before any discussion of the existing semantic networks, let us locate in this diagram the networks that will be developed in the next chapter. Since we are not directly interested in efficiency, and because our networks are intended for the representation of discourse, our main concern must be with expressivity. However, expressivity is a weakly defined notion. It is not even easy to define it in a relative way. When a language is an extension of another, one can reasonably say that it is more expressive than the other. But when two languages are not comparable, because their syntax is different, for example, no one can say which is more expressive than the other. Therefore, in our case, expressivity will simply be understood as proximity to natural language. Contrary to the formalisms that receive their validity from a proximity, and in many case, from a possibility of translation into logic, this proximity with natural language will be our main guarantee of semantic validity.

Turning to the second axis, let us remember that our project is to identify the ideological nature of discourses. This entails that we shall try to discover some 'ideological patterns' in the discourses, and attempt to recognize ideological commitments in the texts. Because we shall look for predefined patterns of evaluations in the texts, rather than try to draw ideological inferences, our methodology can be assimilated to pattern recognition, and not to inference making. Therefore, our networks should belong to the lower right part of the diagram.

To locate more precisely the networks that will fit our project, and to examine in which way they can benefit from the properties of the various existing systems, let us pay attention to the main trends of research concerning semantic networks. Within the above diagram one can distinguish at least seven types of semantic networks.

Inheritance networks

Inheritance hierarchies are the oldest form of semantic networks, since they can be traced as far back as ancient Greek philosophy (Porphyry's tree representing a hierarchy of concepts). Inheritance is also an important field of contemporary research, since it is one of the most basic properties of semantic networks. In the AI literature, inheritance networks are often called *terminological networks*, because they allow us to form terms describing classes of individuals, and to organize these terms in a hierarchy. Inheritance is crucial for AI because it means systems can exploit taxonomic reasoning. With inheritance, the information can be expressed at the most general level, and need not be repeated at all specific levels. However, this substantial economy in the encoding of knowledge may slow down reasoning, since calculus of subsumption may take a considerable amount of time as hierarchies get deeper. The search for efficiency led to NETL (Fahlman 1979) and parallel implementations of inheritance. However, it soon transpired that if the systems were to include, besides IS-A links, IS-NOT-A links too, and above all, if the systems were to support defeasible inheritance (allowing for exceptions), many subtle theoretical problems would arise. The original proposal (Touretsky 1986) for fast, nonmonotonic inheritance finally proved to be intractable. However, some related forms of inheritance have been shown to be tractable (Selman and Levesque 1993).

The relations between inheritance, evaluations, and ideologies have been discussed in Chapter 4. As indicated there, our conclusions and suggestions concerning the use of nonmonotonic logic to formalize ideologies and to store evaluative knowledge will remain at the theoretical level.

Marker-passing parallel networks

These networks, which appear in the upper-left part of our diagram, are intended for fast inference making. They rely on parallel implementations. Originally, that is, in the NETL system, Fahlman's idea was to allow efficient inheritance by means of marker-passing algorithms. This idea has been refined by so-called 'symbolic-marker passing' (Hendler 1992). This paradigm consists in implementing simple logical operations in parallel, by multiplicating markers and rendering the behaviour of each node of the network more complex. Since marker-passing algorithms can be interpreted as graph-searching algorithms, they are close to classical computational paradigms. The networks I develop in the next chapter have little, if anything, to do with this area of research.

Graph-based representations of logic

Examples of this type are higraphs (Harel 1988), and Pierce's Existential Graphs (Roberts 1973). The aim of such networks is to provide an easy and intuitive access to logical reasoning. These formalisms are mainly useful for pedagogical purposes. But they are also a source of inspiration for semantic network design, because they allow us to experiment and compare the various ways of restricting logical languages. They may help in making good decisions concerning the type of logical language that applied systems will support. By contrast, hypergraphs (Courcelle 1990) allow us to study the relation between logic and graph grammars. By means of the correspondence between operations on graphs and logic, many interesting theorems concerning the complexity of graph rewriting have been established. In the AI literature, graph-based representations of logic are often called *assertional networks*, because they give the syntax of the graphical language which states the constraints and the facts applying to a given object domain.

I line with many others, I believe that logic is a handicap rather than a help for discourse modelling. However, the capacity of drawing correct inferences is both an aim and a proof of legitimacy for a semantic theory. Still, this does not entail that these inferences must be logical inferences. They may as well be natural inferences (Jayez 1988) based on semantic games, or argumentative inferences based on topoi (Anscombre 1995). Many graph-representations have been attempts to figure out logics that would be more intuitive. However, between the incentive of being psychologically plausible, and the incentive of being logically sound, the second has often prevailed.

Knowledge representation systems

These are the systems that immediately come to mind when one mentions the term 'semantic networks'. The most famous are KL-ONE (Brachman 1979) and its descendants: NIKL, KRYPTON, KL-TWO, KANDOR, BACK, LOOM and CLASSIC. These systems are characterized by the expressivity of their respective terminological modules, which include a *classifier* automatically organizing the expressions of the terminological language into a taxonomy. In contrast, the strength of SNePS (Shapiro 1979) relies on its assertional language. In particular, SNePS includes propositional nodes and act nodes which correspond respectively to beliefs and intended actions of agents. Thus, SNePS can be seen as an *intensional* model of a semantic network (Shapiro and Rapaport 1987). Another well-known system is CYC, a very large and comprehensive knowledge base. Besides these three systems, at least several hundred sorts of semantic networks have been proposed, and, in some cases, implemented. Some scientists regard this multiplicity as a sign of theoretical immaturity, though others prefer to interpret it as a sign of flexibility and adaptability.

In recent years, the AI community has shifted its attention towards neural networks, and less effort has been devoted to semantic networks. Some smart formalisms seem to have been repudiated by their illustrious authors. This is the case, for example, of the semantic networks with roles and relations (Thomason and Touretsky 1991), which are the victims of the current rush of research on connectionism. Because many sociological theories explain how social *roles* influence social *relations*, Touretsky's formalism could certainly be useful for the representation of simple sociological knowledge. But that is another topic of research.

PDP systems with local representations

By their very structure, semantic networks lend themselves to parallelism. However, because the arcs and the nodes of semantic networks are labelled, both tend to receive fixed and unique meanings. A concept, for example, is identified with a given unit in the net, and not with a pattern of activation. Thus, traditional semantic networks belong to symbolic processing. With the expression *Parallel Distributed Processing* I refer to all the systems that, instead of propagating discrete activations (markers), spread continuous activations along the edges of the network. This class of system takes advantage of the continuous nature of the signals which are exchanged between the units, and of the operations of calculus (summation, normalization, application of signal functions) on real numbers. The underlying idea is that the structure of the net and the adequate local parametrization of the dependencies between units will result in behaviours that, because of the number of parameters and of the complexity of the interactions, would not be easily produced by a set of rules. Structured connectionist networks (Shastri 1992) are knowledge bases which incorporate, in a unique framework, both the information and the means of retrieving this information. Most other systems are devoted to the task of pattern recognition. Several global patterns (for example, several syntactic constructions for a certain class of verbs) are made to compete. The mechanism of spreading activation gradually selects one such pattern under the influence of contextual activations (Waltz and Pollack 1985).

One must distinguish, within the very general class of PDP systems, between those that rely on truly distributed representations, and those that make use of so-called 'local' representations, that is representations in which each unit of the network is in charge of encoding one piece of information. The networks that are proposed in the next chapters belong to the PDP paradigm because they spread continuous activations. But they are PDP systems with local representations, since each node of the network represents a semantic entity.

PDP systems with distributed representations

These are truly distributed realizations of semantic networks. For example, an attribute value for a prototype can be stored in binary associative memories. Most of these systems have, at present, only a theoretical interest. They show how some basic features of semantic networks can be reproduced within various neural network architectures (Hinton 1989; Touretsky 1990). The strength of these systems is that the information, which is spread over the whole pattern of weights and within hidden layers, is automatically incorporated by the net during the learning phase. The limits of these systems are the limits of neural networks themselves: the net often resembles a black box; the knowledge contained in a trained network cannot easily be modified, either by retracting, or by adding knowledge. These limitations appear even more acute in the case of neural implementations of semantic networks, because of the large amount of explicit expert knowledge that semantic networks usually contain. System designers know by experience that expert knowledge is very likely to need substantial and repeated revisions.

I subscribe to the overall project of modelling discourse comprehension within a truly distributed framework. However (as emphasized in Visetti 1990), most of the difficulties attached to this ambitious programme of research are still unsolved. I do not address these difficulties, and I remain strictly within a PDP framework relying on local representations.

Graph-based representations of natural language

The first example of these networks is due to the French linguist Lucien Tesnière, who elaborated a network notation for his dependency grammar. This grammatical formalism was introduced in the US by Hay, who adopted Tesnière's graphs in his research on machine translation. Shank, who quotes Hay, shifted his attention from syntactic to conceptual dependency. De Beaugrande too proposed to build up conceptual networks on top of syntactic networks (de Beaugrande 1980). Sowa, with his conceptual graphs, made a synthesis of previous attempts. Until the end of the 1980s, a large part of the AI community working on NLP had believed that by focusing on the conceptual level, that is, by working on purely semantic constructs, we could represent both knowledge and natural language in an integrated framework. At the beginning of the 1990s, many applied systems inspired by this hope had either revealed their limitations, or simply been abandoned. It became clear that the conceptual structures were too far from syntax to form the basis of NLP systems, and that graph-based representations raised computational problems. Research has now evolved towards a better integration of syntax and semantics, and efficiency has been improved by resorting to operations on trees or acyclic graphs. The best example of this evolution is the use of feature structures in unification grammars, and in particular, in HPSG (Abeillé 1993).

In the next chapter, I propose a graph-based mode of representation which does not impose any restriction on the nature of the graphs. Does this mean that I do not pay attention to recent evolution? Would this not repeat the same error which blocked so much research at the semantic level, during the 1980s? Shouldn't we learn the lessons of this evolution and start with formalisms more akin to syntax?

It is not sure, however, that the movement of computational linguistics from a conceptual level to a syntactic level can be avoided by evaluative semantics. In a sense, it is natural to start by exploring the conceptual nature of evaluative meaning effects, and, only then, to look how language introduces lights and shades in these effects. Obviously, the second step is far beyond the scope of this work, since it implies examining the evaluative behaviour of every single syntactic construction, of every verb, adverb, etc.

Neither is it sure that the inadequacy of semantic networks in representing natural language has not been exaggerated. I show, in the last part of this chapter, that semantic networks such as Sowa's Conceptual Graphs are not as close to language as they ought to be if they are to represent it in a subtle way. But this is more a limitation of logical formalisms with referential semantics, than a limitation of graph-based representations. Once the referential approach is abandoned, it is possible to design formalisms retaining the flexibility of conceptual graphs, and yet stay close to natural language.

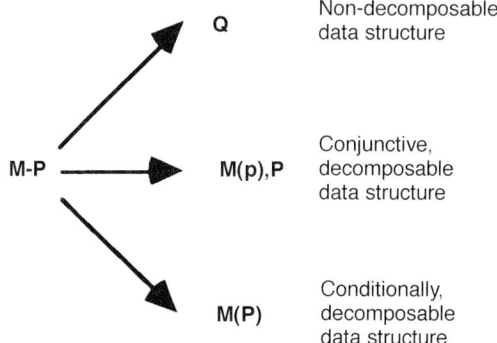

Figure 5.4 Three basic types of data structure.

5 Three basic strategies of content representation

Before recalling the original syntax of Sowa's Conceptual Graphs, the use of such formal languages for the coding of textual information needs to be justified. Formal languages are used as a basis for a semantic theory, which guarantees that the texts are coded unambiguously, and that the coded information can be retrieved without incorrect inferences. A three-strategy framework is presented here to illustrate this fundamental approach, which regards the coding process as a translation of a text into a formal language associated with a semantic theory.

Let us assume that the text to be coded states that Karl Marx believes that the bourgeois class is exploiting the labour class, whatever linguistic form this assertion may take. We have here a composed assertion which consists of a proposition P according to which the bourgeois class is exploiting the labour class, and a modifier M affecting P, according to which P is a belief of Karl Marx. The coding of the whole assertion M-P can be realized in three ways, summarized in Figure 5.4, where the arrows means 'may be represented by', and where p is a pointer to P.

To follow the first strategy means that the assertion according to which the bourgeois class exploits the labour class will not be accessible. This strategy has an advantage: it becomes impossible to infer erroneously a proposition P from the fact that someone believes it. But on the other hand, with modifiers such as 'Marx knows', 'Marx showed', or 'Marx discovered', this inference must be possible, and therefore, the first strategy is inadequate.

The second strategy always allows access to the parts of global information. Therefore, it becomes possible to consider as stand-alone information that the bourgeois class exploits the labour class even if the text considers this as Karl Marx's greatest error. This is clearly an undesirable result, which draws suspicion on the second strategy. As we will see, semantic nets rely fundamentally on the second strategy, and this is where most of their problems come from.

The third strategy allows or forbids access to modified information, depending on the modifier's nature. These dependencies can become rather complex as soon as modifiers are chained, as in sequences such as 'At the beginning, Engels did not know that Marx regarded it possible that...'. At a more general level, logicians tackled the problem of the validity of a transition from one sequence to another by means of so-called 'modal logics'. This type of logic regards modifiers as modal operators, and controls for the inferences on arbitrary sequences of intermingled modal operators,[1] standard quantifiers ($\forall, \exists$) and logical connectives ($\neg, \wedge, \vee$).

Although (Wallen 1990) recently demonstrated that the computational costs of such logics were not higher than that of standard logic, one may question why systems oriented towards natural language should be provided with the capacity of dealing with complex constructions that never happen in natural language, and therefore, that they will never have to cope with. The methods proposed below are inspired by the following idea: restricting the reasoning capacities of the system to the level of logical complexity that characterizes natural language. But the origin of these methodologies, Sowa's Conceptual Structures, must be briefly presented first.

6 The conceptual graph model

Sowa's original syntax is the following:

graph $\longrightarrow$ concept
graph $\longrightarrow$ set of relations
relation $\longrightarrow$ labelled link, ordered n-tuple of concept
concept $\longrightarrow$ type label, #, referent
concept $\longrightarrow$ type label, *, variable
referent $\longrightarrow$ atom
referent $\longrightarrow$ graph

Notations are as indicated in Figure 5.5, which means that 'Rockefeller does not exploit any worker'. By convention, the tag '*' and the variables are omitted in the referent field of generic concepts.

And the counterpart in predicate logic is:

$$\neg(\exists(x,y)(\text{exploit}(x) \wedge \text{worker}(y) \wedge \text{agent}(x, \textit{Rockefeller}) \wedge \text{object}(x,y)))$$

The graphs that contain embedded graphs as the referent of one or several of their concepts or coreference links are called *complex graphs*, in contrast with *simple graphs*, the construction of which does not make use of the last syntactic rule listed above.

SEMANTIC NETWORKS AND DISCOURSE REPRESENTATION

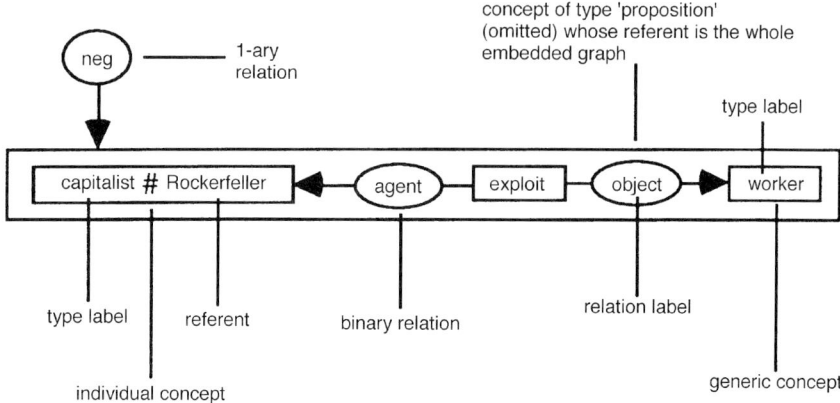

Figure 5.5 An example of a conceptual graph.

The reader will have noted from a comparison between the previous graph and its corresponding formula, that the embedded graph (a simple graph) has an existential meaning. This is due to the fact that a generic concept translates the indefinite 'a' of natural language as 'there exists a *type label*', whilst individual concept translates the definite 'the' or proper nouns, and corresponds to a logical constant.

In addition, within the formula, the logical conjunction is the only connective used. This means that each part of a simple graph (concept or relation) stands in a conjunctive manner with the rest of the graph. To relate it to the general coding framework we designed above, we could say that coding information as a simple graph belongs fundamentally to the second (conjunctive) representational strategy. The existential and conjunctive nature of simple graphs has an important consequence: a simple graph is logically stronger that any of its subgraphs.[2] To put it in an almost similar way, a simple graph logically implies any of its subgraphs.

Another important element shown in the previous example is that Sowa's formalism always indicate the type of constants and variables. The type labels are cast into a lattice structure which expresses their relations of generality. For example, all philosophers are thinkers, and more generally, human beings, while some of them are moralists, others epistemologists, who are also likely to be scientists (see Figure 5.6). In technical terms, the denotational extent of a concept is a subset of the denotational extent of an ancestor concept. From a logical point of view and given the existential reading of conceptual graphs, the lower the label of a concept is in the hierarchy, the greater is the logical strength of the concept. For example if it is true that a philosopher believes a proposition, then it is also true that a thinker believes it, since a philosopher

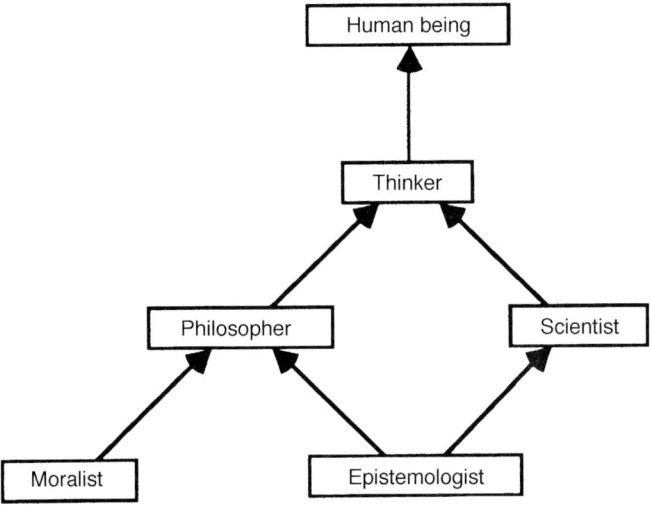

Figure 5.6 An example of type hierachy.

is a thinker. But the fact that a thinker believes a proposition does not entail that a philosopher believes it, since the thinker might be a scientist. The relation 'is an ancestor of' is denoted by '≻'. By definition, this relation is reflexive.

The distinction between individual and generic concepts also presents a trivial logical property: an individual concept is logically stronger than a generic one. Indeed, if it is true that *the* philosopher *Karl Marx* believes a certain proposition, it is also true that there is *a* philosopher (indeed: Karl Marx) who believes this proposition. The operation of transforming a generic concept into an individual one is known as an 'instantiation'.

Sowa combined the latter two properties within the notion of 'restriction' of a concept. One may obtain a restriction of a concept by instantiation, by substituting a new type label T2 such that T1 ≻T2 for the original type label T1, or by combining both operations. For example the individual concept 'the philosopher Karl Marx' is a restriction of the generic concept 'a thinker'.

Finally, Sowa put together all the logical properties of simple graphs already mentioned to produce a practical tool for drawing inferences on conceptual graphs: the *projection* operation. Formally, to project a simple graph u into a simple graph v means to exhibit a subgraph w of v such that:

- The links in w and in u are the same.
- The concepts $c_1 \ldots, c_n$ in w are, respectively, restrictions of the concepts $d_1, \ldots, d_n$ in u.
- If a link ℓ relates two concepts d_i and d_j in u, ℓ relates c_i and c_j in w.

Intuitively, if the projection of a graph into another succeeds, it means that the target graph is bigger and logically stronger than the source graph. For example, the result of the projection of the source graph:

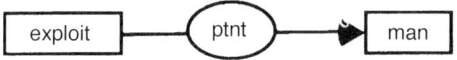

into the target graph:

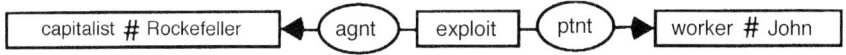

is the graph:

From a practical point of view, the projection operation is an appealing tool since it is equivalent to a very flexible and yet reliable query process. Its reliability is based on the fact that it defines almost *per se* a semantics for simple graphs. In terms of model theory, a model complying to the 'closed-world assumption'[3] can be defined by a set of constants I, and a set T of true conceptual graphs whose concepts all have their referents in I. With these definitions the notion of succeeding projection of a graph g in T is equivalent to the standard notion of the truth of g in a model. Since the model-theoretic counterpart of a text can hardly be viewed as complying to the 'closed-world assumption' it is easy to move to an 'open-world model' by adding a 'false set' F to the model, and by allowing the simple graphs in T and F to have generic concepts.

Definition. An *open-world* W is a triple $\langle T, F, I \rangle$ where T and F are sets of simple graphs and I a set of individual markers.

(a) The graphs in T and F may contain either generic concepts or individual concepts with referents in I.
(b) No individual marker in I occurs in more than one concept in T but there is no such restriction on the referent of F.

Definition. Let S and R be any sets of simple graphs. The *projective extent* of S in R, written $\Pi(S, R)$, is the set of all possible projections from some graph of S into some graph of R.

Those readers more familiar with the realms of social science than with model theory should keep in mind that what we call here an open world is just the content of a text. And what we call a model is nothing but the definition of how this content should be accessed. In particular, we can now easily define the truth and the falsity of an assertion according to a text, and the neutrality and inconsistency of a text with regard to an assertion.

Definition. Let us assume that a text D is represented by an open world $\langle I, T, F \rangle$, and that an assertion A is represented by a simple graph u.
- if $< \Pi(u,T), \Pi(F,u) >=<\emptyset,\emptyset>$, D is said to be *neutral* with respect to A.
- if $< \Pi(u,T), \Pi(F,u) >=< \neg\emptyset,\emptyset>$, A is said to be true according to D.
- if $< \Pi(u,T), \Pi(F,u) >=<\emptyset,\neg\emptyset>$, A is said to be *false* according to D.
- if $< \Pi(u,T), \Pi(F,u) >=<\neg\emptyset,\neg\emptyset>$, D is said to be *inconsistent* with respect to A.

As the careful reader will have noticed, the truth of a simple graph u depends on its projection in T whilst the falsity of u depends on the existence of a projection of a graph of F into u. This reversed direction is intuitive and can be best illustrated by an example. Let us assume that the text to be coded asserts that John, a worker, is exploited by Rockefeller. To code this piece of content, we will set up an open world $W_1 = \langle I_1, T_1, F_1 \rangle$ and we will put the following graph v into T_1:

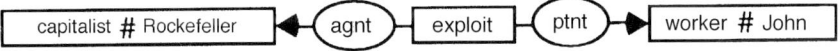

Let us assume now that another text in our sample (represented by $W_2 = \langle I_2, T_2.F_2 \rangle$) asserts that there is no such thing as the exploitation of man (maybe this is an invention of communists). This is easily coded by putting the following graph w into F_2:

Now, suppose we are interested in the opinions of the texts of our sample with respect to the responsibility of the capitalists in exploitation of man. We will set up the query q:

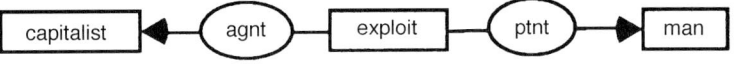

Since there is a projection of q in v we will say that q is true in W_1. And given that there is a projection of w in q, we will say that q is false in W_2.

At this point, we are able to understand why Sowa defines an open world in such a way that no individual marker occurs in more than one concept in the true set, and why the false set is free from this condition. This is because in the true set, two graphs that have one concept in common can be transformed into a single graph by joining the two graphs on their common concept. And within a simple graph, there is no need to use the same concept twice. Therefore the true set can be seen as a collection of 'big graphs' having no elements in common.

On the contrary, in the false set, it would be incoherent to join two graphs since $\neg p \wedge \neg q$ is not logically equivalent to $\neg(p \wedge q)$ (remember that simple graphs are conjunctive formulae). Therefore the false set must be a collection of small graphs. Obviously, if two of these small graphs talk about the same individual, the same individual marker must occur in two different concepts. Hence the inapplicability of the condition.

Projection-based semantics as defined above concerns only simple existential graphs. To deal with complex graphs involving universal quantification, Sowa proposes two different solutions. The first one consists in taking advantage of the fact that $\forall x P(x) \iff \neg(\exists x \wedge \neg P(x))$. Therefore, universal statements can be expressed in terms of negation and existential statements. For example, the sentence 'Rockefeller exploits all his workers' would be translated as 'There is no worker employed by Rockefeller who is not exploited by Rockefeller'. This, however, requires coreference links between generic concepts. These coreference links are represented by undirected dotted lines. A concept c *dominates* a concept c' if there is a dotted path from c to c', and if g', the graph in which c' appears, is embedded in g, the graph in which c appears.

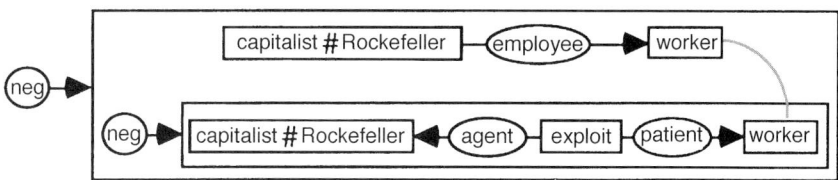

Another solution consists in introducing a universal quantifier directly in concept boxes. However, this does not allow us to distinguish between the scope and the restrictor of a universal quantification. To illustrate this difficulty, consider the following network.

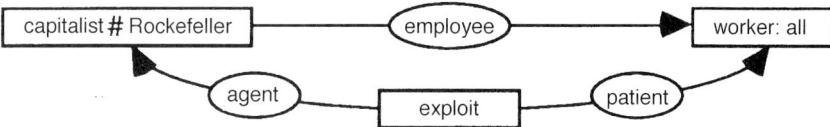

This graph means 'All workers are Rockefeller's employees, and Rockefeller exploits them all', and not 'Rockefeller exploits all his workers'. Stated otherwise, in conceptual graphs, formulae of the form $\forall x(P(x) \Longrightarrow Q(x))$ can be represented only if P is a predicate of the form 'is a *type label*'. Of course, one can form complex type labels to express phrases such as 'a worker employed by Rockefeller'. However, this would probably result in an excessively large number of types.

To provide a semantic interpretation of complex graphs, Sowa proposes an 'evaluation game'. The idea of the game is to decompose a complex graph until simple graphs are found, and then, to apply the projection operation. More precisely, a player called *Credulous* attempts to demonstrate that a set of graphs {U} is supported by the model, while a player called *Sceptic* attempts to demonstrate the opposite. Sowa's game-theoretical semantics is of a rare elegance, though it only concerns the subset of conceptual graphs corresponding to first-order logic (for a discussion of the advantages and drawbacks of the game-theoretical approach over classical model theory the reader is referred to Jackson 1988). Game theoretical semantics can be generalized to the case of modal logic as follows.

> **Definition**: a *complex open world* C is a pair $< \Re, \Omega >$ where Ω is a set of open worlds, and $\Re$ is a set of members of $\Omega \times \Omega$.
> (a) Each element of $\Re$ corresponds to a different modal operator and is called the 'accessibility relation' associated with this modal operator.
> (b) One of the elements of Ω is called the 'real world'.

This definition is clearly inspired by Kripke's semantics for modal logic. The fundamental theorem is that an axiom of modal logic (for the corresponding modal operator) is associated to each property of the accessibility relation. The inverse is not true (Kripke 1963). In the following, it is assumed that modal operators can be classified as either existential or universal. For example, the alethic operators 'possible' and 'necessary', and the temporal operators 'sometimes' and 'always' are respectively existential and universal. The existential operator of a modal logic is often noted $\Diamond$, and the universal operator $\Box$.

> **Definition**: An *evaluation game* G on a complex world $C = < \Re, W >$ *is a two person, zero-sum, perfect information game between two players called Credulous and Sceptic.*
> - The positions of G are 5-tuples $< p, m, s, w, r >$ where the player on move p is a member of {*Credulous, Sceptic*}, m is one of the four 'move types' in the set {*project, select, reduce, select_world*}, s is any set of conceptual graphs, w a world of W, and r a member of $\Re$.
> - The starting positions of G are all 5-tuples <*Credulous, project, s, w, _*> for any set of conceptual graph s, and where w is the real world of W.

The player on move chooses another position among the successors to the current position, which are defined as follows.

- From a position $Q = <p_1, project, \{u_1, ..., u_n\}, w, r>$, the successors are all positions of the form $<p_2, select, \{v_1, ..., v_k\}, w, r>$ where p_2 is the opponent of p_1, and each v_i is a version of u_j modified by the following algorithm:

  for each simple graph u **in** Q **loop**;
    if $\Pi(u, T_w)$ is nonempty **then**
      choose any projection π in $\Pi(u, T_w)$;
      for each concept c in u **do**
        replace *referent*(c) by *referent*(πc);
        for all concepts v dominated by c **do**
          replace referent(v) by referent(πc);
          erase the coreference link between v and c;
      end loop;
    end loop;
    end if;
  end loop;[4]

- From a position $Q = <p_1, reduce, \{u\}, w, r>, w, r>$, the successors are determined by the following algorithm:

  if u is a simple graph **then**
    Q is an ending position;
    case value of $<\Pi(u, T_w), \Pi(F_w, u)>$ is
      when $<\emptyset, \emptyset>$ the game is an 'empty draw'
      when $<\neg\emptyset, \emptyset>$ p_1 wins;
      when $<\emptyset, \neg\emptyset>$ p_2 wins;
      when $<\neg\emptyset, \neg\emptyset>$ the game is a 'nonempty draw'
    end case;
  end if;
  if u is a negative context of the form $\neg c$;
    $s:$ = the set of graphs in *referent*(c);
    the successor to Q is $<p_2, project, s, w, r>$;
  else u is a modal context of the form $\Delta(c)$;
    $s:$ = the set graphs in referent(c);
    $r:$ = the accessibility relation associated with Δ;
    if Δ is an existential modal operator **then**
      the successors to Q are the positions $<p_1, project, s, w', r>$
      where w' is any world such that $w \: r \: w'$;
    else Δ is a universal modal operator
      the successor to Q is $<p_2, select\_world, s, w, r>$;
  end if;
  end if;

- From a position $Q = <p_1, select\_world, \{u_1, ..., u_n\}, w, r>$, the successors are of the form $<p_2, project, \{u_1, ..., u_n\}, w', r>$ where w' is any element of W such that $w \: r \: w'$.

- A position $Q = <p_1, select, \{\}, w, r>$ is an ending position where p_2 wins. From a position $Q = <p_1, select, \{u_1, ..., u_n\}, w, r>$, the successors are the positions of the form $<p_2, reduce, \{u_i\}, w, r>$, where i is any integer from 1 to n.

This evaluation game is roughly the same as that proposed by Sowa. *Credulous* starts with a stack of graphs. If this stack is empty, *Credulous* wins. If the stack is not empty, *Credulous* iterates through the stack, projecting all simple graphs (propagating the substitutions of referents to coreferent concepts) and skipping complex graphs. *Sceptic*'s moves consist in selecting a graph in the modified stack. If the graph selected by *Sceptic* is a simple graph, the game terminates by evaluating the semantic status of this graph in the model defined by the text. If the graph selected by *Sceptic* begins with a negation, *Sceptic* becomes in charge of projecting the nested graphs, which become the new stack. Stated otherwise, entering a negated context launches a new game where the tasks of the players are reversed.

The only difference with Sowa's evaluation game is when *Sceptic* selects a complex graph introduced by a modal operator from the stack. If this is an existential operator, *Credulous* chooses a new world accessible from the first by the relation associated with the modal operator. Then *Credulous* plays again, with a new stack. If the modal operator is a universal operator, it is *Sceptic* who selects a world. These rules reflect the following axioms of possible world semantics:

- $\Diamond P(x)$ is true in w if and only if $P(x)$ is true in at least one of the worlds accessible from w by the accessibility relation associated with the modal operator.
- $\Box P(x)$ is true in w if and only if $P(x)$ is true in all the worlds accessible from w by the accessibility relation associated with the modal operator.

Definition: Let $C = <W,R>$ be a complex open world representing the content of a discourse D. Let G be an evaluation game on C starting from $<Credulous, project, s, w, \_>$.

if *Credulous* has a winning strategy in G, D *supports* statements s.
if *Sceptic* has a winning strategy in G, D *contradicts* statements s
if G is an 'empty-draw', D is *neutral* with respect to statements s.
if G is a 'nonempty-draw', D is *inconsistent* with respect to s.

7 Some critiques of the conceptual graph model

Despite the fact that Sowa's clarification really was a great step forward, I believe that the application of the conceptual graphs to the analysis of social communication is still problematic. Some of these problems are evoked below in the form of a list of seven critiques.

1. Sowa's way of structuring concepts by using a hierarchical lattice is especially *problematic when handling concepts that denote classes*, or sets of individuals. Indeed, the 'bourgeoisie' is a class, while a 'bourgeois' is not, and therefore, it is impossible to regard the second as a child of the first. But on the other hand, we would like to see the second inheriting most of the features of the first. Since it can only be achieved by making 'worker' a child of 'labour class', we face two contradictory requirements. Sowa's approach does not fit well with social discourse, which makes frequent use of social categories and classes.

2. The existential nature of conceptual graphs results, at the semantic level, in an *asymmetric treatment of negative and positive general statements*. While it is possible to give a semantic reality to 'no worker is exploited' by a simple graph placed in F it is impossible do the same with 'all workers are exploited'. As we have seen before, the graph corresponding to the last statement has two levels of nested concepts. Therefore, it can be placed neither in F which accepts only the nested part of one-level nested graphs, nor in T which accepts only simple graphs. We are then constrained to transform the general statement into all the individual statements it subsumes. In practice, it means that we have to put in T as many graphs of the form 'worker #i is exploited' as there are different workers in T. Although such processes can be made automatic, everyone will agree that it is rather inconvenient, especially in terms of information storage.

3. *The asymmetry might lead to faulty generalisations*. If a text mentions an extraordinary case (for example 'surprisingly, the worker John is not exploited') without mentioning any of the ordinary cases (implicit in the adverb 'surprisingly'), and if the coder does not provide the implicit information in the form of at least one of the ordinary cases ('the worker Jim is exploited'), the evaluation game can demonstrate that the extraordinary case is a general rule ('the workers are not exploited')! This is an important practical shortcoming of Sowa's semantics.

4. *The asymmetry allows an exception to block a correct generalization*. Let us imagine that the text indeed speaks of a lot of other workers that are exploited and mentions the exceptional case of John, a non-exploited worker. Then, about the exploitation of the workers, the text will be found inconsistent. Therefore the generalisation is blocked by a single exception. In content analysis, it is easy to see that this awkward handling of weighted assertions could be a real handicap.

5. More fundamentally, if Sowa's game-theoretical semantics easily generalize to non-standard logics, in doing so, they cannot but use

Kripke's possible world semantics. Since *these semantics are useless in practice*, the only solution is to switch to the corresponding proof-theoretic methods. Concretely, it means that the query process has to be handled by a genuine demonstrator in modal logic. Such a demonstrator is a black box in the eyes of the social scientist. This opacity results in an unacceptable loss of control over the query process.

6 The use of nested contexts leads to redundant representations in which the same concepts must appear in many contexts. More economical representations should be adopted.

7 Finally, the intensive use of contexts *weakens the semantic unity* of the graphs. Indeed, the arrows cannot cross the border of the nested contexts. This results in a lack of connexity of the general semantic net representing a text. In fact, since these semantic connections are one of the interests of social scientists, their inability to cross context borders is a real weakness.

All the critiques listed above develop more or less the same idea: when practical problems crop up, the complexity required to achieve logical correctness often turns out to be as dangerous as the lack of logical foundations which characterizes *ad hoc* methods.

Conclusion

The purpose of the first part of this chapter was to give a brief survey of semantic networks. So many kinds of network have been proposed during the last two decades that the expression 'semantic networks' is often more confusing than enlightening. I felt it necessary to circumscribe the research area which will be explored in the following chapters. This area is that of connectionist networks with local representations. These networks are genuine dynamical systems, but use symbolic representations. This may seem disconcerting to the reader who is aware that one of the main interests of the connectionist paradigm is to give a sub-symbolic foundation to cognitive processes. Furthermore, I admit that examples of connectionist approaches to semantic networks are not very numerous. However, in my view, this is regrettable since such types of formalism allow one to articulate symbolic and sub-symbolic processing. To be sure, the main appeal of parallel distributed processing lies in its learning capacities. And no similar learning is possible with symbolic networks, albeit dynamic. However, connectionist symbolic networks are hybrid models, which borrow from the symbolic paradigm its meaningful representations, and from the connectionist paradigm, the flexibility of its continuous representations. One should indeed distinguish, within the desirable features of connectionist sub-symbolic networks, two dimensions. The first one, which is the learning dimension, will not be exploited in this book. The second dimension, which is the expressivity of continuous representation (Victorri 1994), will be intensively exploited. Evaluations, in the model proposed in the following chapters, will indeed be defined on a continuous interval, and the calculus of ideological consistency will use continuous functions. More precisely, evaluation will be defined as a continuous representation, and ideological consistency will be defined as a trajectory on a multi-dimensional continuous space. In this sense, the semantic networks used in this book are connectionist.

Cognitive science has hosted extensive debates on the strength and the limits of the connectionist paradigm. The paradigm itself may be divided between a weak and a strong version. Weak connectionism, which is sometimes called implementational connectionism (Plunkett 1995), assumes that parallel distributed processing is simply a lower level layer of cognition, which, as far as symbolic processes are concerned, is under the control of the symbolic layer. In other words, implementational connectionism is more realistic than traditional, computational models of cognition, but it does not modify our vision of symbolic reasoning. Within this version of connectionism, cognition remains a symbolic engine, with its own, independent logic – except at the implementational level. In contrast, strong connectionism claims that our vision of symbolic processes is deeply modified by the new insights of parallel distributed processing. This book adheres to the strong version of the connectionist paradigm. The models of evaluative cognitive processes which will be presented in the later chapters will indeed have some features that are ordinarily absent from symbolic processing. Among these features, I submit, are non-linearity, connexity, and continuity. These are abstract, formal properties. However, what is at stake is a set of related features, such as non-intentionality, graduality, and unconsciousness of the cognitive processes, which are indirectly achieved by connectionist models.

In the second part of this chapter, I have argued that purely symbolic formalisms, and in particular, logical formalisms, are not adequate for the purpose of linguistic modelling and discourse representation. This position is not new, and I have not reiterated the philosophical and linguistic arguments which support it.[5] Much more simply, I have shown that even conceptual graphs, which are the most elaborate attempt to date to combinine language, logic, knowledge and discourse in a unique and simple framework, still raise a certain number of practical problems when applied to the representation of discourse content. I therefore call for yet another type of formalism, inspired from conceptual graphs, but which is free from the denotational perspective.

6
STYLED SEMANTIC NETWORKS

Introduction

The term 'styled', in the title of this chapter, means neither that styled semantic networks (SSNs) are stylish, nor that they are designed to reflect writing styles – even if they indeed give a flavour of the style of the discourse they represent. In a more prosaic way, the word 'styled' is borrowed from the vocabulary of word processing, where a style summarizes the font, size and face of a piece of text. In SSNs, a large amount of information is conveyed by the style of the text which labels vertices and edges of the networks.

SSNs are not a graph language with a precise syntax. They are not a formalism in which one can easily distinguish between well-formed and ill-formed expressions. They do not have a translation into logic. They are simply a mode of representation of discourse which helps us to experiment on evaluative meaning effects. There is no fixed translation from natural language into SSNs, and I do not claim that this process of translation can be automated. All SSNs provide is a protocol of representation. This protocol consists in a set of rules of thumb, and of typical examples.

SSNs are shaped by two main ambitions. The first one is to allow the representation, at the semantic level, of the information that is necessary to perform discourse-driven evaluative reasoning. This entails that the ambiguities that have an impact on evaluative processes that accompany discourse understanding must be resolved,[1] and that two readings of the same sentence which differ at the evaluative level must lead to two distinct representations.

The second ambition is to propose a mode of representation that, despite its non-logical nature, can support a certain number of inference principles, or at least, a certain number of procedures of information retrieval. This leads me to propose an operation of projection of a graph u into a graph v. If the graph u represents an hypothesis regarding a piece of content, and if the graph v represents the content of a text, then the projection of u into v tests whether the text supports the hypothesis or not. I will briefly discuss the computational problems raised by this operation.

There is a trade off between the two objectives. Increasing the subtlety of the representations in order to allow a better treatment of evaluative meaning effects renders information retrieval more difficult. Among the two objectives, the first one will prevail. I will not attempt to develop a level of information retrieval able to keep pace with the expressivity of the representation. This choice can be justified by the fact that in later chapters, I will provide these representations with another form of evaluative reasoning, which depends crucially on the expressivity of the representations.

1 A relational model

As with all semantic networks, styled networks are relational models. Thus the first question to arise is the following. What parts of discourse should become relations, and what parts should become the arguments of these relations? To answer this question, let us remember that the usual strategy of semantic network designers is to keep the number of relational primitives to a minimum, while putting no limit on the number of types. As a result, standard semantic networks pick up their relational primitives in the set of semantic case relations (TOPIC, AGENT, GOAL, etc.) or within the set of syntactic relations (SUBJECT, ATTRIBUTE, etc.). They select their types within the expressions allowed by their terminological language. Usually, the types are common nouns, verbs, and in the more elaborate cases, constructions such as MAN WITH A CAR OR A MOTORBIKE AND WITH NO BOAT. In addition, the assertional language is often a simple subset of predicate calculus, and therefore, most of the surface structure of a sentence is left out when it is 'translated' from natural language into the formal language of the network.

Because of the scarcity of the relational primitives and because the assertional language if very often limited to the conjunction of existential statements (see, for example, the conceptual graphs, in the last chapter) semantic networks are very rough languages. However, this simplicity is not necessarily a disadvantage. It makes the representation process easier (though less satisfying). More fundamentally, this strategy of simplicity is related to the idea that the conceptual level is simpler than the linguistic level. The underlying conception is that natural language, with all its ambiguities and all its redundancies, is not the language of thought.

Even if I do not share these conceptions, I will follow them to the extent that I, too, limit the number of relational primitives. But my reasons for doing so are different. In the dynamic semantic networks that I propose in the next chapter, the dynamics are parameterized by the weights affecting the relations. Therefore, most of the dynamics are determined by the relations. Thus, keeping the number of relational primitives beneath a certain limit will allow us to keep the number of parameters under a certain limit as well.

The basic idea of the formalism is to represent composition operations by relations:

- Functions of complementation (of a noun, of a verb, or of an adjective) are represented by relational primitives indicating the semantic nature of the complementation. The most common primitives are OBJT (object), PTNT (patient), MEAN, MANR (manner), GOAL, BENF (beneficiary), CAUS (cause), TIME, LOC (location), etc.
- The composition of a verb with its subject is represented by the relational primitives AGENT and TOPIC, and, in case of passive voice, by the primitives OBJT and PTNT.
- The verb *to be* is either represented by a relational primitive expressing attribution (ATTR), or by the primitive expressing predication (PRED) or by the primitive expressing subsumption (ISA).

To determine which kind of linguistic entities can be the terms of the relations, I draw upon the distinction between open- and closed-class forms. I will call 'open-class expression' any linguistic expression that has an open-class item as its lexical head (see Note 2, Chapter 4).

- Concept boxes can contain any open-class expression, or any closed-class item that is a reference to, or an anaphor of an open-class expression.

In other words, a concept box cannot contain a determiner only, an inflexion mark only, or a preposition only. It must contain, as its lexical head, either an open class item, or a pronoun referring to an open-class expression.

Before going further, it may be useful to give an example. Consider the sentence 'He [Caesar] has brought many captives home to Rome, Whose ransoms did the general coffers fill.' (cf. Appendix B, lines 16–17). It can be represented, among several other possibilities, as in Network 6.1.

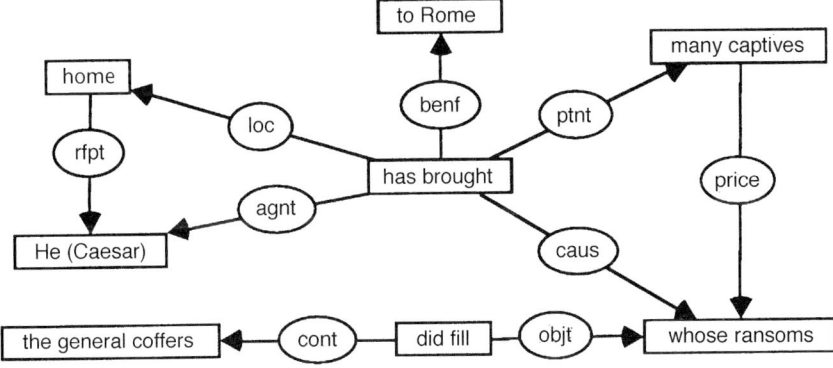

Network 6.1

In this representation, all closed-class items (to, he, whose, the, etc.) are contained within context boxes, along with other open-class items ensuring that the resulting expressions are open-class expressions. All operations of complementation and composition are represented by relational primitives (LOCATION, BENEFICIARY, CONTAINER, PRICE, AGENT, OBJECT, PATIENT). The indexical 'home' is anchored by the relational primitive rfpt, which stands for 'reference point'. A relation of causality has been added between [HAS BROUGHT] and [WHOSE RANSOMS], because it is implicit in the original text. As the reader will notice, although the representation is fairly simple, some coding choice might have been different. Meaning is always a complex matter.

2 Tense

Tense is represented, within the labels, either by the tense of verbs, or by temporal modalities, like 'yesterday'. Again, since not all verbs map to concepts, it is sometimes useful to have another indication of tense rather than the verbal form. A more fundamental reason is that several temporal meanings may correspond to one single verbal form, and that several verbal forms may have the same temporal meaning. I have chosen to represent tense, not just by verbal forms, but also by the colours of the concepts and of the links. Although this is convenient on computer screens, these colours cannot appear in this 'black and white' paper.

One may assign a different colour to each fundamental temporal dimension, past, present and future. Since duration and achievement are important for evaluative processes, aspect must also be taken into consideration. Different intensity of blue, for example, may correspond to different aspects of an action of the past. With this solution, the general temporal orientation always remains available, as well as more subtle indications concerning aspect. Note that colours indicate time and aspect, but no other kind of information conveyed by verbal forms, like the information of alethic nature conveyed by the tenses of verbal moods.

3 Negation

In almost all semantic networks, and even in networks which aim at representing natural language, negation is the logical negation. On the contrary, in SSNs, I draw my inspiration directly from linguistic negation. Thus, negation applies directly to the concepts (most often, to concepts representing verbs), and is visualized, within the labels, by the linguistic negation. However, because semantic networks represent some verbs (in particular auxiliaries) by relations, it is also possible to apply negation to the links. Negation is then visualized, as in logic, by the symbol '¬' preceding the label of the link.

Linguistic negation, because of its flexibility, is potentially ambiguous. To eliminate ambiguities, the scope of negation has to be represented. Relations and concepts that are under the scope of a negation are displayed in italic. It has been shown elsewhere that when negation scope is taken into account, it is possible to generalize Sowa's fundamental operation of projection to graphs incorporating negation (Malrieu 1994).

- *Negation* is represented, either within the concept-boxes, by the linguistic markers of negation, or within the relation label, by the symbol '¬'. The scope of the negation is indicated by the italics in the concept and relation labels. If there is an (undirected) path in italic from a negated concept *u* to another *v*, we will say that *v* is under the scope of the negation affecting *u*. By convention, when the scope of a negation does not extend beyond a particular concept, this concept is displayed in normal face.

Let us give a few examples of the representation of negation. Let us consider the sentence 'I come to bury Caesar, not to praise him.' There are, at least two possible readings of this sentence. This ambiguity is mainly due to that of *to bury*, which can equally mean *to get rid of*, *to forget*, or *to mourn*. If the last sense is retained, and if it is also assumed that Antony does not express any reluctance to praise Caesar, his discourse can be represented as in Network 6.2.

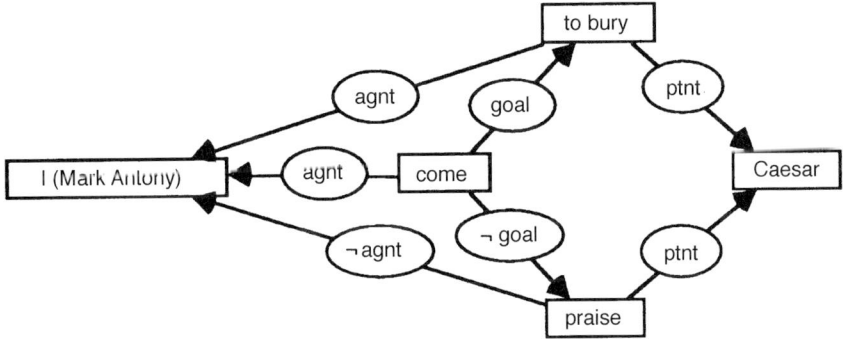

Network 6.2

We may interpret this representation as stating that it is not Antony's goal to praise Caesar. However, we cannot interpret it as stating that Antony's goal is to avoid praising Caesar. If, on the contrary, it is assumed that Antony expresses an intention to forget Caesar, and to deliberately avoid praising him, our sentence must be translated as in Network 6.3.

When, as in network 6.2, negation only applies to relations, we will say that it is *focused*. When negation is focused, it applies to complements of the verb rather than to the verb itself.

Not all primitives are likely to be met under the scope of a negation. I will assume that logical 'meta-primitives', like IMPL, cannot be found under the scope of a negation. I will also assume that the epistemic primitive BELV is never found under the scope of the negation because 'X does not believe in P' can always be transformed into 'X believes in not P'. For some others, this absence from the scope of a negation is the result of the fact that the same

STYLED SEMANTIC NETWORKS

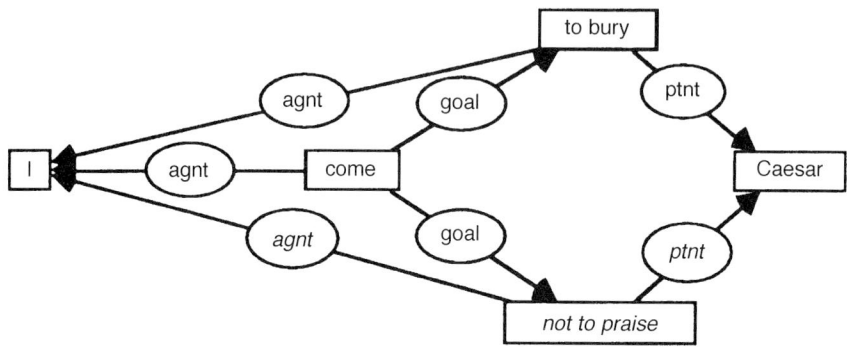

Network 6.3

semantic effect can be achieved by negating them directly. The next proposition describes this alternative as an inference rule.

Proposition: Some relational primitives, like INST (for 'instrument'), MANR, FREQ (for 'frequency'), TIME, MEAN, or QUANT (for 'quantity'), tend to *focus negation*, that is, they enable the following inference:

This property is a simple inferential feature of linguistic negation. When a verb followed by a verb complement of manner, mean, time, quantity, is negated, the negation bears on the complement. For example,

He did not do it on purpose ⇒ He did it, not on purpose.
He did not do it with a knife ⇒ He did it, not with a knife.
He did not do it very often ⇒ He did it, not very often.

On the contrary, some relational primitives do not allow the inference. For example, the relational primitives GOAL and BENF do not focus negation. In addition, there are potential conflicts between several relational primitives that focus negation. Will some primitives have a priority over some others? I will not deal with this problem here because it clearly cannot be solved just at the semantic level, and would require us to go back to the semiotic level, taking into account the order of the complements, punctuation, and accentuation in order to be able to determine which relations negation is focused on.

Remark: Styled representations of scopes are often more convenient than other representations, such as large borders. To illustrate this point, consider the sentence 'He could not avoid the disaster he caused'. If I were using borders to indicate the scope of negations, I would have to choose between several solutions, none of which are really satisfying.

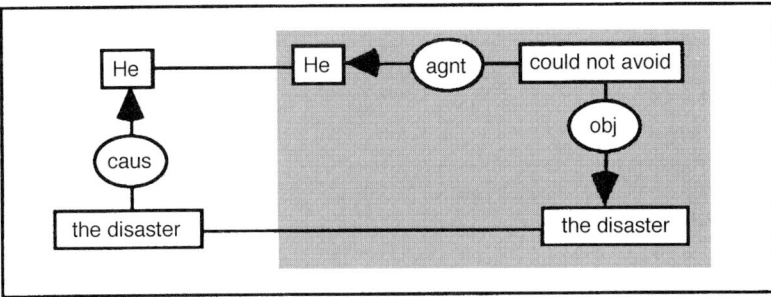

Network 6.4

Network 6.4 has the advantage of making extremely clear the scope of the negation. But it has the drawback of being redundant (concepts must be repeated within and without the scope, and some links must be added to indicate that they are indeed the same).

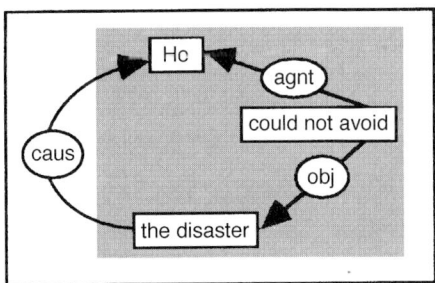

Network 6.5

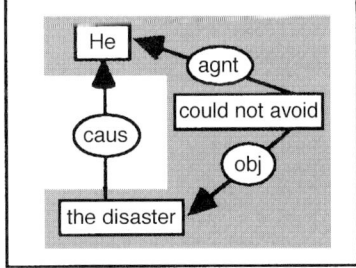

Network 6.6

The two representations numbered 6.5 and 6.6 are more economical. However, curved relations and non-rectangular scopes raise some problems at the level of computer implementations. Because programming graphic interfaces for semantic networks is a cumbersome task with no intrinsic interest, these secondary problems must be avoided by adopting the kind of representation which requires minimal graphic-programming efforts.

4 Quantification and determination

To describe objects and classes of objects, natural language uses determiners (and the absence of determiners) associated with nouns and their marks of number, as in the terms 'a newspaper', 'the newspaper', 'the newspapers' and

STYLED SEMANTIC NETWORKS

'newspapers'. It is also possible to use classifying adjectives, as in the term 'British newspapers'. It is also possible to use complements of the noun, as in the term 'the newspaper of the town', and subordinate propositions, as in 'the newspapers that took his defence'.

When they are included within sentences, these terms receive properties, or enter as arguments in predicates. Logical reconstruction of natural language often assumes that the quantification of these predicates is a threefold phenomenon. It includes a *quantifier*, a *restrictor* and a *scope* (Sowa 1991). The quantifier is sometimes explicit (*all, one, every*, etc.) and often implicit (*the* + plural, *a* + singular, etc.).

I will distinguish, within what Sowa calls the restrictor of a concept, between the type and the restrictor (in a more narrow sense). This distinction corresponds roughly to the distinction between *genus* and *differentiae* in the Aristotelian theory of definition. Therefore, in expressions such as 'the blue-collars', the quantification has a type (blue-collar) and no restrictor. In expressions like 'the blue-collars of the steel industry' or, 'the blue-collars that work in the steel industry', blue-collar is the type, and the rest of the expression is the restrictor.

Finally, I will assume that every relation attached to a quantified concept, and that does not belong to the restrictor of this concept, belongs to the scope of this concept. Therefore, it will not be necessary to indicate graphically the scope of quantification.

- *Linguistics markers of quantification* (adverbs, determiner + inflexions) stand within the concept boxes. The relative pronouns which introduce subordinates that restrict the extension of the concepts stand within the concept boxes too.
- The *restrictor* of a concept is indicated by bold face. If, starting from a quantified concept *u*, one can reach a concept *v* by following an undirected path in bold face, then *v* belongs to the restrictor of *u*.

As a first example of these representational rules, consider the sentence 'the workers that remained voted for the strike'. Its representation could be that of Network 6.7.

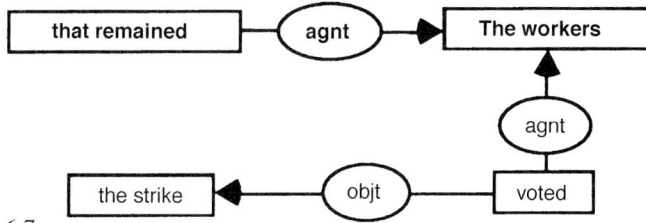

Network 6.7

In this graph, the quantifier is the form *the* + *plural*, the restrictor is the type WORKER and the subgraph (AGNT) → [THAT REMAINED]. The scope of the quantification is the rest of the graph.

A universal quantification may be under the scope of another universal quantification. In that case, since the two restrictors are both indicated by the bold typeface, there are some potential confusions. In practice though, very few ambiguities can arise.

Because typefaces can combine, it is possible to represent in *bold + italic* a quantification which is under the scope of a negation or a negation which belongs to a restrictor. Confusions between these two situations cannot arise because either the scope contains the whole restrictor, or the restrictor contains the whole scope. Still mimicking natural language, it will be assumed that when a quantification is under the scope of a negation, the negation applies to the quantification itself. To represent the sentence 'the government did not help all the people that deserved assistance', Network 6.8 will be drawn. Again, because the concept [ASSISTANCE] is the limit of

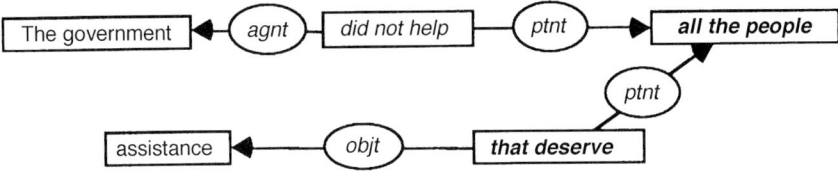

Network 6.8

both the scope and the restrictor, it does not need to be displayed in a special typeface. And for the sentence 'the government did not solve any problems', Network 6.9 will be preferred.

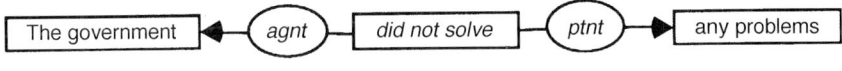

Network 6.9

In natural languages, although there are some unambiguous quantifiers like 'all', quantifiers often get their meaning in context. In French, for example, the determiner 'l' has very different functions in the two sentences 'l'homme entre dans la chambre' and 'l'homme est un roseau pensant'. Until now, I have privileged readability, and in the display of the SSNs, the linguistic form of quantification has been retained. To eliminate ambiguities, a semantic theory of quantification is needed. Since the issue is complex, and would require a whole lifetime of study, a minimal theory of quantification will be adopted. Let us consider the following list of statements:

(a) This American loves his country
(b) John and I love America, our country
(c) There is an American that loves his country
(d) Some Americans love their country
(e) Few (many) Americans love their country

(f) A small (large) proportion (number) of Americans love their country
(g) An American loves his country
(h) Americans love their country
(i) All Americans love their country

It will be assumed that these examples of quantification can be organized into the three traditional categories used in logic.

1. *Individual* statements (a, b) concern definite determiners, either singular or plural. They express factual properties about known individuals and groups of individuals. In logic, this corresponds to the application of a predicate to a constant, which, in model theory, maps onto an individual of the universe of discourse.
2. *Existential statements* (c, d) concern indefinites, either singular or plural. They express factual properties about unknown or unspecified individuals and groups of individuals. In logic, they correspond to the formulae introduced by an existential quantifier. Existential statements are very useful for querying a knowledge base or for information retrieval. In this context, they can be interpreted as queries of the form 'Is there an X of type T that P?'.
3. *Universal statements* express properties that hold for the elements of a class. Within universal statements, one can make several further distinctions.
   - *Gradual* statements (e, f) express to what extent a proposition holds.
   - *Prototypical* and *notional* statements (g) express prototypical properties and properties that characterize a notion.
   - *General* statements (h) express properties that hold for a class of individuals, but with possible exceptions.
   - *Truly universal* statements (i) express general properties without exceptions.

When the quantifier is individual, and when there is a restrictor larger than a simple type, we are facing a phenomenon known in linguistics as determination (by relatives). We have an example of such constructions in Shakespeare's text with the sentence 'The evil that men do lives after them' (cf. Appendix B, line 3). In this sentence, the relative determines (narrows) the meaning of the noun group. It is possible to represent such semantic units in the way that we represent restrictors, that is, by means of the bold typeface (Network 6.10).

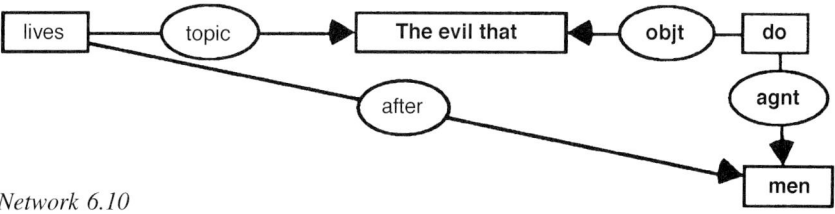

Network 6.10

The categories listed above are working categories, and I do not claim that they form the ground for a satisfactory theory of quantification within natural language. They will be useful later in this chapter, when a projection operation will be defined.

5 Modalities and modal aspectualization

Most modalities are expressed, in natural language, by adverbs. Nothing prevents us from representing each adverb by a concept. However, modalities are also expressed by some special tenses and moods of the verbs. This is the traditional issue, in grammar, of the *value* of verb tenses. Drawing upon this classical approach, the concepts of SSNs will either be *real*, *potential* or *unreal*. However, these notions will receive a slightly different meaning from their usual meaning in grammar. The modality *real* corresponds to asserted facts. The modality *potential* corresponds to facts that, *in the context*, are only hypothetical. The modality *unreal* corresponds to facts that, *in the context*, could not have happened, cannot happen, or are/ were unlikely.

- The modality *real* is displayed by thin, solid concept boxes. The modality *potential* is displayed by thick, hash pattern boxes. The modality *unreal* is displayed in thin, hash pattern boxes.

From an evaluative point of view, hypotheses and alternatives to reality are used either to praise or to criticize some actor, idea or behaviour. Thus, the important point in a supposition is what it reveals about the people, ideas or phenomena concerned. Consider the evaluative effects of the following discourse: 'If the prime minister had done his duty, the poor would suffer less.' The key elements which determine the evaluative effects produced by this sentence are the actor's intentions and his responsibility for the event or absence of event. Since the text seems to reproach the prime minister with his faults, there is certainly something in his intentions, personality, or, simply, in his behaviour, that prevented him from doing his duty. If external, contingent circumstances had imposed this breach of duty, the critique would be weakened. If the prime minister had tried to do his duty, the argument could even be favourable to him.

On the one hand, if we want evaluative semantics to distinguish between all these meanings and to model how they arise, the formal language should incorporate all necessary parameters. Among the parameters that enter into evaluative reasoning, are the actor's intentions, capacities, his knowledge concerning the feasibility of the action, means and manners of the action, etc. On the other hand, these parameters are often lumped together or implicit within natural language, and a formal language should be able to reduce their number whenever some of them are redundant or not available. Contrary to modal operators in logic, which apply to predicates, I propose that different modals should apply to each argument of a predicate. In practice, it means that a modal value is associated with every relation. This modal value represents the contribution of the concepts that surround a supposition to the modal value of the supposition. If the agent, for example, because he wants to perform the action, or because he is able to perform it, renders it possible for the action to happen, the AGNT relation will receive the modal value 'potential'. If the agent tends to render the action impossible, the AGNT relation will receive the modal value 'unreal'.

- The pen pattern of relation ovals indicates the modality of the relation (thin, solid = real; thick, hash = potential; thin, hash = unreal). This modality often indicates the contribution of the relation to the modality of the concepts to which it is attached.

I underline the fact that although this type of semantic information must be inferred by the interpreter, this information is necessary for evaluative reasoning, and therefore, that it should be present in any satisfying semantic representation. This is also a good place to emphasize one of the advantages of semantic networks, and more generally, of relational models over traditional semantic theories based on meaning functions. In these theories, modalities affect predicates as a whole, and it is not possible to decompose the modalities along each argument of the predicate. On the contrary, the aspectualized nature of semantic networks makes it easy to encode each argument as a modal factor. I will therefore call the representation of modalities that has been sketched above, a *modal aspectualization*.

Modal aspectualization helps to represent conditionals. Let us consider the sentence 'If it were so, it was a grievous fault', which refers to Brutus's argument 'Caesar was ambitious' (cf. Appendix B, line 6). The asserted part of the sentence is that ambition, for someone like Caesar, is indeed a grievous fault. Thus the relations (ISA) and (ATTR), in Network 6.11, are *real*. But in any case, it is not sure that Caesar is ambitious, and that he committed this fault. This uncertainty is reflected, within the following SSN, by the *potential* modality of the relations (ATTR) and (AGNT), and the concepts [AMBITIOUS], [FAULT] and [GRIEVOUS].

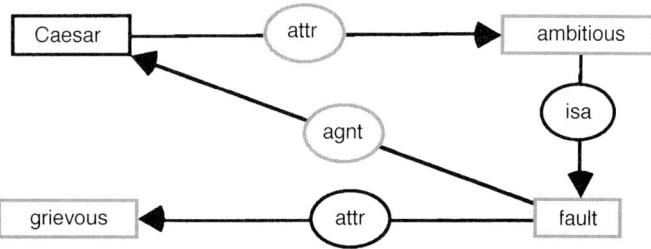

Network 6.11

One may even assume that Caesar was not ambitious and that he therefore did not commit a grievous fault. In that case, we have to modify the modality as in Network 6.12. Here, the *unreal* modality of [AMBITION] and [FAULT]

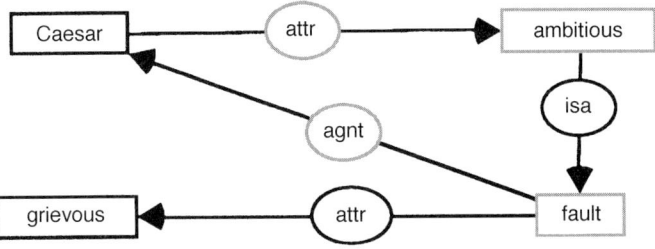

Network 6.12

indicate that we do not believe in Caesar's ambition and guilt. The modality of (ATTR) and (AGNT) is *unreal* because [CAESAR] 'dis-realizes' [AMBITION] and [FAULT].

6 Interrogatives and modalities

Besides their modal value, concepts and relations also have a semiotic status. 'Assertive' is the default semiotic mood. Although it is not as common as in dialogue, the interrogative mood is indeed present in written texts. Intensively studied by pragmatics, it has also some special evaluative effects, and therefore, must be neatly represented within evaluative semantics.

As with negation, interrogation is applied locally. It is marked, within the labels of the concepts, by the '?' tag. Most often, 'yes-no' questions are easily represented by adding an interrogation mark after the main verb of the sentence. When the verb is an auxiliary that does not translate into a concept, the interrogation mark may affect non-verbal concepts. For example the question 'Did this Caesar seem ambitious?', which refers to the fact that Caesar has filled the general coffers of Rome (cf. Appendix B. line 18), would be translated into Network 6.13.[2]

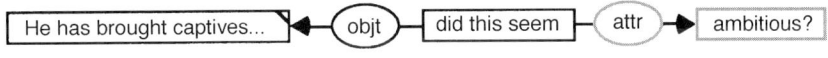

Network 6.13

The concepts affected by an interrogation are not asserted. Therefore, they are not 'real' from the modal point of view. Most often, a question is similar to an hypothesis waiting for confirmation or refutation. Therefore, as in the previous example, the concepts to which interrogation applies, and the links that are attached to them must be considered as 'potential'.

In some contexts, such as rhetorical questions, this modal value need not be 'potential'. The characteristic of rhetorical questions is that they have an implicit answer. In this case, the concept to which interrogation applies is in fact either asserted or negated. In dialogues, even when the question suggests its answer, a denial is always possible. However, within written text with no definite audience, the answers to rhetorical questions are contained within the questions themselves. Therefore, the modal value of the concept representing the interrogation should be either 'real' or 'unreal' rather than 'potential'.

In the case of 'yes-no' rhetorical interrogatives, when the implicit answer is 'yes', this modal value is 'real'. When the implicit answer is 'no', this modal value is 'unreal'. Network 6.14. takes into account the bias internal to the question.

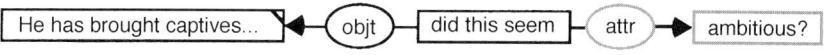

Network 6.14

Interrogatives containing a negation are almost always rhetorical interrogatives suggesting a positive answer. One may even assume that interro-negation has stronger evaluative effects than simple assertion. For example, the rhetorical interrogation 'Did the French not lose the war in Algeria?' has a stronger effect than the statement 'The French lost the war in Algeria', because the interrogation forces the interpreter to actively subscribe to the statement. Interro-negatives can be represented as other rhetorical questions (Network 6.15).

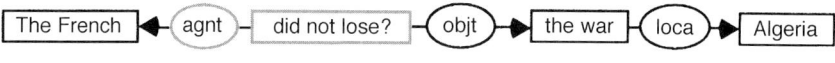

Network 6.15

Since interrogation is applied locally, partial interrogations are also easily represented within DSNs. Returning to Shakespeare, if we assume that the question 'What cause withholds you then to mourn for him?' (cf. Appendix B, line 31) is a true interrogative, then it is naturally translated into Network 6.16.

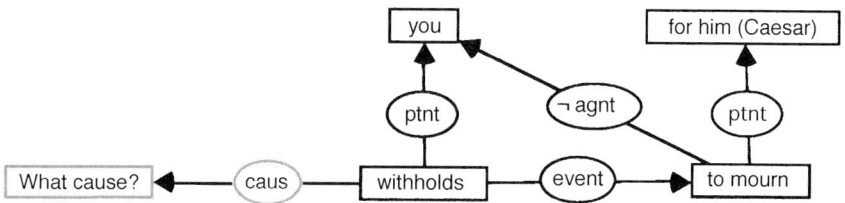

Network 6.16

However, one should not conclude from the previous graph that partial interrogations make no use of modalities. There are indeed a great variety of rhetorical partial interrogations. Once again, the bias contained in the question is expressed by the *unreal* modality (Network 6.17).

In conclusion to this subsection about interrogation, I stress the fact that the conjunction of a local application of interrogation and the use of

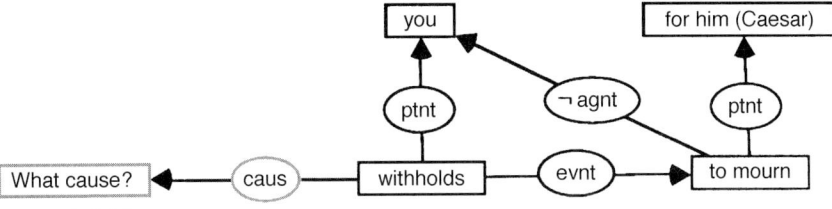

Network 6.17

modalities allows one to propose distinct semantic representations for each reading of interrogatives. Most important perhaps, this task is performed without moving away from the linguistic expression of interrogatives, and without superimposing any artificial taxonomy on the linguistic data.

Despite the ability of SSNs to represent interrogatives, one problem at least remains unsolved. A certain class of rhetoric interrogatives, such as 'Shall we accept the prime minister's disregard?', calls for a moral reaction from the (ideal) audience. The implicit answer is therefore 'We should not' rather than 'not'. And indeed, if a moral reaction is possible, this is because a moral apathy is also considered possible. The action is considered as morally impossible, but effectively possible. Thus, one cannot represent this kind of mixture of possibility and impossibility by the modality 'unreal', and one should stick, as we did in our example, to the modality 'potential', which does not commit us to a definitive reading. The drawback of this prudent strategy is that it becomes impossible to diagnose from the semantic level that this is indeed a rhetorical question, since its representation is the same as non-rhetoric questions. I will show later how, at the level of dynamic representations, the interpretative behaviours of the semantic representation depend on whether we are dealing with a rhetorical or non-rhetorical question.

7 Attitude and speech act reports

When a discourse reports a speech act or a belief, the content of this speech act or of this belief is like another discourse embedded in the first one. Therefore, I choose to represent the content of discourse reports by nested semantic networks. These networks can also be considered as concepts of type DISCOURSE in the embedding network. As concepts, they can enter into relation with other concepts.

- The content of attitude reports and speech act reports are represented by nested semantics networks. By default, acts of belief are represented by the relation BELF (for 'has belief') and speech acts are represented by the relation STMT (for 'makes statement'), or by the relation AUTH (for 'has author').

The pair of relations BELF and STMT does not exhaust the possibilities. If one needs to distinguish between different kinds of beliefs and different kinds of speech acts, other relational primitives must be created.

Let me give an example of the representation of speech act reports. Consider the sentence 'He was my friend, faithful and loyal to me: But Brutus says he was ambitious' (cf. Appendix B, lines 13–14), that we may wish to display as in Network 6.18.

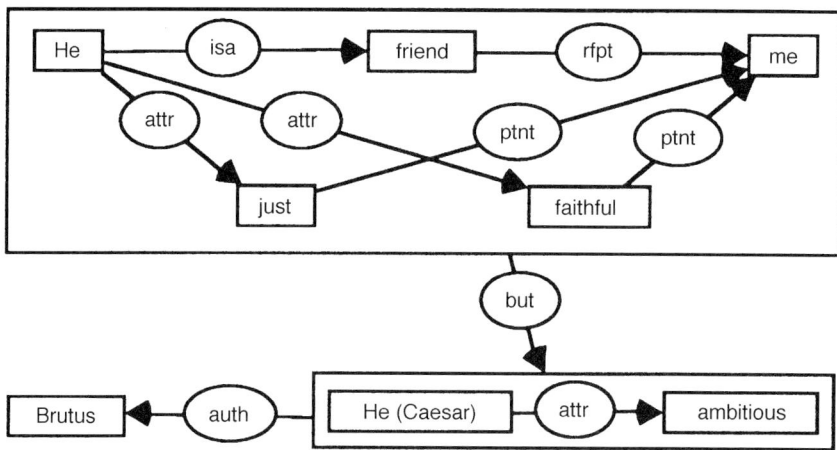

Network 6.18

The drawback of this sort of representation is that the two occurrences of [he] which both refer to Caesar, cannot be connected, or confused. However, these two occurrences are not the same (the first one refers to Mark Antony's perception of Caesar, while the second stands for Brutus' idea of Caesar), and it is therefore legitimate to insulate them. More generally, it is not desirable to draw relations across the enclosing border of a semantic network, because two concepts which are not 'at the same level' are parts of two distinct intentional processes. In particular, the evaluations of the concepts are not necessarily the same in the two intentional processes. The same remarks apply when we regard relations as the channels of meaning effects. It would make no sense to assume that the evaluation of Caesar by Mark Antony would depend on Brutus' evaluation of Caesar. This example leads me to propose that:

- Relations cannot cross the border of nested networks.

This representation rule could have been deduced from the evaluative semantics which has been proposed in Chapter 4, where I argued that verbs expressing speech acts and attitudes introduce 'opaque' contexts. In other words, the evaluation of the attitude and speech act reports does not depend on the evaluation of their content. The representation rule that forbids relations to cross network boundaries is just the 'graphic' equivalent of phenomena of semantic opacity.

Natural language is extremely flexible in the way it uses indirect discourse. One can indeed perfectly understand a sentence like 'But Brutus says that the grand Caesar was ambitious'. In such cases of polyphonic discourse, it may be useful to make an exception to the rule, and to avoid creating nested contexts for the speech act reports, as in Network 6.19. The

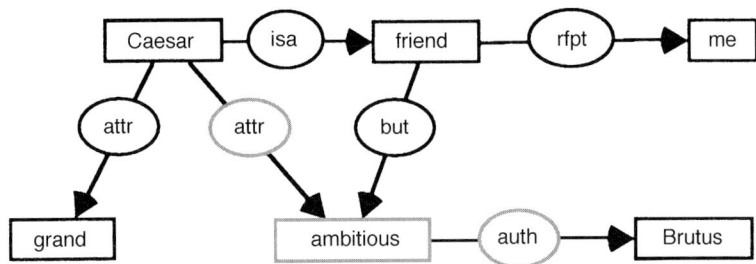

Network 6.19

advantage of this representation is that [GRAND], [CAESAR], and [AMBITIOUS] stand at the same level, and thus, that there is a potential semantic interaction between the three units. The next chapter deals with these interactions.

8 Representing discourse

As stated in Chapter 5, the connexity of network-based representations is a natural correlate of the coherence of discourse. This connexity can be increased by drawing links corresponding to coreference and anaphora. Another solution consists in eliminating all the occurrences that are redundant because they are coreferential, or at least, intentionally coreferential, that is, which refer to the same entity in the author's mind or someone's reported belief. I will adopt this solution, and extend it to anaphora. This leads to a series of simplification rules, which are applied at the last stage of the representation process.

- Within an intentional context (outermost or nested), all coreferential occurrences of pronouns except one are eliminated. The relations that were attached to them are re-attached to the remaining occurrence.
- Within an intentional context (outermost or nested), all anaphoric pronouns are eliminated. The relations that were attached to them are re-attached to the expression of which they were the anaphora.

These rules can be extended to anaphoric expressions in general. For example, to represent the discourse 'I thrice presented him a Kingly crown, which he did thrice refused: was this ambition?' (cf. Appendix B, lines 24–5), one needs first to identify what 'this' stands for. It can be assumed that 'this' refers to Caesar's refusal, as in Network 6.20.

Besides anaphora, the major linguistic instruments of discursive connexity are the connectors. It is usually assumed that connectors relate propositions,

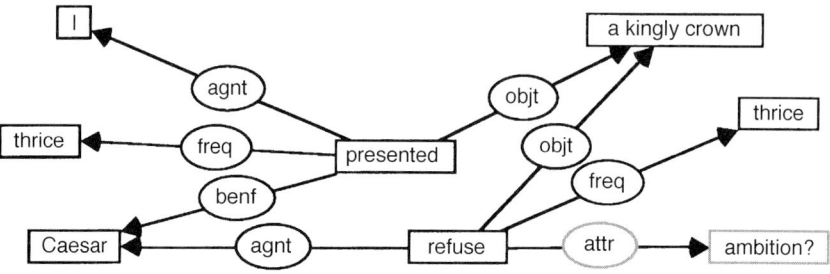

Network 6.20

and that their study belongs either to logic or to argumentation theory. Thus, within SSNs, connectors are represented by relations between propositional nodes. However, within discourses like 'he is brave but stupid', or 'he did it, but slowly' there is only one sentence where logicians would find two underlying propositions. Ducrot, who defends a propositional theory of connectors, remarks that these propositions are not easily identified.

> The elements P and Q, which according to us are coordinated by *mais*, are not necessarily identical with what precedes and what follows this connector. We mean that there is no necessary coincidence between what is articulated by *mais* and its surface environment. This happens because, on the one hand, *mais* selects some specific elements of this environment ... (Ducrot 1980: 123)

This propositional approach leads to circularity. Ducrot himself is perfectly aware of this when he concedes:

> Throughout this research [on the connector *mais*] we found ourselves in a situation which is frequent in linguistics when one attempts to describe an entity having a relational function (which is, according to us, always the case of *mais*). One has, at the beginning, more or less consciously the hope of characterizing this entity by studying the type of elements it relates to (in the case of *mais*, P and Q). However, one often discovers that these elements can only be determined on the basis of a prior conception of the relation. (Ducrot 1980: 125)

I do not claim that this sort of circularity can always be avoided in linguistics. However, for some evaluative uses of the connectors, it can be practically eliminated if instead of introducing certain propositional elements, we just 'select', as the connector does, the linguistic elements it relates. For example, in Network 6.18, I have made a propositional reading of the connector 'but'. In contrast, Network 6.19 represents a non-propositional reading of the connector. Taking my inspiration from language, I will sometimes apply connectors to expressions and not only to propositions. Thus, in SSNs, connectors relate concepts, contexts, and concepts to contexts.

Finally, discourse is sometimes extremely concise, thanks to anaphoric words such as 'so' (e.g. 'So let it be with Caesar', line 5). To represent this type of discursive shortcut, it is often necessary to introduce words that were not in the original discourse, or to duplicate those that were there. To distinguish between the parts of the concept labels that correspond to occurrences of words in the discourse, and the parts that have been added by the representation, the latter are enclosed in brackets.

9 A projection game for styled semantic networks

As noted in the introduction to this chapter, for a formalism of representation, the existence of sound inferential properties is both a guarantee of semantic validity and a good basis for the implementation of deductive systems. For the formalisms, like styled networks, that remain very close to natural language, it is likely that the inferential engine will consist of a very large number of inference rules expressing the relations between the various linguistic expressions of ideas. Because my project is to focus on evaluative inferences, and not to deal with inferences in general, I will not attempt to define a comprehensive deductive engine. Nevertheless, because the use of simple information retrieval tools may be helpful for the purpose of content-oriented analysis of discourse, I propose an operation of projection for styled networks. To facilitate the presentation of the operation, I adopt the vocabulary of game-theory.

In the previous chapter, the definition of the operation of projection on conceptual graphs has been given. Let us recall that in Sowa's formalism, when a graph u has a projection into a graph v, then v logically implies u. In the conceptual graph model, projection is restricted to simple graphs. For complex graphs with negation, Sowa proposes an 'evaluation game'. Roughly speaking, the game defines how one must enter the various nested levels of a complex graph to know whether this graph is supported by the model.

In styled semantic networks, negation and quantification are represented locally, and not by nested graphs. Therefore, styled graphs with negation and quantification are still 'flat' graphs, and are thus much more similar to Sowa's simple graphs than to his complex ones. This remark suggests that the operation of projection could be transposed to the case of styled networks. For the sake of simplicity, I restrict the operation of projection to the case of styled networks with negation, quantification and epistemic modalities. I do not deal with the problems raised by the introduction of alethic modalities. For the same reason, I will also rule out the meta-logical primitives, like IMPL (for 'implication') and OR.

As stated above, SSNs impose very few constraints on the set of possible labels. However, several labels may be occurrences of the same notion. I will therefore assume that concepts have both a *label* and a *type*. For example, the labels HAD DONE HIS DUTY and WILL DO OUR DUTY both correspond to the same type, let's say, TO DO ONE'S DUTY. As in formalisms based on inheritance, a lattice structure is imposed on the set of types. However, I have pointed out (in Chapter 4, section 8) that contrary to Sowa's approach, this lattice structure is not valid in all models because each 'ideology' defines its own type hierarchy. This multiplicity of taxonomies merely reflects the fact that, within social discourse, categories and relations between categories are not always neutral.

Definition: a concept u is a *restriction* of a concept v if

(i) v is negated, then u is negated
(ii) v is under the scope of a negation, then u is under the scope of a negation
(iii) depending on their respective quantifiers, the types and the labels of u and v satisfy the conditions summarized in Table 6.1

This definition is not intuitive, and it can be justified only in the context of the projection game.

Definition: a *projection game* $\pi(u,v)$ is a two person, zero-sum, perfect information game. One of the players is called *Credulous* and the other *Sceptic*. The styled graph u is called *Source*, and the styled graph v is called *Target*.

- At the beginning of the game, *Credulous* moves to a concept in *Source*. *Credulous* also chooses the concept in *Target* where *Sceptic* must start from. This is the first position of the game, and it is *Sceptic*'s turn to move.
- Players move, one after the other, either from a concept to an adjacent relation, or from a relation to an adjacent concept. When a player moves to a relation, he keeps in mind his orientation, that is, whether he goes counter to or along the direction of the relation. At the next turn, he cannot move back to the concept he was previously on.

Table 6.1 Unification and quantification

u\v	Existential	Individual	Universal
Existential	$t(u) \prec t(v)$	$t(u) \prec t(v)$	$t(u) \prec t(v)$
Individual	fails	label(u) = label(v)	fails
Universal	$t(u) \prec t(v)$	$t(u) \prec t(v)$	$t(u) \prec t(v)$

- If, during a move, a player enters or moves out of the restrictor of a universal quantification, then players wait to be either both on a concept or both on a relation, and they change sides, that is, they exchange their position in *Source* and *Target*.
- If, during a move, *Sceptic* enters or moves out of the scope of a negation, then players wait to be either both on a concept or both on a relation, and they change sides.
- Winning positions:
  - A position where both players are on a relation, and these relations have different labels, is a winning position for *Sceptic*. A position where both players are on a relation, and players have a different orientation is a winning position for *Sceptic*.
  - A position where *Sceptic* is on a concept u, *Credulous* on a concept v, and where v is not a restriction of u is a winning position for *Sceptic*.
  - A position where *Sceptic* is on a relation that he occupied earlier in the game is a winning position for *Credulous*.

During the game, *Credulous* wants to demonstrate that *Target* supports *Source*, and *Sceptic* wants to show the opposite. *Sceptic* explores *Source*, trying to make a move that *Credulous* cannot mimic. If *Sceptic* succeeds (provided *Credulous* plays in the best way) there is a path in *Source* that has no equivalent in *Target*, and the projection must fail. To prevent *Sceptic* from moving endlessly and to ensure that the game terminates, it is stipulated that *Sceptic* cannot move twice along the same arc.

Because negation reverses the direction of the projection, when *Sceptic* enters and goes out of the scope of the negation, players change sides. *Credulous* must follow *Sceptic*, entering and exiting negated contexts whenever *Sceptic* does so, otherwise *Sceptic* wins because of the constraints bearing on restrictions. Note that *Credulous* can enter and exit from the scope of a negation without reversing the positions. This is due to the fact that the concepts and relations that are under the scope of a negation but that are not directly negated are in fact asserted. Therefore, they can support some facts asserted in *Source*. Universal quantification also reverses the direction of the projection. But contrary to the case of negation, the direction of the projection is reversed even if *Credulous* only enters within or exits from the restrictor of a universal quantification.

Definition: there is a projection from the SSN u into the SSN v if, in the projection game $\pi(u,v)$, *Credulous* has a winning strategy.

Several examples, corresponding to the most common cases, may serve to illustrate the game.

SSNs without negation and universal quantification

For these SSNs the projection game is roughly equivalent to the projection of simple conceptual graphs. In other words, the definition of the projection game guarantees that if *Credulous* wins, there is graph morphism (in the classical graph theory sense) from u into v which respects the labels of the relations and the subsumption relations between the types of the concepts in u and their image in v by the mapping. However, the definition of the projection game does not ensure that the morphism is injective. Therefore, even if *Sceptic* wins, this does not entail that there is, in *Target*, a subgraph isomorphic to *Source*. To illustrate this point consider the examples in Figure 6.1.

With the *Source* graph – ignoring problems of subsumption – *Credulous* has a winning strategy for both *Target* 1 and *Target* 2, though there is an injective projection from *Source* into *Target* 2, but not into *Target* 1.

Injective projection seems to guarantee more robust inferences because it 'preserves shapes'. However, for computational reasons, ordinary (non-injective) projection may be preferred to injective projection. Let us recall a few results concerning the computational complexity of projection operations.

In general, and as the very nature of the projection game suggests, computing a projection is an NP-hard task. However, the projection from a tree to a graph is computable in polynomial time (Mugnier and Chein 1993). By reduction to the 'subgraph isomorphism problem' (Garey and Johnson 1979), deciding whether there is an *injective* projection from u into v is an NP-Complete problem, even when u is a tree. This is why injective projections may not be workable in practice. If ordinary projection does not seem good enough, there are some intermediate notions of projection, such as the *locally injective* projection from a tree into a graph, for which polynomial algorithms can be given (Mugnier and Chein 1993).

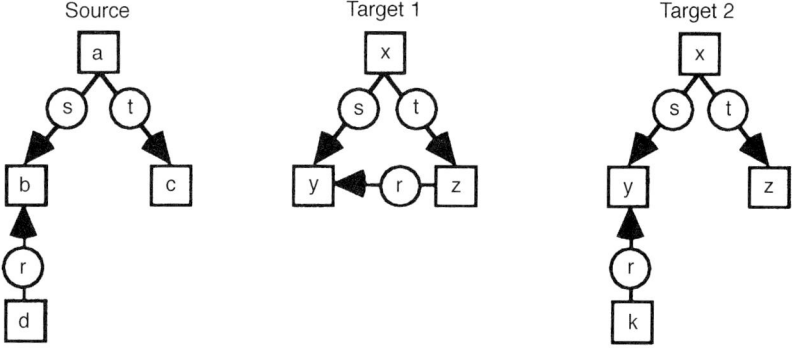

Figure 6.1 Injective and non-injective projection.

STYLED SEMANTIC NETWORKS

SSNs with negation

Let us consider the sentence 'John did not go to Brazil this summer'. This sentence does not imply that John went to Brazil in previous summers (it might well be that John intended to go there and that he finally changed his mind). Therefore, we will not focus the negation on the relation PERD (for 'period'). Our *Source* graph will be Network 6.21. As a *Target* graph, consider the representation of the sentence 'John did not go abroad' (Network 6.22).

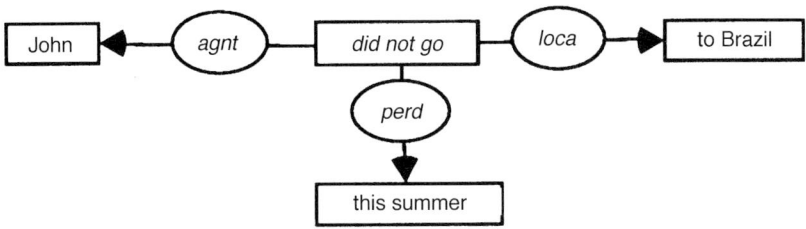

Network 6.21

At the beginning of the game, *Credulous* can move on the concept [DID NOT GO] in *Target*, and force *Sceptic* to position himself on the concept [DID NOT GO] in *Source*. Because, to position himself on [DID NOT GO], *Credulous* has gone through the scope of a negation, and because both players are now on a concept, players change sides. It is *Sceptic*'s turn to move in *Target*. He can go either to the relation labelled DEST, or to the relation labelled AGNT. In both cases, *Credulous* can move to a relation with the same label and orientation. *Sceptic* keeps moving reaching either the concept [JOHN], or the concept [ABROAD]. Again, in both cases, *Credulous* can move to a concept which is a restriction of the concept chosen by *Sceptic* (assuming [BRAZIL] is subsumed by [ABROAD]). At that point, *Sceptic* must move back on a relation that he has already visited. This is a winning position for *Credulous*. Therefore, there is a projection from *Source* to *Target*, despite the fact that *Source* is 'bigger' than *Target*.

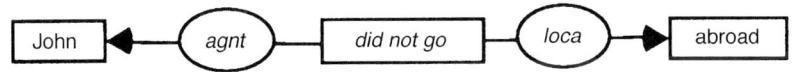

Network 6.22

SSNs with universal quantification

Consider the *Target* graph representing the sentence 'All my new friends are colleagues' (Network 6.23), where the label RFPT means 'reference point'. This graph should support the fact that Paul, a new friend of mine is also a colleague. Therefore, there should be a projection from the *Source* graph (Network 6.24) into the *Target* graph. If, at the beginning of the game, *Credulous* moves to the concept [NEW] in *Target*, and imposes *Sceptic* to

STYLED SEMANTIC NETWORKS

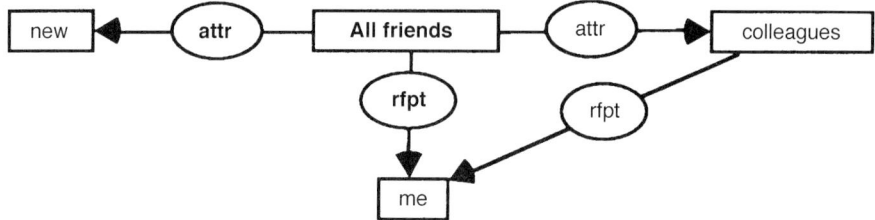

Network 6.23

stand on [NEW] in *Source*, then because *Credulous* has entered within the restrictor of a universal quantification, players change sides. *Sceptic* must move to [MY FRIEND PAUL]. *Credulous* moves to [ALL FRIENDS], which, according to the table given above, is a restriction of the concept [MY FRIEND PAUL]. Whatever sequence of moves *Sceptic* chooses to make afterwards, he will have to go out of the restrictor of the universal quantification. Players will change sides again, and *Sceptic* will finally be blocked. Therefore, *Credulous* has a winning strategy.

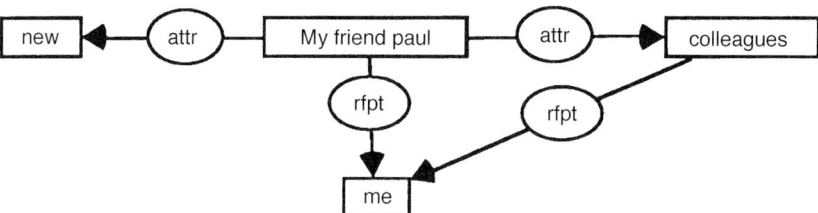

Network 6.24

Note that *Target* should not support the conclusion 'my friend Paul is a colleague', because the information according to which Paul is a *new* friend would be missing. In that case, the projection fails because whatever strategy *Credulous* may adopt, *Sceptic* can force him to enter in the restrictor of the universal quantification. Then, players change sides, and nothing can prevent *Sceptic* from moving in *Target* to the concept [NEW], which has no restriction in *Source*. Therefore, *Sceptic* has a winning strategy, and the projection fails, as expected.

SSNs with a universal quantification under the scope of a negation

Our *Target* graph will be the representation of the sentence 'The government did not solve all social problems' (Network 6.25). As a *Source* graph, let us choose the representation of the sentence 'The government did not solve all the problems' (Network 6.26).

If *Credulous* and *Sceptic* start the game on the concepts labelled [DID NOT SOLVE] respectively in *Target* and *Source*, the first thing they have to do is to change sides. If *Sceptic* moves left in *Target*, he will lose immediately, since

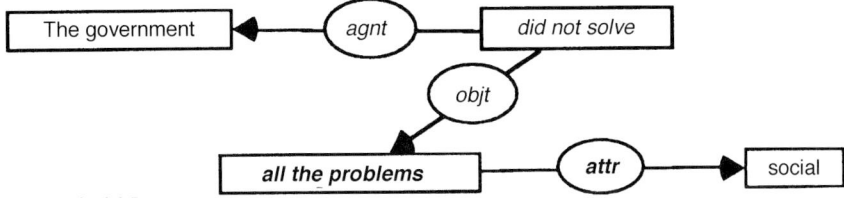

Network 6.25

Credulous can make a similar move on the left in *Source*. If *Sceptic* moves to the right, he will enter into the restrictor of the universal quantification. At that point, players must change sides again. *Sceptic* goes back to *Source*, and *Credulous* to *Target*. That position is a winning position for *Credulous*, since *Sceptic* has no other places to visit in *Source*. Therefore, *Credulous* has a winning strategy, and the projection succeeds, as expected.

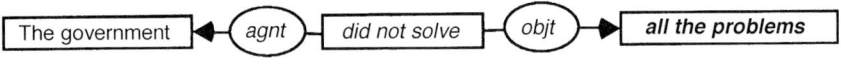

Network 6.26

10 Applications of semantic networks to content analysis

The rest of the discussion is devoted to practical points, such as the reliability of the coding of text into SSNs and the methods of analysis of the coded data.

As far as the coding phase is concerned, the first traditional issue is its cost. Coding into styled semantic networks is a difficult and time consuming task which requires a careful training of the coders. It seems impossible to code large samples of texts, and even with reduced samples, coders should focus on the parts of each text which are relevant for the analysis. Obviously, this selection must be done according to precise rules. For example, one could decide to set up a list of relevant concepts, and decide to leave aside any sentence or paragraph whose coding does not make use of any of the concepts of the list.

The second traditional issue related to the coding phase is the so-called 'inter-coder reliability'. Some experiments carried out at the IRIT[3] with conceptual graphs suggest that the inter-coder reliability is pretty low.[4] This is mainly due to the non-linguistic nature of conceptual graphs. Styled semantic networks, which are much closer to natural language, allow us to achieve a much higher degree of coding reliability. Inter-coder reliability can be achieved by intensive verification procedures. While verification is usually a difficult task, it is rather simple to verify the adequacy of a coding into styled semantic networks. In most cases, it is enough to retranslate the graphs into natural language, and to compare sentences obtained in that way with the original sentences. If they are similar, the coding is satisfactory. If they differ, the coding must be scrutinized and the sources of confusion isolated.

During the analysis phase, SSNs have two naturally associated methods.

Semantic path distributions

The first method benefits from the gain in connexity achieved by styled semantic networks to focus at the level of semantic relations. The method consists in isolating two or more notions (concepts), and computing the semantic paths between them. Such a task can be performed by choosing two projections of the two concepts into a graph, and applying a path-finding algorithm. The algorithm is then repeated with all possible pairs of projections of the concepts. Alternatively, the task can be performed by choosing a projection of the first notion and applying a breadth-first search terminating either when a projection of the second concept is met, or when the path exceeds a certain length.

Both strategies yield (after sorting), a distribution of the semantic relations between two notions, depending on their length. This semantic distance needs to be further analysed by computing, for each length, the distribution of the semantic relations depending on the nature of the relation. I believe that such instruments are a natural way of giving an empirical answer to typical questions like 'what is the relation between these two notions?' or 'how are these two symbols associated in social discourse?' or 'what is the image of this social category or of this institution in social discourse?'.

Discourse clustering

The second method uses the projection operation to test the presence of prototypical conjunctions of ideas or arguments in a text. Before describing it in detail, a last theoretical word must be said about the difference between the role of the projection in Sowa's semantics, and the role of the projection in styled semantic networks.

The most fundamental difference is that, since there are no longer a true set and a false set, the four-valued logic of Sowa's semantics has to be given up. This means that, via the operation of projection on SSNs, an assertion can be found 'true' in a text, or the text can be found 'neutral' towards the assertion. But it is impossible to end up with the 'falsity' of an assertion, and the 'inconsistency' of a text with regard to an assertion. In this new framework, to test whether an assertion is true or false in a text, one needs to perform the projection of the assertion and the projection of its negation.

We here confront one of the classic requirements of content analysis, which demands that all the coding categories should be dichotomies. Still, these coding categories must not necessarily be dichotomies in a logical sense. For example, let one side of a category be 'exploitation of the labour class by the bourgeois class via the appropriation of surplus value'. Should its opposite side be 'exploitation of the labour class by the bourgeois class but not via the appropriation of surplus value', or 'absence of exploitation of the labour class by the bourgeois class'? One may reasonably argue that the choice of the alternative depends on the aims of the analysis. If the analysis aims at differentiating between, let us say, a classical Marxism and a deviant Marxism, it should specify the alternative in the first way. If the analysis contrasts Marxism and non-Marxism, it should specify the alternative in the second way, since the alternative will then be verified in sentences such as 'the labour class is not exploited by the bourgeois class' (regardless of any considerations about surplus value).

In formal terms, one could say that for social purposes, the valid alternative to a set A is not necessarily $\bar{A}$, the complementary of A, but could also be B a subset of $\bar{A}$. The local application of the negation in SSNs allows a very flexible and precise definition of the actual alternative to an assertion. Hence, the analyst can perform a kind of 'parametrization' of the respective sizes of the hypothesis A, its alternative B and the neutral part $\overline{A \cup B}$.

Given the above theoretical clarification about the semantic status of the projection operation in SSNs, the method proceeds as follows. A short fragment of discourse (the hypothesis of the analyst with respect to a text content) is translated into a styled graph, and an alternative is also derived. Next, the projection operation yields a 'score' obtained by the text about the hypothesis and the alternative. This score reflects whether a text supports or not the hypothesis, and gives the strength of this support. The strength depends on the level at which the hypothesis succeeds (general vs. individual for example, or based on the generality of the type labels yielded by the match).

Since the operation of projection is computationally tractable when the *Source* graph is a tree, we can multiply the hypotheses, and obtain a score for each of them. The text is then characterized with respect to a set of prototypic ideas, or arguments, by these scores. Repeating the whole process on a sample of texts, we obtain a population of texts defined by their scores in relation to a set of hypothesis. This kind of data can be analysed by clustering techniques, either numerical or conceptual (Michalsky and Stepp 1983). Ultimately, therefore, the second method is aimed at generating intermediate data so as to perform automatic classification on texts.

The clusters which are obtained from the intermediate data are of great value for a social scientist because they are based on a combination of the hypotheses (or their alternatives). Therefore, each of them represents the high-level association of typical arguments, facts and notions. Each cluster defines a regularity in the combinations of elementary parts of discourse. With such methods, the social scientist can discover the successful combinations of ideas in social discourse, and determine incompatible ideas. It is now the work of sociological interpretation to explain how and why some combinations are used and others neglected.

11 Implementation

To ease the coding of texts into SSNs, a graphic editor called CoCoNet has been implemented. The name CoCoNet stands for 'Colored Conceptual Networks' and refers to Frege's notion of the 'colour' (*farbe*) of a concept. Remember that for Frege, the *sense* of a concept is the part of its meaning which helps us determine its reference, whereas the *colour* of a concept corresponds to the attitude of the speaker towards its reference (Tsohatzidis 1992). The colour is most often evaluative.

The prototype CoCoNet, which runs on Macintosh computers, does not meet the industry standards in terms of efficiency, reliability and programming style. However, it offers the basic functions that one can expect from a graphic editor. Input is made directly on the screen by mouse clicks and typing, and the program transparently manages the internal data structures. Networks can be saved on disk and restored. Networks can be cut and pasted to drawing programs and word-processing programs as PICT images. A tool palette allows us graphically to

- draw and delete concepts, contexts and relations
- select and drag concepts, contexts and relations
- edit concepts, contexts and relations (label, modalities) at any time
- collapse and expand contexts.

When a concept is dragged around the screen and dropped at a new location, relations are updated automatically. When a context is moved, all concepts it contains move with it, and all relations pointing to it are updated automatically.

CoCoNet is a vectorial drawing program, not a paint (pixel-based) program. This saves memory, but slows down scrolling. For large networks with several hundreds of concepts, a pixel-based version would perhaps be more comfortable, though more RAM-consuming.

CoCoNet was first developed in PROLOG++, an object-oriented version of PROLOG by Logic Programming Associates. PROLOG is not a very efficient language, but it is an obvious choice for programs making heavy use of list processing and graph searching. Numerical computations have been implemented as external Pascal routines. LPA PROLOG has powerful graphic capacities, and simplifies interface programming (window and dialogue management). Object-oriented programming was an appealing solution because data structures themselves were hierarchical. In SSNs, for example, a context is both a network and a concept (see Figure 6.2).

Because PROLOG++ implements multiple inheritance, it is straightforward to make contexts inherit their instance variables and their methods from networks and concepts. Another useful feature of PROLOG++, on which the code heavily relies, is the possibility to use recursive functions.

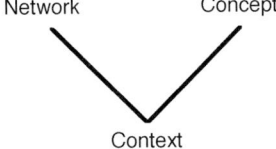

Figure 6.2 Data structures and multiple inheritance.

A C++ version of CoCoNet has been derived from the PROLOG prototype. It retains all the features of the PROLOG version, but adds three important functions. It allows the user to open simultaneous multiple files, and to cut and paste networks (not only PICT images) within or between documents. In addition, the C++ version of CoCoNet implements a highly optimized projection operation. Finally, the C++ version implements a generalized, one-level undo. This version, which is much more efficient than the PROLOG version, is available from the author as a double-clickable application (currently running on Macintosh computers only).[5]

Conclusion

This chapter was aimed at designing a discourse representation formalism capable of integrating the information used in impression formation and evaluative reasoning. Not surprisingly, this information involves the rhetorical structure of discourse, the semantic case relations between linguistic expressions, logical modalities and quantification. All these elements which, as far as their semantic analysis is concerned, are traditionally scattered within existing semantic theories, are incorporated here within a graph-based formalism. The rhetorical structure and speech act reports are represented by rhetorical relations and embedded networks. Negation scope is represented by the italic typeface, and quantification restrictors by the bold typeface. Beside these traditional elements, I have used three modalities (real, potential, and unreal) which are represented by pen patterns. One of the main innovations of the formalism is *modal aspectualization*, which refers to the contribution of expressions to the overall modality of the sentence to which they belong. Modal aspectualization is essential for evaluative reasoning, and cannot be absent from a semantics of evaluation.

The main appeal of styled semantic networks is their simplicity and their proximity to natural language. However, this simplicity should not be obtained at the cost of logical soundness. A projection operation, which is tantamount to a query process, can be defined for SSNs, and has been implemented in CoCoNet, a computer program allowing one to draw and manipulate SSNs.

I hope I have detailed enough the advantages of the use of semantic networks for the representation and the analysis of social discourse. I would like now to put the approach in a wider critical perspective.

An immediate limitation lies in the important time investments which characterize such semi-qualitative methods (or semi-quantitative, according to the reader's preferences). Natural language processing systems now achieve satisfactory levels of reliability. Social scientists interested in factual information extraction would be well advised to experiment with such systems instead of coding the information by hand. Social scientists concerned with subtle associations of ideas have no solution other than manual coding (Cuilemburg *et al.* 1988).

Another important limitation is due to the synchronic feature of semantic networks. All the parts of a net have an equal discursive status, unlike the parts of a human discourse. Being synchronic, the graph-based representations are ill-suited for complex argumentation studies.

A more fundamental problem is that most social communications do not fully make sense outside an ideological context. This context is partially restored by the coder during the coding phase. But most of it remains implicit, and the judgement of values carried by the text are not fully represented in semantic nets. Since this aspect is of invaluable relevance for a social scientist, the advances brought by the use of semantic networks reveal how much is left to be done at the theoretical level, in the field of textual analysis.

In conclusion, styled semantic networks have direct applications, but suffer from some important practical limitations. It is perhaps more interesting to consider them as a bridge between semantic networks and connectionist networks. But before any further work is undertaken in this new direction, it has been important to exhibit a formalism which, because of its flat structure, would lend itself to connectionist computations, but which would remain close to natural language and be semantically reliable. I believe that SSNs are examples of one such formalism, and that they offer a good starting point for further research integrating the symbolic and connectionist aspects of graph-based representations of discourse.

7

DYNAMIC SEMANTIC NETWORKS

Introduction

The purpose of this chapter is to model the ideological consistency of discourse as the stability of evaluations in a dynamic semantic network (DSN). Evaluative meaning effects are modelled as the dynamic modification between units of discourse. Starting from default evaluations, units of discourse interact along semantic channels. After a certain amount of time, the dynamic system eventually reaches an equilibrium. It is then possible to estimate the ideological consistency of the discourse as the difference between the vector of default evaluations and the vector of evaluations on which the dynamic stabilizes. Intuitively, the smaller this difference is, the more consistent discourse is. By trying out several ideological hypotheses, it is possible to determine under which one the discourse is most consistent.

This use of dynamic systems for the estimation of stability must first be situated within the larger context of neural network models of meaning. The fundamental features of DSNs (no hidden units, no global units, connection weights set by hand, synchronic dynamics on the whole system) are made explicit and justified (sections 1 and 2). A specific class of dynamic system is proposed, and its convergence properties are discussed (section 3). A numerical function for the estimation of ideological consistency is proposed (section 4). The meaning of the weights is discussed (section 5).

DSNs are dynamic systems built on top of the SSNs developed in the previous chapter. Transforming SSNs into DSNs requires three types of parametrization. First, semantic relations must be assigned connection weights expressing the evaluative influence between the units of discourse. Secondly, units of discourse must be assigned an *inertia value* representing their stability in a given ideology. Thirdly, the units of discourse must be set up with a default evaluation. A general framework for storing these parameters in a knowledge base and applying them to specific networks is proposed (section 6). In addition, some more specific semantic constraints bearing on weights and inertia coefficients are considered (section 7). Finally, an example is given (section 8).

1 Modelling interpretation as a dynamic process

In this attempt to model evaluative interpretation processes, I draw upon some recent models of polysemy (Victorri and Fuchs 1992, 1996). In these models, the overall meaning of a word is identified with a dynamic system. The various meanings of the word are the attractors of the system. The interpretation processes which pick up one of the meanings on the basis of contextual information are the trajectories of the system. The strength of these models is that the dynamics of the system are not *ad hoc*. In fact, these dynamics are determined *automatically* by a neural network during a training phase in which contexts and meanings are paired. The results of such models on simple words are very convincing. Not surprisingly, combining these sorts of meaning into phrases and sentences is not so straightforward.

Modelling evaluative interpretations as dynamic systems is, on one hand, more complex than modelling meanings because the evaluation of an expression seems to be more context-dependent than the meaning of a word, and, on the other, simpler, because interpreting in general is a more complex task than evaluating. Interpretation combines meanings with the loosely defined task of understanding, whereas evaluation combines meaning in order to achieve ideological consistency. Therefore, it is possible to assume that evaluative processes maximize consistency. More technically, it is possible to model evaluative processes as gradient dynamics of a function of consistency. This function associates a consistency to each vector of local evaluation (the vector of evaluations corresponding to the default evaluations). The local maxima of this function represent possible ideological interpretations of the statement.

To illustrate this very general idea, let us consider the statement 'Individualism is rampant'. When we interpret this discourse, we guess that its author is against individualism, otherwise he would use an expression other than 'rampant' which is a bit frightening. Therefore, we identify a default evaluation of 'individualism' which renders the discourse consistent. But there is also a degree of probability that the author of this discourse is so favourable to individualism that he conceives of its triumph as a good thing. Therefore, we should allow for another reading of this sentence: one in which a very positive evaluation of 'individualism' succeeds in modifying the default evaluation of 'rampant', and turns it into a positive evaluation. Even if we take into account these two interpretations, the second is less likely than the first. Therefore, the inconsistency (c2) of the discourse with pro-individualist ideology should be higher that the inconsistency (c1) with anti-individualist ideology. The diagrams in Figure 7.1 illustrate this situation.

DYNAMIC SEMANTIC NETWORKS

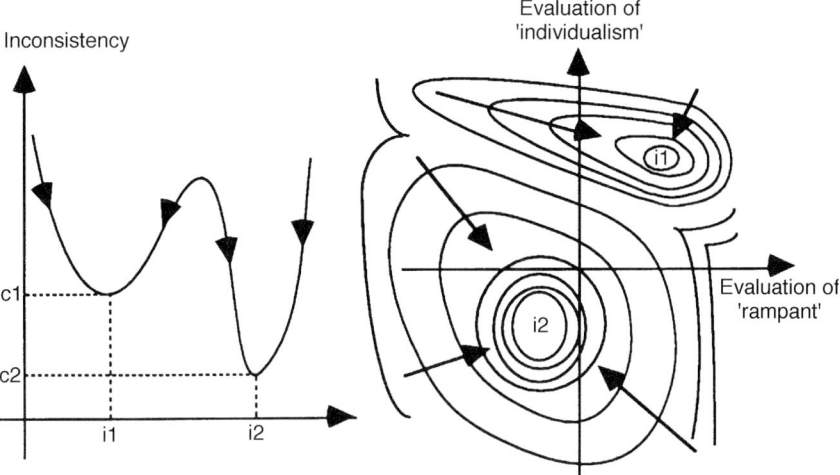

Figure 7.1 The consistency function and a map of the evaluation state space.

In practice, we do not possess a consistency function, but we could arrange to have it 'learned' by a neural network. However, this would imply either training a network for each possible statement, or modelling semantic compositionality as the interaction of dynamic systems. The first solution would be infinite, and the second is still beyond the capacities of current research. This last remark has an important consequence: because evaluative processes are too complex to be 'learned' by current models of neural networks, the networks which are developed later in this chapter do not have hidden units. This strongly restricts the class of dynamics. However, I show below that even without hidden units, the various configurations and combinations of weights produce flexible dynamics with an important expressive power.

Besides hidden units, I also do without 'global' units such as units representing complex phrases and sentences. There are no other units, in DSNs, than the vertices of SSNs. This also restricts the class of dynamics. However, incorporating additional units would require making decisions regarding both syntax and deep cognitive structures underpinning semantics. These decisions would have to be justified, which would lead us far beyond the scope of this research.

In some classes of networks without weight dynamics, weights are set automatically. For example, weights may reflect the probability of association between features (Rumelhart *et al.* 1986). In the networks defined below, weights are set up by hand. To determine a weight, one answers the following question: in this context, and regardless of the evaluation of other units, what is the type of binary interaction between the two units? The answer given to this question allows one to determine the sign and the relative value of the weights. To fine-tune the weights we need to proceed by comparison with the weights that have been previously attributed. I come back, in the next chapter, to the methods used to set up the weights.

2 Estimating ideological consistency

In the absence of a global function of consistency, the dynamics of the networks must be justified by the local behaviours. These local behaviours reflect the evaluative meaning effects. Therefore, the dynamic systems that are proposed later in this chapter are devoted to the calculus of a global evaluation rather than to the maximization of consistency.

What happens to ideological consistency in this framework? It is modelled as the stability of default evaluations during contextual modification. This stability can be measured in various ways. The norm of the field of forces at the initial point of the dynamics, or the maximum of this norm along the trajectory could be good candidates. For the sake of simplicity, I measure stability as a function of the difference between the vector of initial conditions and the vector of activation at which the dynamics stabilize.

We are looking for an estimation of the degree of consistency of a discourse with an ideology. In other words, we make the hypothesis that an ideology inspired the discourse that we have at hand, and we look for an indicator of the validity of this hypothesis. The strategy that we will adopt is to assume that the discourse is a possible emanation of the ideology, and look at the consequences that this has on the evaluations of the concepts it contains. This top-down move is the reverse move of compositional semantics, which would try to derive the evaluation of a proposition from the evaluation of the concepts it contains and from their mode of combination.

In what follows, we never make any hypothesis about the evaluation of the content of a discourse. We only make hypotheses as to the consistency of the discourse with a given ideology. We test the hypothesis against the nature of discourse itself. Indeed, the discourse that we want to position relatively to the ideology is the only 'observed' entity that we have at our disposal. We therefore try to derive from the discourse itself the 'estimated' (final) evaluation of the concepts it contains. Afterwards, we will compare the predicted (initial) evaluations with the 'estimated' (final) evaluations to derive an overall criterion of the conformity of the discourse with the ideology. Since we make no distributional assumptions, this goodness of fit criterion is only *ad hoc*.

I propose to model discourses as dynamic systems where concepts exchange evaluation via some semantic channels. Before examining the technical aspects of these 'neural-like' networks, I would like to give an intuitive justification of the idea of evaluation transfer itself.

Let us consider the sentence 'the government did not help the people that deserved assistance' and focus on the occurrences 'did not help' and 'the people that'. The absence of help will be evaluated on the basis of who is not helped. It is likely that the better the people who did not benefit from this help are evaluated, the more severely the action of not helping them will be judged. Conversely, the more severely the action of not helping them will be judged, the less the people will be judged to deserve being neglected, and therefore, the better they will be evaluated. Focusing on the relation between 'government' and 'did not help', we discover a similar dependency. But in that case, the evaluation of the actor depends positively on the evaluation of its action. The worse the action of neglecting is judged, the worse the government is judged.

The interdependency of the evaluations of the occurrences allows us to consider social meaning as arising from a process of dynamic adjustment. When a social actor receives a message, he starts with default evaluations of the occurrences. During the process of interpretation, these default evaluations evolve by coming in contact with each other. After a certain lapse of time, the interpretation is completed and the evaluations may reach an equilibrium. In the concrete network simulations developed below, the interpretation is supposed to concern the whole discourse. In practice, it means that the evaluation of each occurrence is updated simultaneously at each iteration. Once more, such a choice has been made for expository purposes. Nothing forbids the generalization of the networks proposed here to the case of asynchronous behaviour. It is also possible to think of gradually constructed networks whose nodes would be dynamically created. Such networks would mimic the unfolding dimension of discourse reception. For the sake of simplicity, I assume that the receiver can handle the whole discourse synchronically, before interpretation begins.

The interdependency of occurrences within a discourse can be modelled by a flux of evaluations. At the initial reception of the discourse this flux is null and the evaluation of the occurrences are the predicted evaluations. Immediately, the occurrences start exchanging evaluation with each other. At all successive times, the amount of evaluation that an occurrence sends to all other occurrences is a function of its current level of evaluation. After a certain amount of time, the flux might stabilize, yielding an equilibrium for the network's evaluations.

It is important to realize that this equilibrium does not single out a concept, as 'winner-take-all' networks do. Thus, my networks do not look like those of the original applications of neural networks to lexical perception (Rumelhart *et al.* 1986), semantic-syntactic analysis (Waltz and Pollack 1985), and disambiguation (Kintsch 1991). Neither is this equilibrium an attractor that would have been previously learned by the system (Victorri and Fuchs 1996). In fact, equilibria are not of intrinsic interest. I pay exclusive attention to the 'distance' between the initial state of the network and the equilibrium.

3 Globally asymptotically stable dynamics

Even if equilibria are not interesting in themselves, DSNs still have to converge. In order to measure the variations of evaluation, the trajectory of every initial activation must converge towards a unique equilibrium. In addition, this equilibrium should be stable. When a system satisfies both conditions, it is said to be globally asymptotically stable.

Many systems are convergent, and yet not adequate for modelling semantic effects of contextual modification. It is well known for example, that so-called additive networks with symmetric weights are convergent (Grossberg 1988). However, since evaluative semantic effects are not symmetrical, symmetric weights are not suitable.

I propose to concentrate on a specific class of continuous time networks in which the activation state of a unit $x_i = x(t)$ is influenced by the activation of the other units and by clamped (constant) external input. I therefore consider dynamic systems defined by the following class of differential equations:

$$\dot{x}_i = F(x_1, ..., x_n, I_1, ..., I_s) \tag{7.1}$$

When systems of this type are globally asymptotically stable, they associate an equilibrium to each input vector. More precisely, I focus on a class of systems in which the input vector is also the initial activation vector.

$$\dot{x}_i = F(x_1, ..., x_n, x_1(t_0), ..., x_n(t_0)) \tag{7.2}$$

As in all convergent networks, when they converge, networks defined by (7.2) associate an equilibrium to each vector of initial activations. But this vector of initial activation keeps influencing the trajectories at each moment of the dynamics, thus acting as clamped inputs.

There are some interesting convergence theorems on continuous time networks defined by equation (7.1). Let us denote by $A = DF(y)$ the Jacobian matrix of F. Dynamical systems defined by (7.1) are globally asymptotically convergent if there is a constant $-\mu < 0$ such that $\frac{1}{2}(A + A^T) \leq -\mu$ (Hirsch 1989). By Gerschgorin's circle theorem (Noble and Daniel 1988) this last condition is also fulfilled if

$$A_{ii} + \frac{1}{2}\sum_{j \neq i} |A_{ij} + A_{ji}| \leq -\mu, \quad i = 1, ..., n \tag{7.3}$$

For the sake of semantic modelling, I propose to use networks defined by the following differential equation

$$\dot{x}_1 = -a_i x_i + a_i x_i(t_0) + \sum_{j \neq i} \omega_{ij} S(x_j - x_i). \tag{7.4}$$

The term $-a_i x_i$ corresponds to the passive decay of the system. The term $a_i x_i(t_0)$ corresponds to a constant input signal, depending on the initial state of the system. Taken together, these two terms express the tendency of the system to come back to its initial position. The parameter $a_i > 0$ is the inertia coefficient of the $i^{th.}$ unit. The last term defines the neural feedback of the system. Any deviation from the initial activation state is due to this term. The neural feedback depends on S, a symmetric, monotonous, and bounded signal function. In all computer simulations, S is the bipolar sigmoid[1]

$$S(x) = \frac{2}{1+e^{-x}} - 1.$$

Why does signal function S apply to a difference of evaluations, and not, as in almost all existing neural networks, to the evaluation of a single neuron? The fundamental idea of this chapter is that the more the initial and the final evaluations of each concept differ, the less the discourse conforms to the ideological hypothesis. Ideally, it is therefore expected from a discourse that is fully consistent with the hypothesis that its initial state of evaluation is already a stable equilibrium. As an example of such stability, one may have in mind a simple discourse where an action is attributed to an actor, and where, according to the ideology, both have initially the same evaluation. The evaluation of the action squares with the evaluation of the actor and vice-versa. They should not affect each other, and remain stable. This requirement suggests that the interaction between two semantic entities should be a function of the difference of their evaluations. This requirement also matches a much broader idea, according to which meaning is 'differential'.

Applying (7.3) to differential system (7.4) yields convergence conditions. We are especially interested in conditions expressed in terms of weights and inertia coefficients only. Because the derivative of the bipolar sigmoid is bounded (in our case $S' \leq \frac{1}{2}$), S' can easily be eliminated from the convergence conditions. Let us note $\sum_{-} \omega_{ij}$ (resp. $\sum_{+} \omega_{ij}$) the sum of negative weights (resp. positive) affecting variable x_i. Dynamic systems defined by (7.4) are globally asymptotically stable if

$$-\frac{3}{2}\sum_{-} \omega_{ij} + \frac{1}{4}\sum_{j \neq i} |\omega_{ji}| \leq a_i, \quad i = 1, ..., n.$$

Not surprisingly, to guarantee global asymptotic stability, decay rates must be large enough to compensate for the instability introduced by neural feedback.

In practice, I use discrete time systems defined by the following equations.

$$x_i(t+1) = x_i(t) - a_i(x_i(t) - x_i(t_0)) + \sum_{j \neq i} w_{ij} S(x_j(t) - x_i(t))$$

$$i = 1, ..., n \tag{7.5}$$

Although convergence results for continuous time networks could be transposed to discrete time networks, it is perhaps more convenient to remark that discrete time systems are globally asymptotically stable if the largest eigenvalue of their jacobian is strictly inferior to 1. Applying this condition to (7.5) yields the following convergence condition.[2]

$$-\sum_{-} w_{ij} < a_i < 1 - 2 \sum_{+} w_{ij} \quad i = 1, ..., n \tag{7.6}$$

The above constraint can also be justified at the cognitive and semantic levels. Indeed, DSNs are synchronic representations of diachronic phenomena. Within real discourses, the evaluative transfers are distributed in time. Their effect is therefore not as strong as if they were all taking place at the same time. Furthermore, it is reasonable to think that transfers do not add up linearly. After a certain number of critiques, for example, another critique will not create the same negative effect as the first one. Thus a decreasing rate of argumentative and semantic impact is more plausible than a constant one. The local normalization of the weights reflects this cognitive evidence.

4 A numerical estimation of ideological consistency

The purpose of DSNs is to obtain an estimation of the consistency of a discourse with an ideology. Ideology must first be defined. I limit myself, in this section, to a minimal definition of ideologies as sets of default values and inertia coefficients associated with types.

> **Definition**: a sociological interpretation of an ideology I_m consists of a set of types T and of two assignment functions φ and ψ.
>
> - $T \xrightarrow{\varphi} [-1, 1]$. $\varphi_m(t)$ is the evaluation assigned to type t by ideology I_m.
> - $T \xrightarrow{\psi} [0, 1]$. $\psi_m(t)$ is the inertia coefficient assigned to type t by ideology I_m.

Within an ideology, not all types have the same status. Consider for example the type 'make'. The evaluations of the occurrences of this type are so context-dependent that it would be impossible to stabilize them. Therefore, this type will be assigned a default evaluation close to zero, and a very low inertia coefficient, so that the evaluation of its occurrences easily adapt to different linguistic contexts. In contrast, values which are important for an ideology (for example 'market' or 'competition' for liberal economics) will be stabilized by large coefficients of inertia. Inertia reflects the importance of a notion for an ideology.

Judgements of consistency with an ideology must be based on the observation of the concepts whose type is strongly stabilized by the ideology. However, because the sociologist may wish to test a particular hypothesis, he should be able to focus attention on a few types which he regards as significant.

Definition: a *sociological interpretation* of a discourse d is a function Γ

- $T \xrightarrow{\Gamma} R^+$.

This function associates a weight (called its *significance*) to each unit of the DSN representing the discourse. Because the significance depends on the type of unit, Γ is defined as a function ranging over the set of types. The significance reflects the importance given by the sociologist to this type in his judgement of consistency. Therefore, the ideological consistency of a statement depends on the sociological interpretation of the statement. One of the technical difficulties raised by the notion of ideological consistency is to define a function in which significances have only a relative value.

Let d be a discourse which, under the ideological hypothesis I, is associated with the DSN $D=(X, X(0), W)$. The vector of initial conditions $X(0)$ is defined by φ, and inertia coefficients are defined by ψ. Hence, if t is the typing function,

$$x_i(0) = \varphi(t(x_i)), \text{ and } a_i = \psi(t(x_i)) \qquad i = 1, ..., n.$$

The inconsistency of the discourse d with ideology I must be an increasing function of the variation of evaluations for the most significant types. The simplest function I can think of is

$$g(d) = \sum_i \Gamma(t(x_i))|x_i(\infty) - x_i(0)|.$$

The consistency of discourse d with ideology I must therefore be a decreasing function of $g(d)$. Let us remark first the variation of each occurrence is bounded.[3]

$$|x_i(\infty) - x_i(0)| \leq \frac{1}{a_i} \sum_{j \neq i} |\omega_{ij}|, \qquad i = 1, ..., n.$$

From this, we immediately deduce

$$0 \leq g(d) \leq \sum_i \Gamma(t(x_i)) \frac{1}{a_i} \sum_{j \neq i} |\omega_{ij}|.$$

Let us call m the upper bound of $g(d)$. We are looking for a transform F such that

- $F(g(d))$ is normalized (takes its value between -1 and 1).
- $F(g(d))$ is insensitive to scalar modifications of Γ (significances have only a relative value).
- $F'(g(d)) \leq 0$, because consistency must be a decreasing function of the variations of evaluation.
- $F''(g(d)) \geq 0$, since practice shows that linear transforms underestimate consistency.

I propose the polynomial transform

$$F(x) = \frac{\beta m + 4}{m^3} x^3 - \frac{2\beta m + 6}{m^2} x^2 + \beta x + 1$$

which fulfils the four conditions on $[0, m]$ as soon as we impose $-6/m \leq \beta \leq 0$. As is shown in Figure 7.2, F can be fine-tuned to fit different needs by modifying the value of parameter β, which is the derivative of F at the origin.

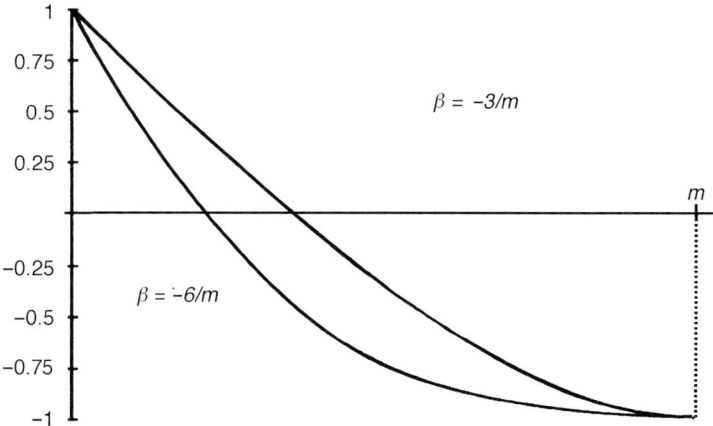

Figure 7.2 Graphs of transform F for two values of β.

It is now possible to propose a numerical estimation of the ideological consistency of a discourse. Let d be a discourse associated with a DSN $D=(X(0),W)$ under the ideological hypothesis I. The consistency of discourse d with ideology I, which is noted $[\![^\wedge d]\!]_I$ by analogy with the notation of Chapter 4, can be estimated by the following formula:

$$[\![^\wedge d]\!]_I = F(\sum_i \Gamma(t(x_i))|x_i(\infty) - x_i(0)|) \tag{7.7}$$

In practice it is observed that the magnitude of the variations depends much on inertia coefficients. Transform F tends to free estimations of consistency from this effect. More precisely, lowering the inertia coefficient of a significant occurrence increases its variation, but this effect is counterbalanced by the fact that F is a decreasing function of the inertia coefficient.

$$\frac{\partial F}{\partial a_i} \leq 0, \quad i = 1, ..., n.$$

Therefore, lowering an inertia coefficient does not necessarily decrease consistency, though because of feedback effects, modifying inertia coefficients is not without effects on consistency.

The major interest of possessing a normalized estimation of consistency is to open the way for a treatment of nested contexts. Remember that in SSNs, nested contexts correspond to belief reports and speech act reports. In Chapter 4, we have given two strategies to deal with opaque contexts. According to the first, the evaluation of a belief report depends on the consistency of the belief. Applying this idea to DSNs leads to the following rule

Let d be a discourse containing a concept c of type PROPOSITION (a nested context).

If c maps to the ith unit in the DSN $D = (X(0),W)$ representing d under ideological hypothesis I,

then

$$x_i(0) = [\![^\wedge c]\!]_I. \tag{7.8}$$

When a DSN contains an embedded DSN, the consistency of the embedded DSN must be estimated first. Then, the consistency of the embedding DSN is estimated, treating the embedded DSN as a single unit. In this second step, the initial value of this unit is the consistency that has been estimated in the previous step. This procedure is applied recursively when there are several levels of nested DSNs. In practice, though, two levels is the maximum that a complex DSN should allow for. The reason for this restriction is that complex DSNs are much less conclusive about the ideological nature of the discourse they represent. Complex DSNs are therefore less relevant for the task of ideological disambiguation. To be convinced of this, the reader may remark that while a sentence such as 'the government does not help the poor' clearly indicates an opposition to the government, the sentence 'trade unions believe that the government does not help the poor' could be favourable or not to the government, depending on the opinion that one has about unions, and depending on the strength of one's faith in the embedded proposition.

Note that in rule (7.8) a consistency is assimilated with a default evaluation. This is not surprising if we remember that consistencies are in fact evaluations of discourse as discourse. However, rule (7.8) implicitly requires that evaluations and consistency have the same kind of values. Because default evaluations belong to the interval $[-1,1]$, consistency should also vary between -1 and 1. This is the purpose of the normalization carried out by transform F.

As stated in Chapter 4, there is a second possibility to deal with attitude and speech act reports. The consistency of 'X believes in P' or 'X says P' with ideology I_1 is the consistency of P with ideology I_2, the ideology attributed to X by ideology I_1. Rule (4.4), given in Chapter 4 (see page 142) applies here without any change. However, this strategy is only applicable when the ideological adherence of X according to I_1 is known.

5 Nature and effects of the links

In the absence of a function that would be both a global Lyapounov function and sociologically meaningful (for example a function of consistency), we are left with justifying our networks at the level of the behavioural equations. To do so, we need to discuss more thoroughly the nature of semantic interactions. The easiest way to get an idea of these interactions is to focus on binary interactions. There are three main cases to consider, corresponding to three possible combinations of signs for the weights.

Mutual attraction

When $\omega_{ij} \geq 0$ and $\omega_{ji} \geq 0$, the evaluation of units i and j attract each other (see Figure 7.3). Mutual attraction is useful for averaging a pair of activations. The term 'averaging' should not confuse. Even if they do not interact with the rest of the network, two mutually attracting units do not end up with the same value. They end up closer to each other than they were initially. Two mutually attracting units are not shifted by the same amount either. If $a_i = a_j$ and $\omega_{ij} \geq \omega_{ji}$, x_i moves more towards x_j than x_j towards x_i.

Figure 7.3 Mutual attraction.

Mutual attraction necessarily damps down because the influence of unit j upon unit i depends on $x_i - x_j$, which decreases along trajectories.

Mutual attraction is the default type of binary interaction. A wide range of semantic compositions are well represented by this kind of link. These include the influence of an action on its actor, the influence of the goal of the action on the action, the influence of the result of the action on the action, the influence of the means of an action on the action, and statements concerning causalities between phenomena.

Mutual repulsion

When $\omega_{ij} \leq 0$ and $\omega_{ji} \leq 0$, units i and j repulse each other (see Figure 7.4). Contrary to mutual attraction, mutual repulsion is self-reinforcing, since the influence of unit j upon unit i depends on $x_i - x_j$, which increases along trajectories. However, the tendency to move away from each other is limited by inertia and by the fact that the signal function S is bounded by 1 and -1. Therefore, after a certain amount of deviation, recall forces necessarily counteract repulsion forces. However, mutual repulsion creates some instability around pairs of almost equal activation.

This kind of behaviour reflects the semantic composition of verbs and noun phrases where the evaluation of the verb depends negatively on the evaluation of its object (*destroy, abolish, neglect, abandon*, for example), and inversely, when the evaluation of the object depends negatively on the evaluation of the verb. Some verbs expressing states (*suffer* for example) also negatively depend on their experiencer, and conversely. Mutual repulsion may reflect the composition of a noun with a noun phrase, when the noun 'reverses' evaluations (for example *defeat, ruin, decrease*, etc.). Finally, mutual repulsion is adequate for the semantic composition of verbs and noun phrases when the evaluation of the verb would depend positively on the evaluation of its object (and inversely) but the verb is negated.

Attraction–repulsion

When $\omega_{ij} \geq$ and $\omega_{ji} \leq 0$, unit i repulses unit j while unit j attracts unit i. As a result, both units are shifted in the same direction. Attraction–repulsion

Figure 7.4 Mutual repulsion.

provides an appealing solution to the complex problem of simulating a comparison with a standard. Let us assume that unit *i* corresponds to an actor, unit *j* to his action, and that the role or the reputation of the actor set up a standard regarding this sort of action. If the action has a similar evaluation to the actor, both will remain stable. The action conforms to the standard associated with the actor. The more the initial evaluation of the action deviates from the evaluation of the actor, the more both will be modified. If the action has a higher evaluation than the actor, this difference will be emphasized, and the action evaluation will be pushed up (we did not expect such good behaviour from the actor). If the action has a lower evaluation than the actor, the action's evaluation will be pushed down (we did not expect him to behave that badly). In both cases, due to the positive link that goes from the action to the actor, the actor's evaluation will tend to follow this movement.

I have argued, in Chapter 2, that evaluative judgements involve global moral attitudes that I called the Jesuit attitude, and the Jansenist attitude. The Jesuit pays more attention to the contrast between actions and reputations, whereas the Jansenist pays more attention to the contrast between actions and normative prescriptions. I give here a slightly different version of opposition between Jesuit and Jansenist attitudes. I assume that we can expect one of two different attitudes from a person facing some new information about the world. He may react softly and quickly adapt to situations which depart from his hopes, his normative beliefs, or his expectation. This first attitude is the Jesuit attitude. He may also stick to his moral values and somehow 'morally reject the world'. He will continuously interpret new data with reference to an ideal state of affairs. Such an attitude can be pure blindness, political fanaticism, totalitarian thinking. However, it can be also moral exigency, incorruptibility, idealism, capacity to give shape to the world. This attitude is the Jansenist attitude. In these new versions, both attitudes can be modelled as dynamical processes, and related to the semantic behaviour of certain connectors.

(a) Jesuit's dynamics When $|\omega_{ij}| \geq |\omega_{ji}|$, and provided inertia does not modify behaviours, unit *i* follows unit *j*, while coming closer to it. The attraction force is stronger than the repulsion force (see Figure 7.5).

Let us illustrate this type of dynamics by the case of a discourse attributing an action to an actor. The actor (unit *i*) is first associated with a standard, represented by his default evaluation. This evaluation is what we expect from him on the basis of his social position, his reputation, or prior knowledge. During message interpretation, some new information is

Figure 7.5 Attraction–repulsion; Jesuit's dynamics.

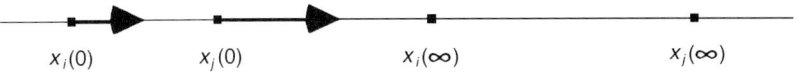

Figure 7.6 Attraction–repulsion; Jansenist's dynamics.

received about the actor. The standard associated with the actor sheds a certain light on this information. The deviation of the new information from the prior information is reinforced. Simultaneously, the evaluation of the actor is updated, moving towards the evaluation of the new information. Thus, the deviation from the standards decreases. This process can be interpreted as a revision of the standard in order to take account of the new information. It can also be interpreted as a weakening of the standard. Receiving some new information about the world, the interpreter convinces himself that the world is really not as it should be. And progressively, this difference matters less and less. This is a sort of moral realism, which evokes the moral flexibility traditionally associated with the Jesuit order.

(b) *Jansenist's dynamics* When $|\omega_{ij}| \leq |\omega_{ij}|$, and provided inertia does not modify behaviours, unit i follows unit j. But in contrast with the previous case, unit i falls behind unit j. The repulsion force is stronger than the attraction force (see Figure 7.6).

To illustrate this type of dynamics, consider again the case of an action (unit i) attributed to an actor (unit i). Unit i's initial activation represents the standard associated with the actor. The Jansenist's interpretation responds to any deviation from this standard by increasing this deviation. The evaluation of the actor is dynamically updated. Such an evaluation, which was initially based on social norms or reputation, becomes a factual evaluation. However, contrary to the Jesuit dynamics, in which the standard fades away, the evaluation of the actor keeps repulsing the evaluation of the action. Stated otherwise, the evaluation of the actor, though being modified, keeps acting as a standard. The deviation between expectations and behaviour, far from being minimized, is emphasized. This sort of evaluative intransigence evokes the uncompromising moral stance of Jansenists

(c) *Applications to semantic modelling* One of the most interesting applications of attraction–repulsion dynamics is the simulation of the semantic behaviour of connectors. Although it is impossible to develop this complex problem in detail, a simple example involving the French connector *mais* will show how connectors can be represented within DSNs. *Mais*, *cependant* and *toutefois*, are the only connectors (indicating opposition) which can be used in purely evaluative uses.

(a) Pierre est beau, mais il ne connait pas son métier
(b) Pierre est beau, pourtant il ne connait pas son métier

Sentence (a) is perfectly correct, but (b) is much less acceptable. The reason is that *pourtant, néanmoins, bien que, malgré*, and *en dépit de*, suggest an objective opposition between the terms they connect.

According to Ducrot's description of *mais*, *P mais Q* presupposes that *P* argues in favour of a conclusion *r*, and that *r* annuls *Q*. In *P mais Q*, the focus is more on *Q* than on *P*. In addition, *Q* is presented as arguing more strongly in favour of *r* than *P* in favour of *r* (Ducrot 1980: 97). Finally *P mais Q* tends to resolve the contradiction between *P* and *Q*, while other connectors, such as *pourtant*, tend to leave the contradiction unsolved.

Instead of explaining *P mais Q* either by a potential or an actual contradiction between *P* and *Q*, I prefer to say that, in the evaluative uses of *mais*, *P* sets an expectation, or a standard, to which *Q* does not conform. I have just pointed out that this kind of interpretative situation based on the deviation from a standard is well represented by attraction–repulsion. Therefore the connector *mais* can be represented by attraction–repulsion links. *P* repulses *Q* (renders it more unexpected), while *Q* attracts *P* (*P* is reconsidered in the light of *Q*). In addition, if we assume that the attraction is stronger than the repulsion (Jesuit dynamics), we also account for the fact that *mais* resolves the evaluative contradictions. This solution is consistent with the argumentative description of *mais*. It has the advantage of combining the most important features of the connector within a simple dynamical framework. Finally, it takes into account some semantic effects usually overlooked by classical argumentative descriptions, such as the reinforcement of the deviation from a standard.

Another interesting application of attraction–repulsion links is the representation of adverbs. Let us consider the following example.

(c) He systematically makes mistakes

Let us assume that the initial value of the unit representing 'systematically' is set to zero, and that there is a negative link from this unit to the unit representing 'makes mistakes'. Starting from a negative default evaluation, the latter becomes even more negative while it interacts with 'systematically'. If the action were positively evaluated, it would be pushed up. Such a behaviour is consistent with the semantic properties of linguistic expressions expressing intensity, frequency, but also intentionality (for example 'deliberately', 'consciously', 'on purpose', etc.). To represent the adverbs that, instead of intensifying the evaluation, tend to moderate it, it is enough to replace the negative link by a positive one. Note that adverbs are not intrinsically catalysts or moderators. An adverb like 'sometimes' may belong to one or the other category depending on the context. But DSNs can handle correctly both cases.

Conclusion

In this rather technical chapter, I have presented the mathematical translation of the semantics of contextual modification sketched in Chapter 4. The dynamic systems used in this book are non-standard, since the interaction between two units depends on the difference of activation between the units. Despite the fact that it is probably the first use of such dynamics, this particular behaviour lends itself to the modelling of evaluative semantics. In addition, under rather weak constraints upon the parameters, the dynamics are globally asymptotically stable, which is a very desirable property, since this guarantees that systems converge whatever their initial state may be.

Various combinations of weights produce several type of dynamics, which simulate a wide range of evaluative semantic effects. This variety ensures the semantic expressivity of the dynamics. In particular, it is possible to represent subtle evaluative properties of adverbs and connectors. The dynamics also allows us to model the semantic effects arising from a comparison with a standard.

A mathematical formula has also been proposed for the estimation of ideological consistency. The calculus basically proceeds by applying a mathematical transform to a measure of the variation between initial and final state of the dynamics. Such is the transform that it tends to render the measure of consistency insensitive to proportional changes in the parameters. Thus, parameters have a relative rather than absolute value, which is another desirable property. The transform also ensures that ideological consistency lies in the same interval as evaluation. This renders it possible to treat the ideological consistency of embedded contexts as their initial evaluation. In this way, we can mathematically and practically solve the problems of semantic opacity that we had only theoretically solved in Chapter 4.

There are numerous potential applications of the method that has been sketched above. The main area of application is obviously the sociological analysis of discourse. However, the method relies on a coding of discourses into conceptual structures (here SSNs), a step which is not yet fully automated even at the level of most ambitious industrial projects. Since the derivation of DSNs is almost as complex, we can only dream (or have nightmares) about a system that would automatically identify the ideological allegiance of a discourse. Even if such a system were never to be realized, working on related topics remains useful since it teaches us a lot about the evaluative effects that occur at the linguistic level.

There are also a few potential applications within AI. It is clear that the social and ideological levels have been strongly underestimated within current research in natural language processing. As an important aspect of textual coherence, ideological consistency ought to be incorporated within NLP systems, where it may prove useful for disambiguation, and more generally, for inference control. The last chapter gives some examples of the disambiguation problems which can be solved by adopting an evaluative approach. However, before turning to these applications, we must be more specific about the parameters of dynamic semantic networks.

8

SETTING THE WEIGHTS

Introduction

In the previous chapter, and for expository purposes, we have used a fairly limited version of ideology as default parameters (evaluation, inertia and significance) associated with types. This restricted definition of ideology does not give us any clue on how connection weights should be set. And indeed, in the last chapter, very little has been said on connection parameters. All we have done until now is to classify relations under three general categories: mutual attraction, mutual repulsion and attraction-repulsion. But in practice, this typology does not provide us with numerical values for relations. How we should set parameters, and in particular, connection weights, is the object of this chapter.

DSNs are obtained from SSNs by specifying an ideological hypothesis. Therefore, an ideological hypothesis complements the semantic information of a SSN with additional information concerning its interpretative dynamics. It is clear that a lot of decisions concerning the meaning of a discourse are in fact taken at this level. In practice, it means that even if we possess the SSN representation of a discourse, we have still determined very little of its evaluative meaning. The three parameter sets that still need to be specified are connection weights, inertia coefficients, and default evaluations.

As we have seen in the last chapter, the large number of parameters is what renders DSNs capable of expressing a wide range of evaluative semantic properties. However, from the point of view of sociological discourse analysis, working with a model incorporating so many parameters can be an important methodological handicap. Indeed, one can achieve any desired result simply by fiddling with the parameters. When the parameter space is complex, this kind of trick cannot easily be discovered. In our case, if a sociologist intends to demonstrate that a discourse is consistent with an ideology, all he needs to do is to customize the DSN representing the text for this specific result. Given the number of parameters, this operation may not be visible.

To avoid this problem, strong constraints must be imposed on the way DSNs are obtained from SSNs. While it is trivial to obtain a SSN from a DSN by neglecting the dynamic part of the DSN, it is much more difficult to obtain a DSN from a SSN and an ideological hypothesis. In other words, the mapping Φ^{-1} which associates SSNs to DSNs is trivially defined, and we look for the mapping Φ_I which associates DSNs to SSNs under an ideological hypothesis I. The problem is in fact to define ideologies in such a way that will allow us to transform SSNs in DSNs.

1 The structure of ideologies

Ideologies will be structured as a lattice of CDSNs. This lattice structure itself, and for expository purposes only, will be organized in three different layers (Figure 8.1). The first layer is the *ontology*. It is made of general categories, which are ideologically neutral. The second layer contains *default parameters for relations and small CDSNs*. This second level is still not strongly ideology-committed. The lower level encodes *ideological knowledge* strictly speaking. The first and second levels correspond to doxa, while the third corresponds to opinion. Opinion is organized according to the Boltanski-Thévenot model presented at the end of the first chapter.
Ontology, relations and ideological knowledge are connected by subsumption links. Any such link from a node a to a node b of the lattice indicates that there is at least one projection of b into a. Conversely, if there

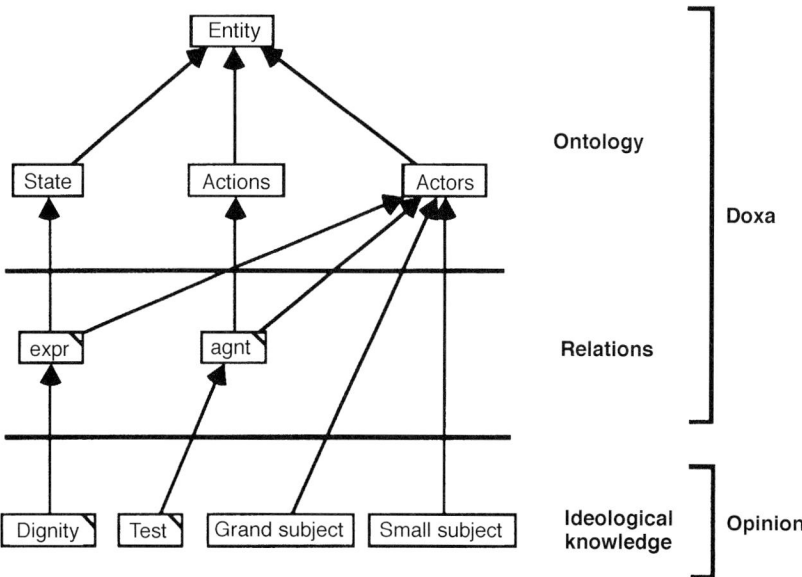

Figure 8.1 The three-layer structure of ideologies.

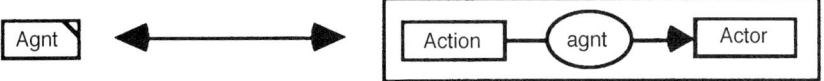

Figure 8.2 Collapsed and expanded view of a context.

is a projection from a node b into a node a, then there should be a path of subsumption links from a to b.

More generally, the partial order which defines the lattice structure is nothing other than the projection operation. An ideology is therefore a lattice of concepts and contexts linked by subsumption links (these links are displayed as arrows without labels). Note that since ideologies and networks contain the same type of data structures, there is no need to create a new type of document for ideologies. Ideologies are simply big networks satisfying lattice properties.

It is important to realize that the lattice structure of ideology concerns both the relation between canonical networks and types. Thus there is in fact no distinction between the type hierarchy and the hierarchy of canonical networks. This unique framework has the advantage of closely integrating ideological categories and their semantic content. In fact, each canonical network can also be considered as a type. For example, the canonical network representing the (AGNT) relation can be seen as the type [AGNT], [AGENT RELATION], or [AGENTIVITY], depending on how we wish to describe it (Figure 8.2). Conversely, most types do have a relational semantic content, which can be made objective by a canonical network. In practice, within CoCoNet, the expanded view of a context can be seen as the definition of the type label which appears in the collapsed view of the same context.

I have criticized, in Chapter 4, the habit of semantic theories to distinguish between the system of language and social norms, or between inherent and afferent semes. These distinctions, I have argued, derive from 'realist' ontological presuppositions, according to which there exists something as a natural, physical world, whose stable and obvious nature is reflected by the more obvious part of the system of language. For a (constructivist) sociologist such as the author of this book, these presuppositions are hardly acceptable. Therefore, my intentions are not to suggest that the ontology can be isolated from ideology. The ontology, in my view, differs from ideological categories exactly to the extent that doxa differs from opinion. In other words, the ontology is just the part of social knowledge that is likely to be accepted by all ideologies. But if we look at a society from the outside, what originally appeared as doxa may perfectly well appear as ideological.

2 A derivation algorithm

Given this lattice structure, it is easy to figure out a derivation algorithm. This algorithm is basically a depth-first search of the lattice. At each step, all projections of the lattice node into the target network are computed. For each projection, all parameters of the lattice node are copied to the relevant parts of the target network. However, if a prior, bigger operation of copy has already been done on a part of the target, then this copy process is skipped. This allows us to be sure that big graphs' parameters prevail over small graphs' ones. Thus, preemption in CoCoNet is implemented through size considerations. To avoid computing projections that cannot succeed, when a node has no projection into the target, the sub-lattice it subsumes is pruned.

Definition: A *derivation* of a SSN called *target* from an ideology I is the result of computing *Derive(target, root(I))* where *root(I)* is the most general concept of I, and *Derive()* is the following procedure:

for all immediate descendants x of root(i) that are unmarked **loop**
  if $\Pi(x, target) \pm \emptyset$ **then** // cf. Ch. 5, section 6.
    for all projections p in $\Pi(x, target)$ **loop**
      for all items i in p **loop**
        if $d(i) < card(x)$ **then** // $d(i)$ stores the size of the graph
                                        // i's parameters are derived from
          do copy the parameters from item y in x that unifies with i in p;
          do $d(i) = card(x)$;
          do *Derive(x, target)*; // recursion on the lattice structure
        end if;
      end loop;
    end loop;
  else
    do mark all descendants of x; // pruning
end loop;

The above algorithm and its associated data structures (the ideology lattice) provides a practical solution to the problem of inputting the evaluative knowledge of an ideology into a knowledge-base and using this knowledge to derive complex DSNs representing discourse. However, this solution is not without problems.

The first difficulty is computational. As stated in Chapter 5, finding a projection of a CDSN in a DSN is an NP-hard problem. The derivation algorithm is therefore not of polynomial complexity. However, the lattice structure helps to keep the computational requirements of the derivation algorithm close to that of the projection algorithm. In the above pseudo-code, most difficulties remain hidden. The main difficulty is to keep track, from one step of the recursion to another, of the unifications that have been made in the projections that occurred at the previous step. When this difficulty is solved, the algorithm is almost as efficient as the projection algorithm itself. In fact, keeping track of previous projections is a problem of data persistence rather than a problem of algorithm design (as far as these two aspects of programming can be separated). The derivation algorithm has been fully implemented in CoCoNet, in a much more straightforward manner than the projection algorithm itself. Indeed, the derivation algorithm is fundamentally a searching algorithm, while the projection algorithm is a genuine backtracking algorithm.

The second difficulty lies in the maintenance of the lattice structure. One has to be sure, when feeding the ideological database with new knowledge, that the consistency of the lattice structure is indeed preserved. In particular, one must make sure that subsumption paths correspond to potential projection operations. Thus, checking the consistency of an ideology may also be computationally demanding.

The third difficulty concerns the CDSNs themselves. Even if we could efficiently derive large DSNs from CDSNs, we still would have to set the parameters of the CDSNs. In theory, connectionist networks could be trained to learn the evaluative behaviour of each simple predicative structure. Despite some promising results obtained in the modelling of meaning by dynamical systems that learn, this objective is still far from being achievable. In practice, there is no solution other than to keep CDSNs small, simple, and general enough to control them on an intuitive basis.

3 Default relation settings

Concerning the intermediate layer of ideologies (that of semantic relations), the following assumptions are made, and rendered explicit by their corresponding CDSNs:[1]

- The evaluative influence of an action on its actor is stronger than the reverse influence:

- The evaluative influence of a state on its experiencer is stronger than the reverse influence:

- Attribution and subsumption are similar to agentivity and experiencing, except that they have a slightly stronger effect.

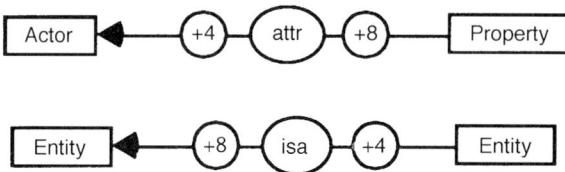

- The evaluative influence of an object or a patient on an action is stronger than the reverse influence:

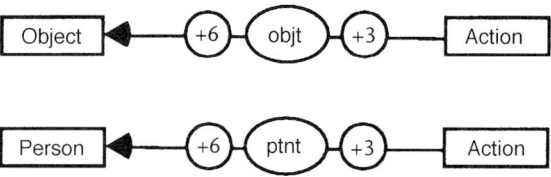

When the evaluation of the action depends negatively on the evaluation of its object, these weights need to change sign. When they become negative, parameters are also divided by two – the reason for this operation will be shown at the end of the next section. Actions that depend negatively on the evaluation of their object are called 'negative actions'. This does mean that they are necessarily negatively evaluated. This expression refers to a certain intrinsic negativity, which determines the type of semantic relation which holds between the relation and its object.

To abandon, for example, is a negative action. Note that no similar rule holds for agentivity relation. Parameters of the (AGNT) relation are the same for both positive and negative action. However, this is not always the case for (EXPR) because states are more often involuntary than actions (for example, 'to suffer'). Thus, actors often cannot be blamed for their negative, involuntary states. We can formulate another default setting corresponding to this last remark:

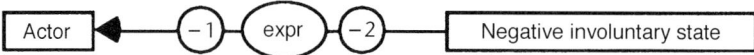

What is involuntary and what of a person's responsibility is highly ideological. Unemployment is a good example of a state upon which commentators hardly reach a consensus.

- The influence of a statement on its author and the influence of an author on his statement are the same (since it is unclear which is stronger):

- The connector *but* is represented by an attraction-repulsion link with Jesuit dynamics (see pages 222–3):

- The influence of the cause on the consequence and the influence of the consequence on the cause is the same. Furthermore, from an evaluative point of view, a causal relation is slightly stronger than a justification (a reason), which is less conclusive. In fact, causality can be seen as a strong justification.

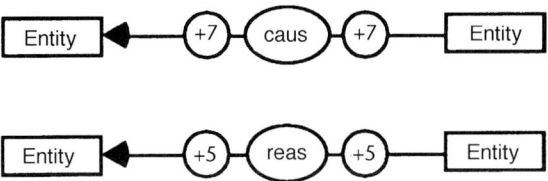

- Catalyst adverbs interact with whatever they apply to by means of a mutual repulsion link (see page 224). The abstract relation (RELA) here stands for all possible relations, and specially intensity, manner, frequency, quantity, location, etc. In practice, if one reduces the positive weight, the impact of the adverb will be stronger.

- Moderator adverbs interact with whatever they apply to by means of a mutual attraction link. Again, lowering the influence bearing the adverb (here equal to +6) will result in a stronger impact of the adverb.

- The influence of the goal upon an action is slightly stronger than the influence of the action upon its goal.

All these settings are default settings. Each adverb, each verb, each expression may override them, and be given more specific parameters. These specific parameters would, to a certain extent, be generic parameters too, since it is only in relation to what they apply that adverbs, verbs and adjectives get their true evaluative meaning. However, this is no longer a purely linguistic issue, and these contextual parameters must be encoded at the ideological level, since they reflect non-universal social norms.

4 An example of ideology

To avoid complexity in the exposition, I will consider only two simple 'ideologies'. The first one, that I will call *tyranny*, corresponds to Antony's character in *Julius Caesar* by Shakespeare. The second one, that I will call the *republican ideology*, reflects Brutus' character in the same play. In order to define more precisely these ideologies, I draw upon the Boltanski-Thévenot model presented in the first chapter of this book (see pages 47–8). I refer the reader to this chapter for a definition of the rhetorical categories listed below. The relations between the categories can be summarized by Network 8.16.

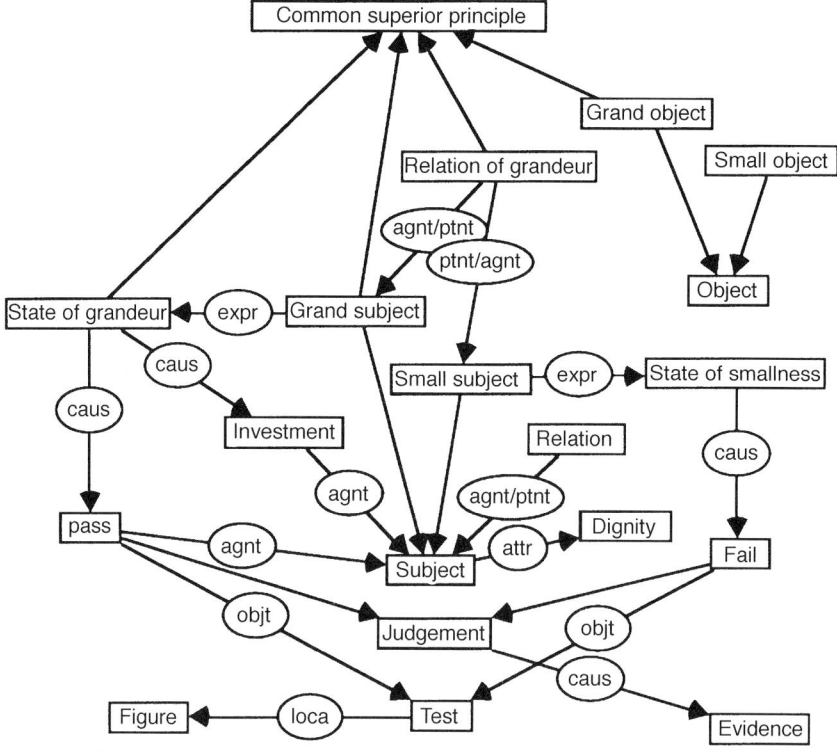

Network 8.16

It is not possible to give here a full account of the way in which these categories translate into a network for *tyranny* and *republic*. In the simulations of the next chapter, each ideology contains more than three hundred concepts, which fill several A3 pages. However, the unique network representing each ideology can be broken into several small networks. Such small networks, which eliminate the two upper layers of ideology, will be used for expository purposes in the rest of this chapter. I will also focus on the part of ideologies that is relevant to Shakespeare's text.

Common superior principle. For tyranny, *power*, or *strength*, is a value in itself. The common superior principle of the republican ideology is *freedom*.

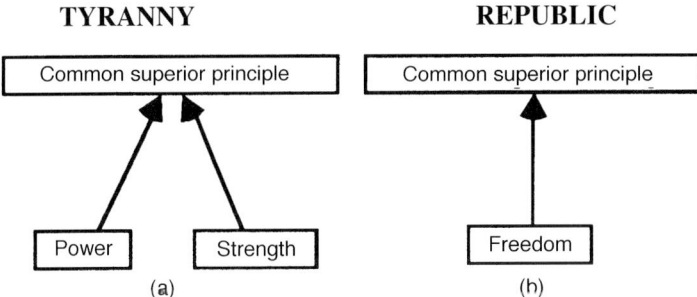

State of grandeur: Within tyranny, this is what Max Weber called *charisma*,[2] while within the republican ideology, this is *reputation*. The republican ideology is close to 'the civic world' of Boltanski and Thévenot. However, in Rome, and in Shakespeare's play, republic is not exactly a synonym for democracy. Republic must be understood as a form of government in which honourable men share the power. Reputation, closely related to morality, is therefore more important than the representative system of government.

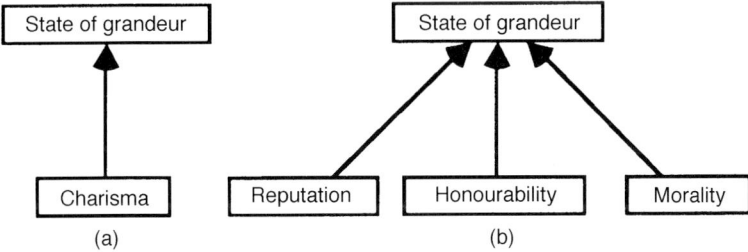

Dignity In a tyrant's view, the feature of human nature which allows subjects to participate in the economy of grandeur is desire and ambition. In a republican's view, this is reason and morality.

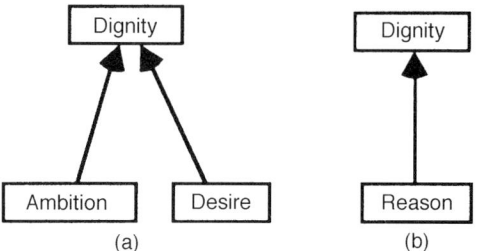

State of smallness For a tyrant, this is to be *weak*, to share his power, which ceases being absolute. On the contrary, within the republican ideology, smallness lies in the eagerness for power. Personal *ambition*, which is a form of dignity within tyranny, becomes a state of smallness within republic. The republican ideology relies on puritan ethics. This entails that greed, lust and debauchery, reveal smallness. On the contrary, within tyranny, the tyrant's sins are like status symbols, which uphold his charisma.

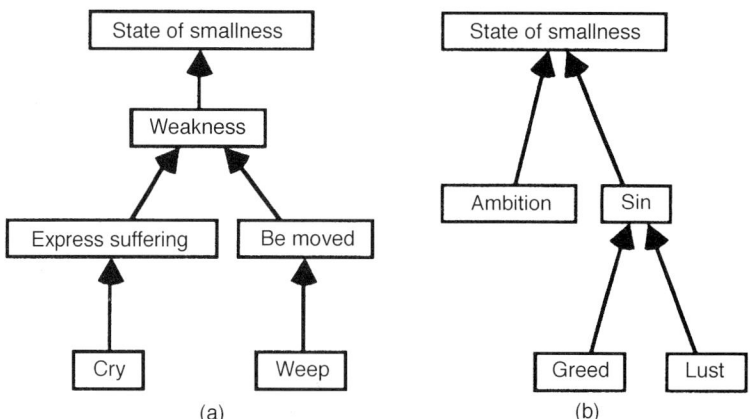

Grand subjects In a tyranny, and besides the tyrant itself, these are the leaders, the military chiefs, the courageous soldiers, the strong men. From a republican perspective, grand beings are representatives, nobles, honourable men, and, more generally, all citizens with good reputation. For Anthony, nobility and honour (being an honourable man, in the social sense of the term) are second-rate values, that do not guarantee nobleness of heart and the true sense of honour. On the contrary, for Brutus, nobility does not go without duties ('noblesse oblige'). Of course, in the context of Shakespeare's play, Caesar is a grand subject for tyranny and Brutus is a grand subject for the republican ideology.

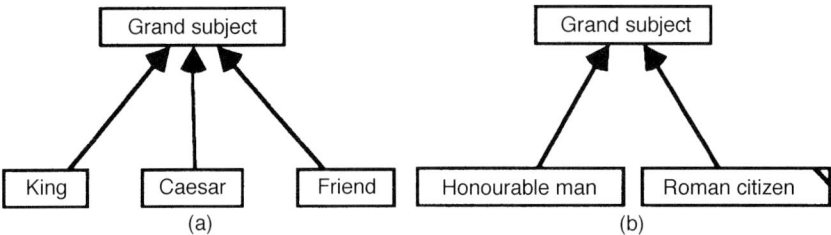

Small subjects A tyrant's small subjects are all the persons that are not his friends, including ordinary citizens, romans, and countrymen. For republic, roman citizens are all equal, and smallness is a matter of social status. Caesar is a small subject for the republican ideology, and Brutus is a small subject for tyranny. More precisely, Brutus and Caesar are fallen idols. For republic, Caesar became a tyrant, and for tyranny, Brutus became a murderer.

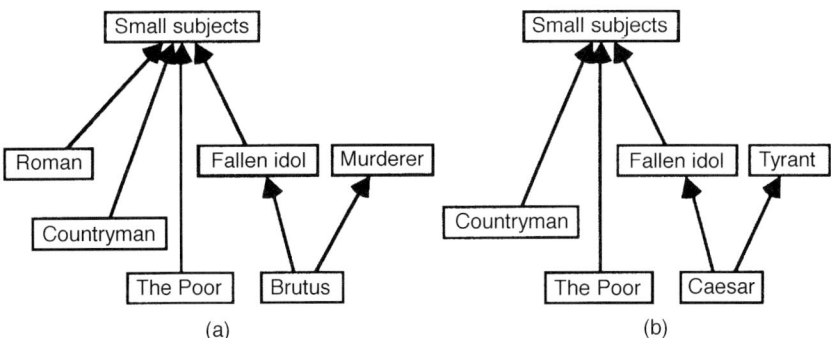

Objects In a tyrant's view, a *kingly crown* is the most valuable achievement. In a republican's view, this is one of the most hated symbols.

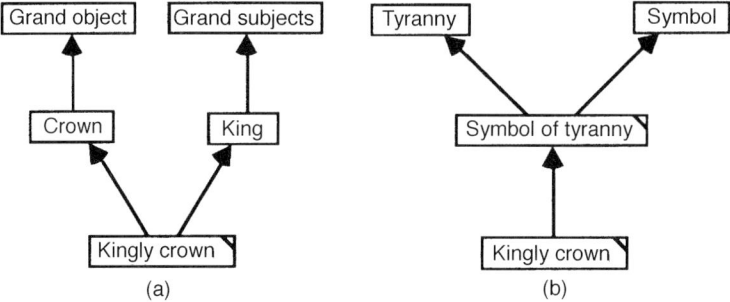

(a)   (b)

Investment A tyrant has to be courageous, tough, even cruel. His main investment is his physical security. He must be made of stern stuff. There is no better way for a republican, in order to bring a tyrant into disrepute, than to suggest that he is a coward – this is why literature abounds with descriptions of tyrants' fears.[3] For a republican, the major investment is the renouncement of all personal advantages granted by power. A representative must be disinterested, unselfish.

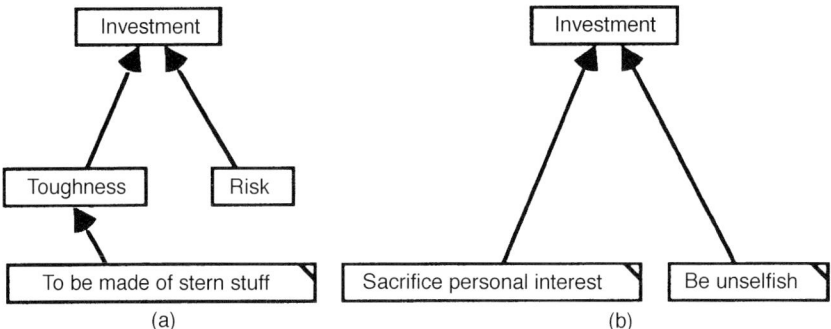

(a)   (b)

Relations of grandeur Tyranny is often close to demagogy. As in absolute monarchy, a tyrant often claims that he can relate directly to his people, without resorting to intermediaries (honourable men, institutions). A tyrant believes that he is able to empathize with his subjects. In particular, he feels *compassion*. But this compassion does not go as far as sharing his subjects' living conditions. Compassion therefore remains an affective disposition, and must be distinguished from the *concern* that the republican experiences for other citizens. Network 8.25 reflects the status of compassion within tyranny. Note that the parameters override default parameters for

CAUS, AGNT and EXPR relations. It is assumed that the harder suffering is, the better compassion (and inversely). The causal link between [EXPRESS SUFFERING] and [BE MOVED] is therefore a mutual repulsion link. A similar reasoning explains the parameters of the AGNT relation. Note finally that empathy is no longer here a weakness. Therefore, even weeping may be judged positively if it is triggered by compassion. In more technical terms, [BE MOVED] will not inherit its initial evaluation from that of [WEAKNESS], because the bigger evaluative pattern of empathy will exert a preemption. Note that the relations between [BE MOVED] as a weakness and [BE MOVED] as a form of compassion need not be made explicit in the ideological knowledge base. The derivation algorithm will automatically select the more specific evaluative pattern.

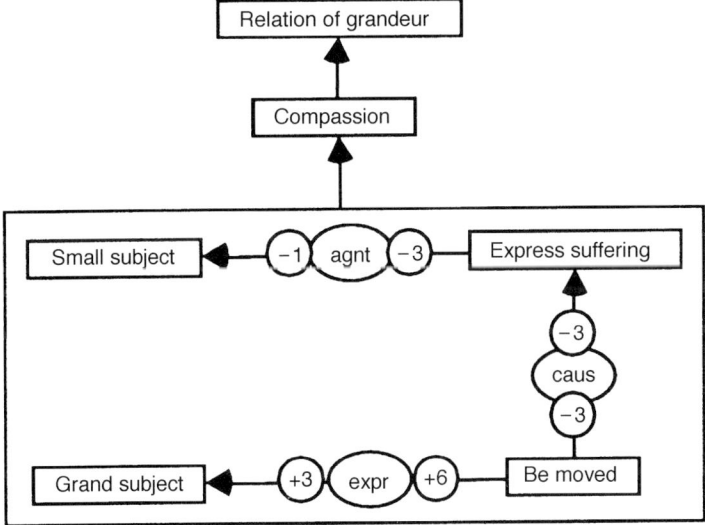

Network 8.25

Besides compassion, a tyrant has other duties, such as his nurturing function. But one must make a difference between a tyrant's *gifts*, which depend on his goodwill, and the *solidarity* of a republican, which is a much more binding requirement. More generally perhaps, tyranny claims to abolish, with the very person of the tyrant, the opposition between public and private sphere. In contrast, the republican discourse is structured by the opposition public/private. Filling the general coffers is a form of prodigality for tyranny, and of solidarity for republic. Note that it is at this level that the information concerning the evaluation of [GENERAL COFFERS] (used in the next chapter) must be stored.

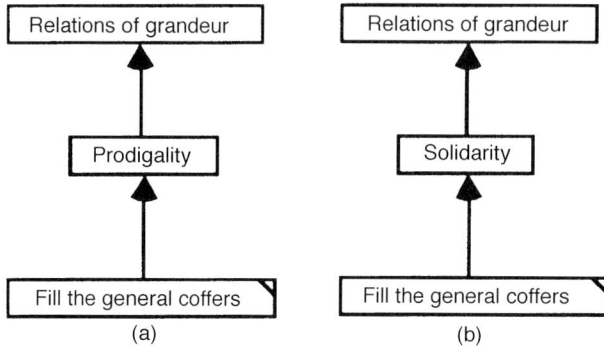

Relations Tyranny emphasizes personal relations, especially friendship and loyalty. The same holds for the republican ideology, although with less intensity, since friendship and loyalty towards friends remains less binding than loyalty to the law.

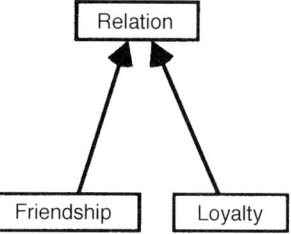

Figures For both ideologies, *Rome* is the ideal context for an optimal distribution of grandeur. However, tyranny views Rome as the head of a military empire, while republic views Rome as the political centre of a democracy. Tyrants also like battlefields, or their surrogates, circus games. Republicans prefer the Lupercal, and all places of public discussion.

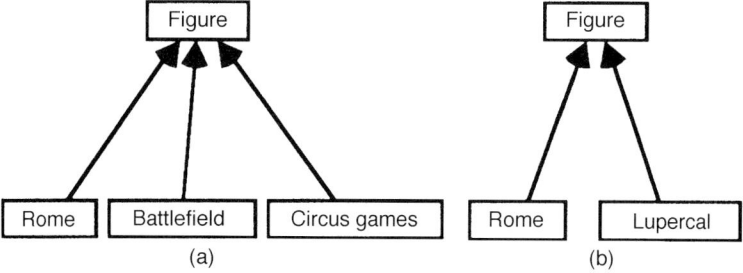

Network 8.28

SETTING THE WEIGHTS

Tests For a tyrant, the most important tests are military battles, and public ceremonies, where they need to exert their charisma. For a republican, the ultimate form of test is voting (irrelevant here). For a dead person, like Caesar in Shakespeare's text, a funeral is a sort of post-mortem test. For the person that buries a grand subject, a funeral is also a sort of test, or a least an obligation.

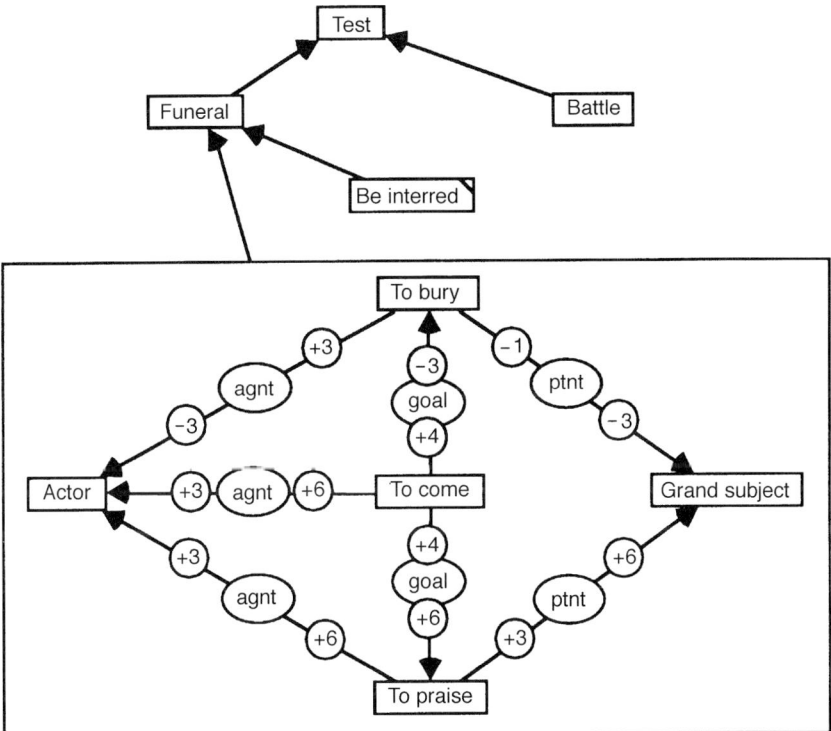

Network 8.29

We could spell out this obligation as 'One should come to the funeral of a grand subject, in order to bury him and to praise him' (see Network 8.29). The unit [TO BURY] depends negatively on its patient, since the better the patient is, the worse it is to bury him. It is reasonable to believe that to bury a person produces a feeling of pity for this person. Therefore, the link [TO BURY] – (PTNT) ⟶ [GRAND SUBJECT] is represented by a mutual repulsion link. It is also assumed that burying a grand subject is a duty, and the harder (sadder) it is to bury him, the better to do this duty.

241

Judgements A tyrant must be applauded, praised and feared. When he is dead, people must mourn for him. In the republican political life, judgement takes the form of voting, or of rhetorical successes in public speeches. Note that Antony pretends that he is not eloquent. Eloquence is an attribute of honourable men. For a tyrant, fate is the ultimate form of judgement. Victory is the positive side of fate, and defeat the negative one.

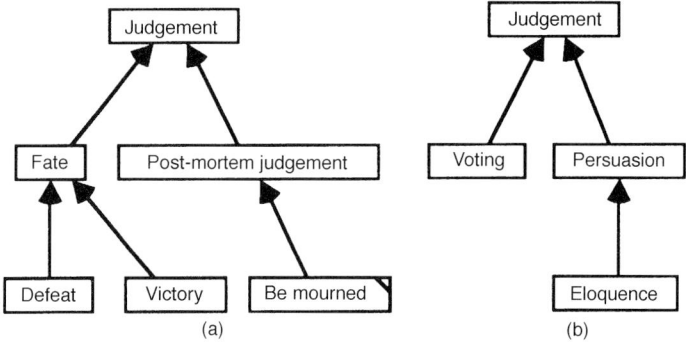

Evidence Within republic, evidence lies in the verdict of the polls (but this is irrelevant to our text). Within tyranny, the evidence supporting judgement tends to be entirely emotional and takes the form of fear and love (see Network 8.31). Captives are also an evidence that military battles (Tests) have been victorious (Judgement). The evaluation of the word 'Captives' is an indexical phenomenon. Captives that are brought to Rome are positively evaluated. Roman captives carried away from Rome would be negatively evaluated. Thus, evaluation is indexical, and it is one of the purposes of ideology to associate indexicality and evaluation.

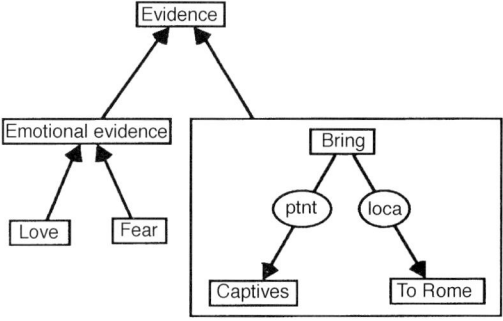

Network 8.31

Several of the dynamic systems listed in this section override the default parameters proposed in section 3. This is usually what happens when social expectations (standards) are attached to a given situation (here the funeral of a grand subject). Thus, the ideology contains the social standards with respect to which behaviours are evaluated. Finally, it contains ideological perspectives strictly speaking, which are translated into default evaluation, inertia, and significance. These parameters need not be specified for each occurrence of a context in the ideology. The parameters are derived from subsumption relations. For example, one need not specify the default evaluation of Caesar, since Caesar will inherit this evaluation from that of grand subjects (in tyranny).

5 Semantic properties

I turn now to another class of evaluative semantic constraints, which is in fact better described as a class of semantic properties than as a class of constraints, since these properties hold for every ideology. These properties allow us to derive the parameters of a complex DSN from the parameters of a simple DSN. In the process of parametrization, these properties are used in a second stage, after a simple DSN has been derived from the CDSNs of an ideology.

Negation

> **Proposition 1.** When a link does not express a comparison with a standard, negating the link label reverses the weights of the link. Let a be a positive coefficient depending on type1 and type2.

- If type2 is not a standard associated with type1, then

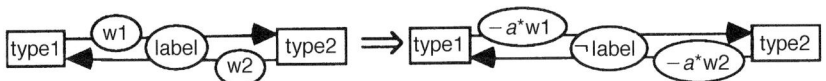

Figure 8.3 Effect of negation.

- If type2 is a standard associated with type1 (i.e. w1 < 0) then

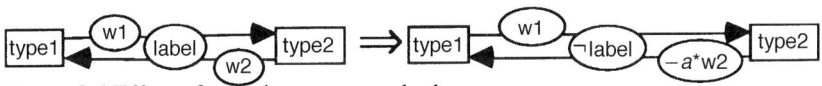

Figure 8.4 Effect of negation on a standard.

When an actor sets up an expectation with respect to an action, performing another action that does not conform to the expectation will imply a comparison with a standard. Not doing the action is just a special case of this

SETTING THE WEIGHTS

deviation from the standard. Thus, when a link expressing a comparison with a standard is negated, the negative weight that expresses this comparison is not modified. On the contrary, when a link does not express a comparison with a standard, the negation reverses the signs of the weights. Such a behaviour will not surprise logicians, accustomed to the effects of logical negation. Coefficient a depends on the types involved in each side of the negated link. In some cases, the negative consequences of not doing something are more extreme than the positive results of doing it. In some other, not doing something is trivial, while doing it is really clever. It is therefore difficult to be more precise about coefficient a, which is here in charge of expressing all these evaluative subtleties. Note that when the negation bears on a concept instead of a link, it is the default evaluation of the negated concept which becomes the parameter of interest. I discuss below what happens to the connection weights when the negation bears on a concept.

Definition. A link is *sensitive* (resp. *insensitive*) *to the scope of a negation* if its weights change signs (resp. do not change) when it is under the scope of the negation. More precisely:

- The link 'label' is *sensitive to the scope of a negation* if

Figure 8.5 Relations sensitive to negation.

- The link 'label' is *insensitive to the scope of a negation* if

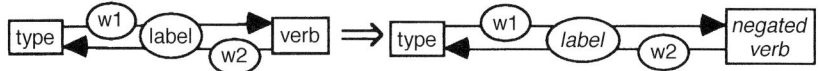

Figure 8.6 Relations insensitive to negation.

This definition immediately raises the question of what determines the 'sensitivity' of a link to the scope of a negation. Interestingly enough this sensitivity only depends on the label of the link.

Proposition 2. Relational primitives can be classified as either sensitive or insensitive with respect to the scope of a negation.

The main difference is between the relational primitive AGENT (and its variants such as EXPERIENCER and ADVISER) and the relational primitive OBJECT (and its variants such as PATIENT). The first one is insensitive, while the second is sensitive to the scope of negations. Such different behaviour shows that, as far as negation is concerned, the verb complement is semantically closer to the verb than the subject. In syntactic terms, one may say that linguistic negation applies first to the *verb phrase*. Only then is the subject composed with the negated verb phrase to produce a *sentence*.

Since the set of relational primitives is open, it is impossible to classify all of them. All other relational primitives used in this chapter are sensitive to the scope of a negation. Nevertheless, not all primitives are likely to be encountered under the scope of a negation. Some primitives like BELIEF, or STATEMENT, because they express attitude verbs, never fall under the scope of a negation. Some others, like IMPLICATION, cannot be found under the scope of a negation because they are 'meta-primitives'. For yet others, this absence from the scope of a negation is the result of the fact that the same semantic effect can be achieved by negating them directly. In the vocabulary employed in Chapter 6 (section 3), some relational primitives tend to 'focus negation'. It is now possible to add another remark concerning this property.

Proposition 3. Relational primitives that express a comparison with a standard do not focus negation.

This comes from the fact that, in some discursive contexts, verb complements have the function of reinforcing a negation bearing on the verb. By making the verb more precise, they evoke a standard from which the actor deviates. Such standards are not so much associated with the actor as with the verb itself, that is, with the situation.

(a) His mother did not come, sweetly as ever, to kiss him in his bed.
(b) Jim did not take her passionately in his arms, he did not kiss her furiously, he did none of that.

In these two examples, the complements 'sweetly as ever', 'passionately', 'furiously' do not focus negation. On the contrary, their effect is to insist on the fact that the actions did not happen. In (a) there is a subjective expectation of sweetness associated with the mother's coming and kissing. In (b), whatever our interpretation of the sentence may be (a critique of Jim's silliness or a praise of his prudence), Jim's behaviour is compared with another, more desirable or simply more plausible behaviour. Thus, because of their complements, the negated verbs appear as deviations from an expected behaviour, or an expected situation. In these cases, the focus of the negation on the complements would lead to misinterpretations.

Propositions 1 to 3 deal with the semantic properties associated with negation. They demonstrate that there are indeed some links between the inferential properties associated with linguistic negation and evaluative properties such as the comparison with a standard. Therefore, it is likely that taking into account the evaluative dimension of discourse could be useful for inference control. More generally, an evaluative perspective may help to choose between several readings of a sentence, and thus, be of benefit to natural language processing. I will come back to this issue in more detail in the next chapter.

Modalities

In Chapters 4 and 5, I have shown how Kripke's possible world semantics for modal logic translates into game-theoretical semantics. Since then, I have given up any reference to model theory, either traditional (Tarskian) or game-theoretical. Nevertheless, modalities are one of the more important dimensions of natural language, and this dimension is closely related to evaluative phenomena. Therefore, any evaluative semantics must take into account modalities, and especially, alethic modalities.

It is reasonable to believe that the evaluative impact of a supposition is not as strong as that of an assertion. For example, 'John made a mistake' argues more strongly against John than 'John might have made a mistake'. This remark reflects the fact that in the first case, both John and the mistake belong to the real world, while in the second case, the mistake only belongs to a possible world.

> **Proposition 4**. Potential facts do not have as much evaluative impact on real facts as real facts themselves. This is achieved, in DSNs, by applying a coefficient $0 < a < 1$, to the weight representing the influence of a potential concept on a real one.

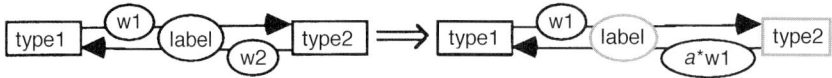

Figure 8.7 Effect of potential modality.

This rule does not apply to 'potential links'[4] relating two 'potential concepts'. Within a given possible world, evaluative semantic relations are the same as they are in a real world. The attenuation of semantic impact concern only the links which bridge the gap between two distinct worlds.

Let us turn now to the case of unreal relations. Consider the following sentences:

(a) The Prime Minister does not do his duty, and thus the poor suffer more.
(b) If the Prime Minister did his duty, the poor would suffer less.

It is clear that the two sentences argue in the same direction, though (a) is perhaps a little stronger than (b). As stated in Chapter 6, sentence (a) can be represented by a negated (AGNT) link between [THE PRIME MINISTER] and [DO ONE'S DUTY], while sentence (b) can be represented by making [DO ONE'S DUTY] and the (AGNT) link unreal. This suggests the following rule:

Proposition 5a. Unreal links behave similarly to negated links, though with less strength. Again, this can be achieved, in DSNs, by applying a coefficient $0 < b < 1$ to the weights.

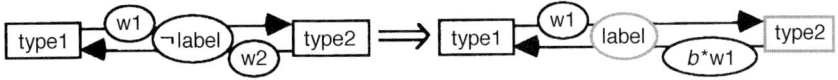

Figure 8.8 Effect of unreal modality.

Thus an event in a counterfactual world has the same type of evaluating impact on the real world as negating the event in the real world, though this effect is slightly attenuated in the first case.

There is another way to deal with the modality *unreal*. One can indeed simply reverse the default evaluation of the *unreal* concept, and diminish connection weights.

Proposition 5b. If the default evaluation of the concept that they contribute to 'dis-realize' is reversed, *unreal* links behave as normal links, though with less strength. This can be achieved, in DSNs, by negating the default evaluation of the *unreal* concept and by applying a coefficient $0 < b < 1$ to the weights.

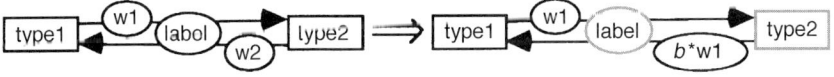

Figure 8.9 An alternative effect of unreal modality.

Proposition 5b is more simple to use than proposition 5a, since it does not require to reverse the sign of the weights. However, it cannot be used when the 'unreal concept' has several relations attached to it, because some of these relations may expect to interact with the 'true' default value of the *unreal* concept and not with the reversed one. Therefore, in this chapter and the next, I will use the following strategy: whenever an *unreal* concept has a single relation attached to it, use proposition 5b, otherwise, use proposition 5a.

Quantification

Most of the evaluative semantic effects of quantification are handled by default evaluations and inertia coefficients in DSNs. Ideologies prescribe default evaluations for important notions, such as fundamental values, and for individuals, such as the historical leaders of the political movements. However, besides the typical expressions, such as 'the workers' or the generic 'a worker', many other expressions, such as 'this worker' or 'the politically uneducated workers', also need to be assigned default evaluations. An easy solution consists in assigning all quantified expression of base type T the default evaluation of type T, but customizing inertia coefficients to suit the extension of the expression. The extension of the expression 'many workers', for example, is close to the extension of 'the workers'. Therefore, it should be almost as well stabilized by an ideology as the expression 'the workers'. On the contrary 'one worker' is only a small subset of the workers, and an ideology does not have the same interest in stabilizing the evaluation of this last expression, since exceptions exist. Similarly, in the expression 'the workers who betray the working class', the expression 'the workers' should be allowed to deviate from its default evaluation to accommodate its restrictor.

Let us assume, as we did in Chapter 6, that all quantifiers can be ordered in terms of generality, and that this order is represented by the relation $\succ$, meaning 'is more general than'.

Proposition 6. In quantified expressions without restrictor, if E[TYPE] > 0 (resp. < 0)

if QUANT1 $\succ$ QUANT2 then E[QUANT1 TYPE] $>$ (resp. $<$) E[QUANT2 TYPE]
if QUANT1 $\succ$ QUANT2, then I[QUANT1 TYPE] $>$ I[QUANT2 TYPE].

In particular, if QUANT is a universal quantifier and E[TYPE] ≤ 0, then E[QUANT TYPE] $<$ E[TYPE]. 'All the problems', for example, is more negatively evaluated than 'problem'.

Proposition 7. In quantified expressions with a restrictor, the first constraint of Proposition 6 holds, but the second is replaced by:

I[QUANT TYPE] $\leq$ I[TYPE]

In particular, in the case of untyped constructs such as 'those who P', the default evaluation of [THOSE WHO] is neutral, and its inertia coefficient is kept low, in order to let it be fully determined by the restrictor.

Negation bearing on quantifiers

Let us consider three simple sentences involving a quantifier under the scope of a negation.

(a) The government did not solve all the problems.
(b) The government did not solve the problems.
(c) The government did not solve any problem.

It is clear that each sentence has a different effect. If we rank them according to the strength of the critique of the government, everyone will agree that (a) is weaker than (b), and, in turn, (b) is weaker than (c). The simulations should reflect this ordering.

Sentence (a) translates into the following SSN:

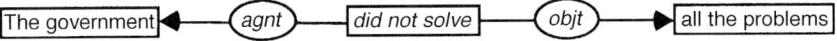

Because [SOLVE] depends negatively on the evaluation of its object, and because (OBJT) is a relational primitive sensitive to the scope of a negation, [DID NOT SOLVE] depends positively on the evaluation of [ALL THE PROBLEMS]. In the reverse direction, [ALL THE PROBLEMS] depends positively on [DID NOT SOLVE]. This is because the worse 'not solving a problem' is considered, the worse the problem is. It is assumed that the government is not expected to solve all problems, and thus, (AGNT) is not a mixed link implementing a comparison with a standard. From the previous SSN, the following DSN is set up:

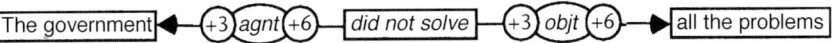

Three successive hypotheses are made as to the evaluation of [THE GOVERNMENT]. The first one is unfavourable, the second one neutral, and the third one favourable to the government. The simulations corresponding to each hypothesis are summarized in Table 8.1.

Table 8.1 Negation and quantifiers – case (a)

	a_i	Hypothesis 1		Hypothesis 2		Hypothesis 3	
		$x_i(0)$	$x_i(\infty)$	$x_i(0)$	$x_i(\infty)$	$x_i(0)$	$x_i(\infty)$
[THE GOVERNMENT]	0.2	−0.5	−0.3595	0.0	−0.1345	0.5	0.0909
[DID NOT SOLVE]	0.2	−0.3	−0.2652	−0.3	−0.2243	−0.3	−0.1838
[ALL THE PROBLEMS]	0.8	−0.2	−0.2103	−0.2	−0.2038	−0.2	−0.1974

Focusing our attention on the variations of evaluation affecting [THE GOVERNMENT], we discover that sentence (a) is slightly more consistent with hypothesis 2 than with hypothesis 1, and more consistent with hypothesis 1 than with hypothesis 3. This is not counter-intuitive, since (a) may be either a very weak critique or a fake critique, as in discourses like 'the government did not solve all the problems, however, it solved most of them'.

Let us turn now to sentence (b). The corresponding DSN reflects the fact that the government is expected to 'solve the problems'.

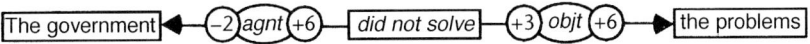

SETTING THE WEIGHTS

Table 8.2 Negation and quantifiers – case (b)

	a_i	Hypothesis 1		Hypothesis 2		Hypothesis 3	
		$x_i(0)$	$x_i(\infty)$	$x_i(0)$	$x_i(\infty)$	$x_i(0)$	$x_i(\infty)$
[THE GOVERNMENT]	0.2	−0.5	−0.4418	0.0	−0.2707	0.5	−0.0966
[DID NOT SOLVE]	0.2	−0.3	−0.4031	−0.3	−0.4515	−0.3	−0.4995
[THE PROBLEMS]	0.8	−0.5	−0.4847	−0.5	−0.4923	−0.5	−0.4999

Table 8.2 gives the results of the simulations for the three hypotheses. This time, the sentence is more consistent with hypothesis 1 than hypothesis 2, and more consistent with hypothesis 2 than hypothesis 3. And this is not surprising since sentence (b) is a genuine critique of the government.

Finally, let us consider sentence (c). It is assumed that 'solving at least one problem' is a standard bearing on the government. The DSN of sentence (c) is thus the same as the DSN of sentence (b). The simulations give very similar results. The only new element is that hypothesis 1 is now too favourable to the government to be absolutely consistent with sentence (c) (Table 8.3).

To convince ourselves that these results fulfil our requirement about the ranking of the sentences, let us position each sentence with respect to the hypotheses (see Figure 8.10).

It is now clear that the expected ranking (c > b > a) is obtained. However, this result is due to two factors. The first one is a difference of DSN between (a) on one side, and (b) and (c) on the other. This factor is not as influential as the second one, which consists in differences of initial evaluations. These differences have not yet been justified. In their respective contexts, the initial evaluations were:

E[ALL THE PROBLEMS] = −0.2,
E[THE PROBLEMS] = −0.5,
E[ANY PROBLEMS] = −0.8.

Note first that, from the logical point of view, 'not all problems' covers a wide range of extensions. This may indeed correspond to 'almost all

Table 8.3 Negation and quantifiers – case (c)

	a_i	Hypothesis 1		Hypothesis 2		Hypothesis 3	
		$x_i(0)$	$x_i(\infty)$	$x_i(0)$	$x_i(\infty)$	$x_i(0)$	$x_i(\infty)$
[THE GOVERNMENT]	0.2	−0.5	−0.5520	0.0	−0.3803	0.5	−0.2046
[DID NOT SOLVE]	0.2	−0.3	−0.5865	−0.3	−0.6350	−0.3	−0.6828
[ANY PROBLEM]	0.8	−0.8	−0.7664	−0.8	−0.7740	−0.8	−0.7815

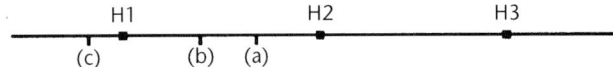

Figure 8.10 Ranking of quantifiers.

problems' as well as to 'a few problems'. Despite this logical ambiguity, within natural inference and in the absence of other indications, 'not all problems' is semantically close to 'some problems'. Under the scope of a negation, the evaluation of 'all problems' should therefore be close to the evaluation of 'some problem'. This is why, in the context of our example, I have assumed that E[ALL THE PROBLEMS] $= -0.2$. From this example we can draw a general rule.

Proposition 8. Under the scope of a negation, E[ALL TYPE] $\approx$ E[SOME TYPE].

Agentivity and passivization

As stated in Chapter 3 (section 4), one of the traditional theses of discourse analysis is that passivization diminishes agentivity. It is easy to incorporate this effect in DSNs.

Proposition 9. Passivization diminishes agentivity. If d is an attenuation coefficient such that $0 < d < 1$, we have

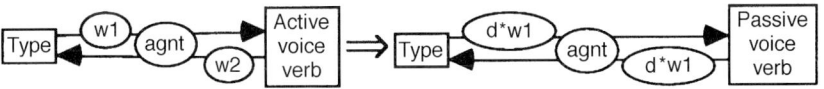

Figure 8.11 Effect of passivization.

Neutralization through presupposition

I evoked, in Chapter 3 (see page 102) another classical thesis of discourse analysis, according to which the referent point of a comparison tends to appear as more natural and more neutral than the term which is the true focus of the comparison. This implies that in a comparison, the evaluation of a reference point appears as the unquestionable, stable part, while evaluative semantic effects centre around the object which is compared. This rhetorical phenomenon can easily be modelled in DSNs.

Proposition 10. Stabilization of the reference point in a comparison can be achieved by increasing the inertia of the reference point.

I[REFERENCE POINT TYPE] > I[TYPE]

More generally, any time a part of discourse appears as 'given' instead of 'new', its evaluation may be stabilized by increasing its inertia. It is therefore possible to model, at the evaluative level, the processes by which a part of discourse is presented as an unquestioned ideological presupposition.

> **Proposition 11**. Stabilization through presupposition. This notion simply extends the scope of proposition 10.

I[TYPE] (GIVEN) > I[TYPE] (NEW)

Of course, we need to define the criteria which will decide which elements are given and which are new at each moment in the process of enunciation.

General proposition

As stated on page 221, mutual attraction interactions naturally damp down, while mutual repulsion interactions are self-reinforcing. It is therefore likely that for connection weights with the same absolute value, mutual repulsion links will produce much more variation of evaluation than mutual attraction links. To counterbalance this effect, and to be able to compare the influence of several links on a unit, it is useful to reduce the absolute value of the weights for mutual repulsion links. A factor of 1/2 is often enough to obtain the same amount of variation with both types of links.

> **Proposition 12**. Mutual repulsion links should have lower connection weights than mutual attraction links.

According to proposition 1, whenever a link is negated, its connection weights should change sign. If they change from positive to negative links, their absolute value should be reduced. This remark also applies to the effect of negation scope and unreal modalities. In practice, in the simulations of the next chapter, we will consistently divide weights by two when they become negative.

> **Proposition 13**: The evaluative effect of an attributive adjective is lower than that of a predicative adjective.

More generally, in a semantic relation, which term influences more the other depends on which term is the theme of the statement. Many other rules could be given. In fact, whenever the same type of meaning effect can be achieved in several syntactic ways, a rule expressing the difference between the different ways could be given. But the purpose of this section is not to be exhaustive.

Conclusion

A general framework for parameter setting has been shown in this chapter. First, a three-layer lattice structure has been adopted to organize the content of ideologies. Given this structure, it is possible to figure out a derivation algorithm that allows us to apply the parameters stored in the ideological knowledge-base to the networks representing discourse. Secondly, we have made explicit a series of semantic rules, which transform the parameters according to modalities, negation, quantification, and some other general rhetorical properties of discourse. Therefore, once we have an ideology, by first running the derivation algorithm, and then applying semantic rules, we have a general and yet practical solution to the question 'how do we set parameters?'.

As defined in this chapter and as implemented in CoCoNet, an ideology is a unique framework incorporating discursive elements belonging to doxa as well as to opinion. More precisely, an ideology contains linguistic information, along with social norms, or standards, which take the form of parameter settings. In order to organize these social standards, and the way in which they are expressed by linguistic means, I have drawn upon Boltanski's conceptual categories. These categories show how the theoretical discussions about ideology can be applied in the context of a formal model of discourse. They also demonstrate that a model of discourse interpretation does not necessarily become trivial or simplistic when it passes the threshold of formalization ... But the reader may now be impatient to see how the model actually performs on a real text, which is the object of the next chapter.

9

EVALUATION AND RHETORICAL ATTITUDES

Introduction

Many statements seem to us evaluatively inconsistent until we understand which particular mood or emotion (optimism, love, hunger, sadness, etc.) their author is experiencing or wishing to express. Some of these moods and emotions are highly socially codified, and may be seen more as communicating devices than as psychological states (indignation, praise, deference, compassion, solidarity, contempt, etc.). Since they usually involve a strong evaluative orientation, I propose to call this last class of communicative attitudes *evaluative attitudes*.

Evaluative attitudes are often related with rhetorical devices. Indignation expresses itself through exclamation and rhetorical questions, deference through specific markers of enunciation, scepticism or contempt through irony. The treatment of these rhetorical devices is among the most difficult problems faced by natural language processing (NLP). From a linguistic point of view, a normal statement does not differ from an ironical statement. In order to determine whether a statement is ironical there seems to be no solution other than to examine the truth, or at least the plausibility of this statement. However, if irony is subtle (and it often is), both ironical and non-ironical readings are plausible. Moreover, NLP systems usually do not possess the knowledge which would be necessary to decide whether a statement is true or false, plausible or not.

Another solution consists in adopting an evaluative perspective. To decide whether or not a statement is ironic, one first assesses its consistency. If the statement is inconsistent, it is ironical, if consistent, it is a normal statement. More generally, ironical statements may be identified by comparing two readings of the same statement, one in which the statement is ironical and one in which it is not. The reading which achieves highest consistency may be retained. The same strategy can be adopted to solve several classes of disambiguation problems.

1 The text

I have chosen to illustrate the application of the notion of ideological consistency to disambiguation with a text from *Julius Caesar*, by William Shakespeare (see Appendix B). I will focus on the first part of Mark Antony's funeral discourse (III, 2). The speech takes place in the Forum. Brutus has justified Caesar's murder. '... as he was ambitious, I slew him' and he has left, allowing Antony to speak.

This passage is rightly famous. It has inspired one of the best known scenes in the history of cinema.[1] It has been commented, among others, by Jakobson, in his paper Linguistics and Poetics (Jakobson 1960), translated and published in French as the last chapter of his *Essai de Linguistique Générale* (1963). Jakobson directs his comments to the sequence of connectors

> *For* Brutus is an honourable man;
> *But* Brutus says he was ambitious;
> *And* Brutus is an honourable man.
> *Yet* Brutus says he was ambitious;
> *And* Brutus is an honourable man.
> *Yet* Brutus says he was ambitious;
> *And, sure,* he is an honourable man.
>
> *But* I am here to speak what I do know.

It is precisely this sequence which interests me, since I claimed in the previous chapter that the evaluative behaviour of connectors can be modelled in DSNs.

Jakobson also shows how Caesar's alleged ambition is progressively denied by Antony through modalization and grammatical effects. First, Caesar's ambition is presented as Brutus' thesis, not as a fact. Then, it becomes a supposition. Later, the adjective *ambitious* is transferred from Caesar to his action 'Did *this*, in Caesar, seem ambitious?'. This adjective is replaced by the more abstract noun *ambition*, which becomes the subject of a passive voice sentence 'Ambition should be made of sterner stuff'. Finally, ambition is turned into the attribute of a rhetorical interrogative 'Was this ambition?'. All these effects should be reproducible within DSNs.

In order to avoid monotony, I will not examine the sentences of the text in purely linear order. Instead, I will group my remarks by topics, postponing to section 6 the discussion of the overall structure of the text. Section 2 is therefore devoted to the communication of Antony's initial evaluative attitude, section 3 to evaluative ambiguity, section 4 to rhetorical interrogatives, and section 5 to the role of connectors.

In the previous chapter, I have attempted to characterize Brutus' and Mark Antony's ideology. I have called the first one the *republican ideology*, and the second one *tyranny*. However, for two kinds of reasons, it would make little sense to estimate the consistency of the text with these ideologies. The first reason is that when he speaks in the forum at Caesar's funeral, Mark Antony is not wishing to express his deep ideological convictions, his vision of the world. All he wants to do is turn the people of Rome against Brutus and the conspirators. To achieve his plans, he dissimulates his own beliefs, and adopts those of its adversaries. Antony is not opposed to personal ambition, for example. Otherwise, he would not have presented Caesar a kingly crown. But, in the particular context of Caesar's funeral, Antony wants to give the impression that he adheres to some parts of the republican ideology. To achieve his goal, he adopts the republican view of ambition (cf. lines 5–7: 'The Noble Brutus hath told you Caesar was ambitious; If it were so, it was a grievous fault.'). Therefore, what we have at hand is not a rhetorical fight between tyranny and republic, but tyranny dressed up as republican discourse.

Besides pragmatic, strategic considerations, a second type of reasons explains why Antony does not speak as a defender of tyranny in his exordium. He has just discovered Caesar's death, and he is revolted by the murder. As a consequence, he cannot fully subscribe to the most cynical version of tyranny, because he is personally affected by violence. The emotional context, I would argue, carries him away from tyranny. In any case, his discourse is a weapon pointed towards Brutus, and this is what matters. I will therefore consider, instead of tyranny and republic, the struggle of the pro-Caesar (which is also anti-Brutus) ideology and the anti-Caesar (pro-Brutus) ideology. Does that mean that all we have said in the first chapter is now outdated? Of course not. Since Antony either proceeds by borrowing from tyranny or from the republican ideology, all his discourse will be derived from either one ideology or the other.

I will proceed by comparing, for each sentence or each discursive unit, its consistency with each ideology (pro- and anti-Caesar). However, the consistency of a sentence with an ideology must be estimated as the consistency of the reading which is most favourable to this ideology. In other words, I compare, on one hand, the consistency of anti-Caesar readings with the anti-Caesar ideology, and, on the other, the pro-Caesar readings with the pro-Caesar ideology.

A last point needs to be clarified at once. Throughout all simulations, Antony's default evaluation will be positive. This may seem strange to the reader, since Antony may be badly evaluated in the anti-Caesar ideology. My purpose here is not so much to assess the consistency of *Antony*'s discourse within each ideology, but the consistency of the *speech act*, regardless of its author. In other words, I question whether such a discourse could be pronounced by an orator unfavourable (i.e. favourable) to Caesar. My intention is to illustrate evaluative disambiguation, not to model discourse reception. As a consequence, Antony's positive evaluation is not *Antony*'s evaluation, but the default evaluation of an abstract orator in his own discourse.

2 Mark Antony's evaluative attitudes

According to Aristotle's rhetorics and to the Latin tradition (Cicero, Quintillion), a discourse should contain four parts: an exordium, which attempts to gain the sympathy of the audience (*captatio benevolentiae*); a narration, which presents the facts or the allegory; a discussion, in which the speaker's theses are proved and opponent's theses are confronted; a peroration, which contains a *recapitulatio*, and an *indignatio*, or final call for pity or sympathy. In the case of Antony's funeral discourse, these rules are not respected. However, the first passage quoted above clearly belongs to the genre of the exordium. At the time Antony starts to talk, the public in the Forum has been fully convinced by Brutus. The citizens are hostile to Caesar, and therefore, to Antony.

> ANTONY:
> For Brutus sake, I am beholden to you. (*Goes into the pulpit*)
> FOURTH CITIZEN:
> What does he say of Brutus?
> FIRST CITIZEN:
> He says for Brutus' sake,
> He finds himself beholden to us all
> FOURTH CITIZEN:
> 'T were best he speak no harm of Brutus here.
> FIRST CITIZEN:
> This Caesar was a tyrant.
> THIRD CITIZEN:
> Nay, that's certain:
> We are blessed that Rome is rid of him.
> SECOND CITIZEN:
> Peace! Let us hear what Antony can say.

Antony's purpose is to render the audience favourable both to Caesar and to himself. To do so, he needs to refute Brutus' accusation that Caesar was ambitious. However, he knows that he cannot overtly argue against Brutus. He first needs to be accepted as a legitimate orator. He therefore begins by dissimulating his intentions ('I come to bury Caesar, not to praise him'). However, the audience may suspect that he is dissimulating. To avoid this suspicion, Antony must demonstrate his good intentions (lines 3–5).

The sentence 'So let it be with Caesar' (line 5) is especially difficult to represent. Given the previous sentence, I assume that it means 'let the evil that Caesar did leave after his death, and let the good be interred with his bones'. This reading is represented in Network 9.1.

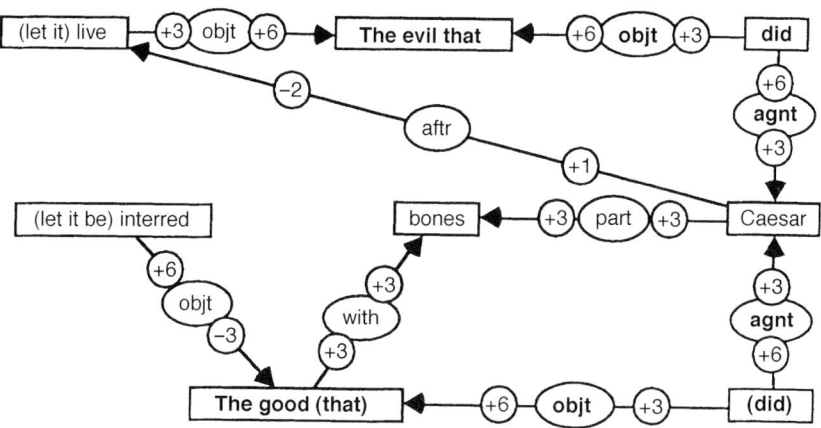

Network 9.1

Connections weights of DSN 9.1 do not call for specific comments, except perhaps for the relation (AFTR). It is assumed that surviving a person who has high evaluation (a grand subject) tends to be negative, while surviving a person who has a low evaluation tends to be positive. Hence the -0.2 connection weight from [CAESAR] to [(LET IT) LIVE]. The fact that the evil that he did lives after him is also a slight negative point for Caesar. Hence the 0.1 connection weight from [(LET IT) LIVE] to [CAESAR].

Not surprisingly, this passage is inconsistent with Antony's ideology (cf. Table 9.1). But it is also inconsistent with the anti-Caesar ideology, because it is not unfavourable to Caesar either (Caesar did some good). The text is slightly more consistent with the anti-Caesar ideology because [(LET IT BE) INTERRED] and [(LET IT) LIVE] are more negative under the pro-Caesar ideology.[2] Both readings are inconsistent because recommending negatively evaluated facts is inconsistent.

To account for this inconsistency, the receiver of this discourse is forced to suppose that Antony has adopted an attitude of *resignation*. From an evaluative perspective, resignation can be identified when a discourse recommends, or suggests accepting a negatively evaluated state of things. This is precisely what happens in lines 2 to 5. Note that resignation is especially plausible in the face of death. In *Lorenzaccio*, by Musset, for example, Louise Strozzi is poisoned by the Duc de Medici, and dies in front of her whole family. Shocked by this death, her father Philip Strozzi, immediately gives up his projects against the Duc, and does not even ask for revenge (III, 7). Resignation, due either to pain

EVALUATION AND RHETORICAL ATTITUDES

Table 9.1 Simulations – lines 3–5

	Γ_i	a_i	Anti-Caesar $x_i(0)$	Anti-Caesar $x_i(\infty)$	Pro-Caesar $x_i(0)$	Pro-Caesar $x_i(\infty)$
The evil that	0.0	0.5	−0.5	−0.3884	−0.5	−0.3616
did	0.0	0.2	0.0	−0.3257	0.0	−0.0157
bones	0.0	0.2	0.0	−0.1330	0.0	0.2831
Caesar	1.0	1.0	−1.0	−0.6367	1.0	0.6741
The good (that)	0.0	0.5	0.5	0.1862	0.5	0.2740
(did)	0.0	0.2	0.0	−0.0581	0.0	0.2810
(let it be) interred	1.0	0.5	0.0	−0.0791	0.0	−0.1154
(let it) live	1.0	0.5	0.0	−0.0764	0.0	−0.2428
Consistency				−0.077		−0.115

or indifference, is also what the conspirators expect from Antony in Act II, scene 1, when they decide not to kill him with Caesar.

> CASSIUS:
> Yet I fear him [Antony]
> For in the ingrafted love he bears to Caesar—
> BRUTUS:
> Alas, good Cassius, do not think of him:
> If he love Caesar, all that he can do
> Is to himself, take thought,[3] and die for Caesar:
> And that were much he should,[4] for he is given
> To sports, to wildness, and much company.
> TREBINIUS:
> There is no fear in him;[5] let him not die;
> For he will live and laugh at this hereafter.

The fact that resignation is here psychologically plausible renders it easier for Antony successfully to communicate to the audience his alleged state of mind. At the end of the text, Antony evokes again his feelings: 'Bear with me; My heart is in the coffin here with Caesar, and I must pause till it come back to me'. I will not attempt to treat this sentence, because any representation I could propose would lose the flavour of the double metaphor. Antony does confirm at the end of the text that he endures Caesar's death, but his attitude is not any more of resignation. Indeed, the previous sentence ('O judgement! thou art fled to brutish beasts, and men have lost their reason') contains no mark of acceptance. On the contrary this sentence is an accusation of the conspirators (*brutish beasts* is here unambiguous, especially because of the homophony *Brutus-brutish*). In DSN 9.2, connection weights are default weights.

Table 9.2 Simulations – lines 32–3

			Anti-Caesar		Pro-Caesar	
	Γ_i	a_i	$x_i(0)$	$x_i(\infty)$	$x_i(0)$	$x_i(\infty)$
O judgement!	0.0	1.0	1.0	0.9337	1.0	0.9332
thou art	0.0	1.0	0.5	0.4844	0.5	0.4800
fled	0.0	0.5	0.0	−0.0312	0.0	−0.0581
brutish	0.0	1.0	−1.0	−0.7729	−1.0	−0.9680
to beasts	0.0	1.0	−0.8	−0.6594	−0.8	−0.8110
men	0.0	1.0	0.0	−0.1042	0.0	−0.1042
have lost	0.0	0.2	0.0	−0.4549	0.0	−0.4549
their reason	0.0	1.0	1.0	1.0976	1.0	1.0976
(Brutus)	1.0	1.0	1.0	0.3566	−1.0	−0.9634
(you)	0.0	1.0	0.0	−0.1042	0.0	−0.1042
Consistency:				−0.573		0.866

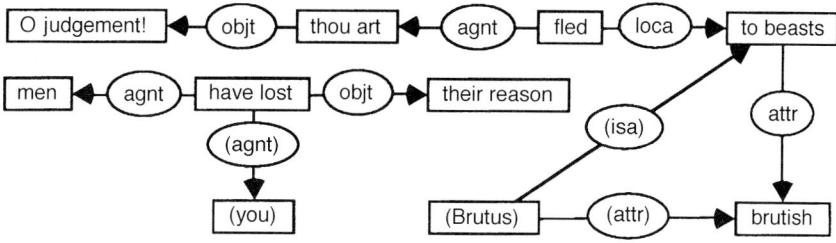

Network 9.2

This veiled accusation is much more consistent with the pro-Caesar ideology than with the anti-Caesar ideology (cf. the consistency in Table 9.2). The audience, here represented as [(YOU)], and indirectly referred to in the text by the word *men*, is admonished for being passive and indifferent to Caesar's death. The text calls for a sharing of emotion, which also implies changing sides, and joining Antony in his condemnation of the conspirators. Therefore, if we compare the beginning and the end of the text, Antony has passed from (alleged) lonely resignation to painful indignation, a change which is expressed through evaluative means.

3 Evaluative ambiguity

As stated in Chapter 3, ambiguity is one of the key notions of the sociological analysis of discourse. The success of a discourse, and more generally, its social function, is indeed often interpreted as a result of its ambiguity. In this section, I intend to show that ambiguity can easily be modelled as the simultaneous consistency with conflicting ideologies.

The second sentence of Shakespeare's text, 'I come to bury Caesar, not to praise him', is especially ambiguous. This ambiguity is mainly due to that of *to bury*, which can equally mean *to get rid of*, *to forget*, or *to mourn*. If the last sense is retained, and if it is also assumed that Antony does not express any reluctance to praise Caesar, his discourse can be represented by DSN 9.3.

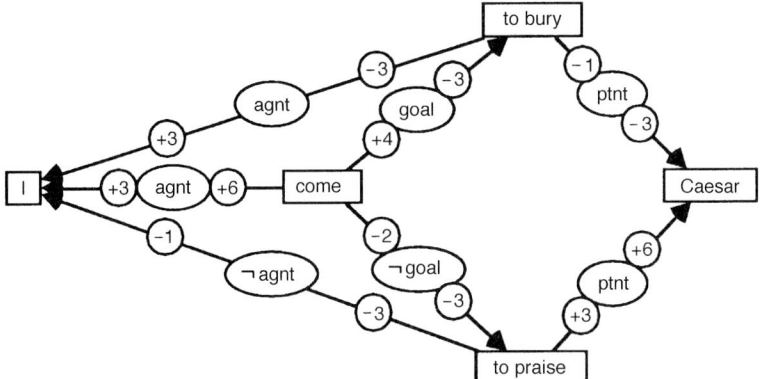

Network 9.3

Weights are obtained by first deriving DSN 9.3 from the CDSN embedded in Network 8.28 (page 240), and by later applying semantic rule 1 (see page 243). Note that the unit [TO BURY] is originally slightly negative, as is suggested by the semantics of the word itself. As Table 9.3 illustrates, this reading of line 2 is perfectly consistent with Antony's ideology.

If, on the contrary, it is assumed that Antony expresses an intention to forget Caesar, and to deliberately avoid praising him, line 2 must be represented by DSN 9.4.

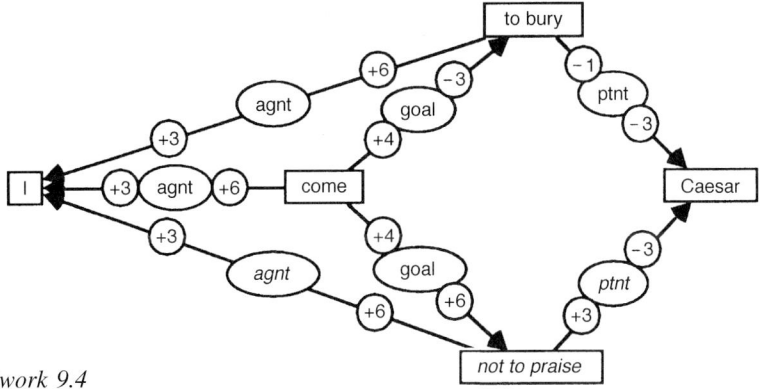

Network 9.4

In that case, [NOT TO PRAISE] depends negatively on Caesar's evaluation. This is prescribed by the successive application of propositions 2 and 12 (see pages 244 and 252). As shown in Table 9.4, this new reading is consistent with that of the audience at the beginning of the exordium.

Table 9.3 Simulations – line 2, first reading

	Γ_i	a_i	$x_i(0)$	$x_i(\infty)$
I	1.0	1.0	1.0	0.9148
come	0.0	0.5	0.5	0.8872
to bury	0.0	0.5	−0.2	0.0881
Caesar	1.0	1.0	1.0	0.9746
to praise	0.0	0.5	0.2	0.3711
		Consistency: 0.679		

Table 9.4 Simulations – line 2, second reading

	Γ_i	a_i	$x_i(0)$	$x_i(\infty)$
I	1.0	1.0	1.0	0.9694
come	0.0	0.5	0.5	0.7421
to bury	0.0	0.2	0.5	1.1376
Caesar	1.0	1.0	−1.0	−0.9045
not to praise	0.0	0.2	−0.2	0.8446
		Consistency: 0.682		

The consistency of DSN 9.4 is very close to that obtained by the previous reading. This is a confirmation of the ideological ambiguity of Antony's first statement.

After stating his intentions, Antony begins to discuss Brutus' argument. Depending on the reading one chooses to make, this piece of discourse can be represented by one of the following:

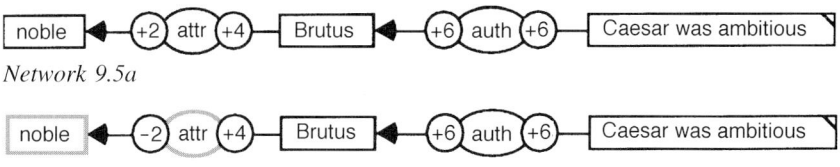

Network 9.5a

Network 9.5b

where the collapsed context [CAESAR WAS AMBITIOUS] can be expanded as

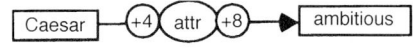

Network 9.5c

Because the expression 'the noble Brutus' is a conventional formula of politeness rather than a true attribution, in DSN 9.5, connection weights between [NOBLE] and [BRUTUS] are not the same as those between [CAESAR] and [AMBITIOUS]. The second DSN is obtained by applying proposition 5a to default weights.

EVALUATION AND RHETORICAL ATTITUDES

Table 9.5 Simulations – lines 5–6

	Γ_i	a_i	Anti-Caesar		Pro-Caesar	
			$x_i(0)$	$x_i(\infty)$	$x_i(0)$	$x_i(\infty)$
Caesar	1.0	1.0	−1.0	−1.0000	1.0	0.5399
ambitious	0.0	1.0	−1.0	−1.0000	−1.0	−0.7699
Consistency:			1.000		−0.847	
Brutus	1.0	1.0	1.0	0.9872	−1.0	−0.9494
Noble	1.0	1.0	0.8	0.8312	−0.8	−0.8702
Caesar was ambitious	0.0	1.0	1.0	0.9972	−0.847	−0.8466
Consistency:			0.906		0.712	

Both readings are consistent with their respective ideology. As Table 9.5 indicates, the normal reading is more consistent with the pro-Caesar ideology than the ironical reading with the anti-Caesar ideology. This reflects the fact that an ironical reading is less 'natural' and perhaps also less efficient than a normal reading.

Let us proceed with lines 7–8. There are several potential readings of this sentence. I will consider only two of them, which arise from two different meanings of the verb 'to answer'. In the first, it is supposed that Caesar was indeed ambitious, and that he atoned for it. This interpretation can be represented by DSN 9.6a, where connection weights are obtained by applying proposition 4 to default weights.

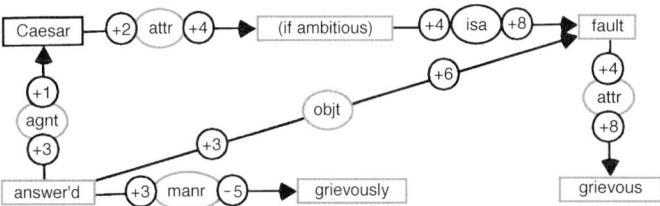

Network 9.6a

In the second interpretation (represented by Network 9.6b), Caesar was not ambitious, though he paid for a fault he did not commit.

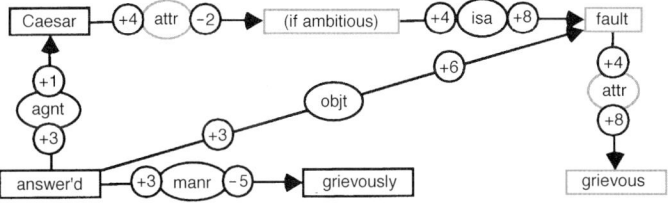

Network 9.6b

EVALUATION AND RHETORICAL ATTITUDES

Table 9.6 Simulations – lines 7–8

			Anti-Caesar		Pro-Caesar	
	Γ_i	a_i	$x_i(0)$	$x_i(\infty)$	$x_i(0)$	$x_i(\infty)$
Caesar	1.0	1.0	−1.0	−0.9155	1.0	0.9293
fault	0.0	0.5	−1.0	−0.9289	−1.0	−0.8544
grievous	0.0	1.0	−1.0	−0.9882	−1.0	−0.9757
(if) ambitious	0.0	1.0	−1.0	−0.9756	−1.0	−0.7895
answer'd	0.0	1.0	0.0	−0.2495	−0.3	0.1989
grievously	0.0	1.0	0.0	−0.0324	0.0	0.0259
Consistency:				0.360		0.516

For the first time, the pro-Caesar reading is more consistent than the anti-Caesar one (see Table 9.6). However, at that stage, it is not sure that the audience has understood Antony's irony, since the non-ironical reading is still consistent with the anti-Caesar ideology.

After this veiled critique of the conspirators, Antony evokes them directly, while simultaneously moving back to a discourse much more acceptable for the audience (lines 9–12). Of course, this sentence too can be interpreted as ironical. The ironical reading is supported by some details, such as the disrespectful 'and the rest' and by the repetition of 'all'. One of the classical ways to achieve irony is indeed to extend the scope of a judgement until it becomes much less plausible than it originally was. This effect cannot easily be simulated in DSN. However, the result (irony) can be represented, and its consistency can be assessed. The first reading can be represented as in Network 9.7a.

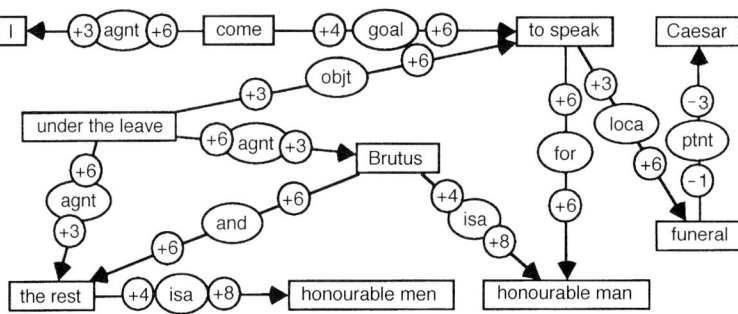

Network 9.7a

The second reading differs from the first only with respect to the modality of the following relations (network 9.7b):

264

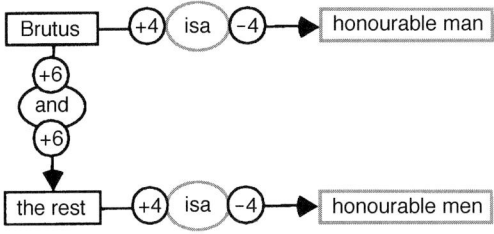

Network 9.7b

As can be seen in Table 9.7, the consistency with pro-Caesar ideology clearly increases with respect to the previous sentence. However, the anti-Caesar reading remains consistent too.

To conclude this section, let us remark that ambiguity and irony are two closely related phenomena. Both require an alternative between two readings of a discourse. Irony is characterized by the fact that one of the readings is much more plausible than the other, while ambiguity is characterized by similar levels of plausibility. When irony is subtle, in particular, when it is not intended to be understood by the person it concerns, irony is close to ambiguity. In those cases, understanding irony requires perceiving ambiguity too.

4 Rhetorical questions

When an NLP systems needs to treat an interrogative without answer, there are fundamentally two basic possibilities.[6] The interrogative is either a true question (the author does not know the answer, or does not know which answer is preferable) or a rhetorical question (both the author and the reader know the answer, or know which answer is preferable). When the question is

Table 9.7 Simulations – lines 9–12

	Γ_i	a_i	Anti-Caesar		Pro-Caesar	
			$x_i(0)$	$x_i(\infty)$	$x_i(0)$	$x_i(\infty)$
I	1.0	1.0	1.0	0.9364	1.0	0.9375
come	0.0	0.2	0.5	0.7237	0.5	0.7287
speak	0.0	0.2	0.7	0.7672	0.7	0.7775
funeral	0.0	0.2	−0.3	0.7913	−0.3	−0.4525
under the leave	0.0	0.2	0.3	0.6116	0.3	0.0074
Brutus	1.0	1.0	1.0	0.9050	−1.0	−1.0131
the rest	0.0	0.5	0.2	0.5093	−1.0	−1.0862
Caesar	1.0	1.0	−1.0	−1.1110	1.0	1.0975
honourable man	0.0	1.0	1.0	0.9409	1.0	0.7326
honourable men	0.0	1.0	1.0	0.9192	1.0	0.7135
Consistency:				0.467		0.590

rhetorical, it may suggest a positive or a negative answer. When the interrogation involves a negation (e.g. 'Aren't we proud of our country?') it is easy to infer that the answer should be positive. In a speech, when the author asks the audience 'Shall we let them *P*?', it is likely that the answer should be negative. Similarly, constructs such as 'What is stopping you (i.e. us) from *P*?' can confidently be interpreted as 'you (i.e. us) should *P*'. For example, in Shakespeare's text, the sentence 'What cause withholds you to mourn for him?' means 'You should mourn for him'.

When the question involves neither negation, nor other specific expressions, it is not easy to determine if it is a rhetorical question, and, if so, of which particular kind. The text we are studying offers an interesting example of rhetorical question for which no particular interpretation can be given on the sole basis of the linguistic context (lines 16–18). 'Did this, in Caesar, seem ambitious?' is a rhetorical question suggesting a negative answer. Therefore, we can represent it by DSN 9.8.

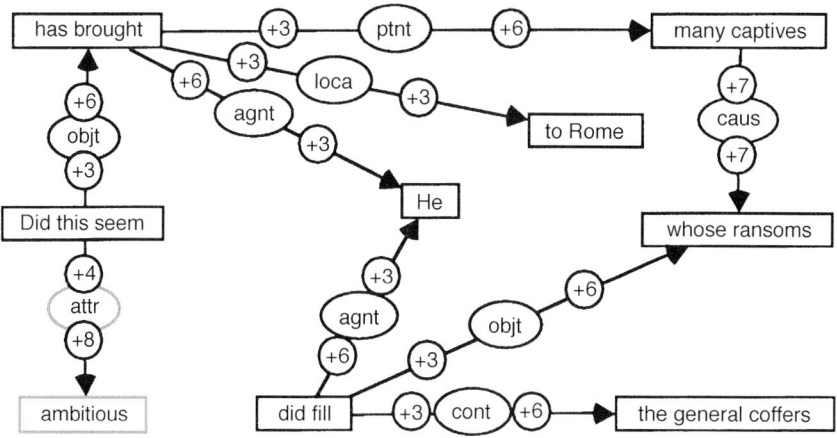

Network 9.8

From an intuitive point of view, there is no alternative reading. However, to give a chance to the anti-Caesar ideology, let us assume that under this ideological hypothesis, the interrogative presupposes that Caesar is ambitious. To represent this reading, all that is necessary is to change the modality of [AMBITIOUS ?] ⟵ (ATTR)— from *unreal* to *real* in Network 9.8, and to modify connection weights appropriately. Note also that Jakobson's remark according to which Antony transfers the adjective ambitious from Caesar to his actions is naturally taken into account within SSNs. The two intermediate nodes between [AMBITIOUS] and [HE] (Caesar) leads to a lighter evaluative effect, even under the anti-Caesar hypothesis. Finally, let us remark that there is no a priori reason to give a highly positive initial value to the unit [MANY CAPTIVES]. However, this positive orientation is deduced, by means of the derivation algorithm, from the fact that bringing captives to Rome is a form of *Evidence* supporting *Judgement* (here victory) as the outcome of *Test* (military campaigns). The initial evaluation of [MANY CAPTIVES] is therefore derived from ideological knowledge. The same remark holds for [THE GENERAL COFFERS] which receives its parameters from the obligation of prodigality (in tyranny) or of solidarity (in republic).

As Table 9.8a indicates, the pro-Caesar reading largely outperforms the anti-Caesar reading in terms of consistency. This result suggests that disambiguation problems arising from interrogatives can be solved by comparing the consistency of the various readings. To illustrate further this point, let us consider all possible readings under both ideological hypotheses. Although the results in Table 9.8b do not differ by very much,[7] they nevertheless conform to intuition.

Consistency-driven disambiguation is not only often correct, but also economical. Consider the amount of information that has been necessary to choose between the different readings. All that was required was to know that bringing many captives to Rome and filling the general coffers was a good thing, and being ambitious a bad thing. On the contrary, if we had chosen a logical approach, we would have had to determine to which extent bringing captives to Rome and filling general coffers is indeed contradictory

Table 9.8a Simulations – lines 16–18

			Anti-Caesar		Pro-Caesar	
	Γ_i	a_i	$x_i(0)$	$x_i(\infty)$	$x_i(0)$	$x_i(\infty)$
He	1.0	1.0	−1.0	−0.5531	1.0	0.9179
has brought	0.0	0.1	0.0	0.3460	0.0	0.7432
many captives	0.0	0.5	1.0	0.8239	1.0	0.8982
whose ransoms	0.0	1.0	0.8	0.7734	0.8	0.8192
did fill	0.1	0.0	0.0	0.4746	0.0	0.7627
the general coffers	0.0	1.0	1.0	0.9325	1.0	0.9691
Did this seem	0.0	0.2	0.0	−0.2532	0.0	0.6703
ambitious?	0.0	1.0	−1.0	−0.8788	1.0	0.9453
to Rome	0.0	1.0	1.0	0.9166	1.0	0.9666
Consistency:				−0.506		0.617

Table 9.8b Simulations of interrogatives

	Anti-Caesar	Pro-Caesar
True interrogative	−0.526	0.496
Rhetorical interrogative (positive answer)	−0.506	0.443
Rhetorical interrogative (negative answer)	−0.575	0.617

with ambition. This would require a much more detailed knowledge than the general evaluative knowledge which has been used.

Consistency-driven disambiguation of rhetorical interrogatives is also more psychologically plausible than logic-based disambiguation. I confess, for example, that I am not capable of following exactly Antony's argument. Because of my ignorance concerning the administration of Rome, it is not clear to me in which sense bringing captives to Rome is incompatible with personal ambition. Nevertheless, I am capable of understanding that Antony strongly suggests such a contradiction. My understanding is based on the evaluative contrast between the two propositions.

The second case of rhetorical question (lines 23–25) can be solved in the same way. The only correct interpretation is clearly that corresponding to DSN 9.9.

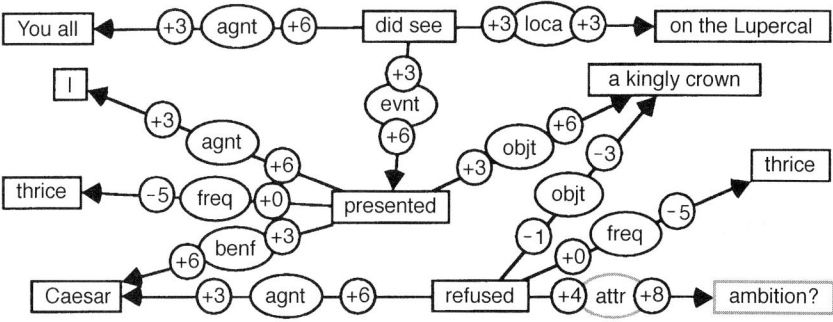

Network 9.9

However, an NLP system would probably not know that this is the only correct interpretation, and would also consider the case in which 'Was this ambition?' is a rhetorical question implying a positive answer. As the results in Table 9.9 demonstrate, an evaluative approach would rule out this hypothesis.

These results call for further remarks. In particular, one may wish to question why the consistency achieved by the pro-Caesar ideology is not higher. This is due to the fact that there is a sort of contradiction within Antony's argument. It is indeed slightly surprising to praise Caesar for refusing a crown that Antony himself wanted him to accept! Either refusing the crown is positive, or presenting it, but not both. In other words, either Caesar was right, or Antony, but not both. The behaviour of DSN 9.9 reflects this contradiction. If we base the estimation of consistency on Caesar only, the consistency almost doubles (= 0.675).

Given the flaw contained in Antony's argument, one may then wish to question why the obtained consistency is not lower. First, under the pro-Caesar ideology, the fact that it is to Caesar that the crown was presented

Table 9.9 Simulations – lines 23–5

	Γ_i	a_i	Anti-Caesar $x_i(0)$	Anti-Caesar $x_i(\infty)$	Pro-Caesar $x_i(0)$	Pro-Caesar $x_i(\infty)$
You all	0.0	1.0	1.0	0.8331	1.0	0.8872
did see	0.0	0.2	0.0	0.2616	0.0	0.5068
on the Lupercal	0.0	1.0	1.0	0.9065	1.0	0.9365
presented	0.0	0.2	0.0	−0.2489	0.0	0.4332
Caesar	1.0	1.0	−1.0	−0.7979	1.0	0.9483
a kingly crown	0.0	1.0	−1.0	−0.9407	−1.0	−0.9348
I	1.0	1.0	1.0	0.7282	1.0	0.8708
refused	0.0	0.2	0.0	−0.3866	0.0	1.0283
thrice	0.0	1.0	0.0	0.0000	0.0	0.0000
thrice	0.0	1.0	0.0	0.0000	0.0	0.0000
ambition ?	0.0	1.0	−0.5	−0.4811	0.5	0.5472
Consistency				−0.360		0.360

renders it more acceptable. Secondly, stressing the fact that the event has been witnessed by the audience somehow dissimulates the inconsistency of the argument. Indeed, such is the emphasis put on the argument that the audience probably will not think of using it against its author. Antony's role becomes part of a matter-of-fact argument. This rhetorical manoeuvre is also carried out by syntactic means. The questionable part of the argument (the fact that Antony did present the crown), far from being dissimulated, is put right into the main sentence, while Caesar's refusal is relegated to a subordinate ('which he thrice refused'). The repetition of the word 'thrice' shifts attention from the nature of the action to the number of times it occurred.[8] This sort of rhetorical strategy, which consists in unmasking in order to mask better, evokes the mix of recognition and misrecognition discovered by Bourdieu in the processes of legitimation. Note finally that the change from *ambitious* to *ambition*, which had been pointed out by Jakobson as further diminishing the impact of Brutus' argument is here reflected by the initial evaluation of [AMBITION], which is not as negative as that of [AMBITIOUS].

The last case of rhetorical question in Antony's exordium is the partial interrogation 'What cause withholds you then to mourn for him?'. As stated above, the correct interpretation of this sentence can be found without resorting to evaluative reasoning. I will therefore consider only the interpretation corresponding to Network 9.10.

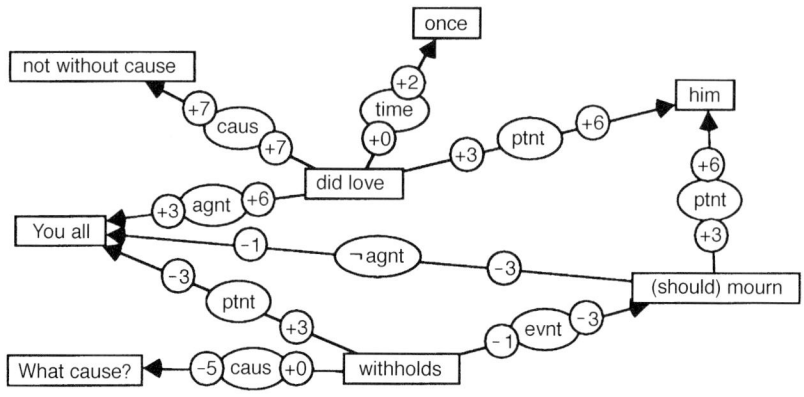

Network 9.10

Since the text suggests that there is no good reason not to mourn for Caesar, the unit [WHAT CAUSE?] can be interpreted as a catalyst of [WITHHOLDS]'s evaluation, and [ONCE] can be interpreted as a moderator of [DID LOVE]. Other connection weights are set in the normal way. Because doing something (either positive or negative) 'with a cause' is better that doing something 'without a cause', [NOT WITHOUT CAUSE] is initially positive, and positively influences [DID LOVE]. In order to determine whether this piece of discourse is favourable to the audience, [YOU ALL] starts with a neutral evaluation.

The final evaluation of [YOU ALL] (Table 9.10) confirms that under the pro-Caesar hypothesis, the text involves a critique of the audience's attitude.

5 The role of connectors

As explained by Jakobson, connectors play an important role in the structure of the text. They allow for an increasing perception of irony. In order to

Table 9.10 Simulations – lines 30–1

	Γ_i	a_i	Anti-Caesar		Pro-Caesar	
			$x_i(0)$	$x_i(\infty)$	$x_i(0)$	$x_i(\infty)$
You all	0.0	1.0	0.0	0.0288	0.0	−0.0436
did love	0.0	0.2	0.2	0.0091	0.2	0.5622
him	1.0	1.0	−1.0	−0.8369	1.0	0.9493
not without cause	0.0	1.0	0.8	0.5993	0.8	0.7385
withholds	1.0	1.0	−0.2	−0.2626	−0.2	−0.6322
What cause?	0.0	1.0	0.0	0.0000	0.0	0.0000
once	0.0	1.0	0.0	0.0000	0.0	0.0000
(should) mourn	0.0	0.2	0.2	−0.5465	0.2	0.9934
Consistency				−0.387		0.763

EVALUATION AND RHETORICAL ATTITUDES

simulate this progression, let us consider successively the four main connectors at line 14, 21, 26, and 29.

At line 13, Antony's speech is for the first time overtly favourable to Caesar. 'He was my friend, faithful and just to me'. However, this sort of appraisal is also overtly subjective, and thus, is not totally conclusive.

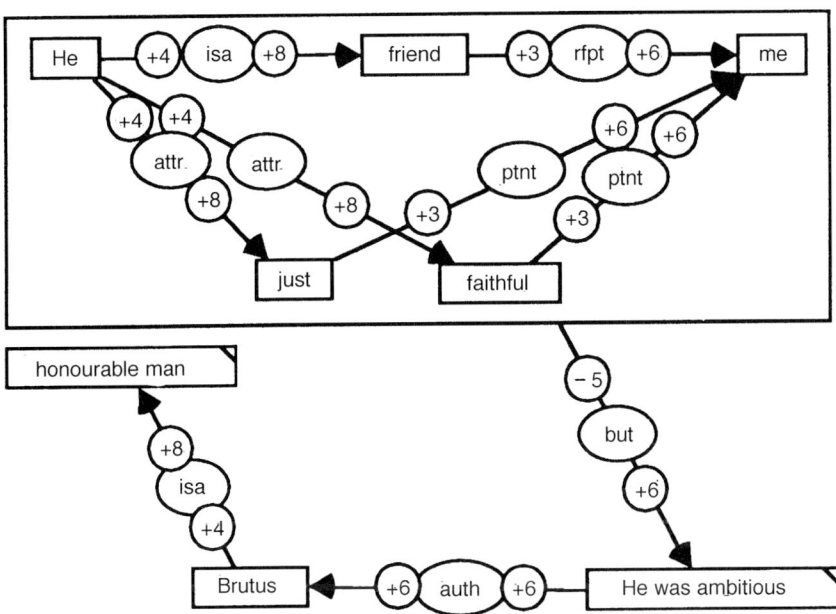

Network 9.11

It is assumed that the connector *but* is adversative, and that it tends to present the second propositions as a valid objection to the first. Therefore, it is adequately represented by an attraction–repulsion link where the consistency of the second proposition modifies the consistency of the first (Network 9.11). The alternative reading is exactly the same, except that Brutus is not an honourable man (the unit [HONOURABLE MAN] and the relation (ISA) between [BRUTUS] and [HONOURABLE MAN] are *unreal*).

As these simulations summarized in Table 9.11 reveal, when the overall discourse is considered, the connector *but* provides satisfying levels of consistency for both ideological hypotheses. However, the second hypothesis is clearly more consistent than the first, especially if we look at the sentence 'He was my friend, faithful and just to me'. In the first hypothesis, this sentence originally has a consistency near to zero, and under the influence of the connector *but*, ends up with a consistency close to 0.3. In the second hypothesis, the same sentence is originally highly consistent, and under the influence of the connector, ends up with a consistency close to 0.5. This

Table 9.11 Simulations – lines 13–15

	Γ_i	a_i	Anti-Caesar		Pro-Caesar	
			$x_i(0)$	$x_i(\infty)$	$x_i(0)$	$x_i(\infty)$
He	1.0	1.0	−1.0	−0.4695	1.0	0.9670
friend	0.0	1.0	0.8	0.6672	0.8	0.8559
me	1.0	1.0	1.0	0.9115	1.0	0.9692
just	0.0	1.0	1.0	0.8062	1.0	0.9893
faithful	0.0	1.0	0.8	0.6673	0.8	0.8559
Consistency:				0.072		0.886
ambitious	0.0	1.0	−1.0	−1.0000	−1.0	−0.7699
He	1.0	1.0	−1.0	−1.0000	1.0	0.5399
Consistency:				1.000		−0.847
He was my friend...	0.0	1.0	0.072	0.3050	0.8862	0.4914
He was ambitious...	0.0	1.0	1.0	1.0000	−0.847	−0.9876
Brutus	1.0	1.0	1.0	1.0168	−1.0	−1.0118
honourable man	0.0	1.0	1.0	1.0029	−0.75	−1.0021
Consistency:				0.929		0.950

example illustrates the fact that a connector alone cannot totally modify the consistency of a statement. Stated otherwise, it is not enough, in order to render a discourse consistent, to articulate its contradicting parts by connectors.

Later in the text, Antony brings more evidence contradicting the idea that Caesar was ambitious. In particular, he recalls Caesar's concern for the state of the poor. For this argument, there is only one possible reading. 'Ambition should be made of sterner stuff' clearly means that Caesar's compassion is incompatible with ambition. This can be represented, in SSNs, by the fact that the unit [SHOULD BE MADE OF STERNER STUFF][9] *dis-realizes* the unit [AMBITION].

Since this is the third point made by Antony against Caesar's alleged ambition, Brutus' argument no longer stands as an unquestionable truth. To stress the fact that Brutus' argument and his own arguments now stand at the same level, Antony chooses to substitute *yet* for *but*.

The connector *yet* is here (Network 9.12) close to 'despite this'. It is assumed that this use is adversative, and that *yet* reinforces the contradiction between the two propositions. This connector is therefore adequately represented by a mutual repulsion link. In the simulations below, [SHOULD BE MADE OF STERNER STUFF] is given a positive default evaluation, as suggested by the usual meaning of the expression.

As in the case of *but*, the important point in the interpretation of Table 9.12 is not the final consistency of the embedding discourse, but the consistency of the embedded graph [WHEN THAT THE POOR ... STERNER STUFF].

EVALUATION AND RHETORICAL ATTITUDES

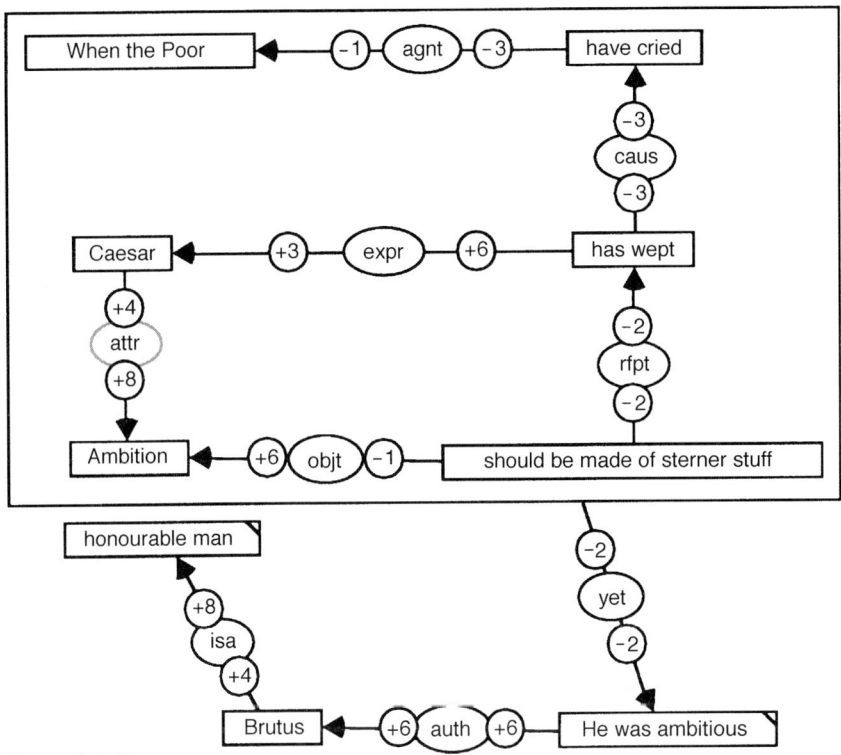

Network 9.12

Table 9.12 Simulations – lines 19–22

			Anti-Caesar		Pro-Caesar	
	Γ_i	a_i	$x_i(0)$	$x_i(\infty)$	$x_i(0)$	$x_i(\infty)$
when that the poor	0.0	1.0	1.0	1.1857	1.0	1.2116
have cried	0.0	0.5	0.0	−0.2611	0.0	−0.5449
Caesar	1.0	1.0	−1.0	−0.7945	1.0	1.0234
has wept	0.0	0.5	0.2	−0.0064	0.2	0.7103
Ambition	0.0	1.0	−0.5	−0.6007	−0.5	−0.3102
should be made of a...	0.0	1.0	0.5	0.2801	0.5	0.2847
Consistency			−0.179		0.830	
When that the poor have...	0.0	1.0	−0.179	−0.2996	0.830	0.9815
Caesar was ambitious	0.0	1.0	1.0	1.0970	−0.846	−0.9983
Brutus	1.0	1.0	1.0	1.0175	−1.0	−0.9999
honourable man	0.0	1.0	1.0	1.0030	−1.0	−0.9999
Consistency			0.926		0.999	

Under the anti-Caesar ideology, this graph starts from −0.179 and ends at −0.299. Therefore, the connector *yet* renders the text even less consistent with the anti-Caesar ideology. On the contrary, under the pro-Caesar ideology, the consistency of the embedded graph is boosted from 0.830 to 0.9815. The connector reinforces the consistency of the text with the second ideology.

The second case of articulation by *yet* is very similar to the first one. The first discursive unit it connects ('You all did see that on the Lupercal ... Was this ambition?') has already been treated in section 4. It is possible to collapse it, as in Network 9.13.

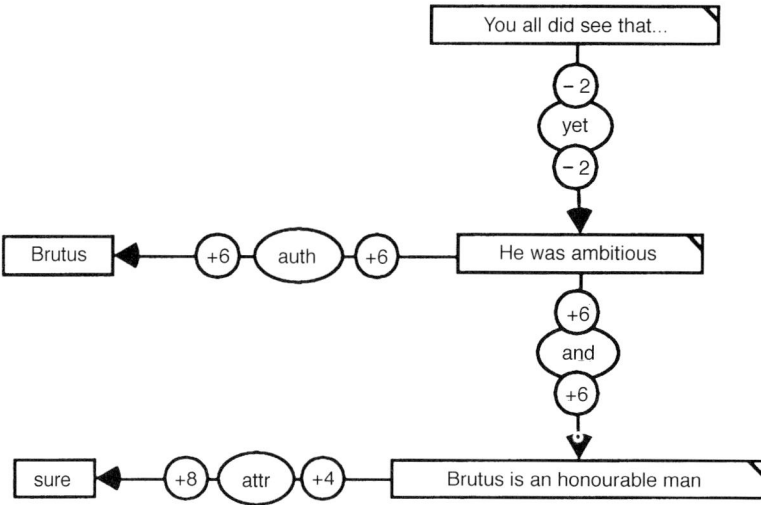

Network 9.13

To represent the ironical reading, it is enough to apply the modality unreal to [SURE]⟵(ATTR)—, and to modify connection weights appropriately (Table 9.13). As previously, the overall discourse is consistent under both ideological hypotheses, but the connector *yet* renders the sentence 'I thrice presented him a kingly crown, which he did thrice refuse', even more inconsistent with the anti-Caesar ideology than it was before.

In a striking symmetry, the text terminates the sequence of connectors *but-yet-yet* by a second *but* at line 29. Again, the behaviour of the connector *but* is represented by an attraction–repulsion dynamics (Network 9.14).

The effect of the connector is symmetrical with respect to the first use of *but*. Instead of attenuating a daring statement, the connector reinforces a weak statement (Table 9.14).

The final inconsistency of the sentence 'I am here to speak what I do know' with the anti-Caesar ideology is partly due to the negative evaluation of [WHAT I DO KNOW], – in the context, 'what I do know' is indeed inconsistent with the anti-Caesar ideology – and partly due to the connector.

EVALUATION AND RHETORICAL ATTITUDES

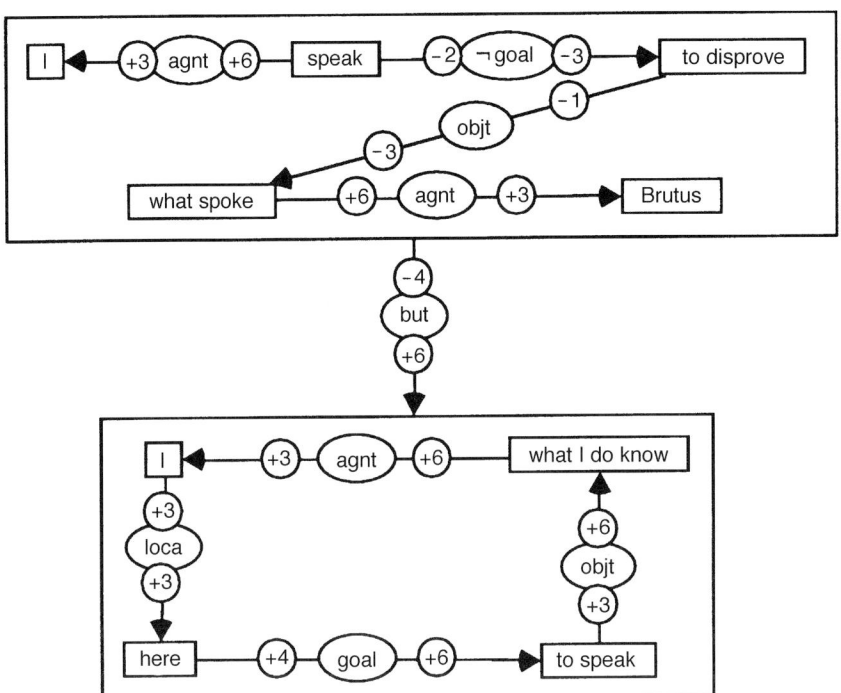

Network 9.14

Table 9.13 Simulations – lines 23–7

	Γ_i	a_i	Anti-Caesar $x_i(0)$	$x_i(\infty)$	Pro-Caesar $x_i(0)$	$x_i(\infty)$
He	1.0	1.0	−1.0	−1.0000	1.0	0.5399
ambitious	0.0	1.0	−1.0	−1.0000	−1.0	−0.7699
Consistency:			1.000		−0.847	
Brutus	0.0	1.0	1.0	1.0000	−1.0	−0.7699
honourable man	1.0	1.0	1.0	1.0000	1.0	0.5399
Consistency:			1.000		−0.847	
You all did see that...	0.0	1.0	−0.360	−0.4902	0.360	0.4816
He was ambitious...	0.0	1.0	1.0	1.0637	−0.847	−0.9295
Brutus			1.0	1.0148	−1.0	−0.9838
Brutus is an honour...	1.0	1.0	1.0	0.9768	−0.847	−0.8578
sure	0.0	1.0	1.0	0.8294	−0.8	−0.8052
Consistency:			0.747		0.843	

EVALUATION AND RHETORICAL ATTITUDES

Table 9.14 Simulations – lines 28–9

	Γ_i	a_i	Anti-Caesar		Pro-Caesar	
			$x_i(0)$	$x_i(\infty)$	$x_i(0)$	$x_i(\infty)$
I	1.0	1.0	1.0	0.8334	1.0	0.7719
speak	0.0	1.0	0.0	0.2631	0.0	−0.0286
to disprove	0.0	0.3	0.0	−1.1213	0.0	1.0062
what spoke	0.0	0.2	0.0	0.7092	0.0	−0.6936
Brutus	1.0	1.0	1.0	0.9331	−1.0	−0.9295
Consistency:			0.045		−0.152	
I	1.0	1.0	1.0	0.6467	1.0	0.9320
here	0.0	0.2	0.0	0.0933	0.0	0.4573
to speak	0.0	0.2	0.0	−0.1152	0.0	0.5300
what do know	0.0	1.0	−0.5	−0.3315	1.0	0.9386
Consistency:			−0.552		0.580	
I speak not...	0.0	0.5	0.0448	−0.2481	−0.1522	0.2044
I am here...	0.0	0.5	−0.5516	−0.7469	0.5800	0.8177

6 Irony at work

It is now possible to gather all the results obtained from sections 3 to 5, and to describe the overall dynamics of the text. Let us compare the consistency of the anti-Caesar reading with the anti-Caesar ideology and the consistency of the pro-Caesar reading with the pro-Caesar ideology. As expected, after line 7, the pro-Caesar reading is everywhere more consistent that the anti-Caesar reading. This result clearly supports the pro-Caesar hypothesis (Figure 9.1).

The various moments of the text are also clearly apparent from the variations of consistency. The initial fall of consistency reflects Antony's wish to persuade the audience of his resignation. From line 7 to line 12, no reading is clearly superior to the other. Therefore, Antony's irony is already present, though not necessarily perceivable given the ambiguity of the text. At line 13, Antony makes a move forward: the text becomes unambiguously favourable to Caesar. Immediately, Antony makes a backward move. The connector used ('but') forces us to reconsider the forward move in the light of the backward move. As a result, Antony's initial argument ceases to be conclusive. Antony then makes another move forward. From there on, the audience knows that Antony rejects the idea of Caesar being ambitious. Antony then twice repeats the strategy of exposing himself and immediately withdrawing. This identity of structure is striking. It suggest a continuity between lines 13–15, lines 19–22, and lines 23–27. However, this similarity is purely formal. The purpose of these rhetorical moves is no longer to attenuate his critiques, but to reinforce them. The change of a single little

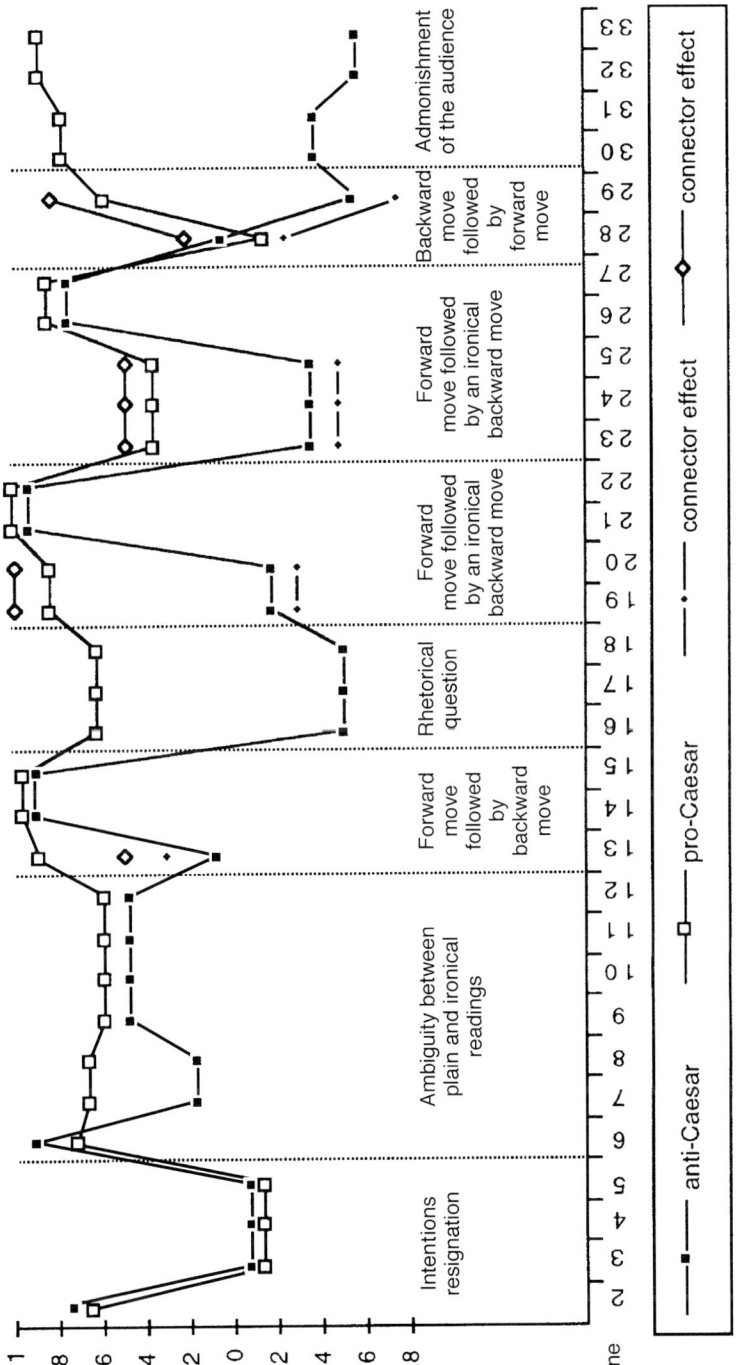

Figure 9.1 The global dynamics of the text.

word to a word which is almost a synonym (*but* replaced by *yet*) reverses the meaning of the sentences 'Brutus says he was ambitious, and Brutus is an honourable man'. Though Antony withdraws from his most daring positions, the audience does not, and draws the conclusion which Antony refuses to draw. This way, Antony attacks Brutus while remaining formally prudent.

It is also noteworthy that if we except the lines corresponding to the backward moves, the gap between the consistency achieved by the two readings continuously increases. This increase illustrates the fact that irony progressively imposes itself. In dialogue, irony is often concentrated in a single sentence, but in written discourse, irony is a often a global dynamics which is better discovered at the textual level.

7 Application to other classes of disambiguation problems

It has been shown that disambiguation problems arising from rhetorical interrogation and irony can benefit from an evaluative approach. Before concluding, I would like to evoke two other classes of disambiguation problems which could also be solved thanks to the notion of ideological consistency.

The first natural candidates for consistency-driven disambiguation are the various uses of *should*. To illustrate the potentially ambiguous uses of *should*, let us turn again to Shakespeare's text. In the sentence 'Ambition should be made of sterner stuff' *should* does not mark, as it usually does, the optative semiotic mood. Therefore, there is a need to choose between *should* as a de-realizing modifier, and *should* as an optative modifier. Since these two readings lead to very different representations in SSNs, it is possible to determine which reading is the correct one by comparing their consistency.

Although similar problems arise in English, I will borrow the second example of consistency-solvable problems from French, and more particularly, from the sentences built around the construction *ne ... que*, which is extremely frequent in French. Let us consider the following sentences

(a) Ne l'engage pas. Il n'a fait que des erreurs.
(b) Ne le condamne pas. Il n'a fait que des erreurs.

In discourse (a), the second sentence means 'everything he did was a mistake', while in discourse (b), it means 'he did nothing other than simple mistakes'. These meanings are clearly different, and should be distinguished by any system hoping to make inferences from these sentences. To decide which reading is correct, it is of course reasonable to base our choice on the consistency of the sentence. In the case of our example, we first need to compute the final evaluation of [IL] in the first sentence. Once this is done, this evaluation serves as the initial evaluation of [IL] in the second sentence. Comparing the consistency of the two readings would allow us to select the correct one. In practice, it is perhaps useful to control whether the choice that has been made also renders consistent the sentences which follow (if there are any).

Conclusion

Whenever a disambiguation process has evaluative consequences, considering these consequences can help in the disambiguation process itself. This last strategy is often superfluous, because the linguistic information, or some simple logical reasoning lets one pick up the correct interpretation among possible ones. However, for some classes of disambiguation problems, such as irony, rhetorical questions, and several others, the syntactic context does not provide the clue. In those cases, an evaluative approach often turns out to be more reliable and more economical in terms of information than a logical approach.

How often will an evaluative approach be helpful? How often will it be necessary? The more NLP systems are concerned with the evaluative dimension of discourse, the more they will need evaluative reasoning skills. Until now, NLP system designers have paid little attention to evaluation in discourse, because this dimension was not fundamental for the purposes of language translation. But if NLP systems are to understand language (not only translate it) or simply communicate with users, they will have to incorporate the evaluative dimension in one way or another. Ideological consistency may be one of the key notions in this area of applied research.

It has been shown that the ideological consistency approach can select a reading among several possibilities. However, nothing has been said about how these possible readings could be obtained. In particular, no proposals have been made concerning the exact location and scope of irony. However, SSNs provide a way to represent this location and this scope in a precise way, and DSNs provide a way to assess the plausibility of these representations. These precise representations and the models of evaluative processes reveal how numerous are the decisions implicitly made by a receiver when he understands the irony of a message. This is one of the virtues of formal representations: they almost naturally help circumscribe problems and generate new areas open to research.

The second purpose of this chapter has been to show that modelling the evaluative behaviour of a discourse can bring us close to 'real' interpretation processes. As I have shown, most of the comments made by Jakobson can be integrated, as evaluative meaning effects, within the model. This capacity to integrate into a unique framework a wide range of rhetorical effects is perhaps the greatest strength of the model.

CONCLUSION

Discourse analysis methods and text processing theories, which oscillate between science and hermeneutics, are seldom both scientific and relevant. The purpose of this research was to find a way out of this dilemma by developing a method which allows us to estimate the consistency of a text with an ideology. This consistency is not the logical consistency of the propositions contained in the text with the doctrine of the ideology. It is the consistency of the evaluations conveyed by the text with the values of the ideology.

To justify this focus on values, sociological theories of ideology have first been discussed (Chapter 1). Pragmatic theories explain beliefs by their material causes (Marx), or by the legitimating effects which they render possible (Bourdieu). However, pragmatic theories do not take seriously the content of discourses (which would be falling into the trap of idealism), and therefore cannot dispute it directly. By focusing on the evaluative dimension of discourse, one extends the scope of criticism to a part of the content of discourse, while still avoiding idealism. In this new perspective, people's ideas are no longer the result of an inculcation, but are simply produced by their attempt to achieve evaluative consistency in a given ideological context.

Studying the role of values in social discourse leads one to reconsider the very nature of sociological explanation. As discussed in the first chapter, I can conceive of three main types of sociological theories of beliefs. The first explains beliefs by the interests they serve. The second postulates that beliefs are only the instrument and the reflex of social distinction. The third assumes that there is a sort of scarcity of cognitive and symbolic resources. I have claimed that there is no such thing as a shortage of symbolic resources in general. The only things that may come in short supply are symbolic resources allowing one to be strategically efficient in public discourse. Evaluative belief systems are a perfect illustration of this. Everyone can create new values, or modify old ones. What is difficult is to produce a consistent global system capable of differentiating itself from other belief systems. Systems which are both ideologically consistent and in conflict with others are strategically efficient. Individuals do not decide on this efficiency, which is tested and enforced at the level of public discourse. Therefore, strategic efficiency is not a quality of the individual's discourse, but of social discourse. To the extent that consistency defines strategic efficiency, the latter is a structural notion. Insofar as capability to confront other discourses is concerned, the strategic efficiency of discourse is a historical notion, which presupposes a given state of ideological conflict.

One of the challenges faced by current sociological theory is to explain how ideologies keep structuring our understanding of the world, and, simultaneously, lose their clear boundaries. It is indeed often difficult to see what makes the difference between left-wing and right-wing positions, for example. Neither political actors nor intellectuals seem principled in their judgement. Thus, there is the widespread impression that political life is unscrupulous, intellectually sloppy, or just strategically smart. Ideologies seem to have been killed by pragmatism. But, if, as I have claimed, this is not entirely true, one must propose an alternative, more flexible interpretation of ideology, which explains how ideologies keep confronting each other, while, at the same time, being capable of blurring into one another. This has led me to propose a specific definition of ideology as a system of evaluations, and of ideological consistency as the compatibility of these evaluations.

The efficiency of ideological discourses rests on their capacity to pervade people's minds. This capacity is due, in a large part, to the mind's permeability to evaluation, which, in turn, stems from the primacy of affects in the mind's development. Social psychology's theories of evaluation and psycholinguistic theories of text processing have been revisited in the light of the connectionist paradigm in cognitive science (Chapter 2). Both seem too functionalist and not in accordance with phenomenological descriptions, psychoanalytical findings, and new evidence regarding the functioning of the brain. In our view, evaluation is a bridge between affects and cognition. Evaluating is almost as basic to human cognition as awareness. It is a form of vigilance, of watchfulness, which operates, so to speak, in the background of our consciousness. A typology of evaluative interpretation has therefore been proposed, where high-level interpretations which attempt to identify the ideological allegiance of a text (ideological disambiguation) are articulated upon low-level interpretations, such as the perception of evaluative meaning effects.

Ideological disambiguation can be seen as a meta-categorization process which differs from ordinary categorization processes in several respects, and should therefore be studied on its own. Classical connectionist theory assumes that categorization can be modelled as a process of consistency maximization between inputs and learned patterns. I have pursued, in this research, a slightly different hypothesis, in which the consistency maximization process is somehow externalized, or at least, performed by a specific module of the system. In this approach, the system which models meaning effects is not a consistency maximization engine. This allows us to come closer to the 'symbolic' nature of meaning effects. Yet, in the case of evaluative meaning effects, I have argued that these semantic processes are also largely sub-symbolic, in the sense that they are often unconscious, and often result from 'impressions' (such as the perception of isotopy) that cannot be located in specific linguistic components (either lexical or grammatical). In addition, I have shown how these meaning effects are under the control of sub-symbolic processes of consistency estimation. I believe that this sort of architecture belongs to a new paradigm in cognitive modelling, in which cognition proceeds by watching itself work. In this paradigm, one may interpret cognition as a polyphonic phenomenon. That is, cognition proceeds by watching itself as if it were somebody else. This cognitive stance seems particularly suited to the interpretation of linguistic messages, which are always somebody else's message. This is why I consider ideological disambiguation as a meta-categorization process rather than as a simple categorization process.

Categorization often relies on prototypes. When prototypes are associated with social or moral standards, categorization processes relying on such prototypes involve moral and evaluative attitudes. Therefore, categorization, even in the traditional sense of the term, depends on evaluative dynamics which have been almost entirely ignored by previous research. More generally perhaps, one must hope that taking into account the evaluative dimension of categorization (which depends on social norms) will help breaking the social solipsism in which cognitive science encloses the subject.

Phenomenological descriptions of evaluative interpretation, as well as connectionist models of cognition, cast doubt upon the strategies of discourse analysis which proceed by a priori selecting relevant elements (for example indexical components). It has been argued that, from an evaluative point of view, there is no such thing as salient elements *per se* (Chapter 3). Salience is an emergent phenomenon, which arises from all levels of textuality. This has led me to stipulate that the analysis be undertaken at the semantic level, and that the semantic level be coextensive with the linguistic data as a whole. This approach radically departs from the theoretical orientations of discourse analysis, which is notoriously anti-semantics. Our critique of discourse analysis should not lead us to neglect the insights of existing methods. On the contrary, the linguistic devices which are traditionally seen as the reflexes of ideological biases (choices regarding categorization, agentivity, passivization, aspectualization, for example) have been listed and successfully integrated within the model. This capacity of encompassing previous methods is one of the most appealing features of the model.

An evaluative semantics has then been sketched (Chapter 4). The major obstacle to this undertaking is evaluative variability (the fact that the evaluation of certain words, such as 'communism', depends on ideological perspective). The solution is to consider evaluations in ideological contexts. A semantics of contextual modification has been proposed, in which *default evaluations*, defined by the ideological context, are transformed into *contextual evaluations* under the influence of the linguistic context.

Concerning the notion of evaluation, many remarks I made in Chapters 2 and 4 were aimed at demonstrating that evaluation, and especially evaluation in language, is synthetic and tends to be uni-dimensional. But evaluation is not always uni-dimensional, and one of the main changes that should be made to the model in future developments is to allow for multi-dimensional spaces of evaluation. This generalization should not lead us to underestimate the close relationships which exist between the different evaluative axes, nor the spill-over effects which take place between the various dimensions of evaluative judgement.

The key notion of evaluative semantics is the *ideological consistency* of discourse, which refers to the evaluation of discourse as discourse (vs. evaluation of the content of discourse). The ideological consistency of discourse has been defined as the evaluative compatibility of its parts. It can be measured as the degree to which discourse fulfils evaluative constraints such as 'the evaluation of agents should square with the evaluation of their actions'. The fundamental hypothesis of this book is that these constraints can be expressed by means of dependencies in a dynamic system representing discourse. The more discourse violates these constraints, the more its associated dynamic system will react when they are applied to it. We can therefore estimate the consistency of a text with an ideology as the variation between default and contextual evaluation of its parts.

Thanks to the notion of ideological consistency, some classical problems of denotational semantics, such as the semantic opacity of intentional contexts, have been given a new solution. I have shown how, in the case of epistemic intentional verbs, for example, by switching from the evaluation of the content of a belief report to the consistency of the belief report itself, compositionality problems can be solved. The same kind of analysis should be carried out in detail for other classes of intentional verbs, a study that I have not undertaken here. More generally perhaps, the ideological consistency of discourse appears as an interesting alternative to the Fregean and Montagovian notion of intension, since it yields similar theoretical results while being much more tractable. It is therefore suggested to pay attention to the world *as it should be* instead of to the world *as it is*, by substituting a finite number of conflicting worlds (ideologies) for Kripke's possible worlds.

Artificial intelligence has always faced the need to model complex, imperfect knowledge. The notion of 'partial model' is one of the answers that have been given to this problem. However, in practice, 'partial model' has always been a synonym for 'small model'. Surprisingly, artificial intelligence has never drawn its inspiration from the way in which human beings deal with global, imperfect information by forming evaluative belief systems. In fact, artificial intelligence has paid little attention to the social and ideological components of knowledge. This is regrettable, since evaluative knowledge is often much simpler, and therefore much more economical than factual knowledge. In addition, some fundamental concepts of artificial intelligence can easily be used to formalize ideologies. The notion of extension, borrowed from nonmonotonic logic, is perhaps best suited to the formalization of ideologies, since it allows us to model conflicts between worlds. Finally, the close relationship between the notions of inheritance and subsumption help us relate evaluative conflicts to propositional conflicts.

As stated in Chapter 4, the purpose of this research was to define ideological consistency in terms of evaluation, and not the opposite way around. Therefore, in the model, default evaluations are exogenous (they depend on the ideological hypothesis), and ideological consistency is endogenous. The model can answer the question 'which evaluations render the text more consistent?' but only by choosing between several predefined possibilities (the ideologies). Another way to proceed would be to put no restriction on the set of possible solutions, and to search for an optimal vector of evaluation. This vector could then be compared with the vector of default evaluation in each ideology in order to determine which is closer. Stated otherwise, evaluations could be defined as maximizing the intrinsic consistency of a text. Although this strategy may seem appealing, it is also much more complex than the one adopted here. In fact, the difference between the two strategies is the same as the difference between a simple calculus and the resolution of an equation.

Labelled semantic networks have been used to represent discourse, and a connectionist extension of these networks is used to model evaluative meaning effects (Chapter 5). More precisely, the model of evaluative interpretation developed in this book relies on parallel networks with non-distributed representation. However, these parallel networks allow for the simultaneous interaction of all the parts of discourse. They also render it possible to use continuous representations, and to model cognitive processes as trajectories of the dynamic systems. The main advantage of using continuous dynamics, is that it emphasizes certain specific features of evaluative cognitive processes (graduality, unconsciousness, unintentionality, resistance to objectivization) which differ from ordinary reasoning.

The discourse representation formalism, called styled semantic networks (SSNs) aims at expressivity (Chapter 6). SSNs contain the essential information needed for evaluative reasoning: the scope of negation, of quantification, of modality, is represented by typography; time and aspect by colours; reported discourses by embedded networks.

Besides its graphical aspect, the formalism brings some interesting innovations. Though less fundamental than the notion of ideological consistency, *modal aspectualization* is an important feature of the representation formalism used in the model. As I have shown, decomposing the modalities bearing on a predicate into the various modal contributions of the predicate's arguments is essential for evaluative reasoning, and should be incorporated in modal representation formalisms in one way or another. The solution which has been adopted in the book for the case of certain alethic modalities (real, potential, unreal) seems to me rather straightforward, and could perhaps be extended to other modalities (optatives, necessity, etc.).

I believe that SSNs are a good compromise between expressivity and semantic clarity, especially for the purpose of the sociological analysis of textual materials. The most important weakness of SSNs is perhaps that they do not provide any way of representing syntactic categories. This was a deliberate choice which aimed to avoid any dependency upon a specific grammar, and therefore, upon any language. However, this choice has the clear drawback of eliminating from the representation of discourse an important part of its structure. A research project attempting to model the processes by which a global evaluation of a sentence's content is derived should perhaps consider representations closer to syntax than SSNs. The same type of remark applies to the cognitive modelling of semantic evaluative processes. It may be useful to introduce intermediate types such as event, action, phenomenon, institution, idea, etc., to structure the representations.

From a more mathematical point of view, the basic idea of this research was to estimate the consistency of a relational structure by means of the stability of an associated dynamical system (Chapter 7). This idea has proved to be successful, especially if we expect from this method estimations that only have a relative value. I repeat that the estimation of a discourse's consistency with an ideology is not so much significant *per se*, but by comparison of the discourse's consistency with other ideologies. This remark has an important consequence for the sociological analysis of textual material, namely, that estimating the consistency of a text under several ideological hypotheses does not yield a set of numerical values, but, rather, a ranking of these hypotheses. However, some well-known methods are available to deal with this sort of data.

SSNs are transformed into dynamical semantic networks (DSNs) by assigning connection weights to each relation. A series of rules allows us to take into account the effects of negation, quantification and modality on connection weights. Under an ideological hypothesis, the dynamics can be initialized. It is then possible to estimate the consistency of the text with the ideological hypothesis as a function of the distance between the initial state of the network representing the text and the attractor of the dynamics. The trajectory of the system can be seen as an interpretation of the text.

Under certain hypotheses concerning the parameters, DSNs are globally asymptotically stable. This is of course a highly desirable feature of dynamic systems, since it tells us that they do converge towards a stable attractor, regardless of their initial state. The constraints insuring convergence are weak enough to allow for various combinations of signs and values of connection weights, and therefore do not significantly lower the expressivity of the dynamics.

The main purpose of the dynamical systems proposed in this work was to model evaluative meaning effects. To this end, I proposed a mode of interaction in which the contrast between the activation states of the units matters more than their intrinsic value. The global dynamics resulting from these interactions have proved to be adequate for a wide range of semantic effects. By playing with the signs of connection weights, one can easily achieve the type of effects produced by classical additive dynamics, for example, as well as some other interesting behaviours, such as mutual attraction, mutual repulsion, and attraction–repulsion. The latter are particularly useful for the semantic modelling of connectors. It is also possible to model the cognitive processes which are based on a comparison with a standard and those which are not in a different way. Any future modelling of semantic effects by the means of dynamical systems should encompass the dynamics studied in this book. More generally, I believe that the results obtained in this work make a strong case in favour of the modelling of discourse by dynamical systems.

Still on the dynamical side, the model has important limitations, which are mainly due to the layout of DSNs representing discourse. Indeed, since DSNs do not possess hidden units, they can have no learning capacities. Future work on evaluation in language should perhaps be more in line with the main streams of connectionist modelling. In other words, one may try to build up systems that learn the associations between a simple predicate (in the context of its various possible arguments), and its evaluation. As demonstrated by similar research on the connectionist modelling of meaning, this sort of project raises many conceptual and technical difficulties. By comparison with connectionist models of meaning, connectionist models of evaluation add another difficulty, namely, variability of evaluations (due to ideological perspectives). On the other hand, this additional difficulty is largely counterbalanced by the fact that focusing on evaluation greatly reduces the complexity of the problem. While each word potentially defines its own semantic space, the evaluative semantic space is shared by all words. This should allow homogeneous systems to be designed, with the same type of hidden layers for all elementary parts of discourse. Furthermore, one can make the hypothesis that the evaluative state space has a limited number of dimensions (truth, feasibility, justice, morality, etc.). This should greatly simplify the conceptual analyses which must always precede the training of the system. Therefore, although ideological phenomena play a part in evaluation, the evaluative dimension of meaning seems to be an interesting starting point for the connectionist modelling of meaning, a paradigm which is still in an early stage of development despite the interest it arouses among computational linguists, computer scientists, and experts in semantics.

The networks proposed in this book are connectionist, and yet have no learning capacities. Thus, one may wonder how connection weights and other parameters are set. The weights of the networks representing discourse are derived from a knowledge-base of small networks (Chapter 8). These 'canonical' networks contain purely semantic information, together with the social expectations and standards attached to a social role or a social situation. Canonical networks also prescribe the initial evaluation of the linguistic unit in restricted 'canonical' contexts. Since expectations and evaluations are ideological, the knowledge base is in fact an ideology, and its content can be organized around the categories proposed in the first chapter of the book. Once the weights of a dynamic semantic network have been set on the basis of an ideological hypothesis, these weights are modified to reflect modalities, negation and quantification in discourse. This modification is performed by the application of a set of explicit rules. At the end of this two-step process, the parameters of a DSN are set in a consistent and reproducible way.

The final application of the model to a text by Shakespeare (Chapter 9) demonstrates why computational linguistics and natural language processing would be well advised to devote more attention to the evaluative dimension of meaning. I have shown how the notion of ideological consistency could help to solve difficult disambiguation problems, such as the identification of irony. The idea here is straightforward. If an NLP system has to choose between two readings that are equally plausible from a syntactic point of view, then the reading which achieves the highest level of evaluative consistency is probably the right candidate. However, much more theoretical work is needed in order to narrow down the readings from which the most consistent will later be selected.

At the end of this work, let me take a last look back. I began this research with the hypothesis that evaluative reasoning had its own logic, and more precisely, a certain autonomy with respect to other forms of reasoning. Although this hypothesis retrospectively seems to be supported by much evidence concerning cognitive processes, at that time this was just a working hypothesis for me, not a certainty. At each turn during the elaboration of the model, I feared I would run into some problems revealing that my hypothesis was wrong. I was surprised by how far the model carried me before its limitations became apparent. When applying the model to real texts, it often turned out that even very simple assumptions concerning parameters produced intuitive results. When the results were counter-intuitive, this was often because I had insufficiently analysed the semantic effects at hand. Modifying parameters to reflect these effects would almost always allow me to achieve satisfying estimations of consistency.

CONCLUSION

Strictly speaking, this does not prove that the hypothesis is correct. Indeed, when I was setting up parameters for a given piece of discourse, I was using some non-evaluative knowledge, sometimes without even realizing. Therefore, if the model eventually did not fail to simulate evaluative interpretation, this is partly because it was backed by my own, global interpretative skills. However, I believe that this is already an important result: it is possible to express in purely evaluative terms (that is, default evaluation, evaluative semantic effects, inertia and ideological significance) the knowledge required for semantic evaluative reasoning. Autonomy of the evaluative sphere is not so much due to the fact that evaluation is the source of reasoning but to the capacity of the evaluative sphere to reflect wider dimensions of knowledge, such as pre-reflexive, pragmatic or theoretical knowledge.

APPENDIX A

This appendix contains the demonstration that when the constraint (6) given in Chapter 7 holds, then the largest eigenvalue of the iteration function has a module stricly inferior to 1.

Let us note that $\sum_{-} w_{ij}$ and $\sum_{+} w_{ij}$ are the sum of negative and positive weights affecting variable x_i respectively. It can be shown that if we impose the constraint

$$\sum_{-} w_{kj} < a_k < 2 - \sum_{+} w_{kj} \quad k = 1, ..., n.$$

then the largest eigenvalue of the Jacobian of the dynamic system defined by equations

$$x_i(t+1) = x_i(t) - a_i(x_i(t) - x_i(t_0)) + \sum_{j \neq i} w_{ij} S(x_j(t) - x_i(t)) \, i = 1, ..., n.$$

is strictly inferior to 1 (in module). Demonstration proceeds as follows:

Let us consider F, the iteration function of the dynamical system

$$X(t) = F(X(t-1)),$$

and its Jacobian $M = J(F)$

$$\begin{cases} m_{ii} = 1 - a_i - \sum_{j \neq i} w_{ij} S'(x_j - x_i) \\ m_{ij} = w_{ij} S'(x_j - x_i) \quad i \neq j \end{cases}$$

To simplify notations, let us assume that

APPENDIX A

$$b_{ij} = \omega_{ij} S'(x_j - x_i).$$

Let us search for the eigenvectors corresponding to the eigenvalue λ.

$$\begin{cases} \left(1 - a_1 - \sum_{j \neq 1} b_{1j}\right) x_1 + b_{12} x_2 + \ldots + b_{1n} x_n = \lambda x_1 \\ b_{i1} x_1 + \ldots + \left(1 - a_i - \sum_{j \neq i} b_{ij}\right) x_i + \ldots + b_{in} x_n = \lambda x_i \\ b_{n1} x_1 + b_{n2} x_2 + \ldots + \left(1 - a_n - \sum_{j \neq n} b_{nj}\right) x_n = \lambda x_n \end{cases}$$

Let us pick up the equation corresponding to the coordinate with larger module:

$$b_{k1} x_1 + \ldots + \left(1 - a_k - \sum_{j \neq k} b_{kj}\right) x_k + \ldots + b_{kn} x_n = \lambda x_k,$$

and let us rewrite it as follows

$$\left(\lambda - 1 + a_k + \sum_{j \neq k} b_{kj}\right) x_k = b_{k1} x_1 + \ldots + b_{k,i-1} x_{i-1} + b_{k,i+1} x_{i+1} + \ldots + b_{kn} x_n.$$

Applying modules to both sides yields:

$$\left|\lambda - 1 + a_k + \sum_{j \neq k} b_{kj}\right| |x_k| = |b_{k1} x_1 + \ldots + b_{k,i-1} x_{i-1} + b_{k,i+1} x_{i+1} + \ldots + b_{kn} x_n|.$$

This entails that

$$\left|\lambda - 1 + a_k + \sum_{j \neq k} b_{kj}\right| |x_k| \leq |b_{k1} x_1| + \ldots + |b_{k,i-1} x_{i-1}| + |b_{k,i+1} x_{i+1}| + \ldots + |b_{kn} x_n|.$$

Because, for all i, $|x_i| \leq |x_k|$, we obtain

APPENDIX A

$$\left|\lambda - 1 + a_k + \sum_{j \neq k} b_{kj}\right| |x_k| \leq \left(\sum_{i \neq k} |b_{ki}|\right) |x_k|,$$

and therefore,

$$\left|\lambda - 1 + a_k + \sum_{j \neq k} b_{kj}\right| \leq \sum_{i \neq k} |b_{ki}|,$$

from which we can deduce that

$$|\lambda| \leq \sum_{i \neq k} |b_{ki}| + \left|-1 + a_k + \sum_{j \neq k} b_{kj}\right|.$$

As before, $\sum_+ b_{kj}$ and $\sum_- b_{kj}$ are the sum of b_{kj} with positive and negative signs respectively.

Two cases must be considered.

Case 1. $-1 + a_k + \sum_{j \neq k} b_{kj} \leq 0.$

Then

$$|\lambda| \leq \sum_{i \neq k} |b_{ki}| + 1 - a_k - \sum_{j \neq k} b_{kj},$$

and therefore,

$$|\lambda| \leq 1 - a_k - 2 \sum_- b_{kj}.$$

Case 2. $-1 + a_k + \sum_{j \neq k} b_{kj} \geq 0$

then

$$|\lambda| \leq \sum_{i \neq k} |b_{ki}| - 1 + a_k + \sum_{j \neq k} b_{kj},$$

and therefore,

APPENDIX A

$$|\lambda| \leq -1 + a_k + 2\sum_+ b_{kj}.$$

Let us impose $|\lambda| < 1$. In each case, this yields a sufficient condition.

Case 1. $|\lambda| \leq 1 - a_k - 2\sum_- b_{kj} < 1,$

and therefore

$$a_k > 2\sum_- b_{kj}.$$

Case 2. $|\lambda| \leq -1 + a_k + 2\sum_+ b_{kj} < 1,$

and therefore

$$a_k < 2 - 2\sum_+ b_{kj}.$$

Because $S' \leq 1/2$, we can rewrite the previous constraints in terms of weights and inertia only.

Case 1. $a_k > \sum_- w_{kj}.$

Case 2. $a_k < 2 - \sum_+ w_{kj}.$

Let us impose that the constraints for each case be satisfied simultaneously. This implies that

$$\sum_- w_{kj} < a_k < 2 - \sum_+ w_{kj} \quad k = 1, ..., n.$$

QED.

APPENDIX B

This appendix contains the exordium of Mark Antony's funeral discourse in *Julius Caesar*, by William Shakespeare (III, 2).

ANTONY:

1   Friends, Romans, countrymen, lend me your ears;
    I come to bury Caesar, not to praise him.
    The evil that men do lives after them,
    The good is oft interred with their bones;
5   So let it be with Caesar. The noble Brutus
    Hath told you Caesar was ambitious;
    If it were so, it was a grievous fault,
    And grievously hath Caesar answer'd it.
    Here, under leave of Brutus and the rest,—
10 For Brutus is an honourable man;
    So are they all, all honourable men,—
    Come I to speak in Caesar's funeral.
    He was my friend, faithful and just to me:
    But Brutus says he was ambitious;
15 And Brutus is an honourable man.
    He has brought many captives home to Rome,
    Whose ransoms did the general coffers fill:
    Did this in Caesar seem ambitious?
    When that the poor have cried, Caesar has wept;
20 Ambition should be made of sterner stuff:
    Yet Brutus says he was ambitious;
    And Brutus is an honourable man.
    You all did see that on the Lupercal
    I thrice presented him a kingly crown,
25 Which he did thrice refuse: was this ambition?
    Yet Brutus says he was ambitious;
    And sure, he is an honourable man.

I speak not to disprove what Brutus spoke,
But I am here to speak what I do know.
30 You all did love him once, not without cause:
What cause withholds you then to mourn for him?
O judgement! thou art fled to brutish beasts,
And men have lost their reason. Bear with me;
My heart is in the coffin there with Caesar,
35 And I must pause till it come back to me.

NOTES

Chapter 1

1. Emphasis is Bourdieu's.
2. 'J'étais avec un musulman en cellule. Là, j'ai appris l'arabe, j'ai bien appris ma religion, l'islam. J'ai appris une grande ouverture d'esprit en connaissant l'islam. Tout s'est écarté. Et je vois ma vie... *pas plus simple*, mais plus cohérente.' *Le Monde*, 7/10/95, no. 15769, p. 12. Emphasis is ours.
3. Social actors are not necessarily aware of their incentives to act, and their discourse upon themselves may be rationalizations or justifications. Nevertheless, they are not necessarily wrong.
4. It has been argued, for example, that social learning is different in the Jewish and in the Catholic tradition, due to different conceptions of text, law, and body (Legendre 1982). More generally, it may be argued that each culture proposes a specific framework (mainly unconscious) for individual learning.
5. This view of language is consistent with the idea that, at the level of discourse, there is no susbstantiality of the phenomena of domination. Symbolic domination is always an artefact because real domination is fundamentally arbitrary. For Bourdieu, domination is social, that is, neither natural nor essential. Domination is reality, that is, a being without substance.
6. 'Il ne faut pas être libéral parce qu'on est contre le dirigisme. Il faut être libéral parce que c'est la théorie de la croissance la plus moderne et la plus complète qui existe'. Valery Giscard d'Estaing, in 'Quel Avenir pour l'Europe?', Paris, Publicis, 1968. 'Libéral' and 'Libéralism', in France, refers to a mix of free enterprise, deregulation and conservatism. Margaret Thatcher is, in the French sense of the term, liberal.
7. In 1968, within the field of economics, 'liberal' theories did not dominate Keynesian theories as they do now. Giscard's appreciation is therefore personal. Today, one of the main ideological functions of scientific economics is to impose upon newcomers (students, future managers) the obligation to work within the intellectual framework of liberal theory.
8. I will sometimes use the word 'compossibility' instead of compatibility, in order to stress that compatibility means here compatibility between values, and not compatibility with a state of society.
9. 'Encompassing' is a principle of model comparison invented and applied in econometrics. It consists of the capacity of a model to predict (statistically) the

results of another model. In the case of nested models, encompassing becomes statistical hypothesis testing. Encompassing is therefore a general framework for model comparison. Applied to semantics, the word 'encompassing' is used, in a much less technical sense, as the pretension of one semantic dimension to 'express' another one.

Chapter 2

1. The CHILDES Project (MacWhinney 1995), for example, which proposes a coding protocol for child speech, does recognize the importance of evaluation. Evaluation is taken into account, at the pragmatic level, by means of speech acts and illocutionary force codes ('DS', for disapproval and scolding, and 'AB' for approval). The coding framework also integrates evaluation at the semantic level, by means of the general code 'EVAL', and its sub-categories.
2. This is not surprising since neither language nor discourse are psychological realities.
3. One may wonder if, in modern society, staying informed requires fewer and fewer retention efforts. The developments of online information and news channels free us from the obligation of retaining knowledge. On the other hand, does this continuous exposure to repeated information lead us to improve our retention skills?
4. In his *Introduction to Metaphysics,* Heidegger explicitly relates the experience of anguish and the awareness of the ontological difference.

Chapter 3

1. *Oceanus Iuris* : title of a collection of texts, Lyon, 1535.
2. Krippendorff argues that the capacity to deal with 'unstructured' symbolic data is one of the main strengths of content analysis (1980, p. 30). This argument is rather surprising since it is hard to conceive of a kind of data that would be more structured than symbolic data.
3. For an introduction to this question, see, for example, the second chapter of Lee 1992. For a discussion of the limits of the Saussurian notion of 'value' and an evocation of the historical evolution of the 'differential' paradigm, see Rastier *et al.* 1994.
4. This is true, at least, of the 'latent ambiguities', that is, ambiguities that are not necessarily perceived as such. There is, of course, another type of ambiguity, that we may call 'manifest ambiguity', and which consists of the ambiguities that, instead of being dissimulated, are specifically encoded in discourse in order to produce a feeling of ambiguity (Riffaterre 1979, p. 14)
5. Sociologism refers to the process by which a sociological description turns into a naturalization, and therefore, into a legitimation, of what it describes.
6. For a perfect illustration of this contrast, see, for example, Achard 1995a.
7. Italics are in the text.
8. Cassirer for example, uses the term 'symbolic' in this broad sense, in his *Philosophie der symbolischen Formen.*
9. *Aesthetic*, vol. II: *Symbolic Art*, introduction: *about the Symbol in general* (my

translation).

10 One cannot justify lexicometric methods by this property. Because most signifiers are not genuine symbols, their meaning depends on their linguistic and pragmatic environment.
11 S. E. XV, p. 165.
12 S. E. XV, pp. 158–9.
13 For example, Pierre Legendre (1988).

Chapter 4

1 For a summary of the positions of several influential semanticians (Greimas, Courtés, Kiefer, the Mu Group, Martin, Kerbrat) on this topic, see Rastier 1987: 45).
2 Broadly speaking, the distinction between closed and open-class forms corresponds to the distinction between grammar and lexicon (Talmy 1987). Closed-class forms are inflexions, particles, modalities, auxiliaries, grammatical categories, grammatical relations and constructions. Open-class forms are the nouns, the adjectives, most of the adverbs, and most of the verbs. It is often assumed that basic semantic notions have correlates within both closed- and open-class forms, while secondary semantic notions only have correlates within open-class forms.
3 Due to some subtle differences between the semantics of 'presque' and 'almost', 'Peter is almost late' may seem meaningless to the English reader, while in French, 'Pierre est presque en retard', is perfectly acceptable, and means 'Pierre has not arrived yet, and may be late'.
4 Throughout this chapter, I use the word 'occurrence' as an abbreviation for 'occurrence of a sememe'.
5 Model-theoretic encoding of data is traditionally seen as much less economical and efficient than its proof-theoretic counterpart. It has recently been shown that this is not always the case (Kautz *et al.* 1995).
6 By monotonicity, I refer to the fact that each argument pushes the result of the function either always upward or always downward.
7 Easier means here 'requiring a lesser amount of information'.

Chapter 5

1 The most common examples of modal operators are the universal operator $\Box$ (meaning 'it is necessary that') and the existential operator $\Diamond$ (meaning 'it is possible that') of the so-called 'alethic' modal logic.
2 A subgraph is obtained by deleting some arcs and nodes of the original graph. It should not be confused with an 'embedded graph', a notion related to complex graphs.
3 As stated in the previous chapter (see pages 127), in a model complying with the 'closed-world assumption', every true atomic fact is asserted and as a consequence, everything which is not asserted or not provable is false. Such models have interesting theoretical properties, but are inapplicable to the formalization of social discourse, which requires partial models.

NOTES

4   This algorithm is a slightly simplified version of that of Sowa, who intends to deal properly with equality between referents (Sowa 1984, p. 168).
5   For a thorough and up-to-date discussion of this point, I refer the reader to the book *Language and Cognition* (Laks 1996).

Chapter 6

1   The requirement that all evaluative ambiguities must be eliminated cannot be totally fulfilled, since many phenomena of ambiguity have not yet been solved by semantics in general. This is the case with many sorts of lexical ambiguity, and in particular, with polysemy, which, despite a large number of theoretical proposals, still awaits a satisfactory treatment.
2   The small triangle at the upper right corner of a concept box indicates that this is in fact a context displayed in collapsed view.
3   Institut de Recherche Informatique de Toulouse.
4   Verbal communication.
5   Send a request to the author at malrieu@ext.jussieu.fr.

Chapter 7

1   Also called the *logistic* function.
2   See Appendix. A
3   Considering (4), note that, at the equilibrium, $x_i(t) = x_i(t+1)$, and that $|S| < 1$.

Chapter 8

1   On each relation, the first number indicates the semantic influence 'in the direction of the arrow', while the second corresponds to the reverse influence. Only the first decimal and the sign are displayed. For example, a connection weight of -0.15 is displayed as -1.
2   Charisma is, according to Weber, the first legitimating principle of domination.
3   For example, the fears of the Prince of Parma, in *La Chartreuse de Parme*, by Stendhal.
4   The expression 'potential link' means here 'link with modality *potential*'.

Chapter 9

1   With Marlon Brando as Mark Antony, under Mankiewiecz's direction.
2   When he says 'So let it be with Caesar', Antony is not talking of the good and the bad that Caesar did, but of the memory that men have of what Caesar did. For those who do not like Caesar, the negative distortion between what Caesar did and what people remember does not matter as much as for those who loved him. Therefore, the fact that [(LET IT BE) INTERRED] and [(LET IT) LIVE] are more negatively evaluated under the pro-Caesar ideology conforms to intuition.
3   take through = grieve.
4   that were much he should = that would be difficult for him.

NOTES

5 no fear = nothing to fear.
6 The pragmatics of interrogation are of course more complex than the skeleton given here.
7 This is due to the fact that the only significant unit ([HE]) is only indirectly related to the unit affected by the changes ([AMBITIOUS]).
8 The emphasis put on the occurrences of 'thrice' is reflected, within our DSN, by the null connection weights from [REFUSED] and [PRESENTED] to [THRICE]. These low connection weights increase the impact of the adverb. Cf. Ch. 8, section 4.
9 The expression 'to be of sterner stuff' has its own, global meaning (usually positive), and need not be decomposed.

BIBLIOGRAPHY

Abeillé A. (1993) Les nouvelles syntaxes. Paris: Armand Colin.
Achard P. (1995a) Registre discursif et énonciation: induction sociologique à partir des marques de personne. *Langage et société*, 71: 5–34.
Achard P. (1995b) Formation discursive et sociologie. *Langage*, 117: 82–95.
Ajzen I. (1974) Effect of information on interpersonal attraction: Similarity versus affective value. *Journal of Personality and Social Psychology*, 29: 374–380.
Althusser L. (1965) *Pour Marx*. Paris: Maspero.
Althusser L. (1970) Idéologie et appareils Idéologiques d'État (notes pour une recherche). *La Pensée*, 151: 3–38.
Anderson N. H. (1981) *Foundations of Information Integration Theory*. New York: Academic Press.
Andrews E. (1990) *Markedness Theory*. Durham: Duke University Press.
Anscombre J. C. (ed.) (1995) *Théorie des Topoi*. Paris: Kimé.
Anscombre J. C. and Ducrot O. (1988) (2nd edition) *L'argumentation dans la langue*. Liège: Mardaga.
Ariety S. (1976) *Creativity; The Magic Synthesis*. New York: Basic Books.
Asher N. (1986) Beliefs in discourse representation theory. *Journal of Philosophical Logic*, 5: 127–185.
Asher N. (1987) A typology for attitude verbs and their anaphoric properties. *Linguistics and Philosophy*, 10: 125–197.
Bakhtine M. (1977) *Le marxisme et la philosophie du langage* (tr. from Russian 1929). Paris: Minuit.
Bakhtine M. (1984) *Esthétique de la création verbale*. Paris: Minuit.
Barrett M. (1996) Early lexical development. In P. Fletcher and B. MacWhinney (eds.) *The Handbook of Child Language*. Cambridge (MA): Blackwell. pp. 363–392.
Barwise J. (1988) *The Situation in Logic*. Stanford (CA): CLSI.
Barwise J. and Perry J. (1983) *Situations and Attitudes*. Cambridge (MA): MIT Press.
Batistella E. L. (1990) *Markedness: The Evaluative Superstructure of Language*. Albany (NY): State University of New York Press.
Baudrillard J. (1993) *Symbolic Exchange and Death*. (G. Hamilton tr.). London: Sage.

Beauvois J. L. (1976) Problématique des conduites sociales d'évaluation. *Connnexions*, 19: 7–30.

Beauvois J. L. and Deschamp J. C. (1990) Vers la cognition sociale. In R. Ghiglione, C. Bonet and J. F. Richard (eds.) *Traité de psychologie cognitive*, Tome 3. Paris: Dunod.

Bem D. J. (1967). Self-perception: an alternative interpretation of cognitive dissonance phenomena. *Psychological Review*, 74: 183–200.

Bodenhausen G. V. and Lichtenstein M. (1987) Social stereotypes and information processing strategies: the impact of task complexity. *Journal of Personality and Social Psychology*, 52: 871–889.

Boltanski L. (1990) *L'amour et la justice comme compétences*. Paris: Métailier.

Boltanski L. (1993) *La souffrance à distance. Morale humanitaire, médias et politique*. Paris: Métailier.

Boltanski L. and Thévenot L. (1983) Finding one's way in social space: a study based on games. *Social Science Information*, 22(4–5): 631–680.

Boltanski L. and Thévenot L. (1991) *De la Justification: les économies de la grandeur*. Paris: Gallimard.

Borgese G. A. (1938) *Goliath: the March of Fascism*. London: Victor Gollancz.

Boudon R. (1982) *The Logic of Social Action. An Introduction to Sociological Analysis*. London: Routledge.

Boudon R. (1986). *L'Idéologie. L'origine des idées reçues*. Paris: Fayard.

Boudon, R. (1990). *l'Art de se persuader. Des idées douteuses fragiles ou fausses*. Paris: Fayard.

Bourdieu P. (1977) *Outline of a Theory of Practice*. Cambridge University Press (translation by Richard Nice of *Esquisse d'une théorie de la pratique, précédé de trois études d'ethnologie kabyle*. 1972. Droz, Genève).

Bourdieu P. (1980a) Le mort saisit le vif. *Actes de la Recherche en Sciences Sociales*, 33: 3–14.

Bourdieu P. (1980b) *Le sens pratique*. Paris: Minuit.

Bourdieu P. (1982) *Ce que parler veut dire; l'économie des échanges linguistiques*. Paris: Fayard.

Bourdieu P. (1990) La domination masculine. *Actes de la Recherche en Sciences Sociales*, September 1–31.

Bourdieu P. (1992) *Les règles de l'art*. Paris: Minuit.

Bourdieu P. (ed.) (1993) *La Misère du monde*. Paris: Seuil.

Bourdieu P. and Boltanski L. (1976). La production de l'idéologie dominante. *Actes de la Recherche en Sciences Sociales*, 2: 4–75.

Boutet J. (1994) *Construire le sens*. Berne: Peter Lang.

Brachman R. (1979) On the epistemological status of semantic networks. In N. Findler (ed.) *Associative Networks*. New York: Academic Press, 3–49.

Breal M. (1897) *Essai de Sémantique*. Paris: Hachette. [reed. 1982, G. Monfort, Brionne].

Breckler S. (1984) Empirical validation of affect, behavior and cognition as distinct components of attitudes. *Journal of Personality and Social Pychology*, 47: 1191–1205.

Breckler S. and Fried S. (1993) On knowing what you like and liking what you smell: attitudes depend on the form in which the object is presented. *Personality*

and Social Psychology Bulletin, 19: 228–249.
Brewer M. (1988) A dual process model of impression formation. In T. K. Srull and R. S. Wyer (eds.) *Advances in Social Cognition, Vol. 1: A dual-process model of impression formation.* Hillsdale (NJ): Laurence Erlbaum Associates.
Brown G. and Yule G. (1983) *Discourse Analysis.* Cambridge: Cambridge University Press.
Carel M. (1995) Trop: argumentation interne, argumentation externe et positivité, in J. C. Anscombre (ed.) *Théorie des Topoi,* Paris: Kimé.
Carnap R. (1942) *Introduction to Semantics.* Cambridge, MA: Harvard University Press.
Carpenter B. (1992) *The Logic of Typed Feature Structures.* Cambridge: Cambridge University Press.
Carrol J. B. (ed.) (1971) *Language, Thought and Reality: Selected Writings of Benjamin Lee Whorf* (first published in 1956). Cambridge (MA): MIT Press.
Clancey W. J. (1993) The biology of consciousness: comparative review of Israel Rosenfield, *The Strange, Familiar and Forgotten: An Anatomy of Consciousness,* and Gerald M. Edelman, *Bright Air, Brilliant Fire, on the Matter of the Mind. Artificial Intelligence,* 60: 313–356.
Clark E. V. (1973) What's in a word? On the child's aquisition of semantics in its first age. In T. E. Moore (ed.) *Cognitive Development and the Aquisition of Language.* NY: Academic Press.
Coffey C. (1984) Language: a transformative key. *Language in Society*, 13: 511–513.
Courcelle B. (1990) Graph rewriting: an algebraic and logic approach. In J. van Leeuwen (ed.) *Handbook of Theoretical Computer Science.* New York: Elsevier. pp. 193–240.
Courtine J. J. (1981) Analyse du discours politique. *Langage,* 62.
Courtine J. J and Marandin J. M. (1981) Quel objet pour l'analyse du discours? *Matérialités discursives,* Presses Universitaire de Lille.
Cuilemburg J. J., Kleinnijenhuis J. and de Ridder J. A. (1988) Artificial intelligence and content analysis. *Quality and Quantity*, 2: 65–97.
Dahlgren K. (1985) The cognitive structure of social categories. *Cognitive Science,* 9: 379–398.
Dahlgren K. (1988) *Naive Semantics for Natural Language Understanding.* Norwell (MA): Kluwer.
Dahlgren K. and McDowell J. (1989) Knowledge representation for common sense reasoning with text. *Computationnal Linguistics,* 15 (3).
De Beaugrande R. (1980) *Text, Discourse and Process.* London: Longman.
Denhiere G. and Rossi, J. P. (eds.) (1992) *Text and Text Processing.* Amsterdam: North Holland.
Dennet D. C. (1992) *Consciousness Explained.* Boston (MA): Little Brown and Company.
Derrida J. (1967) *De la Grammatologie.* Paris: Minuit.
Derrida J. (1996) *Résistances. De la Psychanalyse.* Paris: Seuil.
Derthick M. (1987). Counterfactual reasoning with direct models. *Proc. AAAI-87.*
De Sousa R. (1987) *The rationality of emotion.* Cambridge (MA): MIT Press.
Doise W. (1990) Les représentations sociales. In R. Ghiglione, C. Bonet and J. F.

Richard (eds.) *Traité de psychologie cognitive*, Tome 3. Paris: Dunod.

Dore J. (1985) Holophrases revisited: their 'logical' development from dialog. In M. D. Barrett (ed.) *Children's Single-word Speech*. Chichester: Wiley.

Downs A. (1957). *An Economic Theory of Democracy*. New York: Harper.

Dowty D. R., Wall R. E. and Peters S. (1981) *Introduction to Montague Semantics*. Dordrecht: Reidel.

Dromi E. (1987) *Early Lexical Development*. Cambridge: Cambridge University Press.

Dreben E. K, Fiske S. T. and Hastie R. (1979) The independence of item and evaluative information: Impression and recall order effects in behaviour-based impression formation. *Journal of Personality and Social Psychology*, 37: 1758–1768.

Ducrot O. (1980) *Les mots du discours*. Paris: Minuit.

Ducrot O. (1984) *Le dire et le dit*. Paris: Minuit.

Eagleton T. (1980) Text, ideology, realism. In E. W. Said (ed.) *Literature and Society*. Baltimore: Johns Hopkins University Press.

Eagly A. H. and Chaiken S. (1993) *The Psychology of Attitudes*. Forth Worth (FL): Harcourt Brace Jovanovitz.

Edelman G. M. (1992) *Bright Air, Brilliant Fire: On the Matter of the Mind*. New York: Basic Books.

Fahlman S. (1979) NETL: *A System for Representing and Using Real-World Knowledge*. Cambridge (MA): MIT Press.

Fairclough N. L. (1995) *Critical Discourse Analysis: The Critical Study of Language*. Harlow: Longman.

Fazio R. H. (1990) Multiple processes by which attitudes guide behavior: the MODE model as an interpretative framework. In M. P. Zana (ed.) *Advance in Experimental Social Psychology*, 14: 161–202. San Diego (CA): Academic Press.

Fernald R. (1989) Intonation and communicative intent in mother's speech to infants: is the melody the message? *Child Development*. 60: 1497–1510.

Festinger L. (1957) *A Theory of Cognitive Dissonance*. Stanford (CA): Stanford University Press.

Findler N. V. (ed.) (1979) *Associative Networks: Representation and use of Knowledge by Computers*. New York: Academic Press.

Fishbein M. and Ajzen I. (1975) *Belief, Attitude, Attention and Behavior: An Introduction to Theory and Research*. Reading (MA): Addison Wesley.

Fiske S. T. and Pavelchak M. A. (1986) Category-based vs. piecemeal-based affective responses: Developments in schema-triggered affect. In R. M. Sorentino and E. T. Higgins (eds.) *Handbook of Motivation and Cognition*. New York: Guilford Press.

Fletcher P. and MacWhinney B. (ed.) (1996) *The Handbook of Child Language*. Cambridge (MA): Blackwell.

Foucault M. (1971) Orders of discourse (translated from the French by R. Swyer). *Social Science Information*, 10(2): 7–30.

Foucault M. (1972) *The Archaeology of Knowledge* (translated from the French by A. M. Sheridan Smith). London: Routledge.

Forgas J. P. (ed.) (1991) *Emotion and Social Judgements*. Oxford, New York:

Pergamon Press.

Franzosi R. (1989) From words to numbers: a generalized and linguistic-based coding procedure for collecting textual data. *Sociological Methodology*.

Franzosi R. (1994) From words to numbers: A set theory framework for the collection, organization, and analysis of narrative data. *Sociological Methodology*.

Frege G. (1952) On sense and reference. In P. T. Geach and M. Black (eds.) *Translations from the Philosophical Writings of Gottlob Frege*. Oxford: Basil Blackwell. pp. 56–78. Translated from 'Über Sinn und Bedeutung', *Zeitschrift für Philosophie und philosophiche Kritik*, 100: 25–50 (1892).

Fuchs C. and Leonard A-M. (1979) *Vers une théorie des aspects, les systèmes du français et de l'anglais*. Paris: Mouton.

Garey M. R. & Johnson D. S. (1979) *Computer and Intractability – A Guide to the Theory of NP-completeness*. New York: W. H. Freeman and Co.

Geertz C. (1964). Ideology as a cultural system. In D. Apter (ed.) *Ideology and Discontent*. New York: The Free Press, pp. 47–76.

George A. L. (1959). *Propaganda analysis. A study of Inferences made from Nazi Propaganda in World War II*. Westport (CN.): Greenwood Press.

Girard R. (1977). *Violence and the Sacred*. Baltimore, London: Johns Hopkins University Press.

Gochet P. and Thayse A. (1989) 'Montague's semantics' In A. Tayse (ed.) *From Modal Logic to Deductive Databases. Introducing a Logic Based Approach to Artificial Intelligence*. New York: Wiley.

Gouin-Décarié T. (1962) *Intelligence et Affectivité*. Neuchâtel: Delachaux and Niestlé.

Grammont M. (1933) *Traité de phonétique*. Paris: Delagrave.

Greimas A. (1966) *Sémantique Structurale*. Paris: Larousse.

Greimas A. and Fontanille J. (1991) *Sémiotique des passions. Des états de choses aux états d'âme*. Paris: Seuil.

Grice P. (1989) Meaning revisited. In *Studies in the Way of Words*. Cambridge (MA): Harvard University Press.

Grossberg S. (1988). Nonlinear neural networks: principles, mechanisms and architectures. *Neural Networks*. 1(1): 17–61.

Grosz B. J. and Snider C. L. (1986) Attention, intention, and the structure of discourse. *Computational Linguistics*, 12(3): 175–204.

Guerreiro (de T) R. A., Hemerly A. and Shoham Y. (1990) On the complexity of monotonic inheritance with roles. In *AAAI-90: Proceedings of the Ninth National Conference on Artificial Intelligence*. AAAI, Memlo Park, CA.

Habermas J. (1978) *L'espace Public. Archéologie de la publicité comme dimension constitutive de la société bourgeoise*. Paris: Payot.

Habermas J. (1984) *Theory of Communicative Action*. Boston: Beacon Press.

Hage P. (1979) A further application of matrix analysis to communication structure in oceanic anthropology. *Mathématiques et Sciences Humaines*, 65: 51–70.

Halliday M. (1979) *Language as Social Semiotic: The Social Interpretation of Language and Meaning*. London: Arnold.

Halliday M. and Hasan R. (1985) *Language, Context and Text: Aspects of Language in a Social-semiotic Perspective*. Oxford: Oxford University Press.

Hare R. M. (1964) *The Language of Morals*. Oxford: Oxford University Press.
Harel D. (1988). On visual formalisms. *Communication of ACM*, pp. 514–530.
Harris M., Barrett M. D., Jones D. and Brooke S. (1988) Linguistic input and early word meaning. *Journal of Child Language*. 15: 77–94.
Harris Z. (1968) *Mathematical Structures of Language*, Interscience Publishers.
Heidrich W., Neubaer F., Petöfi J. S. and Sözer E. (1989). *Connexity and Coherence; Analysis of Text and Discourse*. Berlin: De Gruyter.
Hendler J. A. (1992) Massively-parallel marker-passing in semantic networks. *Computers Math. Appl.*, 23(2–5): 277–291.
Hintikka J. (1973) Surface semantics: definition and its motivation. In H. Leblanc (ed.) *Truth, Syntax and Modality*. Amsterdam: North-Holland.
Hinton G. E. (1989) Implementing semantic networks in parallel hardware. In G. E. Hinton and S. A. Anderson (eds.) *Parallel Models of Associative Memories* (updated ed.). Hillsdale, NJ: Erlbaum. pp. 191–221.
Hirsch M. W. (1989) Convergent activation dynamics in continuous time networks. *Neural Networks*, 2: 331–349.
Hirschman A. O. (1991) *The Rhetoric of Reaction: Perversity, Futility, Jeopardy*. Cambridge: Belknap Press.
Hirst G. (1987) *Semantic Interpretation and the Resolution of Ambiguity*. Cambridge: Cambridge University Press
Jackson P. (1988) On game theoretic interactions with first-order knowledge bases. In P. Smets *et al.* (eds.) *Non-Standard Logics for Automated Reasoning*. London: Academic Press.
Jakobson R. (1960). Linguistics and poetics. In T. A. Sebeok (ed.) *Style in Language*. Cambridge (MA): Technology Press of MIT.
Jayez J. (1988) *L'Inférence en Langue Naturelle*. Paris: Hermes.
Kamp H. (1981) Référence temporelle et representation du discours, *Langages*, pp. 39–64.
Karsenti B. (1995) Le sociologue dans l'espace des points de vue. In *Critique*, 579/580, pp. 661–673
Kautz H., Kearns M. and Selman B. (1995) Horn approximations of empirical data. *Artificial Intelligence*, 74: 129–145.
Kintsch W. (1991) The role of knowledge in discourse comprehension, a construction-integration model. In G. Denhiere and J. P. Rossi (eds.) *Text and Text Processing*. Amsterdam: North Holland. pp. 107–153.
Kress G. (1981) Ideological structures in discourse. In M. Janovitz and P. M. Hirsch. *Reader in Public Opinion and Mass Communication*. New York: The Free Press.
Kress G. (1983) Linguistic processes and the mediation of 'reality': the politics of newspaper language. *International Journal of the Sociology of Language*, 40: 43–57.
Kress G. and Hodge R. (1979) *Language as Ideology*. London: Routledge and Keegan Paul.
Kripke S. A. (1963) Semantical considerations on modal logic. *Acta Philosophica Fennica*, Fasc. XVI, pp. 83–94.
Krippendorff K. (1980) *Content Analysis: an Introduction to its Methodology*. Beverley Hills: Sage.
Lakoff G. (1987) *Women, Fire, and Dangerous Things: What Categories Reveal*

about the Mind. Chicago: University of Chicago Press.
Lakoff G. (1995) Metaphors, morality, and politics. Or why conservatives have left liberals in the dust. *Social Research*. 62(2): 177–213.
Lakoff G. and Johnson M. (1980) *Metaphors we Live by*. Chicago: University of Chicago Press.
Lakoff R. (1975) *Language and Women's Place*. New York: Harper and Row.
Laks B. (1996) *Language et Cognition*. Paris: Hermès.
Lebart L. and Salem A. (1990) *Statistique Textuelle*. Paris: Dunod.
Lee D. (1992) *Competing Discourses: Perspective and Ideology in Language*. London: Longman.
Legendre P. (1974) *L'amour du censeur. Essai sur l'ordre dogmatique*. Paris: Seuil.
Legendre P. (1982) *Paroles poétiques échappées du texte. Leçons sur la communication industrielle*. Paris: Seuil.
Legendre P. (1983) *L'empire de la vérité. Introduction aux espaces dogmatiques industriels*. Paris: Fayard.
Legendre P. (1985) *L'inestimable objet de la transmission. Étude sur le principe généalogique en Occident*. Paris: Fayard.
Legendre P. (1988) *Le désir politique de Dieu. Étude sur les montages de l'État et du Droit*. Paris: Fayard.
Lehmann F. (1992) Semantic networks. *Computers Math. Appl.*, 23(2–5): 1–50.
Livet and Thévenot (1993). Modes d'action collective et construction éthique. Les émotions dans l'évaluation. Proceedings of the colloque *Limitation de la rationalité et constitution du collectif,* Cerisy, June.
Luhman N. (1988) The self reproduction of law and its limits. In G. Teubner (ed.) *Dilemmas of Law in the Welfare State*. Berlin: De Gruyter.
MacWhinney B. (1995) (ed.) *The CHILDES Project. Tools for Analysing Talk*. Hillsdale (NJ): Laurence Erlbaum Associates.
Maingueneau D. (1979) *Les Livres d'école de la République, 1870–1914. Discours et Idéologie*. Paris: Le Sycomore.
Maingueneau D. (1984) *Introduction à l'Analyse du Discours. Problèmes et perspectives*. Paris: Hachette.
Maingueneau D. (1987) *Nouvelles tendances en Analyse du Discours*. Paris: Hachette.
Maingueneau D. (ed.) (1995) Les analyses du discours en France. *Language*, 117.
Maldidier D. (1989) Éléments pour une histoire de l'Analyse de Discours en France. *Cahiers de linguistique sociale* (Université de Rouen), 14.
Malrieu J. P. (1994) Coloured semantic networks for content analysis. *Quality and Quantity*, 28: 55–81.
Malrieu J. P. (1995) La Cohérence idéologique du discours. Une méthode d'estimation. *Intellectica*, 20: 185–215.
Malrieu Ph. (1952) *Les émotions et la personalité de l'enfant*. Paris: Vrin.
Mandler G. (1982) The structure of value. In M. S. Clark and S. T. Fiske (eds.) *Affects and cognition* Hillsdale (NJ): Laurence Erlbaum Associates, (pp. 3–38).
Mann W. C. and Thompson S. A. (1987) *Rhetorical Structure Theory: a Theory of Text Organization*. USC/Information Science Institute Technical Report RS-87-190, Marina Del Rey (CA).
Messer D. J. (1994) *The Development of Communication. From Social Interaction to*

Language. New York: Wiley.
Michalski R. S. and Stepp R. E. (1983) Learning from observations: conceptual clustering. In R. S. Michalski, J. Carbone and T. M. Mitchel (eds.) *Machine Learning, and Artificial Intelligence Approach*. Los Altos (CA): Morgan Kaufmann. pp. 333–363.
Michard-Marshall C. and Ribéry C. (1982) *Sexisme et Sciences Humaines, Pratiques linguistiques du rapport de sexage*. Presses Universitaires de Lille.
Minsky M. (ed.) (1968) *Semantic Information Processing*. Cambridge (MA): MIT Press.
Monod J.-C. (1995) Les deux mains de l'État. Remarque sur la sociologie de la misère de Pierre Bourdieu. *Esprit*, 214: 156–171.
Montague R. (1973) The proper treatment of quantification in ordinary English. In J. Hintikka *et al.* (eds.) *Approaches to Natural Language*, Reidel, Dordrecht, pp. 221–242.
Moore J. D. and Pollack M. E. (1992) A problem for RST: the need for multi-level discourse analysis. *Computational Linguistics*, 18(4): 537–544.
Moscovici S. (1961) *La psychanalyse, son image, son public*. Paris: PUF.
Moscovici S. (1986) L'ère des représentations sociales. In W. Doise and A. Palmonari (eds.) *L'étude des représentations sociales*. Neuchatel: Delachaux & Niestlé.
Moscovici S. and Doise W. (1994). *Conflict and Consensus*. London: Sage.
Mugnier M. L. and Chein M. (1993) Polynomial algorithms for projection and matching problems. *7th Annual Workshop on Conceptual Graphs*, New Mexico University, July 1992.
Nisbet R. and Ross N. (1980) *Human Inference*. Englewood Cliffs (NJ): Prentice Hall.
Noble B. and Daniel J. (1988) *Applied Linear Algebra*. Englewood Cliffs (NJ): Prentice Hall.
Nølke H. (1993) *Le Regard du locuteur. Pour une linguistique des traces énonciatives*, Paris: Kimé.
Olson J. M. and Zana M. P. (1993) Attitude and attitude change. *Annual Review of Psychology*, 44: 117–154.
Ortony A. (1991) Value and Emotion. In W. Kesen, A. Ortony and F. Craik (eds.) *Memories, Thoughts and Emotions: Essays in Honor of George Mandler*. Hillsdale (NJ): Laurence Erlbaum Associates.
Ortony A., Clore L. G. and Collins A. (1988) *The cognitive Structure of Emotions*, Cambridge: Cambridge University Press.
Ostrom T. M. (1969). The relationship between the affective, behavioral and cognitive components of attitude. *Journal of Experimental Social Psychology*. 5: 12–30.
Papousek M., Bornstein M. H., Nunzo C., Papousek H. and Symmes D. (1990) Infant responses to prototypical melodic contours in parental speech. *Infant Behaviour and Development*, 13: 539–545.
Pêcheux M. (1982) *Language, Semantics, and Ideology: Stating the Obvious*. London: MacMillan.
Pêcheux M. (1969) *Analyse Automatique du Discours*. Paris: Dunod.
Pêcheux M. (1978) Are the masses an animate object? In D. Sankoff (ed.) *Linguistic*

Variation, New York: Academic Press. pp. 251–266.

Pêcheux M., Henry P., Poitou J. P. and Haroche C. (1979). Un exemple d'ambiguïté idéologique, le rapport Mansholt. *Technologies, Idéologies et Pratiques*, 1(2).

Perelman C. and Olbrechts-Tyteca L. (1988) (5th ed.) *Traité de l'Argumentation*. Éditions de l'Université de Bruxelles.

Perriaux S. and Varro G. (1991) *Les sens d'une catégorisation: 'les O. S. Immigrés' Langage et Société*, 58: 5–36.

Plantin C. (1990) *Essais sur l'argumentation*. Paris: Kimé.

Plunkett K. (1995) Connectionist approaches to language acquisition. In P. Fletcher and B. MacWhinney (eds.) *The Handbook of Child Language*. Cambridge (MA): Blackwell. pp. 36–72.

Pollard C. and Sag I. (1994) *Head Driven Phrase Structure Grammar*, CSLI Series, Chicago: University of Chicago Press.

Pottier B. (1974) *Linguistique Générale. Théorie et description*. Paris: Klincksieck.

Pratkanis A. R. and Greenwald A. G. (1989) A socio-cognitive model of attitude structure and function. *Advances of Experimental Social Psychology*, 22: 245–285.

Raccah P. Y. (1993) Argumentation and language system: presentation and discussion of a few foundational hypotheses. *Proceedings of the Second European Conference on System Sciences, Prague*, October.

Rao A. S. and Foo N. Y. (1987) CONGRES: Conceptual Graph Reasoning System, *Proceedings of the IEEE Conference on AI Applications*, Orlando, FL, pp. 87–92.

Rastier F. (1991) *Sémantique et Recherches Cognitives*. Paris: PUF.

Rastier F. (1987) *Sémantique Interpretative*. Paris: PUF.

Rastier F., Cavazza M. and Abeillé A. (1994) *Sémantique pour L'analyse*. Paris: Masson.

Ricoeur P. (1965) *De l'interpretation: Essai sur Freud*. Paris: Seuil.

Riffaterre M. (1979) *La production du texte*. Paris: Seuil.

Roberts D. D. (1973) *The Existential Graphs of Charles S. Pierce*. The Hague: Mouton.

Rosenfield I. (1992). *The Strange, Familiar and Forgotten: An Anatomy of consciousness*. New York: Alfred A. Knopf.

Rumelhart D. (1975) Notes on a schema for stories. In D. Dobrow and A. Collins (eds.) *Representation and Understanding: Studies in Cognitive Science*. New York: Academic Press.

Rumelhart D. E., Smolensky P., McClelland J. L. and Hinton G. E. (1986) Schemata and sequential thought processes in PDP models. In J. L. McClelland and D. E. Rumelhart and the PDP Research Group *Parallel Distributed Processing*. Vol. 2. *Psychological and Biological Models*. Cambridge (MA): MIT Press. pp. 7-57.

Sabah G. (1989) *L'Intelligence Artificielle et le Langage*. Paris: Hermes.

Saussure F. de. (1972 [1916]) *Cours de Linguistique Générale*. Paris: Payot.

Schank R. (1982) *Reading and Understanding: Teaching from the perspective of artificial intelligence*. Hillsdale (NJ): Laurence Erlbaum Associates.

Scubla L. (1992) Sciences cognitives, matérialisme et anthropologie. In D. Andler (ed.) *Introduction aux sciences cognitives*. Paris: Gallimard. pp. 420–446.

Seidel G. (1985). Political Discourse Analysis. In M. Janovitz and P. M. Hirsch (eds.) *Reader in Public Opinion and Mass Communication*. New York: The Free Press. pp. 43–60.

Selman B and Levesque H. J. (1993) The complexity of path-based defeasible inheritance. *Artificial Intelligence*, 62: 303–339.

Shapin S. (1991) A scholar and a gentleman: the problematic identity of the scientific practitioner in early modern England. *History and Science*, 29: 279–327.

Shapin S. and Schaffer S. (1985) *Leviathan and the Air Pump*. Princeton (NJ): Princeton University Press.

Shapiro S. C. (1979) The SNePS semantic network processing system. In N. V. Findler (ed.) *Associative Networks: The Representation and Use of Knowledge by Computers*. New York: Academic Press. pp. 179–203.

Shapiro S. C. and Rapaport W. J. (1987) SNePS considered as a fully intensional propositional semantic network. In N. Cercone and G. McCalla (eds.) *The Knowledge Frontier*. New York: Springer Verlag.

Shastri L. (1992). Structured connectionists models of semantic networks. *Computers Math. Applic.*, 23(2–5): 293–328.

Sherif C. W. (1973) Social distance as categorization of intergroup interaction. *Journal of Personality and Social Psychology*, 25: 327–334.

Shils E. (1968) The concept and function of ideology, *International Encyclopaedia of the Social Sciences,* vol. 7, pp. 66–76. New York: The Macmillan Company and Free Press.

Silber I. F. (1995) Space, Fields, Boundaries: the role of spatial metaphors in contemporary sociological methodology. *Social Research*, 62(2): 323–355.

Simmel G. (1978) *The Philosophy of Money* (first German ed. 1929). London: Routlcdgc.

Simon H. (1982) *Models of Bounded Rationality*. Cambridge (MA): MIT Press.

Slakta D. (1971) Esquisse d'une théorie lexico-sémantique: analyse d'un texte politique (Cahiers de Doléances). *Langage*. September, pp. 87–131.

Smith E. R. (1992) The role of exemplars in social judgements. In L. L. Martin and A. Tesser (eds.), *The Construction of Social Judgments*. London: Laurence Erlbaum Associates.

Smolensky P. (1986) Information processing in dynamical systems: foundations of harmony theory. In D. E. Rumelhart, J. L. McClelland and the PDP Research Group, *Parallel Distributed Processing, Explorations in the Microstructures of Cognition. Vol. 1, Foundations*. Cambridge (MA): MIT Press.

Sowa J. F. (1984) *Conceptual Structures. Information Processing in Mind and Machine*. Reading (MA): Addison Wesley.

Sowa J. F. (ed.) (1991) *Principles of Semantic Networks, Explorations in the Representation of Knowledge*. San Mateo (CA): Morgan Kaufmann Publishers.

Sowa J. F. (1992) Conceptual graphs as a universal knowledge representation. *Computers and Mathematics with Applications*, 23(2–5): 75–93.

Sowa J. F. and Way EC. (1986) Implementing a semantic interpreter using conceptual graphs, *IBM Journal of Research & Development*, 1: 57–69.

Sperber D. (1992). Les sciences cognitives, les sciences sociales et le matérialisme. In D. Andler (ed.) *Introduction aux sciences cognitives*. Paris: Gallimard pp. 317–420.

Sperber D. (1996) *La contagion des idées*. Paris: Odile Jacob.

Spitz R. A. (1983) *Dialogues from Infancy*. New York : International Universities Press.
Stalin I. V. (1951) On Marxism in linguistics. In *The Soviet Linguistic Controversy* (translation from the Soviet Press by J. V. Murra, R. M. Hankin and F. Holling). New York: King's Crown Press, pp. 70-76.
Stein L. A. (1991) Extensions as possible worlds. In J. F. Sowa (ed.) *Principles of Semantic Networks, Explorations in the Representation of Knowledge*. San Mateo (CA): Morgan Kaufmann Publishers. pp. 267–282.
Stern D. (1989) *Le monde interpersonnel du nourrisson*. Paris: PUF.
Talmy L. (1987) The relation of grammar to cognition. In B. Rudzka-Ostyn (ed.), *Topics in Cognitive Linguistics*. Amsterdam, Philadelphia: John Benjamin Publishing.
Tarski A. (1952) The semantic conception of truth. In L. Lisnsky (ed.) *Semantics and the Philosophy of Language*, pp. 13–47. Urbana: University of Illinois Press. (reprinted from *Philosophy and Phenomenological Research*, 4: 341–375, 1944).
Tesnière L. (1959) *Éléments de syntaxe structurale* (2nd ed. 1965). Paris: Klincksieck.
Teubner G. (ed.) (1987) *Autopoiesis in Law and Society*. Berlin: De Gruyter.
Thayse A. (ed.) (1989) *From Modal Logic to Deductive Databases*. New York: Wiley.
Thomason R. H. and Touretsky D. S. (1991) Inheritance theory and networks with roles. In J. F. Sowa (ed.) *Principles of Semantic Networks. Explorations in the Representation of Knowledge*. San Matteo (CA): Morgan Kaufmann.
Thorndyke P. W. (1977) Cognitive structures in comprehension and memory of narrative discourse. *Cognitive Psychology*, 9: 77–110.
Touretsky D. S. (1986) *The Mathematics of Inheritance Systems*. San Mateo (CA): Morgan Kaufmann.
Touretsky D. S. (1990) BoltzCONS: dynamic symbol structures in a connectionist network. *Artificial Intelligence*, 46: 5–46.
Trew T. (1979a) Theory and ideology at work. In R. Fowler, B. Hodge, G. Kress and T. Trew (eds.) *Language and Control*. London: Routledge & Keegan Paul, pp. 96–116.
Trew T. (1979b) What the papers say: linguistic variation and ideological difference. In R. Fowler, B. Hodge, G. Kress and T. Trew (eds.), *Language and Control*. London: Routledge & Keegan Paul, pp. 117–156.
Tsohatzidis N. (1992) Pronouns of address and truth conditions, *Linguistics*, 30.
Van Dijk T. (1998) *Ideology. A Multidisciplinary Study*. London: Sage.
Van Dijk T. (1999) *Critical Discourse Analysis*. To appear.
Van Dijk T. and Kintsch W. (1983). *Strategies of Text Comprehension*. New York: Academic Press.
Victorri B. (1994) The use of continuity in modelling semantic phenomena. In C. Fuchs and B. Victorri (eds.) *Continuity in Linguistics*. Amsterdam: John Benjamin.
Victorri B. and Fuchs C. (1992) Construction de l'espace sémantique associé à un marqueur grammatical polysémique, *Linguistica Investigationes*, 16(1).
Victorri B. and Fuchs C. (1996) *La Polysémie. Construction dynamique du sens*.

Paris: Hermès.
Visetti Y.-M. (1990). Modèles connexionnistes et représentations structurées. *Intellectica*, 9–10: 167–212.
Wallen L. A. (1990) *Automated Deduction in Nonclassical Logics, Efficient Matrix Proof Methods for Modal & Intuitionistic Logics*. Cambridge (MA): MIT Press.
Wallon H. (1949) *Les origines du caractère chez l'enfant*. Paris: PUF.
Waltz D. and Pollack J. (1985) Massively parallel parsing: a strongly interactive model of natural language interpretation. *Cognitive Science*, 9(1): 57–69.
Whorf B. L. (1971) A linguistic consideration of thinking in primitive communities. In Carroll (ed.) pp. 65–86.
Wilensky R. (1991) Sentences, Situations and Propositions, in Sowa J. F. (ed.), *Principles of Semantic Networks*, pp. 191–227.
Winograd T. (1992) Heidegger et la conception de systèmes informatiques. *Intellectica*, 17: 51–78.
Wyer R. S. and Srull T. K. (1989) *Memory and Cognition in its Social Context*. Hillsdale (NJ): Laurence Erlbaum Associates.
Zadrozny W. (1992) On compositional semantics, in *COLING-92, Proceedings of the fifteenth International Conference on Computational Linguistics*, vol. I, pp. 260–266, Nantes, August.
Zajong R. B. (1980) Preferences need no inferences. *American Psychologist*, 35: 151–175.
Zajong R. B. and Markus H. (1984) Affect and cognition: the hard interface. In C. E. Izard, J. Kagan and R. B. Zajong (eds.) *Emotion, Cognition and Behaviour*. Cambridge: Cambridge University Press.

INDEX

Abeillé A. 165
Achard P. 97, 100, 101, 103, 296
adverb: simulation in dynamic semantic networks 224, 269
Ajzen I. 53
Althusser L. 2, 3, 10, 11, 12, 15, 17, 18, 22, 33, 64, 96, 99
ambiguity 100, 260; and nonmonotonic inheritance 146
analyse du discours 96; and semantics 97, 112
Anderson N. H. 67
Andrews E. 115
Anscombre J. C. 117, 162
argumentation within language 117
Ariety S. 54
Asher N. 158
aspectualization 95
attitude 52; evaluative 75, 254; Jesuit *vs.* Jansenist 75, 222
attitude reports: representation in styled semantic networks
automatic analysis of discourse 97

Bakhtine M. 1, 80, 81, 115, 120
Barrett M. 56
Barwise J. 91, 92, 127
Baudrillard J. 31, 108
Beauvois J. L. 133
Bell D. 4
Bem D. J. 15
Boltanski L. 4, 13, 31–4, 44–8, 82, 100, 235, 253
Borgese G. A. 13
Boudon R. 15, 17, 104
Bourdieu P. 2–4, 6, 11–14, 18-25, 30–46, 51–2, 91, 94, 100, 102, 105–8, 269, 280, 295

Boutet J. 101, 104
Brachman R. 150, 151, 163
Breal M. 119
Breckler S. 53
Brewer M. 67
Brice P, 43, 51
Brow G. 156
Brutus 190, 194, 195, 234, 237, 255–76, 278, 293

Caesar 181, 183, 190–7, 234, 237, 241–3, 255–76, 293, 298
Carel M. 118
Carnap R. 122
Carpenter B. 153
categorization 95, 101
Chaiken S. 54
Chein M. 200
Clancey W. J. 58
Clark. E. V. 116
closed-world 127
CoCoNet 205
Coffey C. 94
cognitive semantics 118
cognitivism 51
comparison: semantic effect of 102
compositionality 128
concept 122; colour 205; in styled semantic networks 181; restriction 198
conceptual graph 167
conditional: representation in styled semantic networks 190
connection weights: 193; attraction-repulsion 224; default settings 231; mutual attraction 220; mutual repulsion 221
connectionism 151, 177, 178
connector: 'mais' *vs.* 'pourtant' 132;

representation in styled semantic networks 196; simulation in dynamic semantic networks 223, 270
connexity 157
context 2
contextual evaluation 135
contextual modification 136
continuity 177
Courcelle B. 162
Courtine J. J. 100
critical discourse analysis 96
Cuilemburg J. J. 208

Dahlgren K. 82
Daniel J. 214
De Beaugrande R. 164
De Sousa R. 52
default evaluation 135
deixis: discursive *vs.* founding 103
Dennet D. C. 66, 67
derivation: algorithm 230
Derrida J. 13, 60
Derthick M. 151
Deschamp J. C. 133
determination by relatives: representation in styled semantic networks 188
dialectics 156, 158
dialogics 156, 158
differential semantics 119
disambiguation 101, 278; ideological 82
discourse clustering 204
discourse representation theory 127, 153
Dore J. 56
Downs A. 15
Dowty D. R. 130
Dreben E. K. 77
Dromi E. 56
Ducrot O. 39, 117, 118, 157, 196, 224
dynamic semantic networks 209; convergence conditions for 215, 289–92; differential equations 215; discrete time equations 216

Eagleton T. 120
Eagly A. H. 54
Edelman G. M. 9, 50, 56, 58, 66–8, 77, 84
emotional development 55
enunciation 103
evaluation: and truth 43
evaluation 1, 134, 148; and objectivism 32, 51; computational metaphor for 66; contextual 147; default 147;

dimensions of 69, 131; non-purposiveness of 79; phenomenology of 80; semantic analysis of the word 'evaluation' 51; variation of 143
expressivity 160
extension 144

Fairclough N. L. 96
Fazio R. H. 78
feature structure 153
Fernald R. 55
Festinger L. 15
Findler N. V. 150
Fishbein M. 53
Fiske S. T. 67
Fontanille J. 31
Forgas J. P. 69
Foucault M. 3, 5, 6, 8, 10, 11, 14, 26, 30, 90, 96, 106
Franzosi R. 153
Frege G. 129, 205
Freud S. 59
Fried S. 53
Fuchs C. 96, 101, 102, 210, 213

game-theoretical semantics 173
Garey M. R. 200
Geertz C. 12, 108
gender 94, 101
genre 97, 103
George A. L. 52, 73, 86
Girard R. 13
Gochet P. 154
Gouin-Décarié T. 55
Grammont M. 115
graph: *vs* tree data structure 155
graph-based representation of logic 162
graph-based representation of natural language 164
Greenwald A. G. 53
Greimas A. 31, 114, 119, 297
Grossberg S. 214
Grosz B. J. 154
Guerreiro (de T) R. A. 147

Habermas J. 18, 79, 107, 123
Hage P. 158
Halliday M. 95, 121
Hare R. M. 119
Harel D. 162
Harris Z. 56, 100
head-driven phrase structure grammar 136

Hegel G. W. F. 109, 111
Hendler J. A. 162
Hintikka J. 127
Hinton G. E. 151, 164
Hirsch M. W. 214
Hirschman A. O. 13
Hirst G. 130

ideological consistency 42, 134, 143, 148; and intension 148; formalization of 138; mathematical formula of 219; principles 137; *vs.* logical 6, 44
ideology: Boltanski and Thévenot's model of 47; boundaries of 49, 281; cold theories of 15; dominant 44; external theories of 13; formalization in nonmonotonic logic 144; internal theories of 13; pro-Ceasar *vs.* anti-Caesar 256; structure of in dynamic semantic networks 228; tyranny *vs.* republic 234
illocutionary transfer 106
indexicality 103
inheritance 145; computational complexity 147
inheritance network 161
intension 140; and ideological consistency 148
intentional verb 139
interpretation 85; and dynamic systems 210
interpretative semantics 120
interrogatives: representation in styled semantic networks 191
irony: global dynamics of 276
isotopy 158; evaluative 121

Jackson P. 173
Jakobson R. 98, 100, 255, 266, 269, 270, 279
Jayez J. 162
Johnson M. 93, 200

Kamp H. 127, 153, 154, 158
Karsenti B. 37
Kautz H. 125, 297
Kintsch and Van Dijk's model, 77, 156
Kintsch W. 77, 78, 156, 213
knowledge representation systems 163
Kress G. 93, 95
Kripke S. A. 5, 140, 148, 173, 177, 246, 283

Krippendorff K. 86, 87, 88, 89, 108, 109, 296

Lacan J. 60
Lakoff G, 60, 93, 94, 118, 119
Lakoff R. 94
Laks B. 178, 298
Lebart L. 97
Lee D. 93, 296
Legendre P. 13, 21, 59, 106, 111, 295, 297
Lehmann F. 159
Leibniz G. W. 108
Levesque H. J. 162
lexicometrics 97
Livet P. 31
Luhman N. 13

MacWhinney B. 56, 296
Maingueneau D. 93, 100, 103
Maldidier D. 96
Malrieu JP. 83, 116, 183
Mandler G. 52, 73, 74
Mann W. C. 154, 155
Marandin J. M. 100
markedness theory 115
marker passing networks 162
memory 67
Michard-Marshall C. 102
modal aspectualization 190
modality: representation in styled semantic networks 190; simulation in dynamic semantic networks 246
model: partial 127
Montague R. 130, 136, 140
Moore J. D. 154
Moscovici S. 13, 81, 101
Mugnier M. L. 200

negation: representation in styled semantic networks 182; simulation in dynamic semantic networks 243
Nisbet R. 15
Nølke H. 157
nominalization 95

occurrence: *vs.* type 121
Olson J. M. 54
opacity 139; of evaluation 140; of ideological consistency 142
open and closed-class forms 181
open world 127, 170
Ortony A. 54, 69, 70, 73

Orwell G. 1
Ostrom T. M. 53

Papousek M. 55
parallel distributed processing 163, 178
passivization 95
Pêcheux M. 18, 30, 96–101
perception: ideological 82
Perelman C. 157
Perriaux S. 134
Perry J. 127
Plantin C. 132, 137
Plunkett K. 178
Pollack J. 151, 154, 164, 213
Pollack M. E. 151, 154, 164, 213
Pollard C. 136
polyphony 157; representation in styled semantic networks 195
possible worlds semantics 140
Pottier B. 119
pragmatics: and evaluation, 123
Pratkanis A. R. 53
pre-emption, 146
presupposition 95
projection 169; computational complexity of 200; projection game for styled semantic networks 198; projective extent 170
proof theory *vs.* model theory 125

quantification: representation in styled semantic networks 186

Raccah P. Y. 118
Rapaport W. J. 163
Rastier F. 78, 83, 93, 114, 120–2, 149–52, 156, 296, 297
register 97, 103
relation: in styled semantic networks 181; sensitivity to negation 244
representation: local *vs.* distributed 163
restrictor 186
retention: and evaluation 77
rhetorical questions: representation in styled semantic networks 191; simulation in dynamic semantic networks 265
rhetorical structure theory 154
Ribéry C. 102
Ricoeur P. 11, 110
Riffaterre M. 101, 296
Roberts D. D. 162

Rosenfield I. 66, 67
Ross N. 15
Rossi JP. 79
Rumelhart D. E. 152, 211, 213

Sag I. 136
Salem A. 97
Saussure F. de, 93
Saussure F. de. 93, 109, 114, 119, 120, 152
Schaffer S. 10
schema: connectionist modelling of 71; consistency-driven 72; generative 45
Scubla L. 17
Seidel G. 93, 95, 96
Selman B. 162
semantic path distributions 204
seme: inherent *vs.* afferent 121
set theory: and the formalization of meaning 124
Shakespeare W. 9, 188, 192, 234, 235, 237, 241, 255, 260, 266, 278, 287, 293
Shapin S. 10
Shapiro S. C. 163
Shastri L. 151, 164
Sherif C. W. 81
Shils R. 10, 13
significance 217
Silber I. F. 23
Simmel G. 13
Simon H. 15
Slakta D. 96, 98
Smith E. R. 67
Smolensky P. 71
Snider C. L. 154
Sowa J. F. 149, 152, 159, 164–76, 183, 186, 197, 198, 204, 298
speech act reports: representation in styled semantic networks 193
Sperber D. 15
Spitz R. A. 55
Srull T. K. 53
Stalin I. V. 1
standard, 74
Stein L. A. 144
Stepp R. E. 205
Stern D. 55
summarizing: and evaluation 77
symbol 108; and sign 109; and value 111; Freud's theory of 110
systematic semantics 130

tactics 159

Talmy L. 116, 297
Tarski A. 127, 246
tense: representation in styled semantic networks 182
Tesnière L. 164
Teubner G. 13
text grammar 152
Thayse A. 154
Thévenot L. 13, 31, 47, 48, 82, 100, 235
Thomason R. H. 147, 163
Thompson S. A. 154, 155
Thorndyke P. W. 152
Touretsky D. S. 147, 159, 161, 163, 164
Trew T. 93, 95, 96
Tsohatzidis N. 205
type hierarchy 169

understanding: and evaluation 76

value-symbols 111

Van Dijk T. 77, 78, 96, 156
Varro G. 134
Victorri B. 178, 210, 213
Visetti Y-M. 71, 164

Wallen L. A. 167
Wallon H. 55, 116
Waltz D. 151, 164, 213
Way E. C. 152
weights *see* connection weights
Wilensky R. 153
Winograd T. 79
Wyer R. S. 53

Yule G. 93, 156

Zadrozny W. 129, 130
Zajong R. B. 53
Zana M. P. 54